Max

M000306418

Domestic Economy

A complete system of English housekeeping

Maximilian Hazlemore

Domestic Economy
A complete system of English housekeeping

ISBN/EAN: 9783742811769

Manufactured in Europe, USA, Canada, Australia, Japa

Cover: Foto ©Lupo / pixelio.de

Manufactured and distributed by brebook publishing software
(www.brebook.com)

Maximilian Hazlemore

Domestic Economy

DOMESTIC ECONOMY;

OR,

A COMPLETE SYSTEM

OF

ENGLISH HOUSEKEEPING:

CONTAINING

The moſt approved Receipts, confirmed by Obſervation and Practice, in every reputable Engliſh Book of Cookery now extant; beſides a great Variety of others which have never before been offered to the Public. Alſo a valuable Collection, tranſlated from the Productions of COOKS of Eminence who have publiſhed in *France*, with their reſpective Names to each Receipt; which, together with the ORIGINAL ARTICLES, form the moſt complete Syſtem of HOUSEKEEPING ever yet exhibited, under the following Heads, *viz.*

ROASTING,	SOUPS,	TARTS,
BOILING,	SAUCES,	PIES,
MADE-DISHES,	GRAVIES,	PASTIES,
FRYING,	HASHES,	CHEESECAKES,
BROILING,	STEWS,	JELLIES,
POTTING,	PUDDINGS,	PICKLING,
FRICASSEES,	CUSTARDS,	PRESERVING, and
RAGOUTS,	CAKES,	CONFECTIONARY.

To which is prefixed, in order to render it as complete and perfect as poſſible,

AN ELEGANT COLLECTION OF LIGHT DISHES FOR SUPPER,

ADAPTED FOR EVERY MONTH IN THE YEAR.

ALSO

THE COMPLETE BREWER;

CONTAINING

Familiar Inſtructions for brewing all Sorts of Beer and Ale; including the proper Management of the Vault or Cellar.

LIKEWISE

THE FAMILY PHYSICIAN;

Being a Collection of the moſt valuable and approved Preſcriptions by MEAD, SYDENHAM, TISSOT, FOTHERGILL, ELLIOT, BUCHAN, and Others.

BY MAXIMILIAN HAZLEMORE.

LONDON:

PRINTED FOR J. CRESWICK, AND CO.

1794.

TO THE PUBLIC.

THE numerous Publications on the ART of COOKERY may appear, on the firſt bluſh, to render any other Treatiſe on that ſubjeEt unneceſſary ; but accurate examination will evince the propriety of the preſent Work.

Without a deſire to depreciate the produEtions of former Writers, on a ſubjeEt apparently ſo much exhauſted, I may venture to aſſert, that this Syſtem of

DOMESTIC ECONOMY;

OR,

COMPLETE ENGLISH HOUSEKEEPING,

will be found to contain the eſſence of all preceding works on that ſubjeEt, enriched with a variety of new and valuable receipts. I have carefully excluded all extravagant, and almoſt impraEticable ones, which too frequently abound in books of this kind; at the ſame time have ſtudiouſly retained every thing that merits preſervation in all the produEtions extant on that ſubjeEt. The moſt frugal and leaſt complicated diſhes have generally been preferred ; though care has been taken that nothing ſhould be omitted that might gratify the appetite of the epicure.

In order to render this performance generally uſeful and acceptable, I have added, by way of ſupplement, INSTRUCTIONS *in the* ART of BREWING *in all its* BRANCHES

together

together with a collection of valuable Medical Receipts, under the title of

THE FAMILY PHYSICIAN;

COMPILED FROM THE WORKS OF

BUCHAN, MEAD, SYDENHAM, FOTHERGILL, TISSOT, &c. &c.

which will be found applicable to the relief of all common complaints incident to families, and which will be particularly useful in the country, where frequent opportunities offer of relieving the Diftreffed, whofe fituation in life will not enable them to call in Medical Aid; concluding with Inftructions for the Recovery of Perfons apparently drowned, as publifhed by the Humane Society.

The whole is intended as a Companion to Young Perfons on the Commencement of Houfekeeping; as well as an Affiftant to Servants entrufted in any Department of a Family.

I cannot omit this opportunity of inviting a candid examination of my Performance, when I flatter myfelf its utility will not be difputed: If it contributes to the inftruction of the uninformed, the general comforts of families, and the relief of thofe who are afflicted with difeafe, my object will be completely attained.

M. HAZLEMORE.

CHAP. II. *Of Roasting.*

CHAP

CHAP. II. *Of Boiling.*

CHAP. III. *Made Dishes of Beef.*

Another

CHAP. IV. *Made Dishes of Veal.*

a 4

To

CHAP. V. *Made Dishes of Mutton.*

CHAP. VI. *Made Dishes of Lamb.*

Chap. VIII. *Made Dishes of Poultry, &c.*

A fowl,

CONTENTS.

Snipes

CHAP. IX.   *Made Dishes of Hares, Rabbits, &c.*

CHAP. X.   *Turtles and Mock Turtle.*

CHAP. XI.   *Of Soups.*

Peas

CHAP. XII. *Soups without Meat.*

CHAP. XIII. *Gravies and Broths.*

CHAP. XIV. *Fricasses.*

CHAP. XVIII. *Of Puddings.*

CHAP.

CHAP. XII. *Soups without Meat.*

CHAP. XIII. *Gravies and Broths.*

CHAP. XIV. *Fricasses.*

Chap. XV. *Of Fish.*

To

CONTENTS.

CHAP. XVI. *Of Sauces.*

CHAP. XVII. *Elegant small Savoury Dishes of Vegetables, Fruits, &c.*

CHAP. XVIII. *Of Puddings.*

CHAP.

CHAP. XX. *Pancakes and Fritters.*

CHAP.

A spi-

CHAP. XXV. *The Art of Confectionary.*

A sweet

CHAP. XXVII. *Possets, Gruels, White-pots, &c.*

CHAP. XXVIII. *Made Wines.*

CHAP. XXIX. *To prepare Bacon, Hams, &c.*

CHAP. XXX. *Vegetables.*

b 3

THE

THE ART OF BREWING.

THE FAMILY PHYSICIAN.

To which is added the useful part of the TOILET.

b 4

To

To

JANUARY.

FIRST COURSE.

Chefnut Soup

Leg of Lamb	Petit Patties	Boiled Chickens
Chickens and Veal Pie	Cod's Head	Roaft Beef
Tongue	Raifolds	Scotch Collops
	Vermicelli Soup	

SECOND COURSE.

Roaft Turkey

Marinated Smelts	Tartlets	Mince Pies
Roafted Sweetbreads	Stands of Jellies	Larks
Almond Tart	Maids of Honour	Lobfters
	Woodcocks	

THIRD COURSE.

Morels

Artichoke Bottoms	Dutch Beef fcraped	Macaroni
Cuftards	Cut Paftry	Black Caps
Scolloped Oyfters	Potted Chars	Stewed Celery
	Rabit fricaffeed	

FEBRUARY.

FIRST COURSE.

Peas Soup

Chickens	Chicken Patty	Mutton Collops
Harrico of Mutton	Salmon and Smelts	Rump of Beef à la daub
Pork Cutlets		
Sauce Robart	Oyfter Patties	Small Ham
	Soup Santé	

SECOND COURSE.

Wild fowl

Cardoons	Dish of Jelly	Stewed Pippins
Scolloped Oyfters	Epergne	Ragout Melé
Comport Pears	Caromel	Artichoke Bottoms
	Hare	

THIRD COURSE.

Two Woodcocks

Cray-fifh	Afparagus	Preferved Cherries
Pigs Ears	Crocant	Lamb Chops larded
Blanched Almonds		
and Raifins	Mufhrooms	Prawns
	Larks á la furprife	

MARCH.

M A R C H.

FIRST COURSE.

Soup Lorrain

Sheeps Rumps	Almond Pudding	Fillet of Pork
Chine of Mutton and stewed Celery	Stewed Carp, or Tench	Lamb's Head
Veal Collops	Beef-steak Pie	Calves Ears
	Onion Soup	

SECOND COURSE.

A Poulard larded and roasted

Asparagus	Blancmange	Prawns
Ragooed Sweetbreads	A trifle	Fricassee of Rabits
Cray-fish	Cheesecakes	Fricassee of Mushrooms
	Tame Pigeons roasted	

THIRD COURSE.

Ox Palates shivered

Tartlets	Potted Larks	Stewed Pippins
Cardoons	Jellies	Spanish Peas
Black Caps	Potted Partridge	Almond Cheesecakes
	Cocks' Combs	

A P R I L.

FIRST COURSE.

Crimp Cod and Smelts.

Chickens	Marrow Pudding	Cutlets à-la Maintenon
Breast of Veal in Rolio	Spring Soup	Beef Tremblant
Lamb's Tails à-la-Bashemel	Pigeon Pie	Tongue
	Whitings boiled and broiled	

SECOND COURSE.

Ducklings

Asparagus	Tartlets	Black Caps
Roast Sweetbreads	Jellies and Syllabubs	Oyster Loaves
Stewed Pears	Tansey	Mushrooms
	Ribs of Lamb	

THIRD COURSE.

Petit Pigeons

Mushrooms	French Plums	Pistachio Nuts
Marinated Smelts	Sweetmeats	Oyster Loaves
Blanched Almonds	Raisins	Artichoke Bottoms
	Calves Ears à-la-braise	

MAY.

MAY.

FIRST COURSE.

Calvert's Salmon broiled

Rabbits with Onions	Veal Olives	Collared Mutton
Pigeon Pie raifed	Vermicelli Soup	Macaroni Tart
Ox Palates	Chine of Lamb	Matelot of Tame Duck
	Mackarel	

SECOND COURSE.

Green Goofe

Afparagus	Cuftards	Cocks' Combs
Green Goofeberry Tarts	Epergne	Green Apricot Tarts
Lamb Cutlets	Blancmange	Stewed Celery
	Roaft Chickens	

THIRD COURSE.

Lamb Sweetbreads

Stewed Lettuce	Rhenifh Cream	Rafpberry Puffs
Lobfters ragooed	Compoft of Green Apricots	Buttered Crab
Lemon Cakes	Orange Jelly	French Beans
	Ragout of Fat Livers	

JUNE.

FIRST COURSE.

Green Peas Soup

Chickens	Haunch of Venifon	Harrico
Lamb Pie	Turbot	Ham
Veal Cutlets	Neck of Venifon	Orange Pudding
	Lobfter Soup	

SECOND COURSE.

Turkey Poults

Peas	Apricot Puffs	Lobfters
Fricaffee of Lamb	Half Moon	Roafted Sweetbreads
Smelts	Cherry Tart	Artichokes
	Roafted Rabbits	

THIRD COURSE.

Sweetbreads à-la-Blanche

Fillets of Soals	Potted Wheat Ears	Ratafia Cream
Peas	Green Goofeberry Tart	Forced Artichokes
Preferved Oranges	Potted Ruff	Matelot of Eels
	Lamb's Tails à-la-braife	

JULY.

JULY.

FIRST COURSE.

Breaſt of Veal à-la-braiſe	Mackarel, &c.	
Veniſon Paſty	Tongue and Turnips	Pulpeton
	Herb Soup	Neck of Veniſon
Chickens	Boiled Gooſe and ſtewed Red Cabbage	Mutton Cutlets
	Trout boiled	

SECOND COURSE.

Stewed Peas	Roaſt Turkey	
Sweetbreads	Apricot Tart	Blancmange
Cuſtards	Jellies	Fricaſſee of Rabits
	Green Codling Tart	Blaized Pippins
	Roaſt Pigeons	

THIRD COURSE.

Apricots	Fricaſſee of Rabbits	
Cray-fiſh ragooed	Pains à-la-Ducheſſe	Forced Cucumbers
Jeruſalem Artichokes	Morel Cherry Tart	Lobſters à-la-braize
	Apricot Puffs	Green Gage Plums
	Lamb Stones	

AUGUST.

FIRST COURSE.

Fillets of Pigeons	Stewed Soals	
French Patty	Ham	Turkey à-la-daube
Chickens	Cray-fiſh Soup	Petit Patties
	Fillet of Veal	Roſard of Beef Palates
	Whitings	

SECOND COURSE.

Macaroni	Roaſt Ducks	
Cheeſecakes	Tartlet	Fillets of Soals
Matelot of Eels	Jellies	Apple Pies
	Orange Puffs	Fricaſſee of Sweetbreads
	Leveret	

THIRD COURSE.

Stewed Peas	Partridge à-la-pair	
Apricot Tart	Potted Wheat Ears	Cray-fiſh
Prawns	Fruit	Cut Paſtry
	Scraped Beef	Blanched Celery
	Ruffs and Rees	

SEPTEMBER.

SEPTEMBER.

FIRST COURSE

	Diſh of Fiſh	
Chickens	Chine of Lamb	Veal Collops
Pigeon Pie	Gravy Soup	Almond Tart
Harico of Mutton	Roaſt Beef	Ham
	Diſh of Fiſh	

SECOND COURSE.

	Wild Fowls	
Peas	Damaſcene Tarts	Ragooed Lobſters
Sweetbreads	Crocant	Fried Piths
Cray-fiſh	Maids of Honour	Fried Artichokes
	Partridges	

THIRD COURSE.

	Ragooed Palates	
Comport of Biſcuits	Tartlets	Fruit in Jelly
Green Truffles	Epergne	Cardoons
Blancmange	Cheeſecakes	Ratafia Drops
	Calves Ears à-la-braiſe	

OCTOBER.

FIRST COURSE.

	Cod and Oyſter Sauce	
Jugged Hare	Neck of Veal à la braiſe	Small Puddings
French Patty	Almond Soup	Fillet of Beef larded & roaſted
Chickens	Tongue and Udder	Torrent de Veau
	Broiled Salmon	

SECOND COURSE.

	Pheaſant	
Stewed Pears	Apple Tarts	Muſhrooms
Roaſt Lobſters	Jellies	Oyſter Loaves
White Fricaſſee	Cuſtards	Pippins
	Turkey	

THIRD COURSE.

	Sweetbread à la braiſe	
Fried Artichokes	Potted Eels	Pig's Ears
Almond Cheeſecakes	Fruit	Apricot Puffs
Amlet	Potted Lobſters	Forced Celery
	Larks	

NOVEMBER.

NOVEMBER.

FIRST COURSE.

Dish of Fish

	Roasted Turkey	Ox Palates
Veal Cutlets	Roasted Turkey	Ox Palates
Two Chickens	Vermicelli	Leg of Lamb
and Brocoli	Soup	and Spinach
Beef Collops	Chine of Pork	Harrico
	Dish of Fish	

SECOND COURSE.

Woodcocks

Sheeps Rumps	Apple Puffs	Dish of Jelly
Oyster Loaves	Crocants	Ragooed Lobsters
Blanc mange	Lemon Tart	Lambs Ears
	Hare	

THIRD COURSE.

Pettit Patties

Stewed Pears	Potted Chars	Fried Oysters
Gallantine	Ice Cream	Collared Eels
Fillets of Whitings	Potted Cray-fish	Pippins
	Lambs' Ears à la braise	

DECEMBER.

FIRST COURSE.

Cod's Head

Chickens	Stewed Beef	Fricandeau of Veal
Almond Puddings	Soup Santè	Calves Feet Pie
Fillet of Pork with sharp sauce	Chine of Lamb	Tongue
	Soals fried and boiled	

SECOND COURSE.

Wild Fowls

Lambs Fry	Orange Puffs	Sturgeon
Gallantine	Jellies	Savoury Cake
Prawns	Tartlets	Mushrooms
	Partridges	

THIRD COURSE.

Ragooed Palates

Savoy Cakes	Dutch Beef Scraped	China Oranges
Lambs Tails	Half Moon	Calves Burs
Jargonel Pears	Potted Larks	Lemon Biscuits
	Fricassee of Cray-fish	

N. B. Be careful to send up all kinds of garden stuff suitable to your meat, &c. in your first course, in different dishes on a water-dish on the side table ; and all your sauce in boats or basons, to answer each other at the corners.

SUPPERS

SUPPERS.

Little Family Suppers of Four Things.

	Minced Veal	
Pat of Butter in a glaſs		Radiſhes
	Poached Eggs on a toaſt	

	Haſhed Mutton	
Anchovy and Butter		Pickles
	Scolloped or roaſted Potatoes	

	Maintenons	
Sliced Ham		Tart
	Rabbit Roaſted	

	Boiled Chicken	
Cold Beef or Mutton ſliced		Pickles
	Scolloped Oyſters	

	Boiled Tripe	
Bologna Sauſage ſliced		Pat of Butter in a glaſs
	Haſhed Hare	

	Gudgeons fried	
Biſcuits		Raſped Beef, and a Pat of Butter in the middle
	Duck roaſted	

	Roaſted Chicken	
Potted Beef		Cheeſecakes
	Sauſages, with Eggs poached	

	Whitings broiled	
Tongue ſliced		Biſcuits
	Calf's Heart	

	Veal Cutlet	
Tart		Radiſhes, and Butter in the middle
	Aſparagus	

	Houſe Lamb Steaks, à-la-fricaſſee, white	
Collared Eel		Pickles
	Chicken roaſted	

Family

Family Suppers of Five Things.

	Scotch Collops	
Potted Pigeon	Salad	Lobster
	Peafe	

	Eels broiled or boiled	
Butter fpun	Tart	Radifhes
	Sweetbread roafted	

	Cold Veal hafhed	
Anchovies and Butter	Plain Fritters	Pickles
	Teal roafted	

	Pigeons roafted	
Prawns	Tarts	Cold Mutton fliced
	Afparagus	

	Poached Eggs and Spinach ftewed	
Slices of Beef	Mince Pies	Baked Sprats
	Chickens roafted	

	Boiled Chickens	
Peafe	Goofeberry Cream	Parfley and Butter, and melted Butter
	Fricaffee of Ox Palates	

	Duck roafted	
Sliced Tongue	Tart	Cray-fifh
	Peafe	

	Boiled Chickens, Lemon-fauce	
Ham fliced	Butter in a glafs	Radifhes
	Lamb's Fry	

	Spitchcock Eel	
Collared Beef	Rafpberry Fritters	Pickles
	Veal Cutlet	

	Giblets ftewed	
Collared Veal fliced	Tart	Crab
	Roafted Pigeons	

	Buttered Lobfter	
Potted Beef	Rafpberry Cream	Collared Pig's Head
	Calf's Heart.	

DOMESTIC

DOMESTIC ECONOMY,

&c. &c. &c.

CHAP. I.—*Of* ROASTING.

General Inftructions.

WHEN you roaft meat of any kind, put a little falt and water in your dripping-pan; bafte your meat a little with it; let it dry, then duft it well with flour; bafte it with frefh butter, and it will make your meat a better colour. Obferve always to have a brifk, clear fire; it will prevent your meat from dazing, and the froth from falling. Keep it a good diftance from the fire. If the meat be fcorched, the outfide will be hard, and prevent the heat from penetrating into the meat, and will appear enough before it be little more than half done. Time, diftance, bafting often, and a clear fire, is the beft method I can prefcribe for roafting meat to perfection. When the fteam draws near the fire, it is a fign of its being enough; but you will be the beft judge of that from the time you put it down. Be careful, when you roaft any kind of wild fowl, to keep a clear brifk fire; roaft them a light brown, but not too much. It is a great fault to roaft them till the gravy runs out of them, as that takes off the fine flavour. Tame fowls require more roafting; they are a long time before they are hot through, and muft be often bafted to keep up a ftrong froth; it makes them rife better, and a finer colour. Pigs and geefe fhould be roafted before a good fire, and turned quick. Hares and rabbits require time and care, to fee the ends are roafted enough; when they are half roafted, cut the neck-fkin, and let out the blood, or when they are cut up they often appear bloody at the neck.

I muft defire the cook to order her fire according to what fhe is to drefs; if any thing very little or thin, then a pretty little brifk fire, that it may be done quick and nice; if a very large joint, then be fure a good fire be laid to cake. Let it be clear at the bottom; and when your meat is half done, move the dripping pan and fpit a little from the fire, and ftir up a good brifk fire; for, according to the goodnefs of your fire, your meat will be done fooner or later.

B   As

As foon as the meat is put to the fire, pour over it fome warm water, which afterwards throw away; this is very neceffary to thofe who are nice in the dreffing their meat, it being a good deal handled in the fpitting; fhake fome flour over it, bafte it with butter, and do not put it too near the fire; this, with frequently bafting it, a brifk fire, and allowing time enough, are the only means of roafting in perfection; when the fteam draws to the fire, the meat is done; flour and bafte it juft before it is fent to the table, that it may have a nice froth; always allow a longer time for the meat to roaft in frofty weather; take particular care to have the fpit clean, as nothing is more difagreeable than a fpit-mark; and remember, when the meat is half done, to remove the dripping-pan and fpit a little from the fire, and ftir it; if it is a good fire before the meat is laid down, once-ftirring it will in general roaft a joint of meat. Never falt the meat before it is put to the fire, it draws out the gravy too much; if it is to be kept fome time before it is dreffed, (and indeed mutton and beef are not good frefh killed) be fure to dry it well with a cloth, and hang it where it will have a thorough air; look at it every day and wipe off all the damp; it will keep a long time. Some pepper it a little.

To roaft Beef.

Be fure to paper the top, and bafte it well all the time it is roafting, and throw a handful of falt on it. When you fee the fmoke draw to the fire, it is near enough; then take off the paper, bafte it well, and dredge it with a little flour to make a fine froth. Never falt your roaft meat before you lay it to the fire, for that draws out all the gravy. Take up your meat, and garnifh your difh with nothing but horfe-radifh.

'To roaft a piece of beef of about ten pounds, will take an hour and an half, at a good fire. Twenty pounds weight will take three hours, if it be a thick piece; but if it be a thin piece of twenty pounds weight, two hours and an half will do it; and fo on, according to the weight of your meat, more or lefs. Obferve, in frofty weather your beef will take half an hour longer. *Glaffe*, 22.

To roaft a Beef-Tongue.

Boil a tongue until it will peel, in broth or water, with falt and pepper, onions, carrots, parfnips, a nofegay*, two cloves of garlic, laurel, and thyme; then lard it as a fricandeau†, and finifh it in roafting; ferve under it a relifhing fauce, or plain. *Dalrymple*, 53.

---

* *A faggot of parfley, onions, fhallots, &c.*
† *A piece of meat larded, brazed, and glazed.*

Cold Roaſt Beef, family faſhion.

Slice three or four onions, and fry them in butter; when done, add a little broth, three ſhallots chopped, pepper and ſalt, then put ſlices of cold beef to it, boil for a moment; when ready, add a liaſon‡ made of three yolks of eggs and a little vinegar. Cold beef is alſo very good with cold ſauce, made of chopped parſley, ſhallots, vinegar, oil, muſtard, minced anchovy, &c. *Dalrymple*, 67.

To roaſt Mutton and Lamb.

As to roaſting of mutton, the loin, the chine of mutton, (which is the two loins) and the ſaddle, (which is the two necks, and part of the ſhoulders cut together) muſt have the ſkin raiſed and ſkewered on; and when near done, take off the ſkin, baſte and flour it, to froth it up. All other parts of mutton and lamb muſt be roaſted with a quick clear fire, without the ſkin being raiſed, or paper put on. You ſhould always obſerve to baſte your meat as ſoon as you lay it down to roaſt; ſprinkle ſome ſalt on, and when near done, dredge it with a little flour to froth it up. Garniſh mutton with horſe-radiſh; lamb with creſſes, or ſmall ſalading.

A leg of mutton of ſix pounds will take an hour and a quarter; of twelve pounds, two hours; a ſmall ſaddle, an hour and an half; a large one, near three hours. Paper a ſaddle. If garlic is not diſliked, ſtuff the knuckle part of the leg with two or three cloves of it; a breaſt will take half an hour at a briſk fire; a large neck, an hour; a ſmall one, a little more than half an hour; a ſhoulder near as much time as a leg. For ſauce—potatoes, pickles, ſalad, celery raw or ſtewed, broccoli, French beans, cauliflower; or, to a ſhoulder of mutton, onion ſauce. *Maſon*, 161.

To roaſt a Haunch of Mutton, Veniſon faſhion.

To dreſs a haunch of mutton, veniſon faſhion, take a hind fat quarter of mutton, and cut the leg like a haunch. Lay it in a pan, with the back-ſide of it down, and pour a bottle of red wine over it, in which let it lay twenty-four hours. Spit it, and roaſt it at a good quick fire, and keep baſting it all the time with the ſame liquor and butter. It will require an hour and an half roaſting; and, when it is done, ſend it up with a little good gravy in one boat, and ſweet ſauce in another. A good fat neck of mutton done in this manner is eſteemed delicate eating. *Farley*, 34.

Another way.

Cut a hind quarter of fat mutton like a haunch of veniſon; let it ſteep in the ſheep's blood for five or ſix hours; then let it

‡ *Conglutinating different liquors without boiling.*

hang.

hang, in cold dry weather, for three weeks, or as long as it will keep fweet; rub it well with a cloth, then rub it over with frefh butter; ftrew fome falt over it, and a little flour; butter a fheet of paper, and lay over it, and another over that, or fome pafte, and tie it round. If it is large, it will take two hours and an half roafting. Before it is taken up, take off the paper, or pafte, bafte it well with butter, and flour it. Let the jack go round very quick, that it may have a good froth. Sauce—gravy and currant jelly. *Mafon*, 161.

Another way.

Get the largeft and fatteft leg of mutton you can, cut out like a haunch of venifon, as foon as it is killed, whilft it is warm, it will eat the tenderer; take out the bloody vein, ftick it in feveral places in the under fide with a fharp pointed knife; pour over it a bottle of red wine; turn it in the wine four or five times a day for five days, then dry it exceeding well with a clean cloth; hang it up in the air, with the thick end uppermoft, for five days; dry it night and morning, to keep it from being damp or growing mufty. When you roaft it, cover it with paper, and pafte it as you do venifon; ferve it up with venifon fauce. It will take four hours roafting. *Raffald*, 107.

To roaft Veal.

As to veal, you muft be careful to roaft it of a fine brown; if a large joint, a very good fire; if a fmall joint, a pretty little brifk fire; if a fillet or loin, be fure to paper the fat, that you lofe as little of that as poffible. Lay it fome diftance ftom the fire, till it is foaked; then lay it near the fire. When you lay it down, bafte it well with good butter; and when it is near enough, bafte it again, and dredge it with a little flour. The breaft you muft roaft with the caul on till it is enough; and fkewer the fweet-bread on the back-fide of the breaft. When it is nigh enough, take off the caul, bafte it, and dredge it with a little flour. Veal will take a quarter of an hour to a pound in roafting; ftuff the fillet and fhoulder with the following ingredients—a quarter of a pound of fuet chopped fine, parfley and fweet herbs chopped, grated bread and lemon peel; pepper, falt, nutmeg, and yolk of egg; butter may fupply the want of fuet; roaft the breaft with the caul on, till it is almoft enough, then take it off; flour it, and bafte it. Veal requires to be more done than beef. For fauce—falad, pickles, potatoes, broccoli, cucumbers raw or ftewed, French beans, peafe, cauliflower, celery raw or ftewed. *Glaffe*, 13. *Mafon*, 137.

To roaft Pork.

Pork muft be well done, or it is apt to furfeit. When you roaft a loin, take a fharp pen-knife, and cut the fkin acrofs, to make the crackling eat the better. The chine muft be cut, and
fo

fo muſt all pork that has the rind on. Roaſt a leg of pork thus :
—Take a knife, as above, and ſcore it ; ſtuff the knuckle part
with ſage and onion, chopped fine, with pepper and ſalt ; or cut
a hole under the twiſt, and put the ſage, &c. there, and ſkewer
it up with a ſkewer. Roaſt it criſp, becauſe moſt people like the
rind criſp, which they call crackling. Make ſome good apple-
ſauce, and ſend it up in a boat ; then have a little drawn gravy
to put in the diſh. This they call a mock-gooſe. The ſpring,
or hand of pork, if very young, roaſted like a pig, eats very
well ; or take the ſpring, and cut off the ſhank or knuckle, and
ſprinkle ſage and onion over it, and roll it round, and tie it with
a ſtring, and roaſt it two hours, otherwiſe it is better boiled.
The ſpare-rib ſhould be baſted with a little bit of butter, a very
little duſt of flour, and ſome ſage ſhred ſmall ; but we never
make any ſauce to it but apple-ſauce. The beſt way to dreſs
pork griſkins is to roaſt them, baſte them with a little butter and
ſage, and a little pepper and ſalt. Few eat any thing with theſe
but muſtard. Pork muſt be well done. To every pound, allow a quarter of an hour. For example—a joint of twelve
pounds weight, three hours ; and ſo on. If it be a thin piece
of that weight, two hours will roaſt it. *Glaſſe*, 322.

Maſon adviſes to rub the pork over with a feather and ſome
oil inſtead of ſcoring.

To roaſt a Pig.

Stick your pig juſt above the breaſt-bone, run your knife to
the heart. When it is dead, put it in cold water for a few minutes, then rub it over with a little roſin beat exceeding fine, or
its own blood ; put your pig into a pail of ſcalding water half a
minute ; take it out, lay it on a clean table, pull off the hair as
quick as poſſible ; if it does not come clean off, put it in again.
When you have got it all clean off, waſh it in warm water, then
in two or three cold waters, for fear the roſin ſhould taſte. Take
off the fore feet at the firſt joint, make a ſlit down the belly, and
take out all the entrails ; put the liver, heart, and lights, to the
pettitoes, waſh it well out of cold water, dry it exceedingly well
with a cloth, hang it up, and when you roaſt it, put in a little
ſhred ſage, a tea-ſpoonful of black pepper, two of ſalt, and a
cruſt of brown bread ; ſpit your pig, and ſew it up ; lay it down
to a briſk clear fire, with a pig-plate hung in the middle of the
fire. When your pig is warm, put a lump of butter in a cloth,
and rub your pig often with it while it is roaſting. A large one
will take an hour and a half. When your pig is a fine brown,
and the ſteam draws near the fire, take a clean cloth, rub your
pig quite dry, then rub it well with a little cold butter, it will
help to criſp it ; then take a ſharp knife, cut off the head, and
take off the collar ; then take off the ears and jaw-bone, ſplit
the jaw in two. When you have cut the pig down the back,

which muſt be done before you draw the ſpit out, then lay your pig back to back on your diſh, and the jaw on each ſide, the ears on each ſhoulder, and the collar at the ſhoulder, and pour in your ſauce, and ſerve it up. Garniſh with a cruſt of brown bread grated. *Raffald*, 55. *Farley*, 34.

Another way to roaſt a Pig.

The pig being prepared, as above, ſpit it, and lay it to the fire, which muſt be a very good one at each end, or hang a flat iron in the middle of the grate. Before you lay it down to the fire, ſhred a little ſage very ſmall, take a piece of butter as big as a walnut, and a little ſalt and pepper; put this into the pig, and ſew it up ſtrongly; then flour it all over, and continue to do ſo till the crackling becomes hard. Take care to ſave all the gravy that comes from it, and for this purpoſe put a large baſon or pan in the dripping-pan as ſoon as the gravy begins to run. When the pig is enough, ſtir up the fire briſkly, take a coarſe cloth, with about a quarter of a pound of butter in it, and rub the pig all over till the crackling is quite criſp, when it muſt be taken up. Lay it in the diſh, and cut off the head with a ſharp knife; and, before you draw out the ſpit, cut the pig in two. Cut off the ears, and lay one at each end; divide the under jaw, and diſpoſe of them in the ſame manner. Put the gravy you ſaved into ſome melted butter, and boil them. Pour it into the diſh, with the brains bruiſed fine, and the ſage mixed all together, and ſerve it up. *Farley*, 34, 35. *Glaſſe*, 3. *Raffald*, 55.

Another way to roaſt a Pig.

Chop ſome ſage and onion very fine, a few crumbs of bread, a little butter, pepper, and ſalt, rolled up together; put it into the belly, and ſew it up before you lay down the pig; rub it all over with ſweet oil. When it is done, take a dry cloth and wipe it; then take it into a diſh, cut it up, and ſend it to table with the ſame ſauce as above.

To roaſt the hind quarter of a Pig, Lamb-faſhion.

At the time of the year when houſe-lamb is very dear, take the hind quarter of a large roaſting pig; take off the ſkin and roaſt it, and it will eat like lamb, with mint-ſauce, or with a ſalad or Seville orange. Half an hour will roaſt it. *Glaſſe*, 4. *Farley*, 36.

To make Sauce for a Pig.

Chop the brains a little, then put in a tea-cup full of white gravy with the gravy that runs out of the pig, a little bit of anchovy; mix near half a pound of butter with as much flour as will thicken the gravy, a ſlice of lemon, a ſpoonful of white wine, a little caper liquor and ſalt; ſhake it over the fire, and pour it into your diſh. Some like currants: boil a few, and
ſend

fend them in a tea-faucer, with a glafs of currant-jelly in the middle of it. *Raffald*, 56.

Different forts of Sauce for a Pig.

Now you are to obferve there are feveral ways of making fauce for a pig. Some do not love any fage in the pig, only a cruft of bread; but then you fhould have a little dried fage rubbed and mixed with the gravy and butter. Some love bread fauce in a bafon, made thus:—take a pint of water, put in a good piece of crumb of bread, a blade of mace, and a little whole pepper; boil it for about five or fix minutes, and then pour the water off; take out the fpice, and beat up the bread with a good piece of butter, and a little milk or cream. Some love a few currants boiled in it, a glafs of wine and a little fugar; but in that you muft do juft as you like. Others take half a pint of good beef gravy, and the gravy which comes out of the pig, with a piece of butter rolled in flour, two fpoonfuls of catchup, and boil them altogether; then take the brains of the pig and bruife them fine; put all thefe together, with the fage in the pig, and pour into your difh. It is a very good fauce. When you have not gravy enough comes out of your pig, with the butter, for fauce, take about half a pint of veal gravy and add to it; or ftew the pettitoes, and take as much of that liquor as will do for fauce, mixed with the other.--N. B. Some like the fauce fent in a boat or bafon. *Glaffe*, 4.

To roaft Venifon.

In order to roaft a haunch of venifon properly, as foon as you have fpitted it, you muft lay over it a large fheet of paper, and then a thin common pafte, with another paper over that. Tie it faft, in order to keep the pafte from dropping off; and if the haunch be a large one, it will take four hours roafting. As foon as it is done enough, take off both paper and pafte, dredge it well with flour, and bafte it with butter. As foon as it becomes of a light brown, difh it up with brown gravy or currant-jelly fauce, and fend up fome in a boat. *Raffald*, 69. *Farley*, 34. *Mafon*, 298.

Another way to roaft Venifon.

Take a haunch of venifon and fpit it; rub fome butter all over your haunch; take four fheets of paper well buttered, put two on the haunch; then make a pafte with fome flour, a little butter and water; roll it out half as big as your haunch, and put it over the fat part; then put the other two fheets of paper on, and tie them with the fame packthread; lay it to a briik fire, and bafte it well all the time of roafting; if a large haunch of twenty-four pounds, it will take three hours and an half, except it is a very large fire, then three hours will do it. Smaller in proportion.

Sweet Sauce for Venison or Hare.

Melt fome currant jelly in a little water and red wine, or fend in currant jelly only ; or fimmer red wine and fugar for about twenty minutes. *Mafon*, 322.

Sweet Sauce of red wine for Venison or roasted Tongue.

Take a gill of water, with a little bit of cinnamon, the crumb of a French roll; add to it half a pint of red port or claret; fweeten it ; let it boil till it is pretty thick, then run it through a fieve. *Mafon*, 322.

Different fort of Sauces for Venison.

You may take either of thefe fauces for venifon. Currant jelly warmed ; or a pint of red wine, with a quarter of a pound of fugar, fimmered over a clear fire for five or fix minutes ; or a pint of vinegar and a quarter of a pound of fugar, fimmered till it is a fyrup. *Glaffe*, 10.

To roast Geese.

To roaft a Green Goofe.

When your goofe is ready dreffed, put in a good lump of butter, fpit it, lay it down, finge it well, duft it with flour, bafte it with frefh butter, bafte it three or four times with cold butter, it will make the flefh rife better than if you was to bafte it out of the dripping pan ; if it is a large one, it will take three quarters of an hour to roaft it ; when you think it is enough, dredge it with flour, bafte it till it is a fine froth, and your goofe a nice brown, and difh it up with a little brown gravy under it. Garnifh it with a cruft of bread grated round the edge of your difh. *Farley*, 38. *Raffald*, 58.

Sauce for a Green Goofe.

Take fome melted butter, put in a fpoonful of the juice of forrel, a little fugar, a few coddled goofeberries, pour it into your fauceboats, and fend it to the table. *Raffald*, 58.

To roaft a Goofe.

Take a few fage leaves and two onions, and chop them as fine as poffible. Mix them with a large piece of butter, two fpoonfuls of falt, and one of pepper. Put this into the goofe, fpit it, and lay it down to the fire ; finge it, and duft it with flour, and when it is thoroughly hot, bafte it with frefh butter. A large goofe will require an hour and an half before a good fire, and when it is done, dredge and bafte it, pull out the fpit, and pour in a little boiling water. *Farley* 38.

Another way to roaft a Goofe.

It muft be feafoned with fage and onion, cut very fmall, and mixed with pepper and falt ; an hour will roaft it. Boil the
fage

fage and onion in a little water before they are cut; it prevents
their eating fo ftrong, and takes off the rawnefs. For fauce—
gravy and apple-fauce. *Mafon.* 268.

When you roaft a goofe, turkey, or fowls of any fort, take
care to finge them with a piece of white paper, and bafte them
with a piece of butter; dredge them with a little flour, and
fprinkle a little falt on; and when the fmoke begins to draw to
the fire, and they look plump, bafte them again and dredge
them with a little flour, and take them up. *Glaffe,* 5.

Sauce for a Goofe or Duck.

As to geefe and ducks. you fhould have fage and onions fhred
fine, with pepper and falt put into the belly.

Put only pepper and falt into wild-ducks, eafterlings. wigeon,
teal and all other fort of wild-fowl with gravy in the difh, or,
fome like fage and onion in one. *Glaffe,* 7.

To roaft a Turkey.

A middle fized one will be roafted in an hour. Make a ftuffing with four ounces of butter or chopped fuet. grated bread, a
little lemon-peel, parfley. and fweet herbs chopped pepper,
falt. and nutmeg. a little cream and yolks of eggs; fill the craw
with this, or with force-meat; paper the breaft till near done,
then flour and bafte it. For fauce—gravy alone. or brown celery fauce, or mufhroom fauce. For a turkey-poult, gravy and
bread fauce. *Mafon,* 258.

A middling turkey will take an hour; a very large one, an
hour and a quarter; a fmall one. three quarters of an hour.
Your fire muft be very good. *Glaffe* 13.

Another way to roaft a Turkey.

Hen turkeys are moftly preferable to cocks, for whitenefs and
tendernefs; the fmall flefhy ones are the moft efteemed, and
they ought to be kept as long as the weather will admit. Make
a forced-meat with the liver chopped, parfley, fhallots, fcraped
lard, yolks of eggs, pepper, and falt. When properly truffed,
give the turkey a few turns over the fire in a large ftew-pan with
butter; ftuff the force-meat under the breaft where the craw was
taken out, and roaft it, with lemon flices upon the breaft to keep
it white; flices of lard, and double paper. Serve with what
ragoo you think proper, as mufhrooms, morels, fmall onions,
or large Spanifh ones, girkins, fmall melons, cucumbers, truffles,
green peas. fmall garden beans, endive, cardoons, roots of any
fort, celery, craw-fifh, or any thing according to the feafon.
Clermont, 226.

Sauce for a Turkey.

Cut the crufts off a penny loaf, cut the reft in thin flices, put
it in cold water, with a few pepper-corns, a little falt and onion;
boil

boil it till the bread is quite foft, then beat it well; put in a
quarter of a pound of butter, two fpoonfuls of thick cream, and
put it into a bafon. *Raffald,* 63.

Another Sauce for a Turkey.

Take half a pint of oyfters, ftrain the liquor, and put the
oyfters with the liquor into a faucepan with a blade or two of
mace; let them juft lump, then pour in a glafs of white wine;
let it boil once, and thicken it with a piece of butter rolled in
flour.   Serve this up in a bafon by itfelf, with good gravy in the
difh, for every body does not love oyfter-fauce.   If you chufe it
in the difh, add half a pint of gravy to it, and boil it up together.   This fauce is good either with boiled or roafted turkies,
or fowls; but you may leave the gravy out, adding as much
butter as will do for fauce, and garnifhing with lemon.

To roaft Fowls.

When the fowls are laid to the fire, finge them with fome
white paper, bafte them with butter, and then dredge over them
fome flour; when the fmoke begins to draw to the fire, bafte
and dredge them over again; let the fire be brifk, and fend
them to table with a good froth.   A large fowl will take three
quarters of an hour; a fmall one twenty minutes.   For fauce—
gravy, egg-fauce, mufhrooms, and white or brown celery-fauce.
Mafon, 262.

Another way to roaft Fowls.

Take your fowls when they are ready dreffed, put them down
to a good fire, finge, duft, and bafte them well with butter.   A
large fowl will be near an hour in roafting.   Make a gravy of
the necks and gizzards, ftrain it, put in a fpoonful of browning.
When you difh them up, pour the gravy into the difh; ferve
them up with egg-fauce in a boat.   *Raffald,* 64.

A large fowl will take three quarters of an hour roafting; a
middling one, half an hour; very fmall chickens, twenty minutes.   Your fire muft be very quick and clear when you lay
them down.   *Glaffe,* 14.

Another way to roaft Fowls.

Make fome force-meat with the flefh of a fowl cut fmall, and
a pound of veal; beat them in a mortar with half a pound of
beef fuet, as much crumb of bread, fome mufhrooms, truffles,
and morels, cut fmall; fome lemon-peel grated fine, fome beaten
mace, a few fweet herbs, and fome parfley, mixed together with
the yolks of two eggs; bone the fowls, fill them with the force-
meat, and roaft them.   For fauce—ftrong gravy, with truffles,
morels, and mufhrooms.   *Mafon,* 263.

To roaft Chickens.

Pluck your chickens very carefully, draw them, and cut off
their

their claws only, and truſs them. Put them down to a good fire, ſinge, duſt, and baſte them with butter. A quarter of an hour will roaſt them; and when they are enough, froth them, and lay them on your diſh. Serve them up hot, with parſley and butter poured over them. *Sarley*, 38. *Raffald*, 65.

A large chicken will take half an hour; a ſmall one, twenty minutes. For ſauce—gravy, parſley and butter, or muſhroom ſauce. *Maſon*, 263.

Another way to roaſt Chickens.

Make a little forced-meat with the livers, ſcraped lard, chopped parſley, ſhallots, pepper and ſalt; ſtuff a couple of chickens with this, truſſed for roaſting; lay a couple of ſlices of lemon on the breaſts, and wrap them up with thin ſlices of lard and paper; roaſt them, and ſerve up what ſort of ſtewed greens you pleaſe, as ſpinach, cucumbers, &c. *Clermont*, 207.

To make Egg Sauce.

Boil two eggs hard, half chop the whites, then put in the yolks, chop them both together, but not very fine; put them into a quarter of a pound of good melted butter, and put it in a boat. *Raffald*, 64.

To roaſt Ducks.

Kill and draw your ducks; then ſhred an onion and a few ſage leaves; ſeaſon theſe with ſalt and pepper, and put them into your ducks. Singe, duſt, and baſte them with butter, and a good fire will roaſt them in twenty minutes; for the quicker they are done, the better they will be. Before you take them up, duſt them with flour, and baſte them with butter, to give them a good frothing and a pleaſing brown. Your gravy muſt be made of the gizzards and pinions, an onion, a tea-ſpoonful of lemon-pickle, a few pepper-corns, a large blade of mace, a ſpoonful of catchup, and the ſame of browning. Strain it, pour it into your diſh, and ſend it up with onion-ſauce in a baſon. *Farley*, 40.

Another way to roaſt Ducks.

Seaſon them with ſage and onion ſhred, pepper, and ſalt; half an hour will roaſt them – gravy-ſauce, or onion-ſauce. Always ſtew the ſage and onion in a little water, as it prevents its eating ſtrong, and takes off the rawneſs. *Maſon*, 273.

A wild duck will take full twenty minutes. *Maſon*, 273. *Raffald*, 66.

If you love them well done, a wild-duck will take twenty-five minutes. *Glaſſe*, 14.

A wigeon or eaſterling will take near twenty minutes. *Maſo*, 273.

A teal will be done in fifteen minutes. *Maſon*, 273.

Teal will take eleven or twelve minutes roaſting. *Glaſſe*, 14.

To

To roaſt wild Ducks or Teal.

When your ducks are ready dreſſed, put in them a ſmall onion, pepper, ſalt, and a ſpoonful of red wine; if the fire be good, they will roaſt in twenty minutes; make gravy of the necks and gizzards, a ſpoonful of red wine, half an anchovy, a blade or two of mace, a ſlice of an end of lemon, one onion, and a little chyan pepper; boil it till it is waſted to half a pint, ſtrain it through a hair ſieve, put in a ſpoonful of browning, pour it on your ducks, ſerve them up with onion-ſauce in a boat. Garniſh your diſh with raſpings of bread. *Raffald*, 67.

The beſt way to dreſs a Wild Duck.

Firſt half roaſt it, then lay it in a diſh, carve it, but leave the joints hanging together; throw a little pepper and ſalt, and ſqueeze the juice of a lemon over it; turn it on the breaſt, and preſs it hard with a plate, and add to its own gravy two or three ſpoonfuls of good gravy; cover it cloſe with another diſh, and ſet it over a ſtove ten minutes; then ſend it to table hot in the diſh it was done in, and garniſh with lemon. You may add a little red wine, and a ſhallot cut ſmall, if you like it; but it is apt to make the duck eat hard, unleſs you firſt heat the wine, and pour it in juſt as it is done. *Glaſſe*, 81.

To roaſt Woodcocks or Snipes.

Having put your birds on a little ſpit, take a round of a threepenny loaf and toaſt it brown; lay it in a diſh under the birds, and when you lay them down to the fire, baſte them with a little butter, and let the trail drop on the toaſt. When they are roaſted enough, put the toaſt in the diſh, and lay the birds on it. Pour about a quarter of a pint of gravy into the diſh, and ſet it over a lamp or chafing-diſh for three or four minutes, when the whole will be in a proper condition to be ſent to the table. Oſerve never to take any thing out of a woodcock or ſnipe.

Another way.

Pluck them, but do not draw them; put them on a ſmall ſpit, duſt, and baſte them well with butter, toaſt a few ſlices of a penny loaf, put them on a clean plate, and ſet it under the birds while they are roaſting. If the fire be good, they will take about ten minutes roaſting. When you draw them, lay them upon the toaſts on the diſh; pour melted butter round them, and ſerve them up. *Raffald*, 66.

Twenty minutes will roaſt woodcocks, and fifteen minutes ſnipes. *Maſon*, 274.

A woodcock will require twenty-five minutes. *Glaſſe*, 6.

A ſnipe will require twenty minutes roaſting. *Glaſſe*, 6.

To roaſt Larks.

Put a ſmall bird-ſpit through them, and tie them on another; roaſt

roaſt them, and all the time they are roaſting, keep baſting them
very gently with butter, and ſprinkle crumbs of bread on them
till they are almoſt done; then let them brown before you take
them up.

The beſt way of making crumbs of bread is, to rub them
through a fine cullender, and put in a little butter into a ſtew-
pan; melt it, put in your crumbs of bread, and keep them
ſtirring till they are of a light brown; put them on a ſieve
to drain a few minutes; lay your larks in a diſh, and the crumbs
all round, almoſt as high as the larks, with plain butter in a cup,
and ſome gravy in another. *Glaſſe*, 6.

Another way to roaſt Larks.

Skewer a dozen of larks, and tie both ends of the ſkewer to
the ſpit. Dredge and baſte them, and let them roaſt ten minutes. Break half a penny loaf into crumbs, and put them,
with a piece of butter of the ſize of a walnut, into a toſſing-
pan, and having ſhaken them over a gentle fire till they are of a
light brown, lay them between the birds, and pour a little melted butter over them. *Farley*, 40.

To roaſt Ruffs and Rees.

Theſe birds are found in Lincolnſhire and the Iſle of Ely;
the food proper for them is new milk boiled, and put over
white bread, with a little fine ſugar, and be careful to keep
them in ſeparate cages. They feed very faſt, and will die of
their fat if not killed in time. Truſs them as you do a woodcock, but draw them, and cover them with vine leaves. *Glaſſe*.
100.

For ſauce—good gravy thickened with butter, and a toaſt
under them. *Maſon*, 285.

Another way.

When you kill them, ſlip the ſkin off the head and neck
with the feathers on, then pluck and draw them. When you
roaſt them, put them a good diſtance from the fire; if the
fire be good, they will take about twelve minutes. When they
are roaſted, ſlip the ſkin on again with the feathers on; ſend
them up with gravy under them, made the ſame as for a
pheaſant, and bread ſauce in a boat, with criſp crumbs of
bread round the edge of the diſh. *Raffald*, 66. *Farley*, 41.

To roaſt Pheaſants or Partridges.

Pheaſants and partridges may be treated in the ſame manner. Duſt them with flour, and baſte them often with freſh
butter, keeping them at a good diſtance from the fire. A good
fire will roaſt them in half an hour. Make your gravy of a
ſcrag of mutton, a tea-ſpoonful of lemon pickle, a large ſpoonful of catchup, and the ſame of browning. Strain it, and put
a little

a little of it into the dish; serve them up with bread sauce in a bason, and fix one of the principal feathers of the pheasant in the tail. *Farley, 39.*

Another way.

Let them be nicely roasted, but not too much; baste them gently with a little butter, and dredge them with flour; sprinkle a little salt on, and froth them nicely up: have good gravy in the dish, with bread sauce in a boat, made thus:—take about a handful or two of crumbs of bread, put in a pint of milk or more, a small whole onion, a little whole white pepper, a little salt, and a bit of butter; boil it all well up, then take the onion out, and beat it well with a spoon. Take poverroy sauce in a boat, made thus:—chop four shallots fine, a gill of good gravy, and a spoonful of vinegar; a little pepper and salt; boil them up one minute, then put it in a boat. *Glasse, 95.*

Another way.

Make a little farcie * with the livres, bread crumbs, scraped lard or butter, chopped parsley, shallots, mushrooms, pepper, and salt; stuff the partridges with it, and wrap them in slices of bacon and paper, or buttered paper only, and roast them. *Dalrymple, 232.*

To roast Pigeons.

Scald, draw, and take the craws clean out of your pigeons, and wash them in several waters. When you have dried them, roll a good lump of butter in chopped parsley, and season it with pepper and salt. Put this into your pigeons, and spit, dust, and baste them. A good fire will roast them in twenty minutes, and when they are enough, serve them up with parsley and butter for sauce, and lay round them bunches of asparagus, if they be in season. *Farley, 39. Raffald, 67.*

Another way to roast Pigeons.

Take some parsley shred fine, a piece of butter as big as a walnut, a little pepper and salt; tie the neck-end tight; tie a string round the legs and rump, and fasten the other end to the top of the chimney-piece. Baste them with butter, and when they are enough, lay them in the dish, and they will swim in gravy. You may put them on a little spit, and then tie both ends together. *Glasse, 6.*

To roast a Hare.

Take your hare when it is cased; truss it in this manner— bring the two hind legs up to its sides, pull the fore legs back, put your skewer first into the hind leg, then in the fore leg, and thrust it through the body; put the fore leg on, and then the hind leg, and a skewer through the top of the shoulders and back part of the head, which will hold the head up.   Make a

* *A French term for force-meat.*

pudding

pudding thus—take a quarter of a pound of beef fuet, as much crumb of bread, a handful of parfley chopped fine, fome fweet herbs of all forts, fuch as bafil, marjoram, winter favory, and a little thyme, chopped fine; a little nutmeg grated, fome lemon-peel cut fine, pepper and falt; chop the liver fine, and put in with two eggs; mix it up, and put it into the belly, and few or fkewer it up; then fpit it and lay it to the fire, which muft be a good one. A good fized hare takes an hour, and fo on in proportion. *Glaffe*, 7.

Another way to roaft a Hare.

Skewer your hare with the head upon one fhoulder, the fore legs ftuck into the ribs, the hind legs double; make your pudding of the crumb of a penny loaf, a quarter of a pound of beef marrow or fuet, and a quarter of a pound of butter; fhred the liver, a fprig or two of winter favory, a little lemon peel, one anchovy, a little chyan pepper, half a nutmeg grated; mix them up in a light force-meat, with a glafs of red wine and two eggs; put it into the belly of your hare, few it up, put a quart of good milk in your dripping-pan, bafte your hare with it till it is reduced to half a gill, then duft and bafte it well with butter. If it be a large one, it will require an hour and an half roafting. *Raffald*, 69. *Farley*, 42.

Different forts of Sauce for a Hare.

Take for fauce, a pint of cream, and half a pound of frefh butter; put them in a faucepan, and keep ftirring it with a fpoon till the butter is melted, and the fauce is thick; then take up the hare, and pour the fauce into the difh. Another way to make fauce for a hare is, to make good gravy, thickened with a little piece of butter rolled in flour, and pour it into your difh. You may leave the butter out, if you do not like it, and have fome current jelly warmed in a cup, or red wine and fugar boiled to a fyrup, done thus—take a pint of red wine, a quarter of a pound of fugar, and fet it over a flow fire to fimmer for about a quarter of an hour. You may do half the quantity, and put it into your fauce-boat or bafon.

To roaft Rabbits.

They will take twenty minutes, or half an hour, according to the fize; hold their heads for a few minutes in boiling water before they are laid down. For fauce—parfley and butter, with the liver parboiled and fhred; but they are beft ftuffed with chopped fuet, the liver part boiled and bruifed, bread crumbs, grated bread, and a little lemon-peel; chopped parfley and fweet herbs, yolk of egg mixed, pepper, falt, and nutmeg; gravy in the difh. *Mafon*, 293.

Another way to roaft Rabbits.

Cafe your rabbits, fkewer their heads with their mouths
upon

upon their backs, ftick their fore legs into their ribs, and fkewer their hind legs double. Break half a penny loaf into crumbs, a little parfley, thyme, fweet marjoram, and lemon peel. Shred all thefe fine, and feafon them with pepper, falt, and nutmeg. Mix them up into a light ftuffing, with two eggs, a little cream, and a quarter of a pound of butter. Put it into their bellies, few them up, and dredge and bafte them well with butter. Take them up when they have roafted an hour; chop the livers, and lay them in lumps round the edge of your difh. Serve them up with parfley and butter for fauce. *Farley*, 42. *Raffald*, 68.

To roaft a Rabbit Hare fafhion.

Lard a rabbit with bacon, roaft it as you do a hare with a ftuffing in the belly, and it eats very well. But then you muft make gravy fauce. But if you do not lard it, white fauce made thus—take a little veal broth, boil it up with a little flour and butter to thicken it; then add a gill of cream; keep it ftirring one way till it is fmooth, then put it in a boat, or in the difh. *Glaffe*, 11. *Mafon*, 294.

To roaft Lobfters.

Put a fkewer into the vent of the tail of the lobfter, to prevent the water getting into the body of it, and put it into a pan of boiling water, with a little falt in it; and if it be a large one, it will take half an hour boiling. Then lay it before the fire, and bafte it with butter till it has a fine froth. Difh it up with plain melted butter in a boat. This is a better way than actually roafting them, and is not attended with half the trouble. *Farley*, 43.

Another way.

Boil your lobfters, then lay them before the fire, and bafte them with butter till they have a fine froth. Difh them up with plain melted butter in a cup. This is as good a way to the full as roafting them, and not half the trouble.

Another way.

Half boil your lobfter, rub it well with butter, and fet it before the fire; bafte it all over till the fhell looks a dark brown; ferve it up with good melted butter. *Raffald*, 40.

Another way.

More than half boil it; fet it in a Dutch oven, bafte it well till nicely frothed; ferve it with melted butter. *Mafon*, 251.

CHAP.

CHAP. II.—*Of* BOILING.

Preliminary Hints and Observations.

NEATNESS being a moſt material requiſition in a kitchen, the cook ſhould be particularly cautious to keep all the utenſils perfectly clean, and the pots and ſaucepans properly tinned. In boiling any kind of meat, but particularly veal, much care and nicety are required. Fill your pot with a ſuffi-cient quantity of ſoft water, duſt your veal well with fine flour, put it into your pot, and ſet it over a large fire. It is the cuſ-tom of ſome people to put in milk to make it white; but this is of no uſe, and perhaps better omitted; for if you uſe hard water, it will curdle the milk, give to the veal a brownish yel-low caſt, and it will often hang in lumps about it. Oatmeal will do the ſame thing: but by duſting your veal, and putting it into the water when cold, it will prevent the foulneſs of the water from hanging upon it. Take the ſcum off clearly as ſoon as it begins to riſe, and cover up the pot cloſely. Let the meat boil as ſlowly as poſſible, but in plenty of water, which will make your veal riſe and look plump. A cook cannot make a greater miſtake than to let any ſort of meat boil faſt, ſince it hardens the outſide before it is warm within, and contributes to diſcolour it. Thus a leg of veal, of twelve pounds weight will take three hours and an half boiling; and the flower it boils, the whiter and plumper it will be. When mutton or beef is the object of your cookery, be careful to dredge them well with flour before you put them into the pot of cold water, and keep it covered; but do not forget to take off the ſcum as often as it riſes. Mutton and beef do not require ſo much boiling; nor is it much minded if it be a little under the mark; but lamb, pork, and veal ſhould be well boiled, as they will other-wiſe be unwholeſome. A leg of pork will take an hour more boiling than a leg of veal of the ſame weight; but, in general, when you boil beef or mutton, you may allow an hour for every four pounds weight. To put in the meat when the water is cold, is allowed to be the beſt method, as it thereby gets warm to the heart before the outſide gets hard. To boil a leg of lamb of four pounds weight, you muſt allow an hour and an half. *Farley*, 16, 17. *Raffald*, 52, 53.

As to all ſorts of boiled meats, allow a quarter of an hour to every pound. Be ſure the pot is very clean, and ſkim it well, for every thing will have a ſcum riſe, and if that boils down, it makes the meat black. All ſorts of freſh meat you are to put in when the water boils, but ſalt meat when the water is warm. *Glaſſe*, 8.

To boil a Ham.

Steep it all night in foft water; a large one fhould fimmer three hours, and boil gently two; a fmall one fhould fimmer two hours, and boil about one and an half. Pull off the fkin, rub it over with yolk of egg, ftrew on bread crumbs, fet it before the fire till of a nice light brown. *Mafon*, 177.

Another way to boil a Ham.

Put your ham into a copper of cold water, and when it boils take care that it boils flowly. A ham of twenty pounds will take four hours and an half boiling; and fo in proportion for one of a larger or fmaller fize. No foaking is required for a green ham; but an old large ham will require fixteen hours foaking in a large tub of a foft water. Obferve to keep the pot well fkimmed while your ham is boiling. When you take it up, pull off the fkin, and rub it all over with an egg, ftrew on crumbs of bread, bafte it with butter, and fet it to the fire till it is of a light brown. *Farley*, 17.

When you boil a ham, put it into your copper when the water is pretty warm, for the cold water draws the colour out; when it boils, be careful it boils very flowly. *Glaffe*, 8.

Another way to boil a Ham.

Steep your ham all night in water; then boil it. If it be of a middle fize, it will take three hours boiling, and a fmall one two hours and an half. When you take it up pull off the fkin, and rub it all over with an egg, ftrew on bread-crumbs, bafte it with butter, and fet it to the fire till it be a light brown. If it be to eat hot, garnifh with carrots, and ferve it up. *Raffald*, 69.

Another way to boil a Ham.

If your ham has been long kept, foak it fome time; if frefh, you need not; pare it round and underneath, taking care no rufty part is left; tie it up with packthread, put it in a brazing-pan much of its own bignefs, with water, a faggot, a few cloves, thyme, and laurel leaves; boil on a flow fire about five hours, then add a glafs of brandy, and a pint of red wine; finifh boiling in the fame manner. If to ferve hot, take up the fkin, and ftrew it over with bread-crumbs, a little parfley finely chopped, and a few bits of butter; give it a colour in the oven, or with a falamander. If to keep cold, it will be better to leave the fkin on. *Clermont*, 169.

To boil a Tongue.

A tongue, if falt, foak it in foft water all night; boil it three hours; if frefh out of the pickle, two hours and an half, and put it in when the water boils; take it out and pull it; trim it; garnifh with greens and carrots. *Glaffe*, 9. *Mafon*, 132.

Another

Another way to boil a Tongue.

If your tongue be a dry one, fteep it in water all night; then boil it three hours. If you would have it eat hot, ftick it with cloves, rub it over with the yolk of an egg, ftrew over it bread-crumbs, bafte it with butter, fet it before the fire till it is a light brown. When you difh it up, pour a little brown gravy, or red-wine fauce, mixed the fame way as for venifon; lay flices of currant jelly round it.—N. B. If it be a pickled one, only wafh it out of water. *Raffald*, 69. *Farley*, 18.

Another way to boil a Tongue.

Lard a tongue with pretty large pieces, and boil it in the broth pot, or in water, with a few onions and roots. When it is done, peel it, and ferve it with broth, fprinkling a little pepper and falt over it.

It is alfo ufed without larding, and being boiled frefh in this manner, is preferable to any thing elfe for mince-pye-meat. *Clermont*, 50.

To boil a Chicken.

Put your chickens into fcalding water, and as foon as the feathers will flip off, take them out, otherwife they will make the fkin hard. After you have drawn them, lay them in fkim-med milk for two hours, and then trufs them with their heads on their wings. When you have properly finged and dufted them with flour, cover them in clofe cold water, and fet them over a flow fire. Having taken off the fcum, and boiled them flowly for five or fix minutes, take them off the fire, and keep them clofe covered for half an hour in the water, which will ftew them fufficiently, and make them plump and white. Before you difh them, fet them on the fire to heat; then drain them, and pour over them white fauce, made the fame way as for boiled fowls. *Farley*, 18. *Mafon*, 262.

A large chicken takes twenty minutes; a very fmall one, fifteen. *Mafon*, 262. *Glaffe*, 9.

Fowls, chickens, and houfe-lamb, fhould be boiled in a pot by themfelves, in a good deal of water; and if any fcum arifes take it off. They will be both fweeter and whiter than if boiled in a cloth. *Glaffe*, 9.

To boil a Fowl.

A large one will be boiled in half an hour. Boil it in a pot by itfelf, fcum it very clean, it will be better than if boiled in a cloth; pour fome melted butter over the breaft; ferve it with tongue, bacon, or pickled pork; cabbages, favoys, broccoli; any greens or carrots, and oyfter fauce, white celery fauce, or white fauce. *Mafon*, 262.

A good fowl will be boiled in half an hour. *Glaffe*.

Another

When you have plucked your fowls, draw them at the rump, cut off the head, neck, and legs, take the breaft-bone very carefully out, fkewer them with the ends of their legs in the body, tie them round with a ftring, finge and duft them well with flour, put them in a kettle of cold water, cover it clofe, and fet it on the fire; when the fcum begins to rife, take it off; put on your cover, and let them boil very flowly twenty minutes; take them off, cover them clofe, and the heat of the water will ftew them enough in half an hour; it keeps the fkin whole, and they will be both whiter and plumper than if they had boiled faft. When you take them up, drain them, and pour over them white fauce, or melted butter. *Raffald, 63. Farley, 19.*

To make Sauce for Fowls.

Boil any bones or bits of veal, with a fmall bunch of fweet herbs, an onion, a flice of lemon, a few white pepper corns, and a little celery; ftrain it; there fhould be near half a pint; put to it fome good cream, with a little flour mixed fmooth in it, a good piece of butter, a little pounded mace, and fome falt; keep it ftirring; add mufhrooms, or a little lemon juice. *Mafon, 326.*

To boil a Turkey.

Make a ftuffing with grated bread, oyfters chopped, grated lemon peel, pepper, falt, nutmeg; about four ounces of butter, or fuet chopped, a little cream, yolks of eggs to make it a light ftuffing; fill the craw; if any is left, make it into balls; flour the turkey, put it into water while cold; take off the fcum as it rifes, and let it boil gently. A middling turkey will take about an hour. Boil the balls, lay them round it, with oyfter fauce in the difh, and in a boat. The ftuffing may be made without oyfters, or it may be ftuffed with forced-meat, or faufage meat, mixed with a few crumbs of bread and yolks of eggs. If oyfters are not to be had, white celery fauce is very good, or white fauce. *Mafon, 257.*

A little turkey will be done in an hour; a large one in an hour and an half. *Glaffe, 9.*

Another way to boil a Turkey.

Let your turkey have no food the day before you kill it. When you are going to kill it, give it a fpoonful of allegar; it will make it white, and eat tender. When you have killed it, hang it up by the legs for four or five days at leaft; when you have plucked it, draw it at the rump; if you can take the breaft-bone out nicely, it will look much better. Cut off the legs, put the end of the thighs into the body of the turkey, fkewer them down, and tie them with a ftring; cut off the head and neck, then

grate

grate a penny loaf, chop a score or more of oysters fine, shred a little lemon-peel, nutmeg, pepper, and salt to your palate. Mix it up into a light forced-meat, with a quarter of a pound of butter, a spoonful or two or cream, and three eggs; stuff the craw with it, and make the rest into balls, and boil them. Sew up the turkey, dredge it well with flour, put it into a kettle of cold water, cover it, and set it over the fire. When the scum begins to rise, take it off, put on your cover, and let it boil very flowly for half an hour; then take off your kettle, and keep it close covered. If it be of a middle size, let it stand half an hour in the hot water, the steam being kept in, will stew it enough, make it rise, keep the skin whole, tender, and very white. When you dish it up, pour over it a little of your oyster-sauce, lay your balls round it, and serve it up with the rest of your sauce in a boat. Garnish with lemon and barberries.—N.B. Observe to set on your turkey in time, that it may stew as above: it is the best way I ever found to boil one to perfection. When you are going to dish it up, set it over the fire to make it quite hot. *Raffald*, 60.

Mr. *Farley*, in his London Art of Cookery, has the same receipt as the above, page 19, excepting a trifling alteration in the language.

Sauce for a boiled Turkey.

The best sauce for a boiled turkey, is good oyster and celery sauce. Make oyster-sauce thus :—take a pint of oysters, and set them off; strain the liquor from them, and put them in cold water, and wash and beard them ; put them into your liquor in a stew pan, with a blade of mace, and some butter rolled in flour, and a quarter of a lemon ; boil them up, then put in half a pint of cream, and boil it all together gently ; take the lemon and mace out, squeeze the juice of the lemon into the sauce, then serve it in your boats or basons. Make celery-sauce thus :—take the white part of the celery, cut it about one inch long ; boil it in some water till it is tender, then take half a pint of veal broth, a blade of mace, and thicken it with a little flour and butter ; put in half a pint of cream, boil them up gently together ; put in your celery, and boil it up, then pour it into your boats. *Glasse*, 9.

To boil a Duck.

As soon as you have scalded and drawn your ducks, let them remain for a few minutes in warm water. Then take them out, put them into an earthen pan, and pour a pint of boiling milk over them. Let them lie in it two or three hours, and when you take them out, dredge them well with flour ; put them into a copper of cold water, and cover them up. Having boiled slowly about twenty minutes, take them out, and smother them with onion-sauce. *Farley*, 20.

Another

Another way to boil a Duck.

Pour boiling milk and water over your duck ; let it lie an hour or two ; boil it gently in plenty of water full half an hour. —Onion-fauce. *Mafon,* 271.

To boil a Duck, or a Rabbit, with Onions.

Boil your duck, or rabbit, in a good deal of water ; be fure to fkim your water, for there will always rife a fcum, which if it boils down, will difcolour your fowls, &c. They will take about half an hour boiling. For fauce—your onions muft be peeled, and throw them into water as you peel them ; then cut them into thin flices, boil them in milk and water, and fkim the liquor. Half an hour will boil **them.** Throw them into a clean fieve to drain ; chop them, and rub them through a cul-lender ; put them into a faucepan, fhake in a little flour ; put to them two or three fpoonfuls of cream, and a good piece of but-ter ; ftew them all together over the fire till they are thick and fine ; lay the duck, or rabbit, in the difh, and pour the fauce all over. If a rabbit, you muft pluck out the jaw-bones, and ftick one in each eye, the fmall end inwards.

Or you may make this fauce for change :—take one large onion, cut it fmall, half a handful of parfley clean w. fhed and picked ; chop it fmall, a lettice cut fmall, a quarter of a pint of good gravy, a good piece of butter rolled in a little flour ; add a little juice of lemon, a little pepper and falt. Let them all ftew together for half an hour ; then add two fpoonfuls of red wine. This fauce is moft proper for a duck. Lay the duck in your difh, and pour the fauce over it. *Glaffe* 82.

To boil Pigeons.

Scald and draw your pigeons, and take out the craw as clean as poffible. Wafh them in feveral waters, and, having cut off the pinions, turn their legs under their wings, dredge them, and put them into foft cold water. Having boiled them very flowly a quarter of an hour, difh them up, and pour over them good melted butter. Lay round them a little broccoli, and ferve them up with butter and parfley. *Farley,* 20.

Pigeons will not take more than a quarter of an hour boiling. They fhould be boiled by themfelves, and may be eaten with bacon, greens, fpinach, afparagus, or parfley and butter. *Mafon,* 275.

Another way.

Boil your pigeons by themfelves for fifteen minutes ; then boil a handfome fquare piece of bacon, and lay in the middle ; ftew fome fpinach to lay round, and lay the pigeons on the fpi-nach. Garnifh your difh with parfley laid in a plate before the fire to crifp. Or you may lay one pigeon in the middle, and
the

the reft round, and the fpinach between each pigeon, and a flice of bacon on each pigeon. Garnifh with flices of bacon, and melted butter in a cup.

To boil a Partridge.

Boil your partridges quick in a good deal of water, and fifteen minutes will be fufficient. For fauce—take a quarter of a pint of cream, and a piece of frefh butter as large as a walnut; ftir it one way till it is melted, and pour it into the difh. *Farley*, 21.

Another way.

Trufs two or three partridges as for boiling; lard them with ham, bacon, and anchovies; braze them as ufual; when done, fkim and fift the fauce, and add a little cullis. When ready to ferve, add the fqueeze of a lemon. *Dalrymple*, 234.

Another way.

Let your partridges be covered with water. Fifteen minutes will boil them. For fauce—celery-fauce, liver-fauce, mufh-room-fauce, or onion-fauce. *Mafon*, 303.

To boil Pheafants.

Boil them in a great deal of water; if large, three quarters of an hour will boil them; if fmall, half an hour. For fauce—white celery ftewed and thickened with cream, and a bit of butter rolled in flour. Lay the pheafants in the difh, and pour the fauce over them. *Mafon*, 306. *Glaffe*, 98.

Obferve fo to ftew your celery, that the liquor may not be all wafted before you put in your cream. Seafon with falt to your palate. Garnifh with lemon.

To boil Woodcocks.

Take a pound of lean beef, cut it into pieces, and put it into a fauce-pan, with two quarts of water, an onion ftuck with three or four cloves, two blades of mace, and fome whole pepper: boil all thefe gently till half is wafted; then ftrain it off into another faucepan. Draw the woodcocks, and lay the trail in a plate; put the woodcocks into the gravy, and let them boil for twelve minutes. While they are doing, chop the trail and liver fmall, put them into a fmall faucepan with a little mace, pour on them five or fix fpoonfuls of the gravy the woodcocks are boiled in; then take the crumb of a ftale roll, rub it fine in a difh before a fire; put to the trail, in a fmall faucepan, half a pint of red port, a piece of butter rolled in flour; fet all over the fire, and fhake it round till the butter is melted; then put in the crumbs of bread, and fhake the faucepan round Lay the woodcocks in the difh, and pour the fauce over them. *Mafon*, 273. *Glaffe*, 99. *Farley*, 21.

To boil Pickled Pork.

Be fure you put your pork in when the water boils. If a

C 4   middling

middling piece, an hour will boil it; if a very large piece, an
hour and an half, or two hours. If you boil pickled pork too
long, it will go to a jelly. You will know when it is done, by
trying it with a fork. *Glasse*, 20.

Pork should be very well boiled; a leg of pork of six pounds
will take about two hours; the hand must be boiled till very
tender. Serve it up with peafe-pudding, favoys, or any greens.
Mason, 175.

To boil Pigs' Pettitoes.

Take up the heart, liver, and lights, when they have boiled
ten minutes, and shred them pretty small; let the feet boil till
they are pretty tender, then take them out and split them;
thicken your gravy with flour and butter, put in your mince-meat
a slice of lemon, spoonful of white wine, a little salt, and boil it
a little; beat the yolk of an egg, add to it two spoonfuls of good
cream, and a little grated nutmeg; put in your pettitoes, shake
it over the fire, but do not let it boil. Lay sippets round your
dish, pour in your mince-meat, lay the feet over them the skin
side up, and send them to the table. *Raffa'd*, 57.

To boil Salmon crisp.

When the falmon is scaled and gutted, cut off the head and
tail, cut the body through into slices an inch and an half thick,
throw them into a large pan of pump-water. When they are
all put in, sprinkle a handful of bay-salt upon the water, stir it
about, and then take out the fish; set on a large deep stew-pan,
boil the head and tail, but do not split the head; put in some
salt, but no vinegar. When they have boiled ten minutes, skim
the water very clean, and put in the slices. When they are
boiled enough, take them out, lay the head and the tail in the
dish, and the slices round. This must be for a large company.
The head or tail may be dressed alone, or with one or two slices;
or the slices alone.

It is done in great perfection in the falmon countries; but if
the falmon is very fresh, it will be very good in London. *Mason*, 213.

Another way.

Scale your falmon, take out the blood, wash it well, and lay
it on a fish-plate; put your water in a fish-pan with a little salt.
When it boils, put in your fish for half a minute, then take it
out for a minute or two. When you have done it four times,
boil it till it is enough. When you take it out of the fish-pan,
set it over the water to drain; cover it well with a clean cloth
dipped in hot water; fry some small fishes, or a few slices of
salmon, and lay round it. Garnish with scraped horse-raddish
and fennel. *Raffald*, 23.

Another

Another way.

Take a bit of falmon, of any bignefs, without being fcaled; tie it up in a cloth, or with packthread; put it in a veffel much of its bignefs, with a good bit of butter or broth, and half red wine, falt, whole pepper, a faggot of parfley, thyme, laurel, two or three cloves, bits of carrots, and fliced onions. When done, drain it, and ferve it upon a napkin, and the fauces in boats. *Clermont*, 358. *Dalrymple*, 294.

To boil a Cod's Head and Shoulders.

Take out the gills and the blood clean from the bone; wafh the head very clean, rub over it a little falt, and a glafs of allegar; then lay it on your fifh-plate. When your water boils, throw in a good handful of falt, with a glafs of allegar; then put in your fifh, and let it boil gently half an hour: if it is a large one, three quarters. Take it up very carefully, and ftrip the fkin nicely off; fet it before a brifk fire, dredge it all over with flour, and bafte it well with butter. When the froth begins to rife, throw over it fome very fine white bread crumbs. You muft keep bafting it all the time to make it froth well. When it is a fine white brown, difh it up, and garnifh it with a lemon cut in flices, fcraped horfe radifh, barberries, a few fmall fifh fried and laid round it, or fried oyfters. Cut the roe and liver in flices, and lay over it a little of the lobfter out of the fauce in lumps, and then ferve it. *Raffald*, 21. *Farley*, 27.

Another way.

Wafh it, ftrew falt over it, put vinegar and falt into the water. If the head be large, it will take an hour's boiling. Oyfter-fauce, and white-fauce, or what other is agreeable. The fifh may be grilled in the following manner:—Strip off the fkin, when boiled, fet it before the fire, fhake flour over it, and bafte it. When the froth rifes, ftrew over it bread-crumbs; let it be a nice brown. Garnifh with fried oyfters, the roe, liver, horfe-radifh, and lemon. *Mafon*, 209.

To boil Cod.

Set on a fifh-kettle of a proper fize for the cod; put in a large quantity of water, with a quarter of a pint, or more, of vinegar, a handful of falt, and half a ftick of horfe-radifh: let thefe boil together, and then put in the fifh. When it is enough (which will be known by feeling the fins. and by the look of the fifh) lay it to drain, put it on a hot fifh-plate, and then in a warm difh, with the liver cut in half and laid on each fide. Sauce—fhrimps, or oyfter-fauce. *Mafon*, 219.

To boil Salt Cod.

Steep your falt fifh in water all night, with a glafs of vinegar; it will take out the falt, and make it eat like frefh fifh. The

next

next day boil it. When it is enough, pull it in flakes into your dish, then pour egg-sauce over it, or parsnips boiled and beat with butter and cream. Send it to the table on a water-plate, for it will soon grow cold. *Raffald*, 22.

To boil Cod Sounds.

Cod sounds, dressed like little turkies, is a pretty side-dish for a large table, or for a dinner in Lent. Boil your sounds as for eating, but not too much. Take them up, and let them stand till they are quite cold; then make a forced-meat of chopped oysters, crumbs of bread, a lump of butter, the yolks of two eggs, nutmeg, pepper, and salt, and fill your sounds with it. Skewer them in the shape of a turkey, and lard them down each side as you would do a turkey's breast. Dust them well with flour, and put them before the fire in a tin oven to roast. Baste them well with butter. When they are enough, pour on them oyster-sauce, and garnish with barberries. *Farley*, 28.

To boil a Turbot.

Lay it in a good deal of salt and water an hour or two, and if it is not quite sweet, shift your water five or six times; first put a good deal of salt in the mouth and belly.

In the mean time set on your fish-kettle, with clean spring-water and salt, a little vinegar, and a piece of horse-radish. When the water boils, lay the turbot on a fish-plate, put it into the kettle, let it be well boiled, but take great care it is not too much done. When enough, take off the fish-kettle, set it before the fire, then carefully lift up the fish-plate, and set it across the kettle to drain. In the mean time melt a good deal of fresh butter, and bruise in either the spawn of one or two lobsters, and the meat cut small, with a spoonful of anchovy liquor; then give it a boil, and pour it into basons. This is the best sauce; but you may make what you please. Lay the fish in the dish. Garnish with scraped horse-radish and lemon. *Glasse*, 177.

Another way.

Make a brine with a handful or two of salt, and a gallon or more of water: let the turbot lie in it two hours before it is to be boiled; then set on a fish-kettle, with water enough to cover it, and about half a pint of vinegar (or less if the turbot is small); put in a piece of horse-radish. When the water boils, put in the turbot, the white side uppermost, on a fish-plate. Let it be done enough, but not too much, which will be easily known by the look. A small one will take twenty minutes; a large one, half an hour. Then take it up, and set it on a fish plate to drain before it is laid in the dish. Sauce—lobster-sauce and white-sauce. *Mason*, 211.

To boil a Pike.

Take a large pike, clean it, and take out the gills; make a stuffing with some crumbs of bread grated fine, some sweet herbs chopped small, some grated lemon-peel, nutmeg, pepper, salt, some oysters chopped small, and a piece of butter. Mix up these ingredients with the yolks of two eggs; put it into the fish, and sew it up; turn the tail into the mouth, and boil it in pump water, with some vinegar and salt in it. When it boils, put in the fish, it will take more than half an hour, if it is a large one. Oyster-sauce. Pour some over the fish, the rest in a boat. *Mason*, 232.

Another way.

Take out the gills and guts, wash it well, then make a good force-meat of oysters chopped fine, the crumb of half-a-penny loaf, a few sweet herbs, and a little lemon-peel shred fine; nutmeg, pepper, and salt, to your taste; a good lump of butter, and the yolks of two eggs; mix them well together, and put them in the belly of your fish; sew it up, skewer it round, put hard water into your fish-pan, add to it a tea-cupful of vinegar, and a little salt. When it boils, put in the fish; if it be a middle size, it will take half an hour's boiling. Garnish it with walnuts and pickled barberries; serve it up with oyster-sauce in a boat, and pour a little sauce on the pike. You may dress a roasted pike in the same way.

To boil a Sturgeon.

Clean your sturgeon, and prepare as much liquor as will just boil it. To two quarts of water, put a pint of vinegar, a stick of horse-radish, two or three bits of lemon-peel, some whole pepper, a bay-leaf, and a small handful of salt. Boil your fish in this, and serve it in the following sauce: —melt a pound of butter, dissolve an anchovy in it, put in a blade or two of mace, bruise the body of a crab in the butter, a few shrimps or craw-fish, a little catchup, a little lemon-juice; give it a boil, drain your fish well, and lay it in your dish. Garnish with fried oysters, sliced lemon, and scraped horse radish; pour your sauce into boats or basons. So you may fry it, ragoo it, or bake it. *Glasse*, 187. *Mason*, 218.

Another way.

Boil the sturgeon in just as much liquid as will do between boiling and stewing; put to this some broth, butter, a little vinegar and white wine, all sorts of sweet herbs, bits of carrots, slices of onions, whole pepper, and salt, according to the bigness of the fish. If a whole one, when properly cleaned, stuff it with all sorts of sweet herbs chopped, pepper and salt, all mixed with good butter, and serve upon a napkin garnished with green parsley.

parfley. Serve what fauce you think proper in boats, fuch as anchovies, capers, &c. *Clermont*, 364.

To boil Mackrel.

Make a fauce with half a pint of white wine, fome weak broth, fweet herbs, bits of roots, flices of onions, pepper and falt ; boil thefe together about an hour ; then boil the fifh therein, and ferve with a fauce made of butter, a little flour, fome fcalded chopped fennel, one fhallot chopped very fine, a little of the boiling liquid, and a lemon fqueeze when ready. *Clermont*, 382.

Another way.

Gut your mackrel, and dry them carefully with a clean cloth, then rub them flightly over with a little vinegar, and lay them ftraight on your fifh-plate (for turning them round often breaks them); put a little falt in the water when it boils ; put them into your fifh-pan, and boil them gently fifteen minutes, then take them up and drain them well, and put the water that runs from them into a fauce-pan, with two tea-fpoonfuls of lemon-pickle, one meat-fpoonful of walnut catchup, the fame of browning, a blade or two of mace, one anchovy, a flice of lemon ; boil them all together a quarter of an hour, then ftrain it through a hair fieve, and thicken it with flour and butter ; fend it in a fauce-boat, and parfley-fauce in another ; difh up your fifh with the tails in the middle. Garnifh it with fcraped horfe-difh and barberries. *Raffald*, 32.

To boil Plaice or Flounders.

Let your water boil, throw fome falt in, then put in your fifh ; boil it till you think it is enough, and take it out of the water in a flice to drain. Take two fpoonfuls of the liquor, with a little falt, and a little grated nutmeg ; then beat up the yolk of an egg very well with the liquor, and ftir in the egg ; beat it well together, with a knife carefully flice away all the little bones round the fifh, pour the fauce over it, then fet it over a chafing-difh of coals for a minute, and fend it hot away. Or, in the room of this fauce, add melted butter in a cup.

Another way.

Put on a ftew-pan, with water fufficient to cover the quantity of flounders, &c. which are to be dreffed ; put in fome vinegar and horfe-radifh. When the water boils, put in the fifh, but let them be well cleaned, and their fins cut off ; do not let them boil too faft, left they break. When they are enough, lay them on a fifh-plate, the tails in the middle. Sauce—parfley and butter. Dabs are boiled in the fame manner. *Mafon*, 248.

To boil Soals.

Take a pair of foals, make them clean, lay them in vinegar, falt,

falt, and water, two hours; then dry them in a cloth, put them into a ftew-pan, put to them a pint of white wine, a bundle of fweet herbs, an onion ftuck with fix cloves, fome whole pepper, and a little falt; cover them, and let them boil. When they are enough, take them up, lay them in your difh, ftrain the liquor, and thicken it up with butter and flour Pour the fauce over, and garnifh with fcraped horfe-radifh and lemon. In this manner drefs a little turbot. It is a genteel difh for fupper. You may add prawns, or fhrimps, or muffels to your fauce. *Glaffe*, 189.

Another way.

Take two or three pair of middling foals; when they are fkinned and gutted, wafh them in fpring-water, then put them on a difh, and pour half a pint of white wine over them; turn them two or three times in it, and pour it away; then cut off the heads and tails of the foals, and fet on a ftew-pan, with a little rich fifh-broth; put in an onion cut to pieces, a bunch of fweet herbs, pepper, falt, and a blade of mace. When this boils, put in the foals, and with them half a lemon, cut in flices with the peel on; let them fimmer flowly, then take out the fweet herbs, and put in a pint of ftrong white wine, and a piece of butter rol'ed in flour; let them all fimmer together till the foals are enough.

While the fifh are doing, put in half a pint of veal gravy, and a quarter of a pint of effence of ham; let it boil a little, take up the foals, and pour this over it. *Mafon*, 224.

Soals, in the common way, fhould be boiled in falt and water. *Mafon*, 224.

Another way.

Take three quarts of fpring water, and a handful of falt; let them boil; then put in your foals; boil them gently for ten minutes, then difh them up in a clean napkin, with anchovy-fauce, or fhrimp-fauce in boats.

To boil Herrings.

Scale, gut, and wafh your herrings; dry them clean, and rub them over with a little vinegar and falt; fkewer them with their tails in their mouths, and lay them on your fifh-plate. When your water boils, put them in, they will take ten or twelve minutes boiling. When you take them up, drain them over the water, then turn the heads into the middle of your difh. Lay round them fcraped horfe-radifh, parfley and butter for fauce. *Raffald*, 30.

Another way.

The propereft time for boiling herrings, is when they come before and at the beginning of the mackrel feafon; they are by

many

many people reckoned better than when full of roe : the flefh is much poorer than at this feafon, when their breeding time is over, and they have had time to feed and recover their flefh

Clean half a dozen herrings, and throw them into a pan of cold water, ftir them about. and change the water once ; fet on a ftew-pan, with water enough to cover them, fome falt, and a little vinegar. When the water boils, put in the herrings ; when they are enough, lay them on a fifh-plate, in a warm difh. Sauce—fennel boiled and chopped fmall, with melted butter.

To boil Eels.

Having fkinned, gutted, and taken the blood out of your eels, cut off their heads, dry them, and turn them round on your fifh-plate.   Boil them in falt and water, and ferve them up with parfley fauce.   *Farley*, 31.

Another way.

Make a brown of butter and flour ; when it is of a good co-lour, add a little broth, cullis, a pint of white wine, one dozen and an half of fmall onions firft blanched, a few mufhrooms, a faggot of parfley and fweet herbs, three cloves, whole pepper and falt ; ftew this until the onions are near done, then put the eels to it, cut in pieces ; ftew on a fmart fire, reduce the fauce to a proper confiftence ; when ready, add a chopped anchovy, and a few whole capers.   Garnifh the difh with fried bread.
Dalrymple, 278.

Chap. III.—MADE DISHES OF BEEF.

A S this is one of the moſt important chapters in the book, it
may not be improper to give the young cook ſome general
hints. It is an important point to take care that all the copper
veſſels be well tinned, and kept perfectly clean from any foulneſs
or grittineſs. Before you put eggs or cream into your white
ſauce, have all your ingredients well boiled, and the whole of
a proper thickneſs; for neither eggs nor cream will contribute
much to thicken it. After you have put them in, do not ſtir
them with a ſpoon, nor ſet your pan on the fire, for fear it
ſhould gather at the bottom, and be lumpy; but hold your pan
at a proper height from the fire, and keep ſhaking it round one
way, which will keep the ſauce from curdling; and be particularly cautious that you do not ſuffer it to boil. Remember to
take out your collops, meat, or whatever you are dreſſing, with
a fiſh-ſlice, and ſtrain your ſauce upon it, which will prevent
ſmall bits of meat mixing with your ſauce, and thereby have it
clear and fine. In browning diſhes, be particularly cautious
that no fat floats on the top of the gravy, which will be the caſe
if you do not properly ſkim it. It ſhould be of a fine brown,
without any one predominant taſte, which muſt depend on the
judicious proportion in the mixture of your various articles of ingredients. If you make uſe of wine, or anchovy, take off its
rawneſs by putting it in ſome time before your diſh is ready; for
nothing injures the reputation of a made-diſh ſo much as raw
wine, or freſh anchovy. Be ſure to put your fried forced-meat
balls to drain on a ſieve, that the fat may run from them, and
never let them boil in your ſauce, as that will ſoften them, and
give them a greaſy appearance. To put them in after the meat
is diſhed up, is indiſputably the beſt method. In almoſt every
made-diſh, you may uſe force-meat balls, morels, trufiles, artichoke-bottoms, and pickled muſhrooms; and in ſeveral made-
diſhes, a roll of force-meat may ſupply the place of balls; and
where it can be uſed with propriety, it is to be preferred.

Browning for Made Diſhes.

Beat ſmall four ounces of treble-refined ſugar, put it in a
clean iron frying-pan, with one ounce of butter; ſet it over a
clear fire, mix it very well together all the time; when it begins
to be frothy, the ſugar is diſſolving, hold it higher over the fire,
have ready a pint of red wine; when the ſugar and butter is of a
deep brown, pour in a little of the wine, and ſtir it well together, then add more wine, and keep ſtirring it all the time; put
in half an ounce of Jamaica pepper, ſix cloves, four ſhallots
peeled, two or three blades of mace, three ſpoonfuls of muſhroom

room catchup, a little falt, the out-rinds of one lemon; boil them flowly for ten minutes, then pour it into a bafon. When cold, take off the fcum very clean, and bottle it for ufe. *Raffald*, 81.

Beef A-la-Mode.

Take fome of the round of beef, the veiny piece, or fmall round (what is generally called the moufe-buttock); cut it five or fix inches thick; cut fome pieces of fat bacon into long bits; take an equal quantity of beaten mace, pepper, and nutmeg, with double the quantity of falt, if wanted; mix them together, dip the bacon into fome vinegar (garlick vinegar, if agreeable), then into the fpice; lard the beef with a larding-pin, very thick and even, put the meat into a pot juft large enough to hold it, with a gill of vinegar, two large onions, a bunch of fweet herbs, half a pint of red wine, and fome lemon-peel. Cover it down very clofe, and put a wet cloth round the edge of the pot, to prevent the fteam evaporating; when it is half done, turn it, and cover it up again; do it over a ftove, or a very flow fire. It will take five hours and an half before it is done.

N. B. Truffles and morels may be added to it. *Mafon*, 123.

Beef A-la-mode another way.

Having boned a rump of beef, lard the top with bacon, and make the following force-meat :—Take four ounces of marrow, the crumb of a penny loaf, a few fweet herbs chopped fmall, two heads of garlick, and feafon them to your tafte with falt, pepper, and nutmeg; then beat up the yolks of four eggs. Mix all together, and ftuff it into the beef at the parts from whence the bone was extracted, and alfo in feveral of the lean parts. Skewer it round, and faften it properly with a ftring. Put it into the pot, throw in a pint of red wine, and tie the pot down with a ftrong paper. Put it into the oven for three or four hours, and when it comes out, if it is to be eaten hot, fkim the fat from the gravy, and add a fpoonful of pickled mufhrooms, and half an ounce of morels. Thicken it with flour and butter, difh it up, and pour on your gravy. Garnifh it with force-meat balls. *Farley*, 91.

Another way.

Cut fome of the round of beef into pieces, lard and fry them, put to them fome beef broth, a bunch of fweet herbs, an onion, a few pepper corns and cloves; ftew this gently till tender, covered clofe, then fkim off the fat, and add a few mufhrooms.— N. B. Water may be ufed inftead of broth. *Mafon*, 123.

Beef A-la-daube.

Take a rump and bone it, or a part of the leg-of-mutton piece, or a piece of the buttock; cut fome fat bacon, as long as the

the beef is thick, and about a quarter of an inch square; take
eight cloves, four blades of mace, a little all-spice, and half a
nutmeg beat very fine; chop a good handful of parsley fine, some
sweet herbs of all sorts chopped fine, and some pepper and salt;
roll the bacon in these, and then take a large larding-pin, or a
small-bladed knife, and put the bacon through and through the
beef with a larding-pin or knife. When that is done, pour it
into the stew-pan with brown gravy enough to cover. Chop
three blades of garlick very fine, and put in some fresh mushrooms or champignons, two large onions, and a carrot: stew it
gently for six hours; then take the meat out, strain off the gravy,
and skim all the fat off. Put your meat and gravy into the pan
again; put a gill of white wine into the gravy, and if it wants
seasoning, season with pepper and salt; stew them gently for
half an hour; add some artichoke bottoms, truffles and morels,
oysters, and a spoonful of vinegar. Put the meat into a soup-
dish, and the sauce over it; or you may put turnips out in
round pieces, and carrots cut round, some small onions, and
thicken the sauce; then put the meat in, and stew it gently
for half an hour with a gill of white wine. Some like savoys
or cabbage stewed, and put into the sauce. *Glass*, 36. *Farley*, 91.

Beef Tremblant, or Trembling Beef.

A rump of beef is the best for this; but it must be vastly cut
and trimmed; cut the edge of the edge-bone off quite close to
the meat, that it may lay flat in your dish; and if it is large,
cut it at the chump-end so as to make it square; hang it up for
three or four days, or more, without salt; prepare a marinade*,
and leave it all night in soak, fillet it two or three times across,
and put it into a pot, the fat uppermost; put in as much water as will a little more than cover it, take care to skim it well,
and season as you would for a good broth, adding about a pint of
white wine; let it simmer for as long a time as it will hang together. There are many sauces for this piece of meat, particularly carrots, herbs, &c. minced. Your carrots should be
cut an inch long, and boiled a little in water, and afterwards
stewed in some cullis proportionate to your meat. When they
are done tender, dish in a glass of white wine, a little minced
shallot and parsley, and the juice of a lemon; take your beef out
upon a cloth, clean it neatly from its fat and liquor, place it
hot and whole in your dish, and pour your sauce hot over it.
Stew some minced parsley over it, it looks prettier. *Verral*, 59.

Another way.

Take the fat end of a brisket of beef, and tie it up close with

* *A pickle.*

D   pack-

packthread ; put it in a pot of water, and boil it fix hours very
gently : feafon the water with a little falt, a handful of all-fpice,
two onions, two turnips, and a carrot : in the mean while, put
a piece of butter in a ftew-pan and melt it, then put in two
fpoonfuls of flour, and ftir it till it is fmooth ; put in a quart of
gravy, a fpoonful of catchup, the fame of browing, a gill of
white wine, carrots and turnips, and cut the fame as for an harrico of mutton ; ftew them gently till the roots are tender, feafon with pepper and falt, fkim all the fat clean off, put the
beef in the difh, and pour the fauce all over. Garnifh with
pickle of any fort, or make a fauce thus :—Chop a handful of
parfley, one onion, four pickled cucumbers, one walnut, and a
gill of capers ; put them in a pint of good gravy, and thicken it
with a little butter rolled in flour, and feafon it with pepper and
falt ; boil it up for ten minutes, and then put it over the beef ;
or you may put the beef in a difh, and put greens and carrots
round it.   *Glaffe*, 33.   *Farley*, 93.

Beef A-la-royal.

. . Bone a rump, firloin, or brifket, and cut fome holes in it at
a little diftance from each other ; fill the holes, one with chopped oyfters, another with fat bacon, and the other with chopped
parfley ; dip each of thefe, before the beef is ftuffed, into a feafoning made with falt, pepper, beaten mace. nutmeg, grated
lemon-peel, fweet-marjoram, and thyme ; put a piece of butter
into a frying-pan, and when it has done hifling, put in the beef,
make it of a fine brown, then put it into fome broth made of
bones, with a bay-leaf, a pint of red wine, two anchovies, and
a quarter of a pint of fmall beer ; cover it clofe, and let it ftew
till it is tender ; then take out the beef, fkim off the fat, and
ftrain the gravy ; add two ox-palates ftewed tender and cut into
pieces, fome pickled gerkins, truffles, morels, and a little mufhroom powder ; let all thefe boil together. Thicken the fauce
with a bit of butter rolled in flour, put in the beef to warm, pour
the fauce over it, and ferve it up.   *Mafon*, 124.

Beef Olives.

Cut fteaks from the rump, or infide of the firloin, half an inch
thick, about fix inches long, and four or five broad, beat them a
little, and rub them over with the yolk of an egg ; ftrew on
bread crumbs, parfley chopped, lemon-peel fhred, pepper and
falt, chopped fuet or marrow, and grated nutmeg ; roll them
up tight, fkewer them, and fry or brown them in a Dutch oven ;
ftew them in fome beef broth or gravy until tender, thicken the
gravy with a little flour ; then add a little catchup, and a little
lemon-juice. To enrich them, add pickled mufhrooms, hard
yolks of eggs, and force-meat balls.   *Mafon*, 128.

Mrs.

Mrs. *Raffald* has given the same receipt in other words, page 117.

Beef A-l'ecarlet *—Scarlet Beef.

A square piece of the middle of the brisket is what is generally provided for this dish, about six or eight pounds. Take half a pound of salt-petre, beat it well, and rub over your beef, wrap it up in a cloth, and bury it in salt for seven or eight days, but not to touch the salt; stew it in the manner of *beef tremblant*, and seasoned so; let it be done very tender, and have some cabbage or savoy, tied up, and stewed with it for an hour, squeeze the fat and liquor well from them, and put them into a stew-pan with a ladle or two of cullis; add a little shallot, minced parsley, and the juice of a lemon; take out your beef upon a cloth to drain it well, dish it up with your cabbage round it, cut it in notches across, and pour your sauce over it very hot.

This is sometimes served to table with lettuce, tops of aspa·ragus, carrots, turnips, or any sort of garden things the sauces are made of. *Verral*, 65.

Another way.

Take a brisket, or the thick part of the thin flank, rub it over well with some salt-petre beat small, then take half a pound of coarse sugar, a pound of common salt, two ounces of bay salt, mix it all together, and rub it well on the beef; turn it every day, and let lie twelve days, or a fortnight.

It eats very good cold, with a weight laid upon it, and then cut into slices. *Mason*, 125. *Glasse*, 36. *Farley*, 96.

A Fricando of Beef.

Cut a few slices of beef five or six inches long, and half an inch thick, lard it with bacon, dredge it well with flour, and set it before a brisk fire to brown; then put it in a tossing pan, with a quart of gravy, a few morels and truffles, half a lemon, and stew them half an hour; then add one spoonful of catchup, the same of browning, and a little chyan; thicken your sauce, and pour it over your fricando. Lay round them force-meat balls, and the yolks of hard eggs. *Raffald*, 115.

Another way.

Take a piece or pieces of beef, of what bigness you please; lard it with coarse pieces of bacon, seasoned with spices; boil it in broth, with a little white wine, a faggot of parsley, sweet herbs, a clove of garlick, shallots, four cloves, whole pepper, and salt. When tender, sift the sauce, skim it well, and reduce it to a glaze, with which you glaze the larded side; and serve it upon what stewed herbs you please. *Dalrymple*, 65.

* *This is erroneously called Beef Escarlet, by Mrs. Glasse and Mr. Farley.—Mrs. Mason calls it Beef Ecarlate.*

To

To ragoo a piece of Beef.

Take a large piece of the flank, which has fat at the top, cut square, or any piece that is all meat, and has fat at the top, but no bones. The rump does well. Cut all nicely off the bone (which makes fine soup); then take a large stew-pan, and with a good piece of butter fry it a little brown all over, flouring your meat well before you put it into the pan; then pour in as much gravy as will cover it, made thus:—take about a pound of coarse beef, a little piece of veal cut small, a bundle of sweet herbs, an onion, some whole black pepper, and white pepper, two or three large blades of mace, four or five cloves, a piece of carrot, a little piece of bacon steeped in vinegar a little while, and a crust of bread toasted brown; put to this a quart of white wine, and let it boil till half is wasted. While this is making, pour a quart of boiling water into the stew-pan, cover it close, and let it be stewing softly; when the gravy is done, strain it, pour it into the pan where the beef is, take an ounce of truffles and morels cut small, some fresh or dried mushrooms cut small, two spoonfuls of catch-up, and cover it close. Let all this stew till the sauce is rich and thick; then have ready some artichoke bottoms cut into four, and a few pickled mushrooms; give them a boil or two, and when your meat is tender, and your sauce quite rich, lay the meat into a dish, and pour the sauce over it. You may add a sweet-bread cut in six pieces, a palate stewed tender cut into little pieces, some cocks'-combs, and a few forced-meat balls. These are a great addition, but it will be good without.

Note—For variety, when the beef is ready, and the gravy put to it, add a large bunch of celery, cut small and washed clean, two spoonfuls of catchup, and a glass of red wine. Omit all the other ingredients. When the meat and celery are tender, and the sauce is rich and good, serve it up. It is also very good this way:—take six large cucumbers, scoop out the seeds, pare them, cut them into slices, and do them just as you do the celery. *Glasse*, 33.

To stew a Rump of Beef.

Half roast your beef, then put it in a large saucepan or cauldron, with two quarts of water, and one of red wine, two or three blades of mace, a shallot, one spoonful of lemon-pickle, two of walnut-catchup, the same of browning. Chyan pepper and salt to your taste; let it stew over a gentle fire, close covered, for two hours, then take up your beef, and lay it in a deep dish, skim off the fat, and strain the gravy, and put in one ounce of morels, and half a pint of mushrooms; thicken your gravy, and pour it over your beef; lay round it force-meat balls. Garnish with horse-radish, and serve it up. *Raffald*, 114.

Another way.

Having boiled it till it is little more than half enough, take it

up,

up, and peel off the fkin; take falt, pepper, beaten mace, grated nutmeg, a handful of parfley, a little thyme, winter favory, fweet marjoram, all chopped fine and mixed, and ftuff them in great holes in the fat and lean, the reft fpread over it, with the yolks of two eggs; fave the gravy that runs out, put to it a pint of claret, and put the meat in a deep pan; pour the liquor in, cover it clofe, and let it bake two hours; then put it into the difh, ftrain the liquor through a fieve, and fkim off the fat very clean; then pour it over the meat, and fend it to table.

Rump au Ragout.

Cut the meat from the bone, flour and fry it, pour over it a little boiling water, and about a pint of fmall beer; add a carrot or two, an onion ftuck with cloves, fome whole pepper, falt, a piece of lemon-peel, and a bunch of fweet herbs; let thefe ftew an hour, then add fome good gravy. When the meat is tender, take it out, ftrain the fauce, thicken it with a little flour; add a little celery ready boiled, and a little catchup; put in the meat, and juft fimmer it up. Or the celery may be omitted, and the ragoo enriched by adding mufhrooms frefh or pickled, artichoke-bottoms boiled and quartered, and hard yolks of eggs.

N. B. A piece of flank, or any piece that can be cut free from bone, will do inftead of the rump. *Mafon*, 125.

Rump of Beef fmoked.

Bone a rump of beef as well as poffible without fpoiling the fhape; falt it with a pound of falt, and two ounces of falt-petre; put it in a falting-pan, length-ways, with all forts of fweet herbs, as parfley, fhallots, thyme, laurel, bafil, winter favory, half an handful of juniper berries, a little coriander, fix cloves, and two cloves of garlick; leave it about a week or ten days in falt, then hang it in the chimney; when dried, keep it in a dry place. When you want to ufe it, boil it in water without falt, with a few onions, cloves, a faggot of fweet herbs, and a little nutmeg: let it cool in the liquor, and ferve it cold upon a napkin. Garnifh with parfley. If you think it will be too falt, foak it fome time before boiling. *Dalrymple*, 68.

To force the infide of a Sirloin of Beef.

Spit your firloin, then cut off from the infide all the fkin and fat together, and then take off all the flefh to the bones; chop the meat very fine with a little beaten mace, two or three fhallots, one anchovy, half a pint of red wine, a little pepper and falt, and put it on the bones again; lay your fat and fkin on again, and fkewer it clofe, and paper it well. When roafted, take off the fat, and difh up the firloin; pour over it a fauce made of a little red wine, a fhallot, one anchovy, two or three flices of horfe-raddifh, and ferve it up. *Raffald*, 113.

D 3   *Another*

Another way.

When it is quite roasted, take it up, and lay it in the dish with the inside uppermost; with a sharp knife lift up the skin, hack and cut out the inside very fine, shake a little pepper and salt over it, with two shallots, cover it with the skin, and send it to table. You may add red wine or vinegar, just as you like.

To broil Beef Steaks.

Cut your steaks off a rump of beef about half an inch thick, let your fire be clear, rub your gridiron well with beef-suet; when it is hot, lay them on, let them broil till they begin to brown, turn them, and when the other side is brown, lay them on a hot dish, with a slice of butter between each steak; sprinkle a little pepper and salt over them, let them stand two or three minutes, then slice a shallot (as thin as possible) into a spoonful of water, lay on your steaks again, keep them turning till they are enough, put them on your dish, pour the shallot and water amongst them, and send them to table. *Farley*, 49.

Another way.

First have a very clear brisk fire: let your gridiron be very clean; put it on the fire, and take a chafing-dish with a few hot coals out of the fire. Put the dish on it which is to lay your steaks on, then take fine rump steaks about half an inch thick; put a little pepper and salt on them, lay them on the gridiron, and (if you like it) take a shallot or two, or a fine onion, and cut it fine; put it into your dish. Keep turning your steaks quick till they are done, for that keeps the gravy in them. When the steaks are enough, take them carefully off into your dish, that none of the gravy be lost; then have ready a hot dish and cover, and carry them hot to the table with the cover on. You may send shallots in a plate, chopped fine.

If you love pickles or horse-radish with steaks, never garnish your dish, because the garnishing will be dry, and the steaks will be cold, but lay those things on little plates, and carry to table. —The great nicety is to have them hot, and full of gravy. *Glasse*, 7.

To fry Beef Steaks.

Take some steaks, cut out of the middle of the rump, fry them in butter; when they are done, put a little small beer into the pan, if not bitter, the gravy which runs from the steaks, a little nutmeg, a shallot, some walnut-catchup, and a piece of butter rolled in flour; shake it round the pan till it boils, and pour it over the steaks. Some stewed oysters may be added, or pickled mushrooms. *Mason*, 127.

Another way.

Cut your steaks as for broiling, put them into a stew-pan with
a good

a good lump of butter, set them over a very slow fire, keep
turning them till the butter is become a thick white gravy, pour
it into a bason, and pour more butter to them When they are
almoft enough, pour all the gravy into your bason, and put more
butter into your pan, fry them a light brown over a quick fire.
Take them out of the pan, put them in a hot pewter dish, slice a
shallot among them, put a little in your gravy that was drawn
from them, and pour it hot upon them. I think this is the best
way of dressing beef-steaks. Half a pound of butter will dress
a large dish. *Raffald*, 71.

Another way.

Take rump-steaks, pepper and salt them, and fry them in a
little butter, very quick and brown: then put them into a dish,
and pour the fat out of the frying-pan. Take half a pint of hot
gravy, half a pint of hot water, and put it into the pan. Add
to it a little butter rolled in flour, a little pepper and salt, and
two or three shallots chopped fine. Boil them up in your pan
for two minutes, and pour it over the steaks. You may garnish
with a little scraped horse-radish round your dish. *Farley*, 54,
from *Glasse*, 39.

To stew Beef Steaks.

Lard the steaks here and there with large pieces of lard, put
them in a stew-pan with chopped parsley, shallots, thyme, laurel,
salt, whole pepper, a little white wine; stew slowly till done;
serve either hot or cold. *Clermont*, 65.

Another way.

Take rump-steaks, pepper and salt them, lay them in a stew-
pan, pour in half a pint of water, a blade or two of mace, two
or three cloves, a little bundle of sweet herbs, an anchovy, a
piece of butter rolled in flour, a glass of white wine, and an
onion; cover them close, and let them stew softly till they are
tender; then take out the steaks, flour them, fry them in fresh
butter, and pour away all the fat; strain the sauce they were
stewed in, and pour into the pan; tofs it all up together till the
sauce is quite hot and thick. If you add a quarter of a pint
of oysters it will make it the better. Lay the steaks into
the dish, and pour the sauce over them. Garnish with any
pickle you like.

Beef Steaks rolled.

Take some beef steaks, what quantity is wanted, beat them
with a cleaver to make them tender; make some force meat
with a pound of veal beat fine in a mortar, the flesh of a fowl,
half a pound of cold ham or gammon of bacon, fat and lean,
the kidney-fat of a loin of veal, and a sweetbread, all cut very
small; some truffles and morels stewed and then cut small, two
shallots, some parsley, a little thyme, some lemon-peel, the

yolks

volks of four eggs, a nutmeg grated, and half a pint of cream. Mix thefe all together, and ftir them over a flow fire for ten minutes; put them upon the fteaks, and roll them up; then fkewer them tight, put them into the frying-pan, and fry them of a nice brown; then take them from the fat, and put them into a ftew-pan with a pint of good drawn gravy, a fpoonful of red wine, two of catchup, a few pickled mufhrooms, and let them ftew for an quarter of an hour; take up the fteaks, cut them in two, lay the cut fide uppermoft. Garnifh with lemon. *Mafon*, 128. *G affe*, 40.

N. B. Before you put the force-meat into the beef, you are to ftir it all together over a flow fire for eight or ten minutes. *Glaffe*, 40.

A Rib of Beef Glaffé, with Spinach.

Provide one of the prime ribs, trim it neatly, and lay it in a marinade for an hour or two; take a ftew-pan exactly its big-nefs, put a flice or two of bacon at the bottom, lay in your beef, and cover it with the fame; to feafon, put in an onion or two, fome bits of carrot, a little fweet bafil, thyme. and parfley, a little pepper, falt, and a blade or two of mace; let it ftew gently till it is very tender, take it out upon a plate, ftrain your braze, clean it well from the fat, put it into a clean ftew pan, and boil it with a ladle of gravy very faft, and you will find it come to a fort of gluey confiftence; then put your beef in, and keep it hot till your dinner-time, and ferve it up with fpinach.

At another time you may ferve it with favoys or red cabbage, ftripped fine and ftewed, and after being blanched, only adding a bit of bacon, with a few cloves ftuck in it in the ftewing, but not to fend to table.

Fillet of the firloin is done pretty much in the fame way, marinaded and roafted, with bacon over it, and the fame fort of fauces. *Verral*, 84.

A Porcupine of the flat Ribs of Beef.

Bone the flat ribs, and beat it half an hour with a pafte pin, then rub it over with the yolks of eggs, ftrew over it bread-crumbs, parfley, leeks. fweet marjoram, lemon-peel, fhred fine; nutmeg, pepper and falt; roll it up very clofe, and bind it hard; lard it acrofs with bacon; then a row of cold boiled tongue, a third row of pickled cucumbers, a fourth row of lemon-peel; do it all over in rows till it is larded all round; it will look like red, green, white. and yellow dice; then fplit it, or put it in a deep pot with a pint of water, lay over the caul of veal to keep it from fcorching, tie it down with ftrong paper, and fend it to the oven. When it comes out, fkim off the fat, and ftrain your gravy into a faucepan; add to it two fpoonfuls of red wine, the fame of browning, one of mufhroom catchup, half a lemon,

thicken

thicken it with a lump of butter rolled in flour, difh up the meat, and pour the gravy on the difh; lay round force-meat balls. Garnifh with horfe-radifh, and ferve it up. *Raffald*, 116.

To bake a Leg of Beef.

Take a large deep pan, and lay your beef at the bottom; then put in a little piece of bacon, a flice or two of carrot, fome mace, cloves, black and white whole pepper, a large onion cut in flices, and a bundle of fweet herbs. Pour in water till the meat be covered, and fend it to the oven covered up. When it is baked, ftrain it through a coarfe fieve; take out all the finews and fat, and put them into a fauce-pan with a few fpoon-fuls of the gravy, a little red wine, a fmall piece of butter roll-ed in flour, and fome muftard; fhake your fauce-pan often, and when the fauce is hot and thick, difh it up, and fend it to table. *Mafon*, 121.

To drefs a Fillet of Beef.

It is the infide of the firloin. You muft carefully cut it all out from the bone, grate fome nutmeg over it, a few crumbs of bread, a little pepper and falt, a little lemon-peel, a little thyme, fome parfley fhred fmall, and roll it up tight; tie it with a piece of packthread, roaft it, put a quart of milk and a quar-ter of a pound of butter into the dripping-pan, and bafte it. When it is enough, take it up, untie it, leave a little fkewer in it to hold it together, have a little good gravy in the difh, and fome fweet fauce in a cup. You may bafte it with red wine and butter, or it will do very well with butter only. *Glaffe*, 40.

Another way.

Soak fix anchovies in water about two hours; fplit them, and lard the fillet with them, intermixed with bacon; ftew it on a flow fire, with a little broth and white wine, a clove of garlick, two cloves, a faggot of parfley, green onions, and fweet herbs. When done, fift the fauce; add a little butter rolled in flour, and a few whole capers; make a liafon of eggs and cream; ferve it up on the fillet. *Clermont*, 76.

Bouille Beef.

Take the thick end of a brifket of beef, put it into a kettle of water quite covered over; let it boil faft for two hours, then keep ftewing it clofe by the fire for fix hours more, and as the water waftes, fill up the kettle; put in with the beef fome tur-nips cut into little balls, carrots, and fome celery cut in pieces; an hour before it is done, take out as much broth as will fill your foup-difh, and boil in it for that hour turnips and carrots cut out in balls, or in little fquare pieces, with fome celery, falt and pepper to your tafte, ferve it up in two difhes, the beef by itfelf, and the foup by itfelf. You may put pieces of fried bread,

if

if you like it, in your foup; boil in a few knots of greens; and
if you think your foup will not be rich enough, you may add a
pound or two of fried mutton chops to your broth when you
take it from the beef, and let it ftew for that hour in the broth;
but be fure to take out the mutton when you fend it to the
table. The foup muft be very clear. *Raffald*, 113.

Beef in Epigram.

Roaft a firloin of beef, take it off the fpit, then raife the
fkin carefully off, and cut the lean parts of the beef out, but
obferve not to cut near the ends or fides. Hafh the meat in the
following manner:—cut it into pieces about as big as a crown
piece, put half a pint of gravy into a tofs-pan, an onion chopped fine, two fpoonfuls of catchup, fome pepper and falt, fix
fmall pickled cucumbers cut in thin flices, and the gravy that
comes from the beef; a little butter rolled in flour; put the
meat in, and tofs it up for five minutes, put it on the firloin,
and then put the fkin over and fend it to table. Garnifh with
horfe raddifh.

You may do the infide inftead of the outfide if you pleafe.
Glaffe, 34. *Mafon*, 126. *Farley*, 95.

To roaft Ox Palates.

Having boiled your palates tender, blanch them, cut them
into flices about two inches long, lard half with bacon; then
have ready two or three pigeons, and two or three chicken-
peepers, draw them, trufs them, and fill them with force-meat;
let half of them be nicely larded, fpit them on a bird-fpit thus:
—a bird, a palate, a fage-leaf, and a piece of bacon; and fo on,
a bird, a palate, a fage-leaf, and a piece of bacon. Take cock's
combs and lambs'-ftones, parboiled and blanched, lard them
with little bits of bacon, large oyfters parboiled, and each one
larded with one piece of bacon; put thefe on a fkewer, with a
little piece of bacon and a fage-leaf between them; tie them on
a fpit and roaft them; then beat up the yolks of three eggs,
fome nutmeg, a little falt, and crumbs of bread: bafte them
with thefe all the time they are roafting, and have ready two
fweetbreads, each cut in two, fome artichoke bottoms cut into
four and fried, and then rub the difh with fhallots; lay the
birds in the middle, piled upon one another, and lay the other
things all feparate by themfelves round about in the difh.
Have ready for fauce a pint of good gravy, a quarter of a pint
of red wine, an anchovy, the oyfter liquor, a piece of butter
rolled in flour; boil all thefe together, and pour into the difh,
with a little juice of lemon. Garnifh your difh with lemon.
Glaffe, 44. *Farley*, 37, from *Glaffe*. *Mafon*, 134.

To ftew Ox Palates.

Wafh four ox-palates in feveral waters, and then lay them in
warm

warm water for half an hour, then wafh them out and put them in a pot, and tie them down with ftrong paper, and fend them to the oven with as much water as will cover them, or boil them till tender; then fkin them and cut them in pieces half an inch broad, and three inches long, and put them in a tofling-pan with a pint of veal gravy, one fpoonful of Madeira wine, the fame of catchup and browning, one onion ftuck with cloves, and a flice of lemon; ftew them half an hour, then take out the onion and lemon, thicken your fauce, and put them in a difh; have ready boiled artichoke bottoms, cut them in quarters, and lay them over your palates, with force-meat balls and morels. Garnifh with lemon, and ferve them up. *Raffald*, 119.

To breil Ox Palates.

Boil in water as many palates as you pleafe; peel them, and foak them in faint menoult, which is thus:—put in a ftew-pan a little butter rolled in flour, falt and pepper, two fhallots, a clove of garlick, two cloves, parfley, a laurel-leaf, thyme, with as much milk as will fimmer your palates till tender; then take them out, and bafte them with yolks of eggs and bread crumbs; broil them flowly, and ferve them with a fharp fauce. *Dalrymple*, 56.

To ragoo Ox Palates.

Take four ox-palates, and boil them very tender, clean them well, cut fome in fquare pieces, and fome long. Make a rich cooley thus:—put a piece of butter in your ftew-pan, and melt it; put a large fpoonful of flour to it, ftir it well till it is fmooth, then put a quart of good gravy to it; chop three fhallots, and put in a gill of Lifbon; cut fome lean ham very fine and put in, alfo half a lemon; boil them twenty minutes, then ftrain it through a fieve, put it into your pan, and the palates, with fome force-meat balls, truffles, and morels, pickled or frefh mufh-rooms ftewed in gravy; feafon with pepper and falt to your liking, and tofs them up five or fix minutes, then difh them up Garnifh with lemon or beet-root. *Glaffe*, 44.

Slices of Fillet of Beef with clear Gravy and Rocombole.

A pound of meat is enough for this difh. Cut it into bits about an inch thick, and flat it down with your knife, or a light cleaver; it is better than flicing; make it very thin, and jag it with the back of your knife crofs and crofs; rub a large ftew-pan with butter, a little green onion and parfley minced, fry your beef brifkly for two or three minutes, tofling it that it may be done on both fides; take it out into a fmall ftew-pan, and pour in a ladle of nice gravy, a little pepper, falt, a morfel of fhallot and parfley; boil it but a moment. When dinner is ready, fqueeze in a lemon or orange, and fend it to table.

The

The infide fillets of loins of mutton or pork are done in the fame manner; and though they feem but trifling matters, yet if care is taken to make them very thin, and nicely fried, and not boiled too much afterwards, they are good and pretty difhes. *Verral*, 112.

To make a mock Hare of a Bullock's Heart.

Wafh a large bullock's heart clean, and cut off the deaf ears, and ftuff it with fome force-meat, as you do a hare; lay a caul of veal or paper over the top to keep in the ftuffing; roaft it either in a cradle fpit or a hanging one; it will take an hour and an half before a good fire; bafte it with red wine. When roafted take the wine out of the dripping-pan, fkim off the fat and add a glafs more of wine. When it is hot put in fome lumps of red currant jelly and pour it in the difh. Serve it up and fend in red currant jelly cut in flices on a faucer. *Raffald*, 318.

To roaft a Bullock's Heart.

Mix bread-crumbs, chopped fuet (or a bit of butter) parfley chopped, fweet marjoram, lemon-peel grated, pepper, falt, and natmeg, with a yolk of an egg; ftuff the heart, and bake or roaft it. Serve it with gravy, a little red wine in it, melted butter, and currant jelly in boats. Some lard it with bacon. *Mafon*, 135.

Cold Roaft Beef marinaded.

Cut flices of cold roaft beef, and make a marinade with a little oil, parfley, chibbol, mufhrooms, a trifle of garlic, and three fhallots, all finely chopped, pepper and falt; foak it along with the beef about half an hour; make as much of the marinade keep to it as you can with a deal of bread crumbs; broil on a flow fire, bafting it with the remaining liquid. Serve with a fharp fauce. *Dalrymple*, 66.

Cold Roaft Beef, family fafhion.

Slice three or four onions, and fry them in butter; when done, add a little broth, three fhallots chopped, pepper and falt; then put flices of cold beef to it; boil for a moment; when ready, add a liafon made of three yolks of eggs and a little vinegar. Cold beef is alfo very good with cold fauce made of chopped parfley, fhallots, vinegar, oil, muftard, minced anchovy, &c. *Clermont*, 68.

To make Collops of Cold Beef.

If you have any cold infide of a firloin of beef, take off all the fat, cut it very thin in little bits, cut an onion very fmall, boil as much water or gravy as you think will do for fauce; feafon it with a little pepper and falt, and a bundle of fweet herbs.— Let the water boil, then put in the meat, with a good piece of butter rolled in flour, shake it round, and stir it. When the sauce is thick and the meat done, take out the sweet herbs, and pour it into your dish. They do better than fresh meat. *Glasse*, 120.

To stew Neat's Tongue.

Put two tongues in water just sufficient to cover them, and let them stew two hours. Then peel them, and put them in again with a pint of strong gravy, half a pint of white wine, a bundle of sweet herbs, a little pepper and salt, some mace, cloves, and whole pepper, tied in a muslin rag; a spoonful of capers chopped, turnips and carrots sliced, and a piece of butter rolled in flour. Let all stew together very softly over a slow fire for two hours, and then take out the spice and sweet herbs, and send the dish to table. You may, just as you like, leave out the turnips and carrots, or boil them by themselves, and lay them in a dish. *Farley*, 67.

Neat's Tongue à la Remoulade—Neat's Tongue with a relishing Sauce.

Scald a fresh tongue and peel it, lard it with large pieces of bacon, boil it in the stock pot, or in broth, with a little salt and a nosegay; split it, but not quite in two; make a sauce with parsley, shallots, capers, anchovies, all very finely chopped, a little vinegar, a few crumbs of bread or raspings, a little cullis and broth, a little salt and pepper; boil all together a little, then put the tongue in it to simmer for a quarter of an hour. When you serve, add a little mustard. *Dalrymple*, 51.

To force a Neat's Tongue.

Boil it till is tender; let it stand till it is cold, then cut a hole at the root end of it, take out some of the meat, chop it with as much beef suet, a few pippins, some pepper and salt, a little mace beat, some nutmeg, a few sweet herbs, and the yolks of two eggs; beat all together well in a marble mortar; stuff it, cover the end with a veal caul, or buttered paper, roast it, baste it with butter, and dish it up. Have for sauce good gravy, a little melted butter, the juice of an orange or lemon, and some grated nutmeg; boil it up, and pour it into the dish.

To marinade Neats' Tongues.

Boil them till tender, and peel them; when cold, put them into a vessel that will hold them at full length; make a pickle of white-wine vinegar (as much as will fill the vessel) some nutmegs, ginger sliced, mace, whole cloves, a bunch of sweet herbs, consisting of parsley, sweet marjoram, sage, winter savory, thyme, and bay-leaves; boil them well. When cold, put them to the tongues, with some salt and sliced lemon; close them up. Serve them in slices in some of the liquor. They may be larded, if agreeable. *Mason*, 153.

A Neat's

A Neat's Tongue en Crepine—A Neat's Tongue in Veal Caul.

Boil a tongue sufficiently to peel; then lard and split it without separating it in two; slice some onions, fry them in hog's lard; put to it three or four spoonfuls of hog's blood, about a quarter of a pound of fresh lard chopped, a few spices, and salt; simmer it, stirring it continually till the blood is well mixed; then lay a caul in the bottom of your dish, and spread upon it part of your preparation, then the tongue, then the same as before on the tongue: roll it up in the caul, and garnish it with bread crumbs; put it in the oven to bake, and take a good colour; clean the dish free from fat, and serve it under a sauce made with cullis, jelly, broth, and lemon. *Clermont*, 53.

To force a Neat's Tongue and Udder.

First parboil the tongue and udder, blanch the tongue, and stick it with cloves. As for the udder, you must carefully raise it, and fill it with force-meat made of veal; first wash the inside with the yolk of an egg, then put in the force-meat, tie the ends close, and spit them; roast them, and baste them with butter; when enough, have a good gravy in the dish, and sweet sauce in a cup.

N. B. For variety, you may lard the udder. *Glasse*, 43. *Farley*, 96.

To pot Neats' Tongues.

Take a neat's tongue, and rub it with an ounce of saltpetre and four ounces of brown sugar, and let it lie two days; then boil it till it is quite tender, and take off the skin and side bits, then cut the tongue in very thin slices, and beat it in a marble mortar, with one pound of clarified butter, mace, pepper and salt to your taste; beat it exceeding fine, then put it close down into small potting pots, and pour clarified butter over them. *Raffald*, 296.

Bouillis des tendrons de Bœuf aux choux—Hodge Podge of Beef with Savoys.

Provide a piece of the middlemost part of brisket beef, of about six pounds, cut it in square pieces so as to make ten or twelve of it; don't put it into too large a pot, but such a one as will be full with a gallon of water to it; take care to skim it well, and season it well with onions, carrots, turnips, leeks, celery, and a little bundle of parsley, and some pepper; when your meat is boiled very tender, strain your broth from it, and put it into a soup-pot or stew-pan; take another, with an ounce, or little more, of butter, melt it, and put in a large spoonful of flour, stir it over the fire till it becomes brown, take the fat off your broth and put to it; boil it a few minutes, and strain to your beef; your savoys should be well blanched, and tied up separate; put them into your meat, and let it stew very gently

till

till your dinner is called; take it off, and clean all from the fpit, place your meat in neat order in your difh, or foup-difh, lay your favoys between, pour your foup or fauce over it, and ferve it up with a little parfley fprinkled gently over it. This difh is frequently fent to table with turnips or carrots, inftead of favoys, cut in neat bits and boiled before you put them to your foup.

Hodge-podge of veal or mutton is done after the fame manner, with this difference only—inftead of making your foup brown, ftir your flour no longer than while it retains its whitenefs, and pour your broth in, and ftrain to your meat. *Verral*, 24.

To marinade a Breast of Veal.

CUT the breast of veal in pieces; stew it in broth till about three quarters done; then marinade about an hour with two spoonfuls of vinegar, a little of its own broth, whole pepper and salt, four cloves, two cloves of garlick, sliced onions, and thyme; then drain it, and fry of a good colour. Garnish with fried parsley. You may also do it with a batter, or baste it with bread-crumbs and yolks of eggs, and fry it as above. *Dalrymple*, 97.

A ragoo of a Breast of Veal.

Half roast the best end of it, flour it, and stew it gently with three pints of good gravy, an onion, a few cloves, whole pepper, and a bit of lemon-peel; turn it while stewing; when very render, strain the sauce; if not thick enough, mix a little more flour smooth; add catchup, chyan, truffles, morels, pickled mushrooms; boil it up, put in hard yolks of eggs. *Mason*, 140.

Another way.

Half roast a breast of veal, then bone it, and put it into a tossing-pan with a quart of veal gravy, one ounce of morels, the same of truffles; stew it till tender; and just before you thicken the gravy, put in a few oysters, pickled mushrooms and pickled cucumbers, cut in small square pieces, the yolks of four eggs boiled hard; cut your sweetbread in slices, and fry it a light brown; dish up your veal, and pour the gravy hot over it; lay your sweet-bread round, morels, truffles, and eggs upon it. Garnish with pickled barberries. This is proper for either top or side for dinner, or bottom for supper. *Raffald*, 90.

To stew a Breast of Veal in its own sauce.

Put a breast of veal into a stew-pan of its own length, with a little broth, a glass of white wine, a faggot of sweet herbs, a few mushrooms, a little coriander tied in a bag, sliced roots, onions, pepper, and salt; stew it slowly till very tender. When ready to serve, strain and skim the sauce, and serve it upon the meat. *Clermont*, 103.

Breast of Veal stewed white.

Cut a piece off each end; make a force-meat as follows:—Boil the sweet-bread, and cut it very small, some grated bread, a little beef suet, two eggs, a little cream, some nutmeg, salt and pepper; mix it well together, and stuff the thin part of the breast with some of it, the rest make up into little balls; skewer the skin close down, flour and boil it in a cloth in milk and water; make some gravy of the ends that were cut off, with half a pint of oysters, the juice of a lemon, and a piece of
butter

butter rolled in flour; when the veal is enough, put it in the difh. Garnifh with the balls ftewed, and pour the fauce over it.

Breaſt of Veal ſtewed with Peas or Aſparagus.

Cut it into pieces about three inches in ſize, fry it nicely; mix a little flour with ſome beef broth, an onion, two or three cloves; ſtew this ſome time, ſtrain it, add three pints or two quarts of peas, or ſome heads of aſparagus like peas; put in the meat, let it ſtew gently; add pepper and ſalt.

Breaſt of Veal in Hodge Podge.

Take a breaſt of veal, cut the briſket into little pieces, and every bone aſunder, then flour it, and put half a pound of good butter into a ſtew-pan; when it is hot, throw in veal, fry it all over of a fine light brown, and then have ready a tea-kettle of water boiling; pour it in the ſtew-pan, fill it up, and ſtir it round; throw in a pint of green peas, a fine lettuce whole, clean waſhed, two or three blades of mace, a little whole pep-per tied in a muſlin rag, a little bundle of ſweet herbs, a ſmall onion ſtuck with a few cloves, and a little ſalt. Cover it cloſe, and let it ſtew one hour, or till it is boiled to your palate, if you would have ſoup made of it; if you would only have ſauce to eat with the veal, you muſt ſtew it till there is juſt as much as you would have for ſauce, and ſeaſon it with ſalt to your palate; take out the onion, ſweet herbs, and ſpice, and pour it all toge-ther into your diſh. It is a fine diſh. If you have no peas, pare three or four cucumbers, ſcoop out the pulp, and cut it into little pieces, and take four or five heads of celery, clean waſhed, and cut the white part ſmall; when you have no lettuces, take the little hearts of ſavoys, or the little young ſprouts that grow on the old cabbage ſtalks, about as big as the top of your thumb.

N. B. If you would make a very fine diſh of it, fill the in-ſide of your lettuce with force-meat, and tie the top cloſe with a thread; ſtew it till there is but juſt enough for ſauce; ſet the lettuce in the middle, and the veal round, and pour the ſauce over it. Garniſh your diſh with raſped bread, made into figures with your fingers. This is the cheapeſt way of dreſſing a breaſt of veal to be good, and ſerve a number of people. *Glaſſe*, 29. *Maſon*, 142.

To collar a Breaſt of Veal.

Take the fineſt breaſt of veal, bone it, and rub it over with the yolks of two eggs, and ſtrew over it ſome crumbs of bread, a little grated lemon, a little pepper and ſalt, a handful of chopped parſley, roll it up tight, and bind it hard with twine; wrap it in a cloth, and boil it one hour and an half; then take it up to cool. When a little cold, take off the cloth, and clip off the twine carefully, leſt you open the veal; cut it in five

E   ſlices, flices, lay them on a dish with the fweetbread boiled and cut in thin flices and laid round them, with ten or twelve force-meat balls; pour over your white fauce, and garnish with barberries or green pickles.

The white fauce muft be made thus:—take a pint of good veal gravy, put to it a fpoonful of lemon pickle, half an anchovy, a tea-fpoonful of mufhroom powder, or a few pickled mufh-rooms: give it a gentle boil; then put in half a pint of cream, the yolks of two eggs beat fine; fhake it over the fire after the eggs and cream are in, but do not let boil, it will curdle the cream. It is proper for a top dish at night, or a fide dish for dinner. *Raffald*, 91.

The Griftles of a Breaft of Veal with a White Sauce.

About the half of a breaft of veal will do for this fmall dish; take off all the upper part, and cut the griftles in fmall bits, blanch them, and put into a ftew-pan to a ladle of broth; ftew it very tender, and put a bit of butter mixed with flour, a bunch of onions and parfley, a blade of mace, pepper, and falt. For your fauce, you may prepare either peas or afparagus; make a liaton; and juft before you ferve, pour it in; add the juice of a lemon, and dish it up.

Breafts of lamb are done in the fame manner, and make a favorite dish. *Verral*, 120.

To ragoo a Neck of Veal.

Cut a neck of veal into fteaks, flatten them with a rolling-pin, feafon them with falt, pepper, cloves, and mace; lard them with bacon, lemon-peel, and thyme; dip them in the yolks of eggs, make a fheet of ftrong cap-paper up at the four corners, in the form of a dripping-pan; pin up the corners, butter the paper and alfo the gridiron, and fet it over a fire of charcoal; put in your meat, let it do leifurely, keep it bafting and turning to keep in the gravy; and when it is enough, have ready half a pint of ftrong gravy, feafon it high, put in mufhrooms and pickles, force-meat balls dipped in the yolks of eggs, oyfters ftewed and fried to lay round and at the top of your dish, and then ferve it up. If for a brown ragoo, put in red wine; if for a white one, put in white wine, with the yolks of eggs beat up with two or three fpoonfuls of cream.

Neck of Veal and fharp Sauce.

Make a marinade with butter and a little flour, fliced onions, roots, and a little coriander-feed, one clove of garlick, three fpice cloves, thyme, laurel, bafil, pepper, and falt; warm it, and put in it a larded neck of veal; let it lie in a marinade about two hours, then wrap it in buttered paper, and roaft it, and ferve with a poivrade or fharp fauce. *Dalrymple*, 102.

Neck of Veal stewed.

Lard it with large pieces of bacon rolled in pepper and salt, shallots and spices; braze it with slices of lard, sliced roots, onions, a laurel leaf, broth, and a little brandy; skim and sift the sauce, and serve it on the meat. *Clermont*, 108.

Neck of Veal stewed with Celery.

Take the best end of a neck, put it into a stew-pan with some beef broth or boiling water, some salt, whole pepper and cloves, tied in a bit of muslin, an onion, a piece of lemon-peel; stew this till tender; take out the spice and peel, put in a little cream and flour mixed, some celery ready boiled and cut into lengths; boil it up.

Neck of Veal à-la-braise.

Take the best end, lard it with bacon rolled in parsley chopped, pepper, salt, and nutmeg; put it into a stew-pan, and cover it with water; put in the scrag-end, with a little lean bacon, or a bit of ham, an onion, two carrots, some shallots, a head or two of celery, and a little Madeira; let these stew gently for two hours, or till tender; strain the liquor, mix a little butter with some flour, stir it in a stew-pan till it is brown; lay in the veal, the upward side to the bottom of the pan, let it do a few minutes till it is coloured, lay it in the dish, stir in some more liquor, boil it up, and squeeze in orange or lemon juice. *Mason*, 141.

Neck of Veal à-la-royal.

Take a neck of veal, and cut off the scrag-end, and part of the chine-bone, in order to make it lie flat in the dish. Then chop very fine a little parsley and thyme, a few shallots and mushrooms, and season with pepper and salt. Cut middling sized lards of bacon, and roll them in the herbs and seasoning. Lard the lean part of the neck, put it in a stew-pan with some lean bacon, or the shank of a ham; and the chine-bone and scrag cut in pieces, with a little beaten mace, a head of celery, onions, and three or four carrots. Pour in as much water as will cover it, shut the pan close, and stew it slowly two or three hours, till it is tender. Then strain half a pint of the liquor through a sieve, set it over a stove, let it boil, and keep stirring it till it is of a good brown; but take care not to let it boil. Then add more of the liquor, strain off the fat, and keep it stirring till it becomes thick and of a fine brown. Then take the veal out of the stew-pan, wipe it clean, and put the larded side down upon the glaze; set it five or six minutes over a gentle fire to take the glaze, and then lay it in the dish with the glazed side upwards. Put into the same stew pan as much flour as will lie on a sixpence, stir it about well, and add some

of

of the braze powder if any be left. Let it boil till it is of a proper thickness, strain it, and pour it into the bottom of the dish. Squeeze in a little lemon juice, and send it to table. *Farley*, 98.

Bombarded Veal.

You must get a fillet of veal; cut out of it five lean pieces, as thick as your hand, round them up a little, then lard them very thick on the round side with little narrow thin pieces of bacon, and lard five sheeps' tongues (being first boiled and blanched) lard them here and there with very little bits of lemon-peel, and make a well seasoned force-meat of veal, bacon, ham, beef suet, and an anchovy beat well; make another tender force-meat of veal, beef suet, mushrooms, spinach, parsley, thyme, sweet marjoram, winter savory, and green onions. Season with pepper, salt, and mace; beat it well, make a round ball of the other force-meat, and stuff in the middle of this, roll it up in a veal caul and bake it; what is left tie up like a Bologna sausage, and boil it, but first rub the caul with the yolk of an egg; put the larded veal into a stew-pan with some good gravy, and stew it gently till it is enough; skim off the fat, put in some truffles and morels, and some mushrooms. Your force-meat being baked enough, lay it in the middle, the veal round it, and the tongues fried and laid between; the boiled cut into slices and fried, and throw all over. Put on them the sauce. You may add artichoke bottoms, sweet-breads, and cock's-combs if you please. Garnish with lemon. *Glasse*, 57. *Mason*, 148.

Bombarded Veal another way.

Cut the bone nicely out of a fillet, make a force-meat of the crumbs of a penny loaf, half a pound of fat bacon scraped, a little lemon-peel, or lemon thyme, parsley, two or three sprigs of sweet marjoram, one anchovy; chop them all very well, grate a little nutmeg, chyan pepper and salt to your palate; mix all up together with an egg and a little cream, and fill up the place where the bone came out with the force-meat; then cut the fillet across, in cuts about one inch from another, all round the fillet; fill one nick with force-meat, a second with boiling spinnach, that is boiled and well squeezed, a third with bread crumbs, chopped oysters, and beef marrow, then force-meat, and fill them up, as above, all round the fillet, wrap the caul close round it, and put it in a deep pot with a pint of water; make a coarse paste to lay over it, to keep the oven from giving it a fiery taste; when it comes out of the oven, skim off the fat, and put the gravy in a stew-pan, with a spoonful of lemon-pickle, and another of mushroom catchup, two of browning, half an ounce of morels and truffles, five boiled ar-

tichoke

tichoke bottoms cut in quarters; thicken the fauce with flour
and butter, give it a gentle boil, and pour it upon the veal into
your difh. *Raffald, 93.*

Veal Olives à-la-mode.

Take two pounds of veal, fome marrow, two anchovies, the
yolks of two hard eggs, a few mufhrooms, and fome oyfters,
a little thyme, marjoram, parfley, fpinach, lemon-peel, falt,
pepper, nutmeg, and mace, finely beaten; take your veal caul,
lay a layer of bacon and a layer of the ingredients, roll it in
the veal caul, and either roaft it or bake it. An hour will do
either. When enough, cut it into flices, lay it in your difh,
and pour good gravy over it. Garnifh with lemon. *Glaffe, 58.*

Fillet of Veal ftewed.

Stuff it, half bake it with a little water in the difh, then ftew
it with the liquor and fome good gravy, and a little Madeira;
when enough, thicken it with flour; add catchup, chyan, a
little falt, juice of orange or lemon; boil it up. *Mafon, 139.*

To ragoo a Fillet of Veal.

Lard your fillet and half roaft it, then put it in a toffing-pan,
with two quarts of good gravy; cover it clofe and let it ftew
till tender, then add one fpoonful of white wine, one of browning, one of catchup, a tea fpoonful of lemon-pickle, a little caper
liquor, half an ounce of morels; thicken with flour and butter,
and lay round it a few yolks of eggs.

Leg of Veal marinated.

Provide a nice leg of white veal and marinate it; roaft it
with four flices of bacon over it, covered with paper; take four
or five heads of endive, cut into bits about an inch in length,
blanch it a little, and ftew it in a little gravy mixed with a ladle of cullis; put a minced fhallot and fome parfley, fqueeze in
the juice of a lemon, and ferve it up with the fauce under it.
Make ufe of capers, olives, or any fort of pickles for a change.
Verral, 67.

Leg of Veal with white Sauce.

Lard a leg of veal with large pieces of bacon, let it foak
twelve hours in marinade made after this manner:—a piece of
butter and flour, a quart of milk, two lemons peeled and fliced,
fix fhallots, two cloves of garlick, fix onions fliced, eight cloves,
three laurel leaves, thyme and parfley, whole pepper and falt.
Warm the marinade, and put into a pot much about the bignefs
of the veal; wipe it dry before fpitting, and cover it with flices
of lard and two fheets of paper, or with buttered paper alone;
and ferve with poivrade, or a cream fauce made of a piece of
butter and flour, a chopped anchovy, chopped parfley and
fhallots, grated nutmeg, pepper and falt, and as much cream as

E 3 necefſary

neceſſary. When ready to ſerve, add the juice of a lemon. It may alſo be done without larding. *Dalrymple*, 103.

Leg of Veal daubed, or à-la-mode.

It is larded and brazed with all ſorts of roots and ſpices; reduce the ſauce to a jelly, and ſerve it with it, either hot or cold. *Dalrymple*, 104.

A Leg of Veal in Diſguiſe.

Lard the veal with ſlips of bacon, and a little lemon-peel cut very thin ; make a ſtuffing as for a fillet of veal, only mix with it half a pint of oyſters chopped ſmall ; put it into a veſſel, and cover it with water ; let it ſtew very gently till quite tender ; take it up, and ſkim off the fat ; ſqueeze ſome juice of lemon, ſome muſhroom catchup, the crumb of a roll grated fine, and half a pint of oyſters, with a pint of cream, and a piece of butter rolled in flour. Let the ſauce thicken upon the fire, put the veal in the diſh, and pour the ſauce over it. Garniſh with oyſters dipped in butter and fried, and with thin ſlices of toaſted bacon. *Maſon*, 143.

A Leg of Veal and Bacon in Diſguiſe.

Lard your veal all over with ſlips of bacon, and a little lemon-peel, and boil it up with a piece of bacon ; when enough, take it up, cut the bacon into ſlices, and have ready ſome dried ſage and pepper rubbed fine; rub over the bacon, lay the veal in the diſh and the bacon round it, ſtrew it all over with fried parſley, and have green ſauce in cups made thus :—take two handfuls of ſorrel, pound it in a mortar and ſqueeze out the juice ; put it into a ſaucepan with ſome melted butter, a little ſugar, and the juice of a lemon. Or you may make it thus:— beat two handfuls of ſorrel in a mortar, with two pippins quartered, ſqueeze the juice out, with the juice of a lemon, or vinegar, and ſweeten it with ſugar. *Glaſſe*, 56.

To ſtew a Knuckle of Veal.

Be ſure you let the pot or ſaucepan be very clean ; lay at the bottom four clean wooden ſkewers, waſh and clean the knuckle very well, then lay it in the pot with two or three blades of mace, a little whole pepper, a little piece of thyme, a ſmall onion, a cruſt of bread, and two quarts of water. Cover it down cloſe, make it boil, then only let it ſimmer for two hours, and when it is enough, take it up, lay it in a diſh, and ſtrain the broth over it.

Leg or Knuckle of Veal and Spinach.

It is larded and brazed with all ſorts of roots, and ſpices as uſual, and ſerved upon ſtewed ſpinach ; it is the garden ſtuff that gives it the name. *Dalrymple*, 103.

Shoulder

Shoulder of Veal à-la-Piedmontoise.

Cut the skin off a shoulder of veal, so that it may hang at one end; then lard the meat with bacon and ham, and season it with pepper, mace, salt, sweet herbs, parsley, and lemon-peel. Cover it again with the skin, stew it with gravy, and when it is just tender enough, take it up. Then take sorrel, some lettuce chopped small, and stew them in some butter, with parsley, onions, and mushrooms. The herbs being tender, put to them some of the liquor, some sweet-breads, and some bits of ham. Let all stew together a little while, then lift up the skin, lay the stewed herbs over and under, cover it again with the skin, wet it with melted butter, strew it over with crumbs of bread, and send it to the oven to brown. Serve it up hot, with some good gravy in the dish. The French, before it goes to the oven, strew it over with Parmesan.— *Farley,* 101.

A shoulder of veal may be dressed in every respect and fashion as the leg. *Clermont,* 111.

A Harrico of Veal.

Take a neck or breast of veal (if the neck, cut the bones short) and half roast it; then put it into a stew-pan just covered with brown gravy, and when it is near done, have ready a pint of boiled peas, six cucumbers pared, and two cabbage-lettuces cut in quarters, stewed in brown gravy, with a few force-meat balls ready fried; put them to the veal, and let them just simmer. When the veal is in the dish, pour the sauce and the peas over it, and lay the lettuce and balls round it. *Mason,* 140.

To roast Sweetbreads with Asparagus.

Two good sweetbreads are enough for this small dish; blanch them, and lay them in a marinade, spit them tight upon a lark spit, and tie them to another, with a slice of bacon upon each, and covered with pepper; when almost done, take that off, and pour a drop of butter upon them, with a few crumbs of bread, and roast them of a nice colour; take two bunches of asparagus, and boil them, not so much as when boiled to eat with butter; dish up your sweetbreads and your grass between them, take a little cullis and gravy, with a jot of shallot and minced parsley; boil it a few minutes, squeeze in the juice of a lemon or orange, and serve it up. *Verral,* 161.

Sweetbreads are very useful in many dishes, as in pies, ragoos, fricassees, &c. and to use alone, either fried, roasted, broiled, or otherwise. They must be soaked in warm water an hour or two, then scalded about an hour or two in warm water, which is commonly called *setting* or *blanching*, which will make them

keep longer, and are ready for any ufe you pleafe to put them
to. *Dalrymple*, 89.

Forced Sweetbreads.

Put three fweetbreads in boiling water five minutes, beat the
yolk of an egg a little, and rub it over them with a feather;
ftrew on bread-crumbs, lemon-peel, and parfley fhred very fine,
nutmeg, falt and pepper to your palate; fet them before the
fire to brown, and add to them a little veal gravy; put a little
mufhroom powder, caper liquor, or juice of lemon, and browning; thicken it with flour and butter, boil it a little, and pour
it into your difh; lay in your fweetbreads, and lay over them
lemon-peel in rings, cut like ftraws. Garnifh with pickles.
Raffald, 98.

Another way.

Parboil them as for a ragoo, put force-meat in a caul in the
fhape of a fweetbread; roaft that in a Dutch oven; thicken a
little good gravy with flour; add catchup, a little grated lemon-
peel, pepper, falt, and nutmeg; boil it up with a few pickled
mufhrooms or lemon-juice. Let the fweetbreads ftew a little in
this gravy; then lay the force-meat in the middle, and the
fweetbreads at the end. *Mafon*, 157.

Sweetbreads as Hedge-hogs.

Scald the fweetbreads, and lard them with ham and truffles,
cut in fmall pieces; fry a fhort time in butter; let the pieces
ftick out a little to make the appearance of briftles; fimmer them
in the fame butter, with broth and a little white wine, very
little falt and pepper; when done, fkim and ftrain the fauce;
add a little cullis, and ferve upon them. You may alfo ufe any
other fauce. As fweetbreads are of an infipid tafte of themfelves, obferve, as a general rule, to ferve a fharp relifhing fauce
with them—either cullis-fauce, fricaffe, or fweet herbs. *Dalrymple*. 90.

To ragoo Sweetbreads.

Rub them over with the yolk of an egg, ftrew over them
bread-crumbs and parfley, thyme, and fweet marjoram, fhred
fmall, and pepper and falt; make a roll of force-meat like a
fweetbread, and put it in a veal caul, and roaft them in a Dutch
oven; take fome brown gravy, and put to it a little lemon-
pickle, mufhroom catchup, and the end end of a lemon; boil
the gravy, and when the fweetbreads are enough, lay them
in a difh, with a force-meat in the middle; take the end of
the lemon out, and pour the gravy into the difh, and ferve
them up.

Sweetbreads with Mushrooms.

Provide two or three veal fweetbreads, blanch them, and cut
them

them in flices ; get a few nice button mufhrooms cleaned upon
a bit of flannel, put them into a ftew-pan together, and let them
ftew gently for half an hour in a ladle of cullis ; but put no
gravy, for the mufhrooms will produce fome liquor ; take a
knot or two, or the yolks of three or four hard eggs, dafh in a glafs
of white wine, a morfel of green onion and parfley minced
fine, pepper, falt, and nutmeg ; fqueeze in the juice of a lemon
or orange, and ferve it up.   Lambs' fweetbreads may be done
the fame way.   *Verral*, 123.

Sweetbreads à-la-daub.

Take three of the largeft and fineft fweetbreads you can
get, put them in a fauce-pan of boiling water for five minutes,
then take them out, and when they are cold, lard them with a
row down the middle, with very little pieces of bacon, then a
row on each fide with lemon-peel, cut the fize of wheat ftraw ;
then a row on each fide of pickled cucumbers, cut very fine ;
put them in a tofling pan, with good veal gravy, a little juice
of lemon, a fpoonful of browning ; ftew them gently a quarter
of an hour ; a little before they are ready, thicken them with
flour and butter, difh them up, and pour the gravy over, lay
round them bunches of boiled celery, or oyfter patties. Garnifh
with ftewed fpinach, green-coloured parfley, ftick a bunch of
barberries in the middle of each fweetbread.   It is a pretty
corner difh for either dinner or fupper.   *Raffald*, 98.

To fry Sweetbreads.

Cut them in long flices, beat up the yolk of an egg, and rub
it over them with a feather ; make a feafoning of pepper, falt,
and grated bread ; dip them into it, and fry them in butter.
For fauce—catchup and butter, with gravy or lemon-fauce.
Garnifh with fmall flices of toafted bacon and crifped parfley.

Loin of Veal in Epigram.

Having roafted a fine loin of veal, take it up, and carefully
take the fkin off the back part of it without breaking ; cut out
all the lean meat, but mind and leave the ends whole, to hold
the following mince-meats : mince all the meat very fine with
the kidney part, put it into a little veal gravy, enough to
moiften it, with the gravy that comes from the loin ; put in a
little pepper and falt, fome lemon-peel fhred fine, the yolks of
three eggs, a fpoonful of catchup, and thicken it with a little
butter rolled in flour ; give it a fhake or two over the fire, and
put it into the loin, and then pull the fkin over.   If the fkin
fhould not quite cover it, give it a brown with a hot iron, or
put it into an oven for a quarter of an hour.   Send it up hot,
and garnifh with barberries and lemon.   *Mafon*, 144. *Glaffe*,
56. *Farley*, 106.

Veal à-la-Bourgeoise.

Lard fome pretty thick flices with bacon, and feafon them with pepper, falt, beaten mace, cloves, nutmeg, and chopped parfley; then cover the ftew-pan with flices of fat bacon, lay the veal upon them, cover it, and fet it over a very flow fire for eight or ten minutes, fo as to be juft hot, and no more; then brifk up your fire, and brown your veal on both fides; then fhake fome flour over it and brown it.   Pour in a quart of good broth or gravy, cover it clofe, and let it ftew gently till it is enough; then take out the flices of bacon, and fkim all the fat off clean, and beat up the yolks of three eggs with fome of the gravy.   Mix all together, and keep it ftirring one way till it is fmooth and thick; then take it up, lay your meat in the difh, pour the fauce over it, and garnifh with lemon.

A Fricando of Veal.

Cut fteaks half an inch thick, and fix inches long, out of the thick part of a leg of veal, lard them with fmall cardoons, and duft them with flour; put them before the fire to broil a fine brown, then put them into a large toffing-pan with a quart of good gravy, and let it ftew half an hour; then put in two tea-fpoon-fuls of lemon-pickle, a meat-fpoonful of walnut catchup, the fame of browning, a flice of lemon, a little anchovy and chyan, a few morels and truffles.   When your fricandos are tender, take them up, and thicken your gravy with flour and butter; ftrain it, place your fricandos in the difh. pour your gravy on them.   Garnifh with lemon and barberries.   You may lay round them force-meat balls fried, or force-meat rolled in a veal caul, and yolks of eggs hard boiled.   *Raffald*, 94.

Veal Rolls.

Take ten or twelve little thin flices of veal, lay on them fome force-meat according to your fancy, roll them up, and tie them juft acrofs the middle with coarfe thread; put them on a bird fpit, rub them over with the yolks of eggs, flour them, and bafte them with butter.   Half an hour will do them. Lay them in a difh, and have ready fome good gravy, with a few truffles and morels, and fome mufhrooms.   Garnifh with lemon.

Calf's Head Surprize.

Take a calf's head with the fkin on, take a fharp knife, and raife off the fkin with as much meat from the bones as you can poffibly get, fo that it may appear like a whole head when ftuffed; then make a force-meat in the following manner :—take half a pound of veal, a pound of beef fuet, the crumb of a two-penny loaf, half a pound of fat bacon, beat them well in a mortar, with fome fweet herbs and parfley fhred fine, fome

cloves,

cloves, mace, and nutmeg, beat fine, fome falt and chyan pepper enough to feafon it, the yolks of four eggs beat up, and
mixed all together in force-meat; ftuff the head with it, and
fkewer it tight at each end; then put it into a deep pot or pan,
and put two quarts of water, half a pint of white wine, a blade
or two of mace, a bundle of fweet herbs, an anchovy, two
fpoonfuls of walnut and mufhroom catchup, the fame quantity
of lemon pickle, a little falt and pepper; lay a coarfe pafte over
it to keep in the fteam, and put it for two hours and an half
into a fharp oven. When you take it out, lay the head in a
foup difh, fkim of the fat from the gravy, and ftrain it through
a fieve into a ftew-pan; thicken it with butter rolled in flour,
and when it has boiled a few minutes, put in the yolks of four
eggs well beaten, and mixed with half a pint of cream; have
ready boiled fome force-meat balls half an ounce of truffles and
morels, but don't put them into the gravy; pour the gravy
over the head, and garnifh with force-meat balls, truffles,
morels, and mufhrooms. *Glaffe*, 60.

Another way.

Drefs off the hair of a large calf's head, as directed in the
mock turtle; then take a fharp-pointed knife, and raife off the
fkin, with as much of the meat from the bones as you can poffibly get, that it may appear like a whole head when it is ftuffed,
and be careful you do not cut the fkin in holes; then fcrape a
pound of fat bacon, the crumb of two penny loaves, grate a
fmall nutmeg with falt, chyan pepper, and fhred lemon-peel to
your tafte, the yolks of fix eggs well beat; mix all up into a
rich force-meat, put a little into the ears, and ftuff the head
with the remainder; have ready a deep narrow pot that it will
juft go in, with two quarts of water, half a pint of white wine,
two fpoonfuls of lemon pickle, the fame of walnut and mufhroom catchup, one anchovy, a blade or two of mace, a bundle
of fweet herbs, a little falt and chyan peper; lay a coarfe pafte
over it to keep in the fteam, and fet it in a very quick oven two
hours and an half. When you take it out, lay your head in a
foup difh, fkim the fat clean off the gravy, and ftrain it through
a hair fieve into a toffing-pan; thicken it with a lump of butter
rolled in flour. When it has boiled a few minutes, put in the
yolks of fix eggs well beat, and mixed with half a pint of cream;
but do not let it boil, it will curdle the eggs. You muft have
ready boiled a few force-meat balls, half an ounce of truffles and
morels, it would make the gravy too dark a colour to ftew them
in it; pour your gravy over your head, and garnifh with the
truffles, morels, force-meat balls, mufhrooms, and barberries,
and ferve it up. This is a handfome top-difh at a fmall expence.
Raffald, 88.

Calf's

Calf's Head boiled.

Wafh it very clean, parboil one half, beat up the yolk of an egg, and rub it over the head with a feather, then ftrew over it a feafoning of pepper, falt, thyme, parfley chopped fmall, fhred lemon-peel, grated bread, and a little nutmeg; ftick bits of butter over it, and fend it to the oven; boil the other half white in a cloth, put them both into a difh; boil the brains in a bit of cloth, with a very little parfley and a leaf or two of fage; when they are boiled, chop them fmall, and warm them up in a fauce-pan with a bit of butter and a little pepper and falt; lay the tongue, boiled and peeled, in the middle of a fmall difh. and the brains round it; have in another difh bacon or pickled pork; greens and carrots in another.

Calf's Head the German way.

Take a large calf's head, with great part of the neck cut with it; fplit it in half, fcald it very white, and take out the jawbone; take a large ftew-pan, or fauce-pan, and lay at the bottom fome flices of bacon, then fome thin beef-fteaks, with fome pepper and falt; then lay in the head, pour in fome beef broth, a large onion ftuck with cloves, and a bunch of fweet herbs; cover the ftew-pan very clofe, and fet it over a ftove to ftew; then make a ragoo with a quart of good beef gravy, and half a pint of red wine; let the wine be well boiled in the gravy; add to it fome fweetbreads parboiled and cut in flices, fome cocks'-combs, oyfters, mufhrooms, truffles, and morels; let thefe ftew till they are tender. When the head is ftewed, take it up, put it into a difh, take out the brains, the eyes, and the bones; then flit the tongue, cut it into fmall pieces, cut the eyes in pieces alfo, and chop the brains; put thefe into a baking-difh, and pour fome of the ragoo over them; then take the head, lay it upon the ragoo, pour the reft over it, and on that fome melted butter; then fcrape fome fine Parmefan cheefe, ftrew it over the butter, and fend it to the oven. It does not want much baking, but only requires to be of a fine brown. *Mafon*, 154.

To ftew a Calf's Head.

Firft wafh it, and pick it very clean, lay it in water for an hour, take out the brains, and with a fharp knife carefully take out the bones and the tongue, but be careful you do not break the meat; then take out the two eyes, and take two pounds of veal and two pounds of beef fuet, a very little thyme, a good deal of lemon-peel minced, a nutmeg grated, and two anchovies; chop all very well together, grate two ftale rolls, and mix all together with the yolks of four eggs; fave enough of this meat to make about twenty balls, take half a pint of
frefh

fresh mushrooms clean peeled and washed, the yolks of six eggs chopped, half a pint of oysters clean washed, or pickled cockles; mix all these together, but first stew your oysters, put your force-meat into the head and close it, tie it tight with a packthread, and put it into a deep stew-pan; and put to it two quarts of gravy, with a blade or two of mace. Cover it close, and let it stew two hours; in the mean time beat up the brains with some lemon-peel cut fine, a little parsley chopped, half a nutmeg grated, and the yolk of an egg; have some dripping boiling, fry half the brains in little cakes, and fry the balls, keep them both hot by the fire; take half an ounce of truffles and morels, then strain the gravy the head was stewed in, put the truffles and morels to it with the liquor, and a few mushrooms; boil all together, then put in the rest of the brains that are not fried, stew them together for a minute or two, pour it over the head, and lay the fried brains and balls round it. Garnish with lemon. You may fry about twelve oysters and put over. *Glasse*, 55.

Mrs. Mason, has the same receipt, though differently expressed, in The Ladies Assistant, page 153.

To roast a Calf's Head.

Wash the head very clean, take out the bones, and dry it very well with a cloth; make a seasoning of beaten mace, pepper, salt, nutmeg, and cloves, some fat bacon cut very small, and some grated bread; strew this over it, roll it up, skewer it with a small skewer, and tie it with tape; roast it, and baste it with butter; make a rich veal gravy, thickened with butter, and rolled in flour. Some like mushrooms and the fat part of oysters, but it is very good without.

To hash a Calf's Head.

Clean your calf's head exceeding well, and boil it a quarter of an hour; when it is cold, cut the meat into thin broad slices, and put it into a tossing-pan, with two quarts of gravy; and when it has stewed three quarters of an hour, add to it one anchovy, a little beaten mace, and chyan to your taste, two tea-spoonfuls of lemon-pickle, two meat-spoonfuls of walnut-catchup, half an ounce of truffles and morels, a slice or two of lemon, a bundle of sweet herbs, and a glass of white wine; mix a quarter of a pound of butter with flour, and put it in a few minutes before the head is enough; take your brains and put them into hot water, it will make them skin sooner, and beat them fine in a bason; then add to them two eggs, one spoonful of flour, a bit of lemon-peel shred fine; chop small a little parsley, thyme, and sage; beat them very well together, strew in a little pepper and salt, then drop them in little cakes

into

into a pan full of boiling hog's lard, and fry them a light brown; then lay them on a fieve to drain; take your hafh out of the pan with a fifh-flice, and lay it on your difh, and ftrain your gravy over it; lay upon it a few mufhrooms, force-meat balls, the yolks of four eggs boiled hard, and the brain-cakes. Garnifh with lemon and pickles. It is proper for a top or fide-difh. *Raffald*, 86. *Farley*, 64.

To hafh a Calf's Head brown.

Half the head only fhould be hafhed, as a whole one makes too large a difh; parboil it; when cold, cut it into thin flices, and the tongue; flour it pretty well, and put it into a ftew-pan with fome good gravy, a quart or more, a glafs of Madeira, an anchovy wiped and boned, a little pounded cloves, chyan, a piece of lemon peel; let thefe ftew gently three quarters of an hour, then add fome catchup, a few truffles and morels, firft wafhed; pickled or frefh mufhrooms; if frefh, a little juice of lemon; ftew thefe together a few minutes; add force-meat balls fried, and hard yolks of eggs. Dip the brains in hot water, fkim them, beat them fine, and mix them with a little grated lemon-peel, parfley chopped, and favoury herbs, favoury fpice, chyan, falt, bread-crumbs, and yolk of egg; fry thefe in fmall cakes; garnifh the hafh with them, oyfters fried. and fliced lemon. If for a arge company, boil the other half of the head, rub it over with yolk of egg, ftrew on bread-crumbs, with pepper, falt, and nutmeg, grated lemon-peel, and chopped parfley; bafte it before the fire, let it be a nice brown, and lay it on the hafh.

To hafh a Calf's Head white.

Take half a pint of gravy, a gill of white wine, a little beaten mace, a little nutmeg, and a little falt; throw into your hafh a few mufhrooms, truffles, and morels, firft parboiled, a few arti-choke bottoms and afparagus tops (if they are in feafon), a large piece of butter rolled in flour, the yolks of two eggs, half a pint of cream. and a fpoonful of mufhroom catchup. Stir thefe all together till it becomes of a tolerable thicknefs, and pour it into the difh. Lay the other half of the head as above-men-tioned, in the middle. *Farley*, 66.

To hafh a cold Calf's Head.

Cut it into flices, flour it, put to it a little boiled gravy, a little white wine, fome cream, a little catchup, white pepper, falt, and nutmeg, a few oyfters and their liquor, fhred lemon-peel, boil this up gently together; a few pickled or frefh mufhrooms, and a little lemon juice, or lemon juice only. This may be en-riched with truffles and morels parboiled, force-meat balls, and hard eggs. *Mafon*, 155.

To

To dreſs a Calf's Head the beſt way.

Take a calf's head with the ſkin on, and ſcald off all the hair and clean it very well; cut in two, take out the brains, boil the head very white and tender, take one part quite off the bone, and cut it into nice pieces with the tongue, dredge it with a little flour, and let it ſtew on a ſlow fire for about half an hour in rich white gravy, made of veal, mutton, and a piece of bacon, ſeaſoned with pepper, ſalt, onion, and a very little mace; it muſt be ſtrained off before the haſh is put in it, thicken it with a little butter rolled in flour; the other part of the head muſt be taken off in one whole piece, ſtuff it with nice force-meat, and roll it like a collar, and ſtew it tender in gravy; then put it in the middle of a diſh, and the haſh all round. Garniſh it with force meat balls, fried oyſters, and the brains made into little cakes dipped in rich butter and fried. You may add wine, morels, truffles, or what you pleaſe, to make it good and rich. *Raffald, 86.*

To grill a Calf's Head.

Waſh your calf's head clean, and boil it almoſt enough, then take it up and haſh one half, the other half rub over with the yolk of an egg, a little pepper and ſalt; ſtrew over it bread-crumbs, parſley chopped ſmall, and a little grated lemon peel; ſet it before the fire, and keep baſting it all the time to make the froth riſe. When it is a fine light brown, diſh up your haſh, and lay the grilled ſide upon it.

Blanch your tongue, ſlit it down the middle, and lay it on a ſoup plate; ſkin the brains, boil them with a little ſage and parſley; chop them fine, and mix them with ſome melted butter and a ſpoonful of cream; make them hot, and pour them over the tongue; ſerve them up, and they are ſauce for the head.

To collar a Calf's Head to eat like Brawn.

Take the head with the ſkin and hair on, ſcald it till the hair will come off, then cleave it down, and take out the brains and the eyes; waſh it very clean and put it into a pot of clean water; boil it till the bones will come out; then ſlice the tongue and ears, and lay them all even; throw a handful of ſalt over them, and roll it up quite cloſe in a collar; boil it near two hours; when the head is cold, put it into brawn pickle. *Ma-ſon, 155.*

Veal Palates.

Provide about two palates, and boil them half an hour; take off the ſkins, and cut them into pieces, as you do ox-palates; put them into a ſtew-pan with a glaſs of Champagne, a little minced green onion, parſley, pepper and ſalt; toſs it often till the wine is gone, pour in a ladle of your cullis mixed with

gravy,

gravy, ſtew them ſoftly in it till very tender, daſh in a ſmall glaſs more of your wine, add the juice of a lemon or orange, and ſend it up. *Verral*, 122.

Calf's Ears with Lettuce.

Six ears will do; ſtew them very tender in a braze, and your lettuce may be done thus:—take as many as you have ears, and blanch them in water, open the leaves, and put into each a bit of the middling bacon, with a clove or two ſtuck in each; cloſe the leaves over, and bind with pack-thread; put them into a ſtew-pan with a ladle of your cullis and a little gravy, pepper, ſalt, and a morſel of ſhallot; ſtew them till very tender, take your ears out, and clear them from greaſe, and put them to your ears; add the juice of a lemon, and ſerve them up. Take care your lettuces are preſerved whole, and laid between the ears. Lambs ears may be done the ſame. *Verral*, 123.

Calf's Ears fried.

Braze the ears in a ſtrong braze to make them tender, and make a batter thus:—take a handful of flour, put into a bowl or ſtew-pan, add one egg, and a little ſalt; mix with as much ſmall beer as will make it of a proper conſiſtence, then add about a table-ſpoonful of fine oil; when well mixed, put the ears to it; have ready a ſtew-pan with hog's-lard properly hot, put in the ears one by one, with as much of the butter as will ſtick to them; fry of a fine colour, and ſerve them with fried parſley; they may alſo be ſtuffed with good force-meat. Inſtead of the above batter, you may baſte them with yolks of eggs and bread-crumbs. *Dalrymple*, 80.

Calf's Ears houſewife faſhion.

Make a ſauce with a little jelly broth and white wine, a little butter, chopped parſley, ſhallots, pepper, and ſalt; boil it to a thick conſiſtence; when done, add the juice of half a Seville orange, and ſerved it upon brazed ears. *Clermont*, 86.

A Midcalf.

Stuff a calf's heart with force-meat, and ſend it to the oven in an earthen diſh, with a little water under it. Lay butter over it, and dredge it with flour. Boil half the liver, and all the lights, for half an hour; then chop them ſmall, and put them in a toſſing pan, with a pint of gravy, a ſpoonful of catchup, and one of lemon-pickle. Squeeze in half a lemon, ſeaſon with pepper and ſalt, and thicken with a good piece of butter rolled in flour. When you diſh it up, pour the mince-meat in the the bottom, and have the other half of the liver ready fried of a fine brown, and cut in thin ſlices, and little pieces of bacon.

Set

Set the heart in the middle, and lay the liver and bacon over the mince-meat. *Farley*, 103.

Calf's Heart roasted.

Having made a force-meat of the crumb of half a penny loaf, a quarter of a pound of beef fuet chopped fmall, a little parfley, fweet marjoram, and lemon-peel, mixed up with a little pepper, falt, nutmeg, and the yolk of an egg; fill the heart with it, and lay a veal caul over the ftuffing, or fheet of writing-paper to keep it in its place. Lay it in a Dutch oven, and keep turning it till it is thoroughly roafted. When you difh it up, lay flices of lemon round it, and pour good melted butter over it. *Cole*, 82.

To roaft a Calf's Liver.

Lard it with bacon, fpit it firft, and roaft it; ferve it up with good gravy. *Glaffe*, 95.

To ftew a Calf's Liver.

Lard the liver and put it into a ftew-pan, with fome falt, whole pepper, a bundle of fweet herbs, an onion, and a blade of mace; let it ftew till tender, then take it up, and cover it to keep hot; ftrain the liquor it was ftewed in, fkim off all the fat, thicken it with a piece of butter rolled in flour, and pour it over the liver. *Mafon*, 158.

Calf's Liver with Shallots.

Chop green fhallots and mufhrooms, cut the liver in thin flices, put all together in a ftew-pan, with a little bit of butter rolled in flour, and a glafs of white wine; ftew flowly for about half an hour; add pepper and falt, and vinegar to your tafte. If you would have it white, make a liafon of yolks of eggs and cream, with lemon or verjuice. *Dalrymple*, 86.

To drefs a Calf's Liver in a Caul.

Take off the under fkins, and fhred the liver very fmall, then take an ounce of truffles and morels chopped fmall, with parfley; roaft two or three onions, take off their outermoft coats, pound fix cloves, and a dozen coriander feeds, add them to the onions, and pound them together in a marble mortar; then take them out and mix them with the liver; take a pint of cream, half a pint of milk, and feven or eight new-laid eggs; beat them together, boil them, but do not let them curdle, fhred a pound of fuet as fmall as you can, half melt it in a pan, and pour it into your egg and cream; then pour it into your liver, then mix all well together, feafon it with pepper, falt, nutmeg, and a little thyme, and let it ftand till it is cold; fpread a caul over the bottom and fides of the ftew-pan, and put in your hafhed liver and cream together; fold it up in the caul in the fhape of a calf's liver, then turn it upfide down carefully, lay it in a difh that

F will

will bear the oven, and do it over with beaten egg; dredge it
with grated bread, and bake it an oven. Serve it up hot for a
firſt courſe. *Glaſſe*, 94.

To dreſs a Calf's Pluck.

Boil the lights and part of the liver; roaſt the heart ſtuffed
with ſuet, ſweet herbs, and a little parſley, all chopped ſmall,
a few crumbs of bread, ſome pepper, ſalt, nutmeg, and a little
lemon-peel; mix it up with the yolk of an egg.

When the lights and liver are boiled, chop them very ſmall,
and put them in a ſaucepan, with a piece of butter rolled in
flour, ſome pepper and ſalt, with a little lemon or vinegar, if
agreeable; fry the other part of the liver as before-mentioned,
with ſome little pieces of bacon; lay the mince at the bottom,
the heart in the middle, and the fried liver and bacon round,
with ſome criſped parſley. For ſauce—plain butter. It is a
large diſh, but it may eaſily be diminiſhed. *Cole*, 84.

Calf's Feet with force-meat.

Bone them, and fill them with force-meat, made of whatever
you pleaſe; tie them in ſlices of lard, ſtew them ſlowly in broth
and white wine, a faggot of ſweet herbs, a few cloves, roots,
and onions. When done, ſerve with what ſauce you pleaſe.
Dalrymple, 89.

Calf's Feet with lemon-ſauce.

Take calve's feet, plain boiled, put them in a ſtew-pan with
a little oil or butter, half a lemon, peeled and ſliced, and as
much broth or cullis as will ſimmer them on a ſlow fire for
about half an hour; take them out and wipe them, ſift the
ſauce, ſkim it well, add a little butter rolled in flour, a little
cullis, a chopped anchovy, and the juice of half a lemon.
Clermont, 94.

Ragoo of Calves Feet.

Boil the feet, bone and cut the meat in ſlices; brown them
in the frying-pan, and then put them in ſome good gravy, with
morels, truffles, pickled muſhrooms, the yolks of four eggs
boiled hard, ſome ſalt, and a little butter rolled in flour. For
a ſick perſon, a calf's foot boiled, with parſley and butter, is
eſteemed very good. *Cole*, 84.

Calves Feet and Chaldron after the Italian way.

Take the crumb of a three-penny loaf, one pound of ſuet, a
large onion, two or three handfuls of parſley, mince it very ſmall,
ſeaſon it with ſalt and pepper, three or four cloves of garlick,
mix with eight or ten eggs; then ſtuff the chaldron, take the
feet and put them in a ſtew-pan; it muſt ſtew upon a ſlow fire
till the bones are looſe; then take two quarts of green peas,
and put in the liquor; and when done, you muſt thicken it
with

with the yolks of two eggs, and the juice of a lemon. It muſt
be feaſoned with pepper, ſalt, mace, and onion, ſome parſley
and garlick. You muſt ſerve it up with the aforeſaid pudding
in the middle of the diſh, and garniſh the diſh with fried
ſuckers and ſliced onion. *Glaſſe*, 383.

Veal Cutlets.

Cut your veal into pieces about the thickneſs of half a crown,
and as long as you pleaſe; dip them in the yolk of an egg, and
ſtrew over them crumbs of bread, a few ſweet herbs, ſome
lemon-peel, and a little grated nutmeg, and fry them in freſh
butter. While they are frying, make a little gravy, and when
the meat is done, take it out, and lay it in a diſh before the
fire, then ſhake a little flour into the pan, and ſtir it round.
Put in a little gravy, ſqueeze in a little lemon, and pour it
over the veal. Make uſe of lemon for your garniſh. *Farley*, 55.

Another way.

Cut part of the neck into cutlets; ſhorten them, fry them
nicely brown, ſtew them in ſome good gravy till tender, with
a little flour mixed ſmooth in it; then add catchup, chyan,
ſalt, a few truffles and morels, pickled muſhrooms. Force-
meat balls may likewiſe be added. *Maſon* 147.

Veal Cutlets in Ragoo.

Take ſome large cutlets from the fillet, beat them flat; and
lard them; ſtrew over them ſome pepper, ſalt, crumbs of
bread, and ſhred parſley; then make a ragoo of veal ſweet-
breads and muſhrooms; fry the cutlets in melted butter of a
fine brown; then lay them in a hot diſh, and pour the ragoo
boiling hot over them. *Cole*, 85.

A ſavory diſh of Veal.

Having roaſted a fine loin of veal, take it up, and carefully
take the ſkin off the back part without breaking it. Cut out
all the lean meat, but leave the ends whole, to hold the following mince-meat:— mix all the meat very fine with the kidney part, put it into a little veal gravy, enough to moiſten it
with the gravy that comes from the loin. Put in a little pep-
and ſalt, ſome lemon-peel ſhred fine, the yolks of three eggs,
and a ſpoonful of catchup. Thicken it with a little butter rolled
in flour; give it a ſhake or two over the fire, and put it into
the loin, and then pull the ſkin over. If the ſkin ſhould not
quite cover it, give it a brown with a hot iron, or put it in an
oven for fifteen minutes. Send it up hot, and garniſh with
barberries and lemon. *Farley*, 106.

Calf's Brains fried.

Cut the brains in four pieces, braze them about half an hour in broth and white wine, two flices of lemon, pepper and falt, thyme, laurel, cloves, parfley, and fhallots; then drain and foak them in batter made of white wine, a little oil, and a little falt, and fry them of a fine colour; you may likewife bafte them with eggs and bread-crumbs. Garnifh with fried parfley. *Dalrymple*, 83.

Calf's Brains with Rice.

The brains of two heads are enough for a good difh; blanch them, and take off the little bloody fibres, cut into two pieces each, and foak them in a marinade of white wine and vinegar, &c. for an hour; boil your rice in water a few minutes, ftrain it off, and ftew it in broth till it is tender, with a little falt and a bit of mace; difh up the brains, and pour fome of the fauce to the rice; fqueeze in a lemon or orange, and pour over for ferving to table.

When you procure two or three pair of eyes, they make an excellent difh done in the manner of doing the fweetbreads. *Verral*, 127.

Veal Griftles and Green Peas.

Cut the griftles of a breaft of veal in pieces; fcald them, if you would have them white; ftew them in broth with a few flices of lard, half a lemon peeled and fliced, whole pepper and falt, and a faggot of fweet herbs; when done, wipe them clean, and ferve the ftewed peas upon them. You may alfo, when the meat is about a quarter done, take it out of the braze, and put it in a ftew-pan with the peas, a little butter, parfley, a little winter-favoury, a flice of ham, and a few cabbage lettuces cut fmall; add a little cullis and flour; reduce the fauce pretty thick; falt only a little before you ferve. *Dalrymple*, 92.

To drefs Scotch Collops white.

Cut them off the thick part of a leg of veal, the fize and thicknefs of a crown piece, put a lump of butter into a toffing-pan, and fet it over a flow fire, or it will difcolour your collops; before the pan is hot, lay the collops in, and keep turning them over till you fee the butter is turned to a thick white gravy; put your collops and gravy into a pot, and fet them upon the hearth, to keep warm; put cold butter again into your pan every time you fill it, and fry them as above, and fo continue till you have finifhed. When you have fried them, pour your gravy from them into your pan, with a teafpoonful of lemon-pickle, mufhroom-catchup, caper liquor, beaten mace, chyan pepper, and falt; thicken with flour and butter. When it has well boiled, put in the yolks of two eggs well beat and mixed, with a tea-fpoonful of rich cream; keep fhaking your pan over the fire till your gravy looks of a fine

thicknefs,

thicknefs, then put in your collops, and fhake them; when they are quite hot, put them on your difh, with force-meat balls, ftrew over them pickled mufhrooms. Garnifh with barberries and pickled kidney beans. *Raffald, 96.*

Another way.

Cut the veal the fame as above directed, throw the collops into a ftew-pan, put fome boiling water over them, and ftir them about; then ftrain them off, take a pint of good veal broth, and thicken it; add a bundle of fweet herbs with fome mace; put fweetbread, force-meat balls, and frefh mufhrooms; if no frefh to be had, ufe pickled ones wafhed in warm water; ftew them about them fifteen minutes, add the yolks of two eggs and a pint of cream; beat them well together with fome nut-meg grated, and keep ftirring it till it boils up; add the juice of a quarter of a lemon, then put it in your difh. Garnifh with lemon. *Glaffe, 22.*

To drefs Scotch Collops brown.

Cut your collops the fame way as the white ones, but brown your butter before you lay in your collops, fry them over a quick fire, fhake and turn them, and keep them on a fine froth; when they are a light brown, put them into a pot, and fry them as the white ones; when you have fried them all brown, pour all the gravy from them into a clean toffing-pan, with half a pint of gravy made of the bones and bits you cut the collops off, two tea-fpoonfuls of lemon-pickle, a large one of catchup, the fame of browning, half an ounce of morels, half a lemon, a little anchovy, chyan, and falt to your tafte; thicken it with flour and butter, let it boil five or fix minutes, then put in your collops, and fhake them over the fire; if they boil, it will make them hard. When they have fimmered a little, take them out with an egg fpoon, and lay them on your difh, ftrain your gravy, and pour it hot on them; lay over them force-meat balls, and little flices of bacon curled round a fkewer and boiled; throw a few mufhrooms over. Garnifh with lemon and barberries, and ferve them up. *Cole, 88.*

Another way.

Take a piece of fillet of veal, cut it in thin pieces about as large as a crown piece, but very thin; fhake a little flour over it, then put a little butter in a frying-pan, and melt it; put in your collops, and fry them quick till they are brown, then lay them in a difh. Have ready a good ragoo made thus:—take a little butter in your ftew-pan, and melt it, then add a large fpoonful of flour, ftir it about till it is fmooth, then put in a pint of good brown gravy; feafon it with pepper and falt, pour in a fmall glafs of white wine, fome veal fweetbreads, force-

meat

meat balls, truffles and morels, ox-palates, and mushrooms; stew them gently for half an hour, add the juice of half a lemon to it; put it over the collops, and garnish with rashers of bacon. Some like the Scotch collops made thus:—put the collops into the ragoo, and stew them for five minutes. *Cole*, 88.

To dress Scotch Collops the French way.

Take a leg of veal, and cut your chops pretty thick, five or six inches long, and three inches broad, rub them over with the yolk of an egg, put pepper and salt, and grate a little nutmeg on them, and a little shred parsley; lay them on an earthen dish, and set them before the fire; baste them with butter, and let them be a fine brown; then turn them on the other side, and rub them as above; baste and brown them the same way. When they are thoroughly enough, make a good brown gravy with truffles and morels, dish up your collops, lay truffles and morels, and the yolks of hard boiled eggs over them. Garnish with crisp parsley and lemon.— *Raffald*, 97.

To hash Veal.

Cut your veal into round thin slices, of the size of half a crown, and put them into a sauce-pan with a little gravy; put to it some lemon-peel cut exceedingly fine, and a tea spoonful of lemon-pickle; put it on the fire, and thicken it with butter and flour; put in your veal as soon as it boils, and just before you dish it up, put in a spoonful of cream, and lay sippets round the dish. *Farley* 66.

N. B. The same receipt as the preceding, though conveyed in language somewhat different, is to be found in Mrs. *Raffald's* Experienced English Housekeeper, page 73.

To toss up cold Veal white.

Cut the veal into little thin bits, put milk enough to it for sauce, grate in a little nutmeg, a very little salt, a little piece of butter rolled in flour; to half a pint of milk, the yolks of two eggs well beat, a spoonful of mushroom pickle, stir all together till it is thick, then pour it into your dish, and garnish with lemon.

Cold fowl, skinned and done this way, eats well; or the best end of a cold breast of veal; first fry it, drain it from the fat, then pour this sauce to it. *Glasse* 119.

To fry cold Veal.

Cut your veal into pieces of the thickness of an half-crown, and as long as you please; dip them in the yolk of an egg, and then in crumbs of bread, with a few sweet herbs and shred lemon-peel in it; grate a little nutmeg over them, and fry them in fresh butter. The butter must be hot, just enough to fry
them

them in. In the mean time, make a little gravy of the bone of the veal, and when the meat is fried, take it out with a fork, and lay it in a difh before the fire. Then fhake a little flour into the pan, and ftir it round. Then put in a little gravy, fqueeze in a little lemon, and pour it over the veal. Garnifh with lemon. *Cole,* 90.

To mince Veal.

Cut your veal in flices, then cut it in little fquare bits, but do not chop it; put it into a fauce-pan, with two or three fpoonfuls of gravy, a flice of lemon, a little pepper and falt, a good lump of butter rolled in flour, a tea-fpoonful of lemon-pickle, and a large fpoonful of cream; keep fhaking it over the fire till it boils, but do not let it boil above a minute; if you do, it will make your meat eat hard: put fippets round your difh, and ferve it up. *Raffald,* 73. *Farley,* 66.

Calf's Chitterlings.

Clean fome of the largeft of the calf's guts, cut them into lengths proper for puddings, tie one of the ends clofe, take fome bacon, and cut it like dice, and a calf's udder, and fat that comes off the chitterlings; chaldrons blanched and cut alfo; put them into a ftew-pan, with a bay-leaf, falt, pepper, fhallot cut fmall, fome pounded mace, and Jamaica pepper, with half a pint or more of milk, and let it juft fimmer; then take off the pan, and thicken it with four or five yolks of eggs, and fome crumbs of bread; fill the chitterlings with this mixture, which muft be kept warm, and make the links like hogs'-puddings. Before they are fent to table they muft be boiled over a moderate fire; let them cool in their own liquor. They ferve in fummer when hogs'-puddings are not to be had. *Mafon,* 159.

Veal Steaks, Venetian fashion.

Cut thick flices of veal pretty large; marinade an hour in a little oil, with chopped parfley, fhallots, mufhrooms, fweet herbs, pepper and falt; make as much of the marinade ftick to them as poffible; roll them in bread crumbs, and boil flowly, bafting with the remainder of the marinade. Serve with the fqueeze of a lemon or Seville orange. *Dalrymple,* 110.

Slices of Veal, Venetian fashion.

Cut thin flices of veal, and between every two put a flice of ham of the fame fize, firft dipped in eggs, chopped parfley, fhallots, mufhrooms, truffles, and a little pepper; roll them in flices of lard, and ftew flowly with a little broth and white wine; when done take off the bacon, fkim and ftrain the fauce, add a little butter and flour, and ferve with a relifhing fauce. Inftead of bacon you may bafte them with eggs and bread crumbs,

F 4 and

and fry or bake them. Serve with a fauce as above, and garnifh with parfley. *Clermont,* 116.

To make Calf's foot Jelly.

Boil two calf's feet in a gallon of water till it comes to a
quart, then ftrain it, let it ftand till cold, fkim off all the fat
clean and take the jelly up clean. If there is any fediment at
the bottom, leave it; put the jelly into a fauce-pan with a pint
of mountain wine, half a pound of loaf fugar, the juice of four
large lemons; beat up fix or eight whites of eggs with a whifk,
then put them into a fauce-pan, and ftir all together till it boils.
Let it boil a few minutes. Have ready a large flannel bag, pour
it in, it will run through quick; pour it in again till it runs
clear; then have ready a large China bafon, with the lemon-
peel cut as thin as poffible; let the jelly run into that bafon,
and the peels both give it a fine amber colour, and alfo a flavour; with a clean filver fpoon fill your glaffes. *Glaffe,* 295.
Farley, 320.

Another way.

To two calf's feet, put three quarts of water, boil it to one
quart; when cold, take off the fat, and take the jelly from the
fediment; put to it one pint of white wine, half a pound of
fugar, the juice of three lemons, the peel of one. Whifk the
whites of two eggs, put all into a fauce-pan, boil it a few minutes; put it through a jelly bag till it is fine. *Cole,* 91.

To make favoury Calf's-foot Jelly.

Boil either two or four calf's feet, according to the quantity
which is wanted, with ifing-glafs to make it a ftiff jelly; one
ounce of picked ifing-glafs to two feet is about fufficient, if the
ifing-glafs is very good; boil with thefe a piece of lemon-peel,
an onion, a bunch of fweet herbs, fome pepper corns, a few
cloves, a bit of mace, nutmeg, and a little falt. When the
jelly is enough, ftrain it, and put to it juice of lemon, and white
wine to your tafte; boil it up, pulp it through a bag till fine;
the white of an egg may be added before it is boiled. *Mafon,*
160.

Another way.

Spread fome flices of lean veal and ham in the bottom of a
ftew-pan, with a carrot and turnip, or two or three onions;
cover it, and let it fweat on a flow fire till it is as deep a brown
as you would have it; then put to it a quart of very clear broth,
fome whole pepper, mace, a very little ifing-glafs, and falt to
your tafte; let this boil ten minutes, then ftrain it through a
French ftrainer; fkim off all the fat, and put it to the whites of
three eggs; run it feveral times through a jelly bag, as you do
other jellies. *Cole,* 92.

Veal

Veal Collops.

Cut thin flices of fillet of veal, put them in a ftew-pan with a little oil or butter, fweet herbs chopped, pepper and falt; let them catch a little, then add a little good broth; you may add fome good force-meat balls, either fried or blanched. If for brown make a liafon with flour and butter; let your collops ftew flowly till done. If you want them white, when ready to ferve, add a liafon made of eggs and cream, a few bits of good butter, and the juice of half a lemon. *Dalrymple*, 105.

).

To dress a Leg of Mutton to eat like Venison.

TAKE a hind quarter of mutton, and cut the leg in the shape of a haunch of venison; save the blood of the sheep, and steep it for five or six hours; then take it out, and roll it in three or four sheets of white paper, well buttered on the inside; tie it with a packthread, and roast it, basting it with good beef dripping or butter. It will take two hours at a good fire, for your mutton must be fat and thick. About five or six minutes before you take it up, take off the paper, baste it with a piece of butter, and shake a little flour over it to make it have a fine froth, and then have a little good drawn gravy in a bason, and some sweet sauce in another. Do not garnish with any thing. *Glasse*, 49.

Another way.—See under the Chapter of Roasting, *p.* 3.

Leg of Mutton, Modena fashion.

Bone a leg of mutton all to the end, which you leave very short; boil it to three parts in water or broth; then take it out, and cut the upper part crossways, into which you stuff butter and bread-crumbs, seasoned with pepper, salt, and sweet herbs chopped; then put it in a stew-pan, with a little of the broth, and a little white wine; finish it, and add the juice of a Seville orange to the sauce. *Dalrymple*, 136.

Leg of Mutton à-la-mode.

Lard a leg of mutton through and through with large pieces rolled in chopped sweet herbs and fine spices; braze it on a pan of the same bigness, with slices of lard, onions, and roots; stop the steam very close. When done, add a glass of white wine, and sift the sauce to serve it. *Clermont*, 143.

Leg of Mutton à-la-haut-gout.

Take a leg of mutton, and let it hang for a fortnight in any place; then stuff every part of it with some cloves of garlick, rub it with pepper and salt, and then roast it. When it is properly roasted, send it up with some good gravy and red wine in the dish. *Farley*, 110.

Mrs. Mason has given the same receipt in other words, page 162; and *Mrs. Glasse*, page 45.

Leg of Mutton à-la-daube.

Take a leg of mutton and lard it with bacon, half roast it, and then put it in as small a pot as will hold it, with a quart of mutton gravy, half a pint of vinegar, some whole spice, bay-leaves,

leaves, fweet-marjoram, winter-favory, and fome green onions. When it is tender, take it up, and make the fauce with fome of the liquor, mufhrooms, fliced lemon, two anchovies, a fpoonful of colouring, and a piece of butter; pour fome over the mutton, and the reft in a boat. *Mafon, 162.*

To ragoo a Leg of Mutton.

Take all the fkin and fat off, cut it very thin the right way of the grain, then butter your ftew-pan, and fhake fome flour into it; flice half a lemon and half an onion, cut them very fmall, a little bundle of fweet herbs, and a blade of mace. Put all together with your meat into the pan, ftir it a minute or two, and then put in fix fpoonfuls of gravy, and have ready an anchovy minced fmall; mix it with fome butter and flour, ftir it all together for fix minutes, and then difh it up. *Glaffe, 92. Farley, 79.*

To drefs a Leg of Mutton à-la-royale.

Having taken off all the fat, fkin, and fhank-bone, lard it with bacon, feafon it with pepper and falt, and a round piece, of about three or four pounds, of beef or leg of veal, lard it, have ready fome hogs'-lard boiling, flour your meat, and give it a colour in the lard, then take the meat out, and put it into a pot with a bundle of fweet herbs, fome parfley, an onion ftuck with cloves, two or three blades of mace, fome whole pepper, and three quarts of gravy; cover it clofe, and let it boil foftly for two hours; meanwhile get ready a fweetbread fplit, cut into four and broiled, a few truffles and morels ftewed in a quarter of a pint of ftrong gravy, a glafs of red wine, a few mufhrooms, two fpoonfuls of catchup, and fome afparagus tops; boil all thefe together, then lay the mutton in the middle of the difh, cut the beef or veal into flices, make a rim round your mutton with the flices, and pour the ragoo over it. When you have taken the meat out of the pot, fkim all the fat off the gravy, ftrain it, and add as much to the other as will fill the difh. Garnifh with lemon. *Glaffe, 45.*

To roaft a Leg of Mutton with Oyfters.

Make a force-meat of beef-fuet chopped fmall, the yolks of eggs boiled hard, with three anchovies, a fmall bit of onion, thyme, favoury, and fome oyfters, (a dozen or fourteen) all cut fine; fome falt, pepper, grated nutmeg, and crumbs of bread, mixed up with raw eggs; ftuff the mutton under the fkin in the thickeft part, under the flap, and at the knuckle. For fauce—fome oyfter-liquor, a little red wine, an anchovy, and fome more oyfters ftewed, and laid under the mutton. *Le Maitre, 74,*

Another

Another way.

Cut feveral holes in the mutton, beard fome oyfters, and roll them in crumbs of bread and nutmeg; put three oyfters into each hole; if it is roafted, cover it with a caul; but if it is boiled, put it in a cloth, and pour oyfter-fauce over it. *Cole,* 95.

Leg of Mutton with Cockles.

Stuff your mutton in every part with cockles, roaft it, and garnifh with horfe-radifh. *Glaffe,* 46. *Farley,* 110.

To force a Leg of Mutton.

Raife the fkin, and take out the lean part of the mutton, chop it exceeding fine, with one anchovy; fhred a bundle of fweet herbs, grate a penny loaf, half a lemon, nutmeg, pepper, and falt to your tafte; make them into a force-meat, with three eggs and a large glafs of red wine; fill up the fkin with the force-meat, but leave the bone and fhank in their place, and it will appear like a whole leg; lay it on an earthen difh, with a pint of red wine under it, and fend it to the oven; it will take two hours and an half. When it comes out, take off all the fat, ftrain the gravy over the mutton, lay round it hard yolks of eggs, and pickled mufhrooms. Garnifh with pickles, and ferve it up. *Raffald,* 106.

Split Leg of Mutton and Onion fauce.

Split the leg from the fhank to the end, ftick a fkewer in to keep the nick open, bafte it with red wine till it is half roafted, then take the wine out of the dripping-pan, and put to it one anchovy; fet it over the fire till the anchovy is diffolved, rub the yolk of a hard egg in a little cold butter; mix it with the wine, and put it in your fauce-boat; put good onion fauce over the leg when it is roafted, and ferve it up. *Du Pont,* 116.

To make Mutton Hams.

Take a hind quarter of mutton, cut it like a ham, take an ounce of falt-petre, a pound of coarfe fugar, a pound of common falt; mix them and rub your ham, lay it in a hollow tray with the fkin downwards, bafte it every day for a fortnight, then roll it in faw-duft, and hang it in the wood-fmoke a fortnight; then boil it, and hang it in a dry place, and cut it out in rafhers, and broil it as you want. It eats better broiled than boiled. *Cole,* 96.

Jiggot of Mutton with Spanifh Onions.

A jiggot of mutton is the leg with part of the loin; provide fuch a one as has been killed two or three days at leaft, thump it well, and bind it with packthread, that you keep whole when you take it out; put it into a pot about its bignefs, and pour in a little of your broth, and cover it with water; put in about a

dozen

dozen of Spanish onions with the rinds on, three or four carrots, a turnip or two, fome parfley, and any other herbs you
like; cover down clofe, and ftew it gently for three or four
hours; but take your onions after an hour's ftewing, and take
the firft and fecond rinds off; put them into a ftew-pan, with
a ladle or two of your cullis, a mufhroom or two, or truffles
minced, and a little parfley; take your mutton and drain clean
from the fat and liquor, make your fauce hot and well feafoned, fqueeze in a lemon, and ferve it up with the onions round
it, and pour the fauce over it. *Verral*, 47.

Shoulder of Mutton furprifed.

Put a fhoulder of mutton, having firft half boiled it, into a
tofsing pan, with two quarts of veal gravy, four ounces of rice,
a little beaten mace, and a tea-fpoonful of mufhroom powder.
Stew it an hour, or till the rice is enough, and then take up
your mutton and keep it hot. Put to the rice half a pint of
cream, and a piece of butter rolled in flour. Then fhake it
well, and boil it a few minutes. Lay your mutton on the difh,
and pour your gravy over it. You may garnifh with either
pickles or barberries. *Farley*, 107. *Mafon*, 164.

N. B. The above receipt is inferted in page 103 of *Mrs.
Raffald's* Englifh Houfe-keeper, with the phrafeology a little
different.

A Shoulder of Mutton in epigram.

Roaft it almoft enough, then very carefully take off the fkin
about the thicknefs of a crown piece, and the fhank-bone with
it at the end; then feafon that fkin and fhank-bone with pepper and falt, a little lemon-peel cut fmall, and a few fweet
herbs and crumbs of bread; then lay this on the gridiron, and
let it be of a fine brown: in the mean time take the reft of the
meat, and cut it like a hafh about the bignefs of a fhilling;
fave the gravy and put to it, with a few fpoonfuls of ftrong
gravy, half an onion cut fine, a little nutmeg, a little pepper
and falt, a little bundle of fweet herbs, fome gerkins cut very
fmall, a few mufhrooms, two or three truffles cut fmall, two
fpoonfuls of wine, either red or white, and throw a little flour
over the meat: let all thefe ftew together very foftly for five
or fix minutes, but be fure it does not boil; take out the fweet
herbs, and put the hafh into the difh; lay the broiled upon it,
and fend it to table. *Glaffe*, 46.

A Shoulder of Mutton called Hen and Chickens.

Half roaft a fhoulder, then take it up, and cut off the blade
at the firft joint, and both the flaps, to make the blade quite
round; fcore the blade round in diamonds, throw a little pepper and falt over it, and fet it in a tin oven to broil; cut the
flaps

flaps and the meat off the fhank, in thin flices, into the gravy
that runs out of the mutton, and put a little good gravy to
it, with two fpoonfuls of walnut catchup, one of browning, a
little chyan pepper, and one or two fhallots. When your meat
is tender, thicken it with flour and butter, put your meat in the
difh with the gravy, and lay the blade on the top, broiled a
dark brown. Garnifh with green pickles, and ferve it up.
Raffald, 104.

Mrs. *Mafon* has got this receipt under the title of " A Shoulder of Mutton in Difguife," page 164.

To boil a Shoulder of Mutton and Onion Sauce.

Put your fhoulder in when the water is cold ; when enough
fmother it with onion-fauce, made the fame as for boiled ducks.
You may drefs a fhoulder of veal the fame way. *Cole*, 98.

Breaft of Mutton grilled.

Half boil it, fcore it, pepper and falt it well, rub it with yolk
of egg, ftrew on crumbs of bread and chopped parfley ; broil
it, or roaft it in a Dutch oven. Serve it with caper fauce.
Mafon, 167.

Another way.

Mrs. *Raffald* has, in page 105, a receipt fomewhat fimilar
to the above, but as it differs in one or two particulars, I have
thought proper to give it in her own words. They are as follow :—Score a breaft of mutton in diamonds, and rub it over
with the yolk of an egg ; then ftrew on a few bread crumbs
and fhred parfley, put it into a Dutch oven to broil, bafte it
with frefh butter, pour in the difh good caper fauce, and ferve
it up. *Raffald*, 105.

To collar a Breaft of Mutton.

Take the fkin off and bone it, roll it up in a collar like the
breaft of veal, put a quart of milk and a quarter of a pound of
butter in the dripping-pan, and bafte it well while it is roafting.
Sauce—good gravy in the difh and in a boat, and currant jelly
in another. *Le Maitre*, 216.

Mutton Kebobbed.

Take a loin of mutton and joint it between every bone ; feafon it with pepper and falt moderately, grate a fmall nutmeg all
over, dip them in the yolks of three eggs, and have ready
crumbs of bread and fweet herbs ; dip them in, and clap them
together in the fame fhape again, and put it on a fmall fpit ;
roaft them before a quick fire, fet a difh under, and bafte it
with a little piece of butter, and then keep bafting it with what
comes from it, and throw fome crumbs of bread and fweet herbs
all over them as it is roafting. When it is enough, take it up,
lay

lay it in the difh, and have ready half a pint of good gravy, and what comes from it. Take two fpoonfuls of catchup, and mix a tea-fpoonful of flour with it, and put to the gravy; ftir it together, give it a boil, and pour over the mutton.

Note.—You muft obferve to take off all the fat of the infide, and the fkin off the top of the meat, and fome of the fat if there be too much. When you put in what comes from your meat into the gravy, obferve to pour out all the fat. *Glaffe*, 104. *Mafon*, 166.

A Harrico of Mutton.

Take a neck or loin of mutton, cut it into thick chops, flour them, and fry them brown in a little butter; take them out, and lay them to drain on a fieve, then put them into a ftew-pan, and cover them with gravy; put in a whole onion, and a turnip or two, and ftew them till tender; then take out the chops, ftrain the liquor through a fieve, and fkim off all the fat; put a little butter in the ftew-pan, and melt it with a fpoonful of flour; ftir it well till it is fmooth, then put the liquor in, and ftir it well all the time you are pouring it, or it will be in lumps; put in your chops and a glafs of Lifbon; have ready fome carrot about three quarters of an inch long, and cut round with an apple corer, fome turnips cut with a turnip fcoop, a dozen fmall onions all blanched well; put them to your meat, and feafon with pepper and falt; ftew them gently for fifteen minutes, then take out the chops with a fork, lay them in your difh, and pour the ragoo over it. Garnifh with beet root. *Cole*, 99.

Another way.

Cut a neck of mutton, or a loin, into fhorts fteaks; fry them, flour them, put them into a ftew-pan with a quart or three pints of beef broth, a carrot fliced, a turnip, an onion ftuck with cloves, a few pepper corns, and fome falt; let them ftew till tender, they will take three hours, as they fhould do gently: take out the mutton, ftrain the fauce, put to it carrots cut in wheels, or any fhape, turnips in balls, and celery cut to pieces, all boiled ready; fimmer thefe a minute or two in the fauce, lay the mutton in the difh, and pour the fauce over. If it cannot be ferved immediately, put the mutton into the fauce to keep hot. *Mafon*, 166.

A Harrico of a Neck of Mutton.

Cut the beft end of a neck of mutton into chops, in fingle ribs, flatten them, and fry them a light brown; then put them into a large fauce-pan with two quarts of water, a large carrot cut in flices, cut at the edge like wheels; when they have ftewed a quarter of an hour, put in two turnips cut in fquare flices, the white part of a head of celery, a few heads of afparagus,

two

two cabbage lettuces fried, and chyan to your taste; boil them
all together till they are tender; the gravy is not to be thickened; put it into a tureen or soup-dish. It is proper for a top
dish. *Du Pont,* 89.

Neck of Mutton called The Hasty Dish.

Take a large pewter or silver dish, made like a deep soup-dish,
with an edge about an inch deep on the inside, on which the
lid fixes (with a handle at top) so fast that you may lift it up
full by that handle without falling. This dish is called a necro-
mancer. Take a neck of mutton of about six pounds, take off
the skin, cut it into chops, not too thick, slice a French roll
thin, peel and slice a very large onion, pare and slice three or
four turnips, lay a row of mutton in the dish, on that a row of
roll, then a row of turnips, and then onions, a little salt, then
the meat, and so on; put to it a little bundle of sweet herbs,
and two or three blades of mace; have a tea-ketle of water
boiling, fill the dish, and cover it close; hang the dish on the
back of two chairs by the rim, have ready three sheets of brown
paper, tear each sheet into five pieces, and draw them through
your hand, light one piece, and hold it under the bottom of
the dish, moving the paper about; as fast as the paper burns,
light another till all is burnt, and your meat will be enough.
Fifteen minutes just does it. Send it to table hot in the dish.

N. B. This dish was first contrived by Mr. Rich, and is much
admired by the nobility. *Glasse.*

To dress a Neck of Mutton like Venison.

Cut a large neck before the shoulder is taken off, broader
than usual, and the flap of the shoulder with it, to make it
look handsomer; stick your neck all over in little holes with a
sharp pen-knife, and pour a little red wine upon it, and let it
lie in the wine four or five days; turn and rub it three or four
times a day, then take it out and hang it up for three days in
the open air out of the sun, and dry it often with a cloth to
keep it from musting; when you roast it, baste it with the
wine it was steeped in, if any is left; if not, fresh wine; put
white paper three or four folds to keep in the fat, roast it
thoroughly, and then take off the skin, and froth it nicely, and
serve it up.

Neck of Mutton larded with Ham and Anchovies.

Lard the fillet of a neck of mutton quite through with ham
and anchovies, first rolled in chopped parsley, shallots, sweet
herbs, pepper and salt; then put it to braze or stew in a little
broth, with a glass of white wine; when done sift and skim the
sauce, and add a little cullis to give it a proper consistence; add
the juice of half a lemon, and serve it upon the neck of mutton.
Dalrymple, 123.

To

To drefs a Neck of Mutton.

Lard it with lemon-peel cut thin in fmall lengths, boil it in falt and water, with a bunch of fweet herbs and an onion ftuck with cloves; when it is boiled, have ready for fauce a pint of oyfters ftewed in their own liquor, as much veal gravy, two anchovies diffolved and ftrained into it, and the yolks of two eggs beat up in a little of the gravy; mix thefe together till they come to a proper thicknefs, and put it over the meat. *Mafon,* 166.

A Bafque of Mutton.

Lay the caul of a leg of veal in a copper difh of the fize of a fmall punch-bowl, and take the lean of a leg of mutton that has been kept a week. Having chopped it exceedingly fmall, take half its weight in beef marrow, the crumb of a penny loaf, the rind of half a lemon grated, half a pint of red wine, two anchovies, and the yolks of four eggs. Mix it as you would faufage-meat, and lay it in the caul in the infide of the difh. · Faften the caul, bake it in a quick oven, and when it comes out, lay your difh upfide down, and turn the whole out. Pour over it brown gravy; pour venifon-fauce into a boat, and make ufe of pickles for garnifh. *Raffald,* 107. *Farley,* 108, with very inconfiderable alterations.

Fillet of Mutton with Cucumbers.

Provide one large or two fmall necks of mutton, cut off a good deal of the fcrag, and the chine and fpay-bones clofe to the ribs, tear off the fat of the great end, and flat it with your cleaver, that it may lay neat in your difh, foak it in a marinade, and roaft it wrapped up in paper well buttered. For your fauce in the fpring and fummer, quarter fome cucumbers nicely, and fry them in a bit of butter, after laying in the fame marinade, ftew them in a ladle or two of your cullis, a morfel of fhallot or green onion, pepper and falt, a little minced parfley, the juice of a lemon, and ferve it. The only difference between this and the celery-fauce is, inftead of frying your celery, boil it very tender in a little water, or broth if you have plenty, and ftew it for a quarter of an hour. Be cautious you do not break the cucumbers. *Verral,* 81.

To french a hind Saddle of Mutton.

It is the two chumps of the loins. Cut off the rump, and carefully lift up the fkin with a knife. Begin at the broad end, but be fure you do not crack it nor take it quite off; then take fome flices of ham or bacon chopped fine, a few truffles, fome young onions, fome parfley, a little thyme, fweet marjoram, winter favory, a little lemon-peel, all chopped fine, a little mace, and two or three cloves beat fine; half a nutmeg, and a

G
little

little pepper and falt. Mix all together, and throw over the meat where you took off the fkin; then lay on the fkin again, and faften it with two fine fkewers at each fide, and roll it in well-buttered paper. It will take two hours roafting : then take off the paper, bafte the meat, ftrew it all over with crumbs of bread, and when it is of a fine brown, take it up. For fauce, take fix large fhallots, cut them very fine, put them into a fauce-pan with two fpoonfuls of vinegar, and two of white wine ; boil them for a minute or two, pour it into the difh, and garnifh with horfe-radifh. *Glafs*, 47.

To drefs a Saddle à St. Menehout.

Take the fkin off the hind part of a chine of mutton, lard it with bacon, feafon it with pepper, falt, mace, beaten cloves, and nutmeg, fweet herbs, young onions, and parfley, all chopped fine : take a large oval or gravy-pan, lay layers of bacon, and then layers of beef all over the bottom ; lay in the mutton, then layers of bacon on the mutton, and then a layer of beef; put in a pint of wine, and as much good gravy as will ftew it ; put in a bay-leaf and two or three fhallots, and cover it clofe; put fire over and under it, if you have a clofe pan, and let it ftand ftewing for two hours; when done, take it out, ftrew crumbs of bread all over it, and put it into the oven to brown; ftrain the gravy it was ftewed in, and boil it till there is juft enough for fauce ; lay the mutton into a difh, pour the fauce in, and ferve it up. If you have not an oven, you muft brown it before a fire. *Mafon*, 165.

Mrs. Glaffe, in page 69 of her Art of Cookery, has the fame receipt, though the language is fomewhat different.

Mutton the Turkifh way.

Let the meat be cut in flices, wafh it in vinegar, put it in a pot, with whole pepper, rice, and two or three onions ; ftew thefe very flowly, and fkim them very often. When it is tender, take out the onions, and put fippets in the difh under them. *Cole*, 103.

Saddle of Mutton matted.

Take up the fkin, fcarify the meat, and ftick in it fliced fat livers, truffles, frefh pork, fliced onions, and anchovies; cover this all over with a good force-meat, made of rafped lard, fuet, or marrow, fweet herbs chopped, mufhrooms, pepper and falt, and three yolks of eggs, all pounded together ; cover it over with the fkin well faftened, braze it (with the fkin undermoft) with broth, and a faggot of fweet herbs ; when done, reduce the fauce to caramel or glaze. Glaze all the upper fide. *Dalrymple*, 133.

Mutton

Mutton à-la-Maintenon.

Cut fome fhort fteaks from a leg of mutton, make a force-meat with crumbs of bread, a little fuet chopped, or a bit of butter, lemon-peel grated, fhred parfley, pepper, falt, and nutmeg, mixed up with the yolk of an egg; pepper and falt the fteaks, lay on the force-meat; butter fome half fheets of writing paper, in each wrap up a fteak, twifting the paper neatly; fry them, or do them in a Dutch oven; ferve them in the paper, a little gravy in the difh, and fome in a boat. Garnifh with pickles. *Le Maitre,* 119.

Chine of Mutton with Cucumber Sauce.

You muft provide the two fore-quarters of mutton, fmall and fat; cut it down the fides, and chop through the fhoulders and breafts, fo that it may lay even in your difh; raife the fkin all off, without cutting or tearing; fcrape a little fat bacon, and take a little thyme, marjoram, favory, parfley, three or four green onions, a mufhroom or two, and a fhallot; mince all very fine, and fry them gently in the bacon; add a little pepper, and when it is almoft cold, with a pafte-brufh daub it all over the back of your meat, fkewer the fkin over it, fpit it with three or four large fkewers, and wrap fome paper over it well buttered; roaft it enough very gently, and for fauce provide fome cucumbers, (if in feafon) nicely quartered and fried in a bit of butter to a brown colour; ftrain them upon a fieve for a minute or two, and put them into a ladle or two of your cullis; boil them a little while, and throw in fome minced parfley, the juice of a lemon, and ferve it up. For your fauce of herbs, prepare juft fuch matters as are fried for the firft part of it, take a ftew-pan, with as much of your cullis as is neceffary, and ftrew all in, and boil about half an hour very foftly; take the paper and fkin off your chine, and fend it to table with the fauce poured over it, adding the juice of a lemon; and tafte it to try if it is well flavoured. *Verral,* 49.

Mutton Rumps and Kidnies.

Boil fix fheeps' rumps in veal gravy, then lard your kidnies with bacon, and fet them before the fire in a tin oven; when the rumps are tender, rub them over with the yolk of an egg, a little chyan and grated nutmeg, fkim the fat off the gravy, put it in a clean tofing-pan, with three ounces of boiled rice, a fpoonful of good cream, a little mufhroom-powder or catch-up, thicken it with flour and butter, and give it a gentle boil; fry your rumps a little brown. When you difh them up, lay them round on your rice, fo that the fmall ends may meet in the middle, and lay a kidney between every rump. Garnifh with red cabbage or barberries, and ferve it up. It is a pretty

fide

fide or corner difh. *Raffald*, 106. *Farley*, 108. *Du Pont,* 165.

Mutton Rumps à-la braise.

Boil fix mutton rumps for fifteen minutes in water; then take them out and cut them in two, and put them into a ftew-pan, with half a pint of good gravy, a gill of white wine, an onion ftuck with cloves, and a little falt and chyan pepper. Cover them clofe, and ftew them till they are tender. Take them and the onion out, and thicken the gravy with a little butter rolled in flour, a fpoonful of browning, and the juice of half a lemon. Boil it up till it is fmooth, but not too thick. Then put in your rumps, give them a top or two, and difh them up hot. Garnifh with horfe-radifh and beet-root. For variety, you may leave the rumps whole, and lard fix kidnies on one fide, and do them the fame as the rumps, only not boil them, and put the rumps in the middle of the difh, and kidnies round them, with the fauce over all. The kidnies make a pretty fide difh of themfelves. *Far-ley*, 190.

To hafh Mutton.

Cut your mutton in little bits as thin as you can, ftrew a little flour over it, have ready fome gravy (enough for fauce) wherein fweet herbs, onion, pepper, and falt have been boiled; ftrain it, put in your meat, with a piece of butter rolled in flour, and a little falt, a fhallot cut fine, a few capers and ger-kins chopped fine; tofs all together for a minute or two; have ready fome bread toafted and cut into thin fippets, lay them round the difh, and pour in your hafh. Garnifh your difh with pickles and horfe-radifh.

Note.—Some love a glafs of red wine or walnut pickle. You may put juft what you will into a hafh. If the fippets are toafted, it is better. *Cole*, 105.

Another way.

Cut mutton in flices, put a pint of gravy or broth into a tofling-pan, with one fpoonful of mufhroom catchup, and one of browning; flice in an onion, a little pepper and falt, put in over the fire, and thicken it with flour and butter; when it boils, put in your mutton, keep fhaking it till it is thoroughly hot, put it into a foup-difh, and ferve it up. *Cole*, 106.

To hafh cold Mutton.

Cut your mutton with a very fharp knife in very little bits, as thin as poffible; then boil the bones with an onion, a little fweet herbs, a blade of mace, a very little whole pepper, a little falt, a piece of cruft toafted very crifp; let it boil till there is juft enough for fauce, ftrain it, and put it into a fauce-pan, with a piece of butter rolled in flour; put in the meat; when

it

it is very hot, it is enough. Seafon with pepper and falt.
Have ready fome thin bread toafted brown, cut three-corner
ways, lay them round the difh, and pour in the hafh. As to
walnut-pickle, and all forts of pickles, you muft put in according to your fancy. Garnifh with pickles. Some love a
fmall onion peeled, cut very fmall, and done in the hafh. Or
you may ufe made gravy, if you have not time to boil the bones.
Glaffe, 119.

Oxford John.

Take a ftale leg of mutton, cut it in as thin collops as you
poffibly can, take out all the fat finews, feafon them with mace,
pepper, and falt; ftrew among them a little fhred parfley,
thyme, and two or three fhallots; put a good lump of butter
into a ftew-pan. When it is hot, put in all your collops, keep
ftirring them with a wooden fpoon till they are three parts
done, then add half a pint of gravy, a little juice of lemon,
thicken it a little with flour and butter, let them fimmer four
or five minutes, and they will be quite enough. If you let
them boil, or have them ready before you want them, they
will grow hard. Serve them up hot, with fried bread cut in
dice, over and round them. *Raffald*, 108. *Farley*, 113.

A Hodge-podge of Mutton.

Cut a neck or loin of mutton into fteaks, take off all the
fat, then put the fteaks into a pitcher, with lettuce, turnips,
carrots, two cucumbers cut in quarters, four or five onions,
and pepper and falt; you muft not put any water to it, and
ftop the pitcher very clofe; then fet it in a pan of boiling water,
let it boil four hours, keep the pan fupplied with frefh boiling
water as it waftes. *Cole*, 107.

Mutton Cutlets Lover's fafhion.

Make the cutlets pretty thick, lard them with ham and bacon,
then give them a few turns in a little butter, chopped parfley,
and a little winter favory; then put them in a ftew-pan, with
fmall bits of ham, fliced onions, carrots, and parfnips, which
you firft give a fry in oil or butter; add a glafs of white wine
and a little cullis. When done, fkim the fauce, and ferve with
all the roots and ham. *Dalrymple*, 125.

Mutton Cutlets en Surtout, or in Difguife.

Cut cutlets in the common way, and fimmer them with broth
to about three parts, with a faggot of fweet herbs; reduce the
fauce till no more remains than what will bathe the cutlets;
garnifh them with force meat round, made of fillet of veal,
fuet, chopped parfley, fhallots, pepper and falt, and bread-
crumbs foaked in cream, all being well pounded; add three
yolks of eggs, then bafte your cutlets with eggs and bread-

G 3   crumbs;

crumbs; bake in the oven till of a good colour; ferve with con-fomme fauce, gravy, &c. *Clermont*, 133.

Mutton Chops in Difguife.

Take as many mutton chops as you want, rub them with pepper, falt, nutmeg, and a little parfley; roll each chop in half a fheet of white paper, well buttered on the infide, and rolled on each and clofe. Have fome hog's-lard, or beef-dripping, boiling in a ftew-pan; put in the fteaks, fry them of a fine brown, lay them in your difh, and garnifh with fried parfley; throw fome all over, have a little good gravy in a cup, but take care you do not break the paper, nor have any fat in the difh; but let them be well drained.

To broil Mutton Steaks.

Cut your fteaks half an inch thick; when your gridiron is hot, rub it with frefh fuet, lay on your fteaks, keep turning them as quick as poffible; if you do not take great care, the fat that drops from them will fmoak them. When they are enough, put them into a hot difh, rub them well with butter, flice a fhallot very thin into a fpoonful of water, pour it on them with a fpoonful of mufhroom catchup and falt; ferve them up hot. *Raffald*, 71.

Mutton fleaks baked.

Cut a loin of mutton into fteaks, feafon them with pepper and falt, butter a difh and lay them in; take a quart of milk, fix eggs well beat, and four fpoonfuls of flour; beat the flour and eggs together in a little milk, and then put the reft to it; put in fome beaten ginger and falt, pour it over the fteaks, and fend it to table. Half an hour will bake it. *Mafon*, 167.

Sheeps' Tongues Provence fafhion.

Fry fliced onions in butter; when half done, add a little flour, chopped parfley, a clove of garlick, pepper and falt, a little cullis, and a glafs of white wine; let it ftew till the onions are done, then add as many fplit tongues (being ready boiled) as you think proper; ftew them a quarter of an hour in the fauce; ferve all together. Garnifh the difh with fried bread. *Dalrymple*, 117.

Sheeps' Tongues Royal fafhion.

Boil as the former; then lard them quite through; marinade them an hour in a little pepper and falt, chopped parfley, fhallots, and mufhrooms; put a few flices of lard under and over, add a little gravy, a glafs of white wine, with all the feafonings. When done, take out the flices of lard, fkim the fauce, add a little cullis, or butter rolled in flour, the juice of half a lemon, and ferve it upon the tongues. *Dalrymple*, 118.

Sheeps'

Sheeps' Tongues plain Family fashion.

Split ready boiled tongues in two; marinade in melted butter, pepper and salt, chopped parsley, and shallots; roll them in bread-crumbs, and broil them slowly; serve them with a sauce made of a spoonful of vinegar, a bit of butter rolled in flour and broth. grated nutmeg, and chopped shallots; reduce the sauce, and serve it under the tongues. *Du Pont*, 116.

Sheeps' Trotters of different fashion.

When well scalded, boil them in water till you can take out the great bone; then split and clean them properly; boil them again till they are very tender, and dress them in what manner you please, either as a fricassee, or with a cullis sauce, &c. taking care to make the sauce relishing. *Clermont*, 129.

Sheeps' Trotters fried in paste.

The trotters being first brazed or stewed, bone them without cutting them; roll them in good force-meat, then dip them in thick batter made of flour, white wine, one egg, and a little oil, pepper, and salt; fry them of a good colour, and garnish with fried parsley.

Sheeps' Trotters Aspic.

Aspic is a sharp sauce or jelly, wherein is commonly used elder or tarragon vinegar, chopped parsley, shallots, tarragon leaves, pepper and salt, oil, mustard, lemon, any forts of cold meat. Poultry or game may be served in aspic, either hot or cold. *Dalrymple*, 122.

G 4   CHAP

To dre/s a Lamb's Head.

BOIL the head and pluck tender, but do not let the liver be too much done. Take the head up, hack it cro/s and cro/s with a knife, grate /ome nutmeg over it, and lay it in a di/h before a good fire; then grate /ome crumbs of bread, /ome /weet herbs rubbed, a little lemon-peel chopped fine, a very little pepper and /alt, and ba/te it with a little butter; then throw a little flour over it, and ju/t as it is done do the /ame, ba/te it and dredge it. Take half the liver, the lights, the heart and tongue, chop them very /mall, with /ix or eight /poonfuls of gravy or water; fir/t /hake /ome flour over the meat, and /tir it together, then put in the gravy or water, a good piece of butter rolled in a little flour, a little pepper and /alt, and what runs from the head in the di/h; /immer all together a few minutes, and add half a /poonful of vinegar; pour it into your di/h, lay the head in the middle of the mince-meat, have ready the other half of the liver cut thin, with /ome /lices of bacon broiled, and lay round the head. Garni/h the di/h with lemon, and /end to table. *Gla//e,* 27.

Lamb's Head and Purtenances.

Skin the head and /plit it, take the black part out of the eyes, then wa/h and clean it exceeding well, lay it in warm water till it looks white, wa/h and clean the purtenance, take off the gall, and lay them in water; boil it half an hour, then mince your heart, liver, and lights, very /mall; put the mince-meat in a to//ing-pan, with a quart of mutton gravy, a little catchup, pepper and /alt, half a lemon; thicken it with flour and butter, a /poonful of good cream, and ju/t boil it up. When your head is boiled, rub it over with the yolk of an egg, /trew over it bread-crumbs, a little /hred par/ley, pepper, and /alt; thicken it well with butter, and brown it before the fire, or with a /alamander; put the purtenance on your di/h, and lay the head over it. Garni/h with lemon or pickle, and /erve it up. *Raffald,* 109. *Farley,* (without any material alterations,) 113.

Lamb's Head, Pontiff Sauce.

Take a lamb's head, about three parts boiled, chop /ome mu/hrooms, and fat livers cut in dice; put them in a /tewpan with a little culli/s and white wine, a faggot of /weet herbs, a little chopped /hallot, pepper and /alt; cut the tongue in dice, which you mix with the /auce; then take the brains out of the head, and put it in the ragoo or /auce; cover it over with the brains cut in /lices; ba/te them with a little of the /auce,

bread-

bread-crumbs, and melted butter; bake in the oven till of a good colour; ferve with *Pontiff Sauce*. *Dalrymple*, 166.

To ftew a Lamb's Head.

In order to ftew a lamb's head, wafh it and pick it very clean. Lay it in water for an hour, take out the brains, and with a fharp knife carefully extract the bones and the tongue; but be careful to avoid breaking the meat. Then take out the eyes. Take two pounds of veal, and two pounds of beef fuet, a very little thyme, a good piece of lemon-peel minced, a nutmeg grated, and two anchovies. Having chopped all thefe well together, grate two ftale rolls, and mix all with the yolks of four eggs. Save enough of this meat to make about twenty balls. Take half a pint of frefh mufhrooms, clean peeled and wafhed, the yolks of fix eggs chopped, half a pint of oyfters clean wafhed, or pickled cockles. Mix all thefe together; but firft ftew your oyfters, and put to them two quarts of gravy, with a blade or two of mace. Tie the head with packthread, cover it clofe, and let it ftew two hours. While this is doing, beat up the brains with fome lemon-peel cut fine, a little chopped parfley, half a nutmeg grated, and the yolk of an egg. Fry the brains in little cakes in boiling dripping, and fry the balls, and keep them both hot. Take half an ounce of trufles and morels, and ftrain the gravy the head was ftewed in. Put to it the trufles and morels, and a few mufhrooms, and boil all together; then put in the reft of the brains that are not fried, and ftew them together for a minute or two. Pour this over the head, lay the fried brains and balls round it, and garnifh with lemon. *Farley*, 63.

Lamb's Head Condè fafhion.

Take a lamb's head, being done in a white braze; ferve with a fauce made of verjuice, three yolks of eggs, pepper, falt, and a piece of butter, fcalded chopped parfley, and a little nutmeg, if agreeable; make thefe articles in a liafon without boiling, and ferve upon the head. *Clermont*, 174.

To force a Leg of Lamb.

Carefully take out all the meat with a fharp knife, and leave the fkin whole, and the fat on it. Make the lean you cut out into a force-meat, thus:—To two pounds of meat add two pounds of beef fuet cut fine, and beat it in a marble mortar till it is very fine; take away all the fkin of the meat and fuet, and then mix it with four fpoonfuls of grated bread. eight or ten cloves, five or fix large blades of mace dried and beaten fine, half a large nutmeg grated, a little pepper and falt, a little lemon-peel cut fine, a very little thyme, fome parfley, and four eggs. Mix all together, put it into the fkin again juft as it was,

in

in the fame fhape; few it up, roaft it, and bafte it with butter. Cut the loin into fteaks, and fry it nicely; lay the leg on the difh, and the loin round it, with ftewed cauliflowers all round upon the loin; pour a pint of good gravy into the difh, and fend it to table. If you do not like the cauliflower, it may be omitted. *Glaffe*, 31. *Mafon*, 170. *Farley*, 114.

To boil a Leg of Lamb, and Loin fried.

Cut your leg from the loin, boil the leg three quarters of an hour, cut the loin in handfome fteaks, beat them with a cleaver, and fry them a good brown; then ftew them a little in ftrong gravy; put your leg on the difh, and lay your fteaks round it; pour on your gravy, lay round lumps of ftewed fpinach and crifped parfley on every fteak. Send it to the table with goofeberry fauce in a boat. *Raffald*, 108.

Another way.

Let the leg be boiled very white. An hour will do it. Cut the loin into fteaks, dip them into a few crumbs of bread and egg, fry them nice and brown, boil a good deal of fpinach and lay in the difh; put the leg in the middle, lay the loin round it, cut an orange in four, and garnifh the difh, and have butter in a cup. Some like the fpinach boiled, then drained, put into a fauce-pan with a good piece of butter, and ftewed. *Glaffe*, 31.

To fry a Loin of Lamb.

Cut your lamb into chops, rub it over on both fides with the yolk of an egg, and fprinkle fome bread crumbs, a little parfley, thyme, marjoram, and winter favory, chopped very fine, and a little lemon-peel chopped fine; fry it in butter of a nice light brown, and fend it up in a difh by itfelf. Garnifh with a good deal of fried parfley. *Cole*, 114.

To ragoo a Fore-quarter of Lamb.

Cut off the knuckle-bone, take off the fkin, lard it all over with bacon, and fry it of a nice light brown, then put it in a ftew-pan, and juft cover it with mutton gravy, a bunch of fweet herbs, fome pepper, falt, beaten mace, and a little whole pepper; cover it clofe, and let ftew for half an hour; pour out the liquor, and take care to keep the lamb hot; ftrain off the gravy, and have ready half a pint of oyfters fried brown, pour all the fat from them, add them to the gravy, with two fpoonfuls of red wine, a few mufhrooms, and a bit of butter rolled in flour; boil all together, with the juice of half a lemon; lay the lamb in the difh, and pour the fauce over it. *Mafon*, 173.

Mrs. Glaffe has a receipt very much refembling the above, in page 53.

To force a Hind-quarter of Houfe Lamb.

Cut off the flank, and with a knife raife the thick part of the meat from the bone. Make a force-meat with fome fuet, a

few

few fcalded oyfters cut fmall, fome grated bread, a little beaten mace, pepper and falt, mixed up with the yolks of two eggs; ftuff it with this under where the meat is raifed up, and under the kidney. Let it be half roafted, then put it in a large ftew-pan, with a quart of mutton gravy; cover it, and let it ftew very gently. When it is enough, take it up and keep it hot, fkim off the fat, and ftrain the gravy; add to it a glafs of Madeira, one fpoonful of walnut catchup, half a lemon, a little chyan, half a pint of ftewed oyfters, with a piece of butter rolled in flour; pour it over the lamb. *Mafon*, 173.

Two Hind quarters of Lamb with Spinach.

Take your two quarters of lamb, trufs your knuckles in nicely, and lay it in foak two or three hours in fome milk, coriander feed, a little falt, two or three onions, and parfley; put it in but little boiling water, fkim it well, put in fome flour and water well mixed, a lemon or two pared and fliced, a bit of fuet, and a little bunch of onions and parfley; ftir it well from the bottom, and boil it gently and thefe ingredients will make it as white as a curd. Prepare your fpinach as for the ham with this difference—inftead of cullis with that feafoning, put to it about a pint of cream, a bit of butter mixed with flour, a little pepper, falt, and nutmeg; ftir it over a flow ftove till it is of a nice confiftence, fqueeze in the juice of a lemon, pour it into the difh, and lay your lamb upon it, after draining it from fat and water, and take off any of your feafonings that may chance to hang to it.

A neck of veal is frequently done in the fame way, taking the chine-bone off, and trimming it neatly. *Verral*, 53.

To force a Hind-quarter of Lamb.

Take a hind-quarter and cut off the fhank, raife the thick part of the flefh from the bone with a knife, ftuff the place with white force-meat, and ftuff it under the kidney; half roaft it, then put it in a toffing-pan, with a quart of mutton gravy; cover it clofe up, and let it ftew gently. When it is enough, take it up, and lay it in your difh, fkim the fat off the gravy, and ftrain it; then put in a glafs of Madeira wine, one fpoonful of walnut catchup, two of browning, half a lemon, a little chyan, half a pint of oyfters; thicken it with a little butter rolled in flour; pour your gravy hot on your lamb, and ferve it up. *Raffald*, 109.

To bake Lamb and Rice.

Take a neck or loin of lamb, half roaft it, take it up, cut it into fteaks, then take half a pound of rice boiled in a quart of water ten minutes, put it into a quart of good gravy, with two or three blades of mace, and a little nutmeg. Do it over a ftove or flow fire till the rice begins to be thick; then take it off,

off, ftir in a pound of butter, and when that is quite melted, ftir in the yolks of fix eggs, firft beat ; then take a difh and butter it all over ; take the fteaks and put a little pepper and falt over them ; dip them in a little melted butter, lay them into the difh, pour the gravy which comes out of them over them, and then the rice ; beat the yolks of three eggs, and pour all over ; fend it to the oven, and bake it better than half an hour. *Glaffe*, 52.

Mrs. Mafon, in page 72 of the Lady's Affiftant, has the above receipt, with only a little variation of the language.

Shoulder of Lamb neighbour fafhion.

Prepate the fhoulder as the preceding ; make a force meat of roafted fowls, calf's udder or fuet, bread crumbs foaked in cream, chopped parfley, fhallots, pepper, falt, and four yolks of eggs ; then fill the fhoulder with it, and make it as round as poffible ; faften it well, that the force-meat may not get out ; then lard it, and ftew it in broth, with a faggot of fweet herbs. When done, ftrain the fauce through a lawn fieve, reduce it to a glaze, and glaze the larded part. Serve with what fauce or ragoo you pleafe. *Cole*, 116.

Lambs' Sweetbreads.

Blanch your fweetbreads, and put into cold water a while, put them into a ftew-pan with a ladle of broth, with pepper, falt, a fmall bunch of green onions and parfley, and a blade of mace ; ftir in a bit of butter with flour, and ftew all about half an hour. Make ready a liafon of two or three eggs and cream, with a little minced parfley and rutmeg ; put in tops of afparagus that you are to have ready boiled, and pour in your liafon, and take care it does not curdle ; add fome juice of lemon or orange, and fend it to table. You may make ufe of peas, young goofeberries, or kidney beans for this, and all make a pretty difh. *Verral*, 118.

To drefs a Difh of Lambs' Bits.

Skin the ftones and fplit them, lay them on a dry cloth with the fweetbreads and liver, and dredge them well with flour, and fry them in boiling lard or butter a light brown ; then lay them on a fieve to drain ; fry a good quantity of parfley, lay your bits on the difh, and the parfley in lumps over it. Pour melted butter round them. *Raffald*, 282. *Farley*, 113.

Lamb Chops en Cafarole.

Having cut a loin of lamb into chops, put yolks of eggs on both fides, and ftrew bread crumbs over them, with a little cloves and mace, pepper and falt, mixed ; fry them of a nice light brown, and put them round in a difh, as clofe as you can ; leave a hole in the middle to put the following fauce in :—all

forts

forts of fweet herbs and parfley chopped fine, ftewed a little in
fome good thick gravy. Garnifh with fried parfley. *Glaſſe,*
54. *Maſon,* 172. *Farley,* 114.

Lamb Chops larded.

Cut the beſt end of a neck of lamb in chops, and lard one
fide; feafon them with beaten cloves, mace, and nutmeg, a
little pepper and falt; put them into a ftew-pan, the larded fide
uppermoſt; put in half a pint of gravy, a gill of white wine, an
onion, a bundle of fweet herbs, ftew them gently till tender;
take the chops out, fkim the fat clean off, and take out the onion
and fweet herbs; thicken the gravy with a little butter rolled in
flour; add a fpoonful of browning, a fpoonful of catchup, and
one of lemon-pickle. Boil it up till it is fmooth, put in the
chops, larded fide down, ftew them up gently for a minute or
two; take the chops out, and put the larded fide uppermoſt in
the difh, and the fauce over them. Garnifh with lemon, and
pickles of any fort. You may add truffles and morels, and
pickled mufhrooms, in the fauce, if you pleaſe; or you may do
the chops without larding. *Cole,* 117.

Grafs Lamb Steaks.

Pepper and falt them, fry them. When enough, lay them in
a difh, pour out the butter, fhake a little flour into the pan, pour
in a little beef broth, a little catchup and walnut-pickle; boil
this up, ftirring it; put in the fteaks, and give them a fhake
round. *Cole,* 118.

Houſe Lamb Steaks.

Seafon them with pepper, falt, nutmeg, grated lemon-peel,
and parfley chopped (but dip them firſt in egg); fry them quick,
thicken fome good gravy, add a very little red wine, catchup,
and fome oyſters; boil theſe together, put in the fteaks; juſt
heat them. Palates may be added ftewed tender, force-meat
balls, and hard eggs.

N. B. It is a very good difh, and convenient, when poultry
are dear. *Maſon,* 171.

To fry a Neck or Loin of Lamb.

Cut it into thin fteaks, beat them with a rolling-pin, fry them
in half a pint of ale, feafon them with a little falt, and cover
them clofe. When enough, take them out of the pan, lay
them in a plate before the fire to keep hot, and pour all out of
the pan into a bafon; then put in half a pint of white wine, a
few capers, the yolks of two eggs beat, with a little nutmeg and
a little falt; and to this the liquor they were fried in, and keep
ftirring it one way all the time till it is thick, then put in the
lamb, keep fhaking the pan for a minute or two, lay the fteaks
in the difh, pour the fauce over them, and have fome parfley in
a plate

a plate before the fire to crisp. Garnish your dish with that and lemon. *Glasse*, 53.

Lambs' Ears with Sorrel.

In London such things as these, or calves' ears, tails, or the ears of sheep, ready for use, or perhaps in some other great markets, are always to be had of the butchers or tripemen.

About a dozen of lamb's ears will make a small dish, and they must be stewed tender in a braze; take a large handful of sorrel, chop it a little, and stew it in a spoonful of broth and a morsel of butter; pour in a small ladle of cullis, a little pepper and salt, and nutmeg; stew it a few minutes, and dish up the ears upon it, nicely twisted up. *Verral*, 119.

Lambs' Rumps fried of a bright colour.

The rumps being brazed or boiled, make a light batter of flour, one egg, a little salt, white wine, and a little oil; fry them of a good colour, and serve with fried parsley round. You may also put them to any sauce you think proper, being first brazed or boiled. *Clermont*, 179.

To barbecue a Pig.

DRESS a pig of ten weeks old as if it were to be roasted; make a force-meat of two anchovies, six sage-leaves, and the liver of the pig, all chopped very small; then put them into a marble mortar, with the crumb of half a penny loaf, four ounces of butter, half a tea-spoonful of chyan pepper and half a pint of red wine; beat them all together to a paste, put it in your pig's belly, and sew it up; lay your pig down at a good distance before a large brisk fire, singe it well, put in your dripping-pan three bottles of red wine, baste it with the wine all the time it is roasting. When it is half roasted, put under your pig two penny loaves; if you have not wine enough, put in more. When your pig is near enough, take the loaves and sauce out of your dripping-pan, put to the sauce one anchovy chopped small, a bundle of sweet herbs, and half a lemon. Boil it a few minutes, then draw your pig, put a small lemon or apple in the pig's mouth, and a leaf on each side; strain your sauce, and pour it on them boiling hot; lay barberries and slices of lemon round it, and send it up whole to table. It is a grand bottom dish. It will take four hours roasting. *Raffald,* 111. *Farley,* with the alteration of a few words, 114.

Mrs. Glasse, page 67, has the above receipt, with only this difference—she recommends two bottles of port and one of Madeira for basting. *Mrs. Raffald* three bottles of port, and no Madeira.

Another way.

Take a pig of nine or ten weeks old, scalded, &c. as for roasting; make a stuffing with a few sage leaves, the liver of the pig, and two anchovies boned, washed, and cut very small; put them into a mortar with some crumbs of bread, a quarter of a pound of butter, a very little chyan pepper, and half a pint of Madeira wine; beat them to paste, and sew it up in the pig. lay it down at a great distance to a large brisk fire, singe it well; put into the dripping-pan two bottles of Madeira wine, and baste it well all the time it is roasting. When it is half roasted, put into the dripping-pan two French rolls. If there is not wine enough in the dripping-pan, add more. When the pig is near enough, take the rolls and sauce, and put them into a sauce pan; add to them one anchovy cut small, a bunch of sweet herbs, and the juice of a lemon. Take up the pig, put an apple in its mouth, and a roll on each side; then strain the sauce over it.

Some barbecue a pig of six or seven months old, and stick blanched almonds all over it; but baste it with Madeira in the same manner. *Mason,* 185.

To dress a Pig au Pere Duillet.

Cut off the head, and divide it into quarters; lard them with bacon, season them with mace, cloves, pepper, nutmeg, and salt. Lay a layer of fat bacon at the bottom of a kettle, lay the head in the middle, and the quarters round; then put in a bay-leaf, an onion sliced, lemon, carrots, parsnips, parsley, and chives; cover it again with bacon, put in a quart of broth, stew it over the fire for an hour, and then take it up. Put your pig into a stew-pan or kettle, pour in a bottle of white wine, cover it close, and let it stew for an hour very softly. If you would serve it cold, let it stand till it is cold, then drain it well, and wipe it that it may look white, and lay it in a dish with the head in the middle and the quarters round; then throw some green parsley all over. Or any one of the quarters is a pretty little dish, laid in water cresses. If you would have it hot, whilst your pig is stewing in the wine, take the first gravy it was stewed in, and strain it, skim off all the fat, then take a sweetbread cut into five or six slices, some truffles, morels, and mushrooms; stew all together till they are enough, thicken it with the yolks of two eggs, or a piece of butter rolled in flour; and when your pig is enough, take it out and lay it in your dish; put the wine it was stewed in to the ragoo, then pour all over the pig, and garnish with lemon. *Mason*, 185. *Glasse*, 66. *Farley*, 67.

A Pig Matelot.

Gut and scald your pig, cut off the head and pettitoes, then cut your pig in four quarters, put them with the head and toes into cold water; cover the bottom of a stew-pan with slices of bacon, and place over them the said quarters, with the pettitoes and the head cut in two. Season the whole with pepper, salt, thyme, bay-leaf, an onion, and a bottle of white wine; lay over more slices of bacon, put over it a quart of water, and let it boil. Take two large eels, skin and gut them, and cut them about five or six inches long. When your pig is half done, put in your eels, then boil a dozen of large craw-fish, cut off the claws, and take off the shells of the tails; and when the pig and eels are enough, lay first your pig and the pettitoes round it, but do not put in the head (it will be a pretty dish cold); then lay your eels and craw-fish over them, and take the liquor they were stewed in; skim off all the fat, then add to it half a pint of strong gravy, thicken with a little piece of butter rolled in flour, and a spoonful of browning, and pour over it; then garnish with craw-fish and lemon This will do for a first course, or remove. Fry the brains and lay round, and all over the dish. *Cole*, 121.

Collared Pig.

Kill a fine young roasting pig, dress off the hair and draw it, and wash it clean; rip it open from one end to the other, and
take

take out all the bones; rub it all over with pepper and falt, a little cloves and mace beaten fine, fix fage leaves and fweet herbs chopped fmall; roll up your pig tight, and bind it with a fillet; fill the pot you intend to boil it in with foft water, a bunch of fweet herbs, fome pepper-corns, fome cloves and mace, a handful of falt, and a pint of vinegar; when the liquor boils, put in your pig; boil it till it is tender; take it up, and when it is almoft cold, bind it over again, put it into an earthen pan, and pour the liquor your pig was boiled in over it, and always keep it covered. When you want it, take it out of the pan, untie the fillet as far as you want to cut it, then cut it in flices, and lay it in your difh. Garnifh with parfley. *Glaffe*, 65. *Mafon*, 186.

To bake a Pig.

When neceffity obliges you to bake a pig, lay it in a difh, flour it well all over, and rub the pig over with butter. Butter the difh in which you intend to put it, and put it in the oven. Take it out as foon as it is enough, and having rubbed it over with a butter cloth, put it into the oven again till it is dry; then take it out, lay it in a difh, and cut it up. Take off the fat from the difh it was baked in, and fome good gravy will remain at the bottom. Add to this a little veal gravy, with a piece of butter rolled in flour, and boil it up; put it into the difh, with the brains and fage in the belly. *Farley*, 46.

A Pig in Jelly.

Cut it into quarters, and lay it into your ftew-pan; put in one calf's foot, and the pig's feet, a pint of Rhenifh wine, the juice of four lemons, and one quart of water, three or four blades of mace, two or three cloves, fome falt, and a very little piece of lemon-peel; ftove it, or do it over a flow fire two hours; then take it up, lay the pig into the difh you intended for it, then ftrain the liquor, and when the jelly is cold, fkim off the fat, and leave the fettling at the bottom. Beat up the whites of fix eggs, and boil up with the jelly about ten minutes, and put it through a bag till it is clear; then pour the jelly over the pig, and ferve it up cold in the jelly. *Glaffe*, 65.

To drefs a Pig like a fat Lamb.

Take a fat pig, cut off its head, flit and trufs it up like a lamb. When it is flit through the middle and fkinned, parboil it a little, then throw fome parfley over it, roaft it and dredge it. Let your fauce be half a pound of butter, and a pint of cream, ftirring it all together till it is fmooth; then pour it over, and fend it to table. *Cole*, 123.

To drefs a Pig the French way.

Spit your pig, lay it down to the fire, let it roaft till it is thoroughly warm, then cut it off the fpit, and divide it into twenty pieces. Set them to ftew in half a pint of white wine and a pint

H of

of ftrong broth, feafoned with grated nutmeg, pepper, two onions
cut fmall, and fome ftriped thyme. Let it ftew an hour; then
put it to half a pint of ftrong gravy, a piece of butter rolled in
flour, fome anchovies, and a fpoonful of vinegar or mufhroom-
pickle. When it is enough, lay it in your difh, and pour the
gravy over it; then garnifh with orange and lemon. *Cole*, 123.

To drefs Pigs' Pettitoes.

Put your pettitoes into a fauce-pan with half a pint of water,
a blade of mace, a little whole pepper, a bundle of fweet herbs,
and an onion. Let them boil five minutes, then take out the
liver, lights, and heart, mince them very fine, grate a little nutmeg over them; and fhake a little flour on them; let the feet
do till they are tender, then take them out and ftrain the liquor, put all together with a little falt, and a piece of butter as
big as a walnut; fhake the face-pan often, let it fimmer five or
fix minutes, then cut fome toafted fippets and lay round the
difh; lay the mince-meat and fauce in the middle, and the pettitoes fplit round it. You may add the juice of half a lemon,
or a very little vinegar. *Cole*, 123.

Another way.

Boil the heart, liver, and lights, a few minutes (let the feet
do till tender); fhred them, take a little of the liquor they were
boiled in, fome pepper, falt, and nutmeg, a little grated lemon-
peel; ftir in the mince with a bit of butter and flour, and give
it a boil up. Serve it with the feet fplit, laid on the top, and
toafted fippets. *Mafon*, 187.

A ragoo of Pigs' Feet and Ears.

Having boiled the feet and ears, fplit the feet down the middle, and cut the ears in narrow flices. Dip them in butter and
fry them brown. Put a little beef gravy in a toffing-pan, with
a tea-fpoonful of lemon-pickle, a large one of mufhroom catchup, the fame of browning, and a little falt. Thicken it with a
lump of butter rolled in flour, and put in your feet and ears
Let them boil gently, and when they are enough, lay your feet
in the middle of the difh, and the ears round them; then ftrain
your gravy, pour it over them, and garnifh with curled parfley.
Farley, 79.

Another way.

Take them out of the fauce, fplit them, dip them in egg, then
in bread crumbs and chopped parfley; fry them in hogs' lard,
drain them; cut the ears in long narrow flips, flour them, put
them into fome good gravy; add catchup, morels, and pickled
mufhrooms; ftew them, pour them into the difh, and lay on
the feet.

Or they are very good dipped in butter and fried, eat with
melted butter and muftard. *Cole*, 124.

To

To barbecue a Leg of Pork.

Lay down your leg to a good fire, put into the dripping-pan two bottles of red wine, baste your pork with it all the time it is roasting. When it is enough, take up what is left in the pan, put to it two anchovies, the yolks of three eggs boiled hard and pounded fine, with a quarter of a pound of butter and half a lemon, a bunch of sweet herbs, a tea-spoonful of lemon-pickle, a spoonful of catchup, and one of tarragon vinegar, or a little tarragon shred small; boil them a few minutes, then draw your pork, and cut the skin down from the bottom of the flank in rows an inch broad, raise every other row, and roll it to the shank; strain your sauce, and pour it in boiling hot, lay oyster patties all round the pork, and sprigs of green parsley. *Raffald*, 111.

Mrs. Mason, page 175, has nearly the same receipt as the above; the only difference is, that she omits the lemon-pickle and tarragon, as well as the green parsley for garnish.

To stuff a Chine of Pork.

Take a chine of pork that has hung four or five days; make four holes in the lean, and stuff it with a little of the fat leaf, chopped very small, some parsley, thyme, a little sage and shallot cut very fine, seasoned with pepper, salt, and nutmeg. It must be stuffed pretty thick. Have some good gravy in the dish. For sauce—apple-sauce and potatoes. *Cole*, 125.

Another way.

Take a chine that has been hung about a month, boil it half an hour, then thicken it up and make holes in it all over the lean part, one inch from another, stuff them betwixt the joints with shred parsley, rub it all over with the yolk of eggs, strew over it bread crumbs, baste it, and set it in a Dutch oven. When it is enough, lay round it boiled broccoli, or stewed spinach. Garnish with parsley. *Raffald*, 112.

Hog's Head au Sanglier, or Wild-boar fashion.

Cut the head close to the shoulder, bone the neck part, part the flesh from the nose as far as the eyes, cut off the bone, lard the inside with bacon, season with pepper, salt, and spices; rub it all over with salt, and half an ounce of pounded salt-petre; put it in a pickle-pan, with half a handful of juniper-berries, sweet herbs, six laurel-leaves, basil, eight cloves, whole pepper, and half a handful of coriander-seed; let it lie for about eight days, rubbing it every day; then take it out and wipe it dry; tie it well, boil it with three pints of red wine, and as much water as will properly boil it, with onions, carrots, a large faggot of sweet herbs, two cloves of garlick, four cloves, and two pounds of hogs' lard; when near done, taste the braze,

and

and add falt, if neceſſary; when it gives under the finger, it is done; let it cool in the braze; ſerve cold upon a napkin. You may garniſh with bay-leaves or parſley, according to fancy. *Cole*, 123.

N. B. You may dreſs it without the hogs' lard, as directed. *Dalrymple*, 143.

A Hog's Head like Brawn.

Waſh it well, boil it till the bones will come out; when cold, put the inſide of the cheeks together, with ſalt between; put the ears round the ſides, put the cheeks into a cloth, preſs them into a ſieve, or any thing round, put on a weight for two days; have ready a pickle of falt and water, with about a pint of malt boiled together; when cold, put in the head. *Cole*, 126.

Ham à-la-braze.

Take off the ſkin, clear the knuckle. and lay it in water to freſhen. Then tie it about with a ſtring, and take ſlices of bacon and beef; beat and ſeaſon them well with ſpices and ſweet herbs, and lay them in the bottom of a kettle. with onions, parſnips, and carrots ſliced, with ſome chives and parſley. Lay in your ham the fat ſide uppermoſt, and cover it with ſlices of beef, and over that with ſlices of bacon. Then lay on ſome ſliced roots and herbs. the ſame as under it. Cover it, and ſtop it clôſe with paſte. Put fire both over and under it, and let it ſtew twelve hours with a very ſlow fire. Put it into a pan, dredge it well with grated bread, and brown it with a hot iron; or put it into the oven, and bake it an hour. Then ſerve it upon a clean napkin. Garniſh with raw parſley. If it is to be eaten hot, make a ragoo thus:—take a veal ſweetbread, ſome livers of fowls, cocks'-combs, muſhrooms, and truffles. Toſs them up in a pint of good gravy, ſeaſoned with ſpice to your taſte; thicken it with a piece of butter rolled in flour, and a glaſs of red wine. Then brown your ham as above, and let it ſtand a quarter of an hour to drain the fat out. Take the liquor it was ſtewed in, ſtrain it, ſkim off all the fat, put it into the gravy, and boil it up with a ſpoonful of browning. Sometimes you may ſerve it up with carp-ſauce, and ſometimes with a ragoo of craw-fiſh. *Farley*, 135.

To roaſt a Ham, or a Gammon of Bacon.

Half boil your ham or gammon, then take off the ſkin, dredge it with oatmeal ſifted very fine, baſte it with freſh butter; it will make a ſtronger froth than either flour or bread-crumbs, then roaſt it. When it is enough, diſh it up, and pour brown gravy on your diſh. Garniſh with green parſley, and ſend it to table. *Raffald*, 112.

To force Hogs' Ears.

Take two or three pairs of ears, parboil them, or take them ſouſed; then take an anchovy, ſome ſage, ſome parſley, half a
pound

pound of fuet chopped fmall, fome crumbs of bread, and a little pepper; mix all of them together with the yolk of an egg, ftuff them, and fry them in frefh butter till they are of a light brown; then pour away all the fat, and put to them half a pint of very rich gravy, a glafs of Madeira, three tea-fpoonfuls of muftard, a little bit of butter rolled in flour, a fmall onion whole, and a little pepper; cover them clofe, ftew them very gently for half an hour, and fhake the pan often. When they are enough, take them out, and pour the fauce over them, but firft take out the onion. To improve the difh, the meat may be fliced from the feet. and added. Put in falt enough to give it a proper flavour. *Mafon*, 180.

Mock Brawn.

Take two pair of neat's feet, boil them very tender, and pick the flefh entirely from the bones; take the belly-piece of pork, boil it till it is near enough, then bone it, and roll the meat of the feet up in the pork very tight; then take a ftrong cloth, with fome coarfe tape, and roll it round very tight; tie it up in a cloth, boil it till it is fo tender that a ftraw may run through it; let it be hung up in a cloth till it is quite cold, after which put it into fome foufing liquor, and keep it for ufe.

Chine of Pork, poivrade fauce.

Salt it about three days; then roaft it, and ferve with fauce-poivarde. You may alfo fend Robert fauce in the fame boat. *Dalrymple*, 145.

Hogs' Tails of different fafhions.

Stew the tails very tender in broth, with a clove of garlick, whole pepper, falt, a little thyme, and two laurel-leaves. When done, ferve with what fauce you pleafe; or broiled with crumbs of bread, with muftard-fauce in a fauce-boat, alfo with ftewed cabbages, &c.

Hogs' Feet brazed and broiled.

Clean the feet very well, and cut them in two; put thin flices of lard between each two halves; tie them two and two together; then fimmer them about fix hours, with two glaffes of white wine, one of brandy, a little hogs'-lard, fpices, a faggot of parfley and fweet herbs, three fhallots, and one clove of garlick. When done, let them cool in the braze; untie them, bafte with their own fat, and ftrew them over with bread-crumbs; broil of a fine colour; ferve with or without fauce.

N. B. They may alfo be fried, baked, ragooed, &c. *Dalrymple*, 146.

To broil Pork Steaks.

Pork fteaks require more broiling than mutton fteaks.

When

When they are enough, put in a little good gravy. A little sage, rubbed very fine, strewed over them, gives them a fine taste. Do not cut them too thin. *Farley*, 72.

Pork Cutlets.

Skin a loin of pork, and divide it into cutlets ; strew some parsley and thyme cut small, with some pepper, salt, and grated bread over them ; boil them of a fine brown ; have ready some good gravy, a spoonful of ready-made mustard, two shallots shred small ; boil these together over the fire, thicken with a piece of butter rolled in flour, and a little vinegar, if agreeable. Put the cutlets into a hot dish, and pour the sauce over them. *Mason*, 176.

Pork Steaks.

Cut a neck of pork which has been kept some time, and pare the steaks properly : you may dress them in the same manner, in every respect, as veal cutlets, and in as many different ways, serving them with any sort of stewed greens or sauces. *Clermont*, 171.

Toasted Bread and Ham with Eggs.

Toast bits of bread of what bigness you please, fry them in butter of a good colour ; take as many slices of ham, and soak them over a slow fire in butter till they are done, turning them often ; then lay them upon bread, put a little cullis into the stew-pan, give it a boiling, skim the fat clear off, and add a little broth and vinegar ; boil a moment, and serve upon the toast. The ham is prepared the same, if you would serve it with poached eggs, or any sort of stewed greens. *Cole*, 129.

Goose à-la-mode.

PICK a large fine goose clean, skin and bone it nicely, and take off the fat. Then take a dried tongue, and boil and peel it. Take a fowl and treat it in the same manner as the goose; season it with pepper, salt, and beaten mace, and roll it round the tongue. Season the goose in the same manner, and put both tongue and fowl into the goose. Put it into a little pot that will just hold it, with two quarts of beef gravy, a bundle of sweet herbs, and an onion. Put some slices of ham, or good bacon, between the fowl and goose; then cover it close, and let it stew over the fire for an hour very slowly. Then take up your goose, and skim off all the fat; strain it, and put in a glass of red wine, two spoonfuls of catchup, a veal sweetbread cut small, some truffles, mushrooms, and morels, a piece of butter rolled in flour, and, if wanted, some pepper and salt. Put the goose in again, cover it close, and let it stew half an hour longer. Then take it up, pour the ragoo over it, and garnish with lemon. You must remember to save the bones of the goose and fowl, and put them into the gravy when it is first set on. It will be an improvement if you will roll some beef-marrow between the tongue and the fowl, and between the fowl and goose, as it will make them mellow and eat the finer. Before we conclude this article, it may not be amiss to observe, that the best method to bone a goose or fowl of any sort is to begin at the breast, and take out all the bones without cutting the back; for when it is sewed up, and you come to stew it, it generally bursts in the back, whereby the shape of it is spoiled *Farley*, 117. *Glasse*, 86. *Mason*, without any material alteration, 269.

To marinade a Goose.

Cut your goose up the back-bone, then take out all the bones, and stuff it with force-meat, and sew up the back again; fry the goose a good brown, then put it into a deep stew-pan, with two quarts of good gravy, and cover it close, and stew it two hours; then take it out, and skim off the fat; add a large spoonful of lemon pickle, one of browning, and one of red wine; one anchovy shred fine, beaten mace, pepper, and salt to your palate; thicken it with flour and butter, boil it a little, dish up your goose, and strain your gravy over it.

N. B. Make your stuffing thus:—take ten or twelve sage-leaves, two large onions, two or three large sharp apples, shred them very fine, mix them with the crumb of a penny loaf, four ounces of beef-marrow, one glass of red wine, half a nutmeg

grated,

grated, pepper, falt, and a little lemon-peel fhred fmall; make a light ftuffing with the yolks of four eggs. Obferve to make it one hour before you want it. *Raffald*, 126.

To ragoo a Goofe.

Flat the breaft down with a cleaver, then prefs it down with your hand, fkim it, dip it into fcalding water; let it be cold, lard it with bacon, feafon it with pepper, falt, and a little beaten mace; then flour it all over, take a pound of good beef-fuet cut fmall, put it into a deep ftew-pan, let it be melted, then put in your goofe; let it be brown on both fides. When it is brown, put in a quart of boiling gravy, an onion or two, a bundle of fweet herbs, a bay-leaf, fome whole pepper, and a few cloves. Cover it clofe, and let it ftew foftly till it is tender. About an hour will do, if fmall; if a large one, an hour and an half. In the mean time make a ragoo. Boil fome turnips almoft enough, fome carrots and onions quite enough; cut your turnips and carrots the fame as for a harrico of mutton, put them into a fauce-pan with half a pint of good beef gravy, a little pepper and falt, a piece of butter rolled in flour, and let this ftew all together a quarter of an hour. Take the goofe and drain it well; then lay it in the difh, and pour the ragoo over it.

Where the onion is difliked, leave it out. You may add cabbage boiled and chopped fmall. *Glaffe*, 85. *Mafon* almoft in the fame words, 269.

To fmoke a Goofe.

Take a large ftubble-goofe, take off all the fat, dry it well infide and out with a cloth, wafh it all over with vinegar, and then rub it over with common falt, faltpetre, and a quarter of a pound of coarfe fugar; rub the falts well in, and let it lie a fortnight; then drain it well, few it up in a cloth, dry it in the middle of a chimney. It fhould hang a month. Sauce—onions, greens, &c. *Cole*, 132.

To ftew Giblets.

Scald and clean them well, cut off the bill, divide the head, fkin the feet, ftew them with water (enough for fauce) a fprig of thyme, fome whole black pepper, an onion; let them do till very tender, ftrain the fauce; add a little catchup and flour, if the fauce is not thick enough. Lay fippets toafted round the difh. *Mafon*, 270.

Another way.

Cut your pinions in two, the neck in four pieces, flice the gizzard, clean it well, ftew them in two quarts of water, or mutton broth, with a handful of fweet herbs, one anchovy, a few pepper corns, three or four cloves, a fpoonful of catchup,

and

and an onion. When the giblets are tender, put in a fpoonful of good cream, thicken it with flour and butter, ferve them up in a foup-difh, and lay fippets round it. *Raffald*, 57.

Giblets à-la-Turtle.

Let three pair of giblets be well cleaned and cut, as before, put them into your ftew-pan, with four pounds of fcrag of veal, and two pounds of lean beef, covered with water; let them boil up, and fkim them very clean; then put in fix cloves, four blades of mace, eight corns of all-fpice, beat very fine, fome bafil, fweet marjoram, winter favory, and a little thyme, chopped very fine, three onions, two turnips, and one carrot; ftew them till tender, then ftrain them through a fieve, and wafh them clean out of the herbs in fome warm water; then take a piece of butter, put it in your ftew-pan, melt it, and put in as much flour as will thicken it; ftir it till it is fmooth, then put your liquor in, and keep ftirring it all the time you pour it in, or elfe it will go into lumps, which if it happens, you muft ftrain it through a fieve; then put in a pint of Madeira wine, fome pepper and falt, and a little chyan pepper; ftew it for ten minutes, then put in your giblets; add the juice of a lemon, and ftew them fifteen minutes; then ferve them in a tureen. You may put in fome egg-balls made thus :—Boil fix eggs hard, take out the yolks, put them in a mortar, and beat them; throw in a fpoonful of flour, and the yolk of a raw egg, beat them together till fmooth; then roll them in little balls, and fcald them in boiling water, and juft before you ferve the giblets up, put them in.

N. B. Never put your livers in at firft, but boil them in a fauce-pan of water by themfelves. *Glaffe*, 87.

Turkey à-la-daube, to be fent up hot.

Cut the Turkey down the back, juft enough to bone it, without fpoiling the look of it, then ftuff it with a nice force meat, made of oyfters chopped fine, crumbs of bread, pepper, falt, fhallots, a very little thyme, parfley, and butter; fill it as full as you like, and few it up with a thread, tie it up in a clean cloth, and boil it very white, but not too much. You may ferve it up with oyfter-fauce made good, or take the bones, with a piece of veal, mutton, and bacon, and make a rich gravy, feafoned with pepper, falt, fhallots, and a little bit of mace; ftrain it off through a fieve, and ftew your turkey in it (after it is half-boiled) juft half an hour, difh it up in the gravy after it is well fkimmed, ftrained, and thickened with a few mufhrooms, ftewed white, or ftewed palates, force-meat balls, fried oyfters or fweetbreads, and pieces of lemon. Difh them up with the breaft upwards. If you fend it up garnifhed with palates, take care to have them ftewed tender firft. Before you add them to

the

the turkey, you may put a few morels and truffles in your sauce, if you like it, but take great care to wash them clean. *Raffald*, 122. *Farley*, 119.

Turkey à-la-daube, to be sent up cold.

Bone the turkey, and season it with pepper and salt, then spread over it some slices of ham, upon that some force-meat, upon that a fowl, boned and seasoned as above; then more ham and force-meat, then sew it up with thread; cover the bottom of the stew-pan with veal and ham, then lay in the turkey, the breast down; chop all the bones to pieces, and put them on the turkey, cover the pan, and set it on the fire five minutes; then put in much clear broth as will cover it, let it boil two hours; when it is more than half done, put in one ounce of ising-glass and a bundle of herbs. When it is done enough, take out the turkey, and strain the jelly through a hair sieve, skim off all the fat, and when it is cold, lay the turkey upon it, the breast down, and cover it with the rest of the jelly. Let it stand in some cold place When you serve it up, turn it on the dish it is to be served in. If you please, you may spread butter over the turkey's breast, and put some green parsley or flowers, or what you please, and in what form you like. *Cole*, 133.

To stew a Turkey brown the nice way.

Bone it, and fill it with a force-meat thus :—Take the flesh of a fowl, half a pound of veal, and the flesh of two pigeons, with a well-pickled or dry tongue, peel it, and chop it all together: then beat it in a mortar, with the marrow of a beef bone, or a pound of the fat of a loin of veal; season it with two or three blades of mace, two or three cloves, and half a nutmeg dried at a good distance from the fire, and pounded, with a little pepper and salt. Mix all these well together, fill your turkey, fry them of a fine brown, and put it into a little pot that will just hold it ; lay four or five skewers at the bottom of the pot, to keep the turkey from sticking ; put in a quart of good beef and veal gravy, wherein was boiled spice and sweet herbs, cover it close, and let it stew half an hour; then put in a glass of white wine, one spoonful of catchup, a large spoonful of pickled mushrooms, and a few fresh ones, if you have them, a few truffles and morels, a piece of butter as big as a walnut, rolled in flour; cover it close, and let it stew half an hour longer ; get the little French rolls ready fried, take some oysters, and strain the liquor from them, then put the oysters and liquor into a sauce-pan, with a blade of mace, a little white wine, and a piece of butter rolled in flour ; let them stew till it is thick, then fill the loaves, lay the turkey in the dish, and pour the sauce over it. If there is any fat on the gravy, take it off, and lay the loaves on each side of the turkey. Garnish with lemon when you have no loaves,

and

and take oyſters dipped in butter and fried. *Glaſſe*, 73. *Far-*
ley, 68.

Note.—The ſame will do for any white fowl.

Another way.

Take a ſmall turkey and bone it; fill it with a force-meat
made as follows:—Take half a pound of veal, and the meat of
two pigeons, a tongue out of the pickle, boiled and peeled; chop
all theſe ingredients together, and beat them in a mortar, with
ſome marrow from a beef bone, or a pound of ſuet from a loin
of veal; ſeaſon them with two or three cloves, two or three
blades of mace, and half a nutmeg dried at the fire and pounded,
with ſome ſalt. Mix all theſe well together, fill the turkey,
and fry it of a fine brown; put it into a pot that will juſt hold it,
lay ſome ſkewers at the bottom of the pot to keep the turkey
from ſticking; put in a quart of good beef gravy, cover it cloſe,
and let it ſtew for half an hour very gently; then put in a glaſs
of red wine, one ſpoonful of catchup, a large ſpoonful of pickled
muſhrooms, ſome truffles, morels, and a piece of butter rolled
in flour; cover it cloſe, and let it ſtew half an hour longer. Fry
ſome hollow French loaves, then take ſome oyſters, ſtew them
in a ſauce-pan with a bit of mace, their liquor, a little white
wine, and a piece of butter rolled in flour; let them ſtew till
they are pretty thick, fill the loaves with them; lay the turkey
in the diſh, pour the ſauce over it, and lay the loaves on each
ſide. *Maſon*, 258.

To ſtew a Turkey with Celery.

Stuff the turkey as when ſtewed brown (leaving out the oyſters) or with force-meat; boil it till near enough, with an onion,
a little whole pepper, a piece of lemon-peel, and a bunch of
ſweet herbs in the water; have ſome celery cut into lengths and
boiled till near enough; put them into ſome of the liquor the
the turkey was boiled in, lay in the turkey breaſt downwards,
ſtew it a quarter of an hour, or till it is done; but do not over-
do it. Take it up, thicken the ſauce with a piece of butter rolled in flour, and ſome good cream; add ſalt and chyan. *Cole*, 135.

Another way.

Take a large turkey, and make a good white force-meat of
veal, and ſtuff the craw of the turkey; ſkewer it for boiling,
then boil it in ſoft water till it is almoſt enough, and then take
up your turkey, and put it in a pot with ſome of the water it
was boiled in, to keep it hot; put ſeven or eight heads of celery,
that are waſhed and cleaned very well, into the water that the
turkey was boiled in, till they are tender; then take them up,
and put in your turkey with the breaſt down, and ſtew it a
quarter of an hour; then take it up, and thicken your ſauce
with half a pint of butter and flour to make it pretty thick, and
a quar-

a quarter of a pint of rich cream, then put in your celery; pour the sauce and celery hot upon the turkey's breast, and serve it up. It is a proper dish for dinner or supper. *Raffald*, 120.

Turkey à-l'ecarlate.—Turkey of a scarlet colour.

Take up the skin of a small turkey from the flesh without breaking it, and stuff as much craw-fish and butter under it as possible; stuff the inside with a ragoo made of the liver, mushrooms, pepper, and salt, prepared in a good cullis short sauce; sew it up, and wrap it with slices of lard and pepper. Serve with a craw-fish cullis. *Clermont*, 230.

Turkey with Onions and pickled Pork.

Scald two dozen of small white onions, and boil them in broth, with half a pound of pickled pork cut into thin slices, a faggot of parsley, green shallots, thyme, a bay-leaf, two cloves, whole pepper, and salt. When done, drain them all, stuff the turkey therewith, and wrap it in slices of lard and paper to roast. Make a sauce with a bit of butter, a slice of ham, two shallots, and a few mushrooms; soak it awhile, then add two spoonfuls of broth, and as much cullis; simmer it about an hour, skim it, and sift it. When ready, add a small spoonful of mustard, a little pepper and salt. *Clermont*, 227.

To roast a Turkey the genteel way.

Cut your turkey down the back, and bone it with a sharp pen-knife; then make your force-meat thus:—take a large fowl, or a pound of veal, as much grated bread, half a pound of suet, cut and beat very fine, a little beaten mace, two cloves, half a nutmeg grated, about a large tea-spoonful of lemon-peel, and the yolks of two eggs; mix all together with a little pepper and salt, fill up the places where the bones came out, and fill the body, that it may look just as it did before; sew up the back and roast it. You may have oyster sauce, celery-sauce. or just as you please. Put good gravy in the dish, and garnish with lemon. Be sure to leave the pinions on. *Glasse*, 32.

A Turkey in Jelly.

Boil a turkey or a fowl as white as you can, let it stand till cold, and have ready a jelly made thus:—take a fowl, skin it, take off all the fat, do not cut it to pieces, nor break the bones; take four pounds of a leg of veal, without any fat or skin, put it into a well tinned sauce pan, put to it full three quarts of water, set it on a very clear fire till it begins to simmer; be sure to skim it well, but take great care it does not boil. When it is well skimmed, set it so as it will but just seem to simmer; put to it two large blades of mace, half a nutmeg, and twenty corns of white pepper, a little bit of lemon-peel as big as a sixpence. This will take six or seven hours doing. When you think it is

a stiff

a ftiff jelly, which you will know by taking a little out to cool, be fure to fkim off all the fat, if any, and be fure not to ftir the meat in the fauce-pan. A quarter of an hour before it is done, throw in a large tea fpoonful of falt, fqueeze in the juice of half a Sevelle orange or lemon. When you think it is enough ftrain, it off through a clean fieve, but do not pour it off quite to the bottom, for fear of fettlings. Lay your turkey or fowl in the difh you intend to fend it to the table in, beat up the whites of fix eggs to a froth, and put the liquor to it, then boil it five or fix minutes, and run it through a jelly bag till it is quite clear, then pour the liquor over it; let it ftand till quite cold, colour fome of the jelly in different colours, and when it is near cold, with a fpoon fprinkle it over in what form or fancy you pleafe, and fend it to table. A few naftertium flowers ftuck here and there look pretty, if you can get them; but lemon, and all thofe things, are entirely fancy. This is a very pretty difh for a cold collation, or a fupper.

All forts of birds or fowls may be done this way. *Glaffe,* 348. *Mrs. Mafon,* page 261, has the fame receipt in different words; but we have chofen the above as being rather more explicit.

A Turkey the Italian way.

Mince the liver of a young turkey very fine, with fome chopped parfley, and two or three handfuls of frefh mufhrooms, fome pepper, falt, and more than an ounce of butter; mix thefe well together, and put them into the body of the turkey; put on a ftew-pan with a piece of butter, fome fhallots, fome pepper and falt; when it is hot, put in the turkey, turn it often that it may be of a fine brown, and lay it to cool; then wrap fome flices of bacon over it, and cover it all over with paper; put it upon a fpit, and lay it down to roaft. For fauce—cut fome large mufhrooms very fine, with twice the quantity of parfley, a few green onions cut fmall. Put on a fauce-pan with half a pint of white wine; when it is hot, put in thefe ingredients; add fome pepper and falt, the juice of a lemon, two cloves of garlick whole; let them boil, and then put in a quarter of a pint of rich gravy, and a fmall tea-cupful of oil; let all boil up once or twice, then take out the garlic, and put in a piece of butter rolled in flour. Lay the turkey in the difh, and pour the fauce over it. *Mafon,* 259.

Turkey in a hurry.

Trufs a turkey with the legs inward, and flatten it as much as you can; put it in a ftew-pan, with melted lard, chopped parfley, fhallots, mufhrooms, and a little garlick; give it a few turns on the fire, and add the juice of half a lemon to keep it white; then put it in another ftew-pan, with flices of veal, one

flice

flice of ham, the melted lard, and every thing as ufed before, adding whole pepper and falt; cover it over with flices of lard, and foak it about half an hour on a flow fire; then add a glafs of white wine and a little broth, and finifh the brazing; fkim and fift the fauce, add a little cullis to make it a liafon, reduce it to a good confiftence, and ferve upon the turkey. *Clermont*, 231.

Turkies and Chickens after the Dutch way.

Boil them, feafon them with falt, pepper, and cloves; then to every quart of broth, put a quarter of a pound of rice or vermicelli. It is eat with fugar and cinnamon. The two laft may be left out. *Cole*, 138.

Turkey ftuffed after the Hamburg way.

Take one pound of beef, three quarters of a pound of fuet, mince it very fmall, feafon it with falt, pepper, cloves, mace, and fweet marjoram; then mix two or three eggs with it; loofen the fkin all round the turkey, and ftuff it. It muft be roafted. *Glaffe*, 383.

To drefs a Turkey or Fowl to perfection.

Bone them, and make a force meat thus :—take the flefh of a fowl, cut it fmall, then take a pound of veal, beat it in a mortar, with half a pound of beef fuet, as much crumbs of bread, fome mufhrooms, truffles, and morels, cut fmall, a few fweet herbs and parfley, with fome nutmeg, pepper, and falt, a little mace beaten, fome lemon-peel cut fine; mix all thefe together with the yolks of two eggs, then fill your turkey, and roaft it. This will do for a large turkey, and fo in proportion for a fowl. Let your fauce be good gravy, with mufhrooms, truffles, and morels in it. Then garnifh with lemon, and, for variety fake, you may lard your fowl or turkey. *Cole*, 139.

A glazed Turkey.

The turkey muft be young, but not fmall. When it is pick-ed, drawn and finged, lay it a little while over a clear charcoal fire, but turn it often; have ready a ragoo of fweetbreads, take off the turkey, fplit it down the back, fill it with this ragoo, few it up, and lard it with bacon; then lay at the bottom of a deep ftew-pan, firft fome flices of ham, then fome flices of veal, and then fome flices of beef; lay the turkey upon thefe, ftrew over fome fweet herbs, and cover them clofe; let thefe ftew over a flow fire. When they are enough, take off the ftew-pan, take out the turkey, and then pour into the turkey a little good broth, ftir it about and ftrain off the liquor; fkim off the fat, fet it over the fire again, and boil it to a jelly; then put in the turkey, and fet the pan over a gentle fire or ftove; it will be

foon

soon well glazed; then pour into the diſh ſome eſſence of ham, and then put in the turkey. *Maſon*, 261.

To roaſt a Turkey with Cray-fiſh.

Take a young turkey, in October or November, let it be truſſed as for roaſting; make ſome force-meat with ſome fat bacon, ſuet, and the white of a chicken, all cut as fine as poſſible, and ſome freſh muſhrooms, minced very fine; mix theſe ingredients well together, with ſome ſalt, pepper, the leaves of ſweet herbs picked clean from the ſtalks, and a little grated nutmeg; chop them all together after they are mixed, then boil ſome crumb of bread in rich cream, put it to the force-meat; then take the yolks of two new laid eggs, beat them well, and mix the force-meat with them; ſtuff the crop of the turkey, raiſe the ſkin a little upon the breaſt, and put as much of the force-meat as will go in without tearing it; if any is left, put it into the body, and with it a ragoo of cray-fiſh made as follows:—waſh ſome cray-fiſh, and boil them in water, then pick out the tails and bodies; cut ſome muſhrooms, but not ſmall, ſome truffles in thin ſlices, ſome artichoke bottoms and aſparagus tops, boiled and cut in pieces; mix all theſe together with the cray-fiſh, put them into a ſauce-pan, with a piece of butter, ſome nutmeg cut in ſlices, pepper, ſalt, three or four ſlices of lemon, a little onion cut ſmall; let theſe all ſimmer over a ſlow fire, and when enough, put in ſome cullis of cray-fiſh to thicken it. Put ſome of this ragoo into the body of the turkey, tie up both ends; ſkewer and ſpit it for roaſting; ſtrew ſome ſtuffing over it, then ſome ſlices of bacon, and over all ſome buttered paper; let it have a good fire, and be thoroughly done. When it is enough, take off the paper and bacon, and pour over it the reſt of the ragoo. *Cole*, 139.

To haſh a Turkey.

Take off the legs, cut the thighs in two pieces, cut off the pinions and breaſt in pretty large pieces, take off the ſkin, or it will give the gravy a greaſy taſte; put it into a ſtew-pan with a pint of gravy, a tea-ſpoonful of lemon-pickle, a ſlice of the end of a lemon, and a little beaten mace; boil your turkey ſix or ſeven minutes (if you boil it any longer, it will make it hard) then put it on your diſh; thicken your gravy with flour and butter, mix the yolks of two eggs with a ſpoonful of thick cream, put in your gravy, ſhake it over the fire till it is quite hot, but do not let it boil; ſtrain it, and pour it over your turkey. Lay ſippets round, ſerve it up, and garniſh with lemon or parſley. *Raffald*, 74.

Another way.

Mix ſome flour with a piece of butter, ſtir it into ſome cream
and

and a little veal gravy till it boils up; cut the turkey in pieces, not too fmall, put it into the fauce, with grated lemon-peel, white pepper, and mace pounded, a little mufhroom powder or catchup; fimmer it up. Oyfters may be added. *Mafon, 261.*

To roaft a Fowl with Chefnuts.

Firft take fome chefnuts, roaft them very carefully, fo as not to burn them; take off the fkin, and peel them; take about a dozen of them cut fmall, and bruife them in a mortar; parboil the liver of the fowl, bruife it, cut about a quarter of a pound of ham or bacon, and pound it; then mix thefe all together, with a good deal of parfley chopped fmall, a little fweet herbs, fome mace, pepper, falt, and nutmeg; mix thefe together, and put into your fowl, and roaft it. The beft way of doing it is to tie the neck, and hang it up by the legs to roaft with a ftring, and bafte it with butter. For fauce—take the reft of the chef-nuts, peeled and fkinned, put them into fome good gravy, with a little white wine, and thicken it with a piece of butter rolled in flour; then take your fowl, lay it in the difh, and pour in the fauce. Garnifh with lemon. *Glaffe, 75.*

Mrs. Mafon gives the above receipt, differently expreffed, page 263.

To force a Fowl with a Ragoo of Oyfters.

Prepare a force-meat, to which add a dozen oyfters, ftuff the craw; cover the breaft of the fowl with bacon fliced, then a fheet of paper, roaft it; take fome cullis, or good gravy, put in the oyfters, with their liquor ftrained, a little mufhroom powder or catchup, lemon juice, thicken it with flour; add chyan and falt, if wanted, boil it up. When the fowl is done, take off the bacon. Serve the fauce in the difh.

This fauce is proper for any roafted fowls or chickens.

A Fowl with a fharp Sauce.

Trufs a fowl for roafting; make a force-meat with fcraped lard or butter, a little tarragon, chervil, burnet, garden-crefs, pepper, falt, and the yolks of two or three eggs; ftuff the fowl with it, make a fauce with a little cullis, a few of the above herbs pounded, two anchovies, and a few capers. When done, ftrain it, then add a little more cullis, and a little muftard, pep-per, and falt; warm, without boiling, and ferve with your roaft-ed fowl. *Dalrymple, 214.*

A Fowl à la-braze.

Skewer your fowl as for boiling, with the legs in the body, then lay over it a layer of fat bacon, cut in pretty thin flices, then wrap it round in beet leaves, then in a caul of veal, and put it into a large fauce pan with three pints of water, a glafs of Madeira wine, a bunch of fweet herbs, two or three blades

of

of mace, and half a lemon; ftew it till quite tender, take it up, and ſkim off the fat; make your gravy pretty thick with flour and butter, and ſtrain it through a hair ſieve, and put to it a pint of oyſters, a tea-cupful of thick cream; keep ſhaking your toſſing-pan over the fire, and when it has ſimmered a little, ſerve up your fowl with the bacon, beet-leaves, and caul on, and pour your ſauce hot upon it. Garniſh with barberries, or red beet-root. *Raffald*, 123. *Farley*, 119.

Another way.

Truſs your fowl with the legs turned into the belly, ſeaſon it, both inſide and out, with beaten mace, nutmeg, pepper, and ſalt; lay a layer of bacon at the bottom of a deep ſtew-pan, then a layer of veal, and afterwards the fowl; then put in an onion, two or three cloves ſtuck in a little bundle of ſweet herbs, with a piece of carrot; then put at the top a layer of bacon, another of veal, and a third of beef; cover it cloſe, and let it ſtand over the fire for two or three minutes, then pour in a pint of broth or hot water; cover it cloſe, and let it ſtew an hour; afterwards take up your fowl, ſtrain the ſauce, and after you have ſkimmed off the fat, boil it down till it is of a glaze, then put it over the fowl. You may add juſt what you pleaſe to the ſauce. A ragoo of ſweetbreads, cocks'-combs, truffles, and morels; or muſhrooms, with force-meat balls, look very pretty. *Glaſſe*, 74.

A Fowl with its own gravy.

Truſs a fowl for boiling; lard it through and through with bacon, ham, and parſley; put it in a pan of much its bigneſs, with a little butter, two or three ſlices of peeled lemon, a faggot, three cloves, ſliced onions, and carrots, pepper and ſalt, a little broth, and a glaſs of white wine; ſtew ſlowly till done; ſkim and ſtrain the ſauce, and ſerve with the fowl. You may alſo do it the ſame without larding. *Dalrymple*, 214.

A ragoo of Fowls.

Take a large capon, or two pullets, and blanch nicely in a morſel of butter or ſcraped bacon, but cut off your pinions and feet, and tuck in the legs. Prepare your ragoo in the following manner: get a ſweetbread of veal, or two of lambs, the fat livers of a turkey or fowls, ſome cocks' combs, three or four muſhrooms, a thin ſlice or two of lemon; blanch all well with a knot or two of eggs, cut all into very ſmall dice, and ſtew in a ladle of cullis; you may add to it three or four gizzards, and a few cock's combs, boiled very tender; fill up the bellies of your fowls or capon, and ſew it up at both ends, but make a reſerve of ſome of your ragoo to pour over; put them upon a lark-ſpit acroſs, and tie upon another; lard them with bacon,

I   cover

cover with paper, and roaft them foftly, that they may be nice and white; ftrew in a little minced parfley, a morfel of fhallot; fqueeze in the juice of a lemon or orange, and ferve up with the ragoo under. Remember to draw the threads out. *Verral*, 89.

To force a fowl.

Take a large fowl, pick it clean, and cut it down the back, take out the entrails, and take the fkin off whole; cut the flefh from the bones, and chop it with half a pint of oyfters, one ounce of beef marrow, a little pepper and falt; mix it up with cream, then lay the meat on the bones, and draw the fkin over it, and few up the back; then cut large thin flices of bacon, and lay them over the breaft of your fowl, tie the bacon on with a packthread in diamonds; it will take an hour roafting by a moderate fire. Make a good brown gravy fauce, pour it upon your difh, take the bacon off and lay in your fowl, and ferve it up. Garnifh with pickles, mufhrooms, or oyfters.— It is proper for a fide difh for dinner, or top for fupper. *Raffald*, 124.

Mr. *Farley*, in page 120, gives the above receipt, with only the following addition:—" Serve it up garnifhed with oyfters, mufhrooms, or pickles."

A Fowl fervant fafhion.

Trufs a fowl for roafting, make a force meat with the liver, chopped parfley, fhallots, butter, pepper and falt; ftuff the fowl with it, wrap it in buttered paper, and roaft it. When three parts done, take off the paper, bafte it with yolks of eggs beat up with melted butter, and a good deal of bread crumbs; finifh roafting; it muft be of a fine yellow colour. Make a fauce with a little butter, one anchovy chopped, a few capers, a little flour, broth, pepper, and falt, and a little nutmeg; thicken with a liafon, and ferve under the fowl. *Dalrymple*, 215.

To marinade a Fowl.

Raife the fkin from the breaft bone of a large fowl with your finger, then take a veal fweetbread and cut it fmall, a few oyfters, a few mufhrooms, an anchovy, fome pepper, a little nutmeg, fome lemon peel, and a little thyme; chop all together fmall, and mix it with the yolk of an egg, ftuff it in between the fkin and the flefh, but take great care that you do not break the fkin; and then ftuff what oyfters you pleafe into the body of the fowl. You may lard the breaft of the fowl with bacon, if you chufe it. Paper the breaft, and roaft it. Make good gravy, and garnifh with lemon. You may add a few mufhrooms to the fauce. *Glaffe*, 78. *Farley*, 123.

Fowls

Fowls stuffed.

Make a force meat with half a pound of beef suet, as much crumb of bread grated fine, the meat of a fowl cut very small; beat these in a mortar, and a pound of veal with them, some truffles, morels, and mushrooms, cut small, a few sweet herbs and parsley shred fine, some grated nutmeg, pepper, salt, and grated lemon-peel; bone the fowls, fill them with this force-meat, and roast them. For sauce—good gravy, with truffles and morels. The fowls may be larded.

To hash Fowls.

Let your fowl be cut up as for eating, put it into a tossing-pan, with half a pint of gravy, a tea-spoonful of lemon pickle, a little mushroom catchup, a slice of lemon, thicken it with flour and butter; just before you dish it up, put in a spoonful of good cream, lay sippets round your dish, and serve it up. *Cole*, 145.

Another way.

Cut your fowl to pieces, and put it into some gravy, with a little cream, catchup, or mushroom powder, grated lemon-peel, and nutmeg, a few oysters and their liquor, a piece of butter mixed with flour; keep it stirring till the butter is melted, lay sippets round the dish. *Mason*, 264.

Pullets à-la-St. Menehout.

After having trussed the legs in the body, slit them along the back, spread them open on a table, take out the thigh-bones, and beat them with a rolling-pin; then season them with pepper, salt, mace, nutmeg, and sweet herbs; after that, take a pound and an half of veal cut into thin slices, and lay it in a stew-pan of a convenient size to stew the pullets in; cover it, and set it over a stove or slow fire; and when it begins to cleave to the pan, stir in a little flour, shake the pan about till it be a little brown; then pour in as much broth as will stew the fowls, stir it together, put in a little whole pepper, an onion, and a little piece of bacon or ham; then lay in your fowls, cover them close, and let them stew half an hour; then take them out, lay them on the gridiron to brown on the inside; strew them over with the yolk of an egg, some crumbs of bread, and baste them with a little butter; let them be of a fine brown, and boil the gravy till there is about enough for sauce; strain it, put a few mushrooms in, and a little piece of butter rolled in flour. Lay the pullets in the dish, and pour in the sauce. Garnish with lemon.

Note.—You may brown them in an oven, or fry them, which you please. *Glasse*, 75.

To stew a Fowl.

Truss a fowl for boiling; put it in a stew-pan with a piece of butter, chopped parsley, shallots, and mushrooms; soak it on a slow fire about a quarter of an hour, turning it often; then put it in another stew-pan, first garnished with slices of veal and ham, and all the first seasoning; cover with slices of bacon; soak it for a quarter of an hour longer, then add a little whole pepper and salt, a little broth and white wine; finish it on a slow fire, then skim and strain the braze. When ready, add the squeeze of a lemon, and serve upon the fowl, being well wiped from fat. *Dalrymple*, 219.

A nice way to dress a cold Fowl.

Peel off all the skin of the fowl, and pull the flesh off the bones in as large pieces as you can; then dredge it with a little flour, and fry it a nice brown in butter; toss it up in rich gravy, well seasoned, and thicken it with a piece of butter rolled in flour. Just before you send it up, squeeze in the juice of a lemon. *Raffald*, 75.

To dress a cold Fowl or Pigeon.

Cut them in four quarters, beat up an egg or two, according to what you dress, grate a little nutmeg in, a little salt, some parsley chopped, a few crumbs of bread; beat them well together, dip them in this batter, and have ready some dripping hot in a stew-pan, in which fry them of a fine light brown. Have ready a little good gravy, thickened with a little flour, minced with a spoonful of catchup; lay the fry in the dish, and pour the sauce over. Garnish with lemon, and a few mushrooms, if you have any. A cold rabbit eats well done thus.

Chickens in savoury Jelly.

Take two chickens and roast them. Boil some calves' feet to a strong jelly; then take out the feet, and skim off the fat; beat up the whites of three eggs, and mix them with half a pint of white wine vinegar, the juice of three lemons, a blade or two of mace, a few pepper-corns, and a little salt. Put them to your jelly, and when it has boiled five or six minutes, strain it several times through a jelly-bag till it is very clear. Then put a little in the bottom of a bowl large enough to hold your chickens, and when they are cold, and the jelly set, lay them in with their breasts down. Then fill your bowl quite full with the rest of your jelly, which you must take care to keep from setting, so that when you pour it into the bowl it will not break. Let it stand all night; and the next day put your bason into warm water, pretty near the top. As soon as you find it loose in the bason, lay your dish over it, and turn it out whole. *Farley*, 120.

Chickens

Chickens Cavalier fashion.

Truss as for boiling as many chickens as you want; marinade them two hours in oil, with slices of peeled lemon, parsley, shallots, a clove of garlick, thyme, laurel, salt, and spices: tie them up in slices of lard and paper, with as much of the marinade as you can; broil on a slow fire. When done, take off the paper, lard, and herbs. Serve with what sauce you think proper. *Dalrymple*, 188.

To make artificial Chickens or Pigeons.

Make a rich force-meat with veal, lamb, or chickens, seasoned with pepper, salt, parsley, a shallot, a piece of fat bacon, a little butter, and the yolk of an egg; work it up in the shape of pigeons or chickens, putting the foot of the bird you intend it for in the middle, so as just to appear at the bottom; roll the force-meat very well in the yolk of an egg, then in the crumbs of bread, send them to the oven, and bake it a light brown; do not let them touch each other; put them on tin plates well buttered, as you send them to the oven. You may send them to table dry, or gravy in the dish, just as you like. *Raffald*, 126. *Farley*, 120.

Chicken in Jelly.

Pour some jelly into a bowl; when cold, lay in a cold roasted chicken, breast downward; fill up the bowl with jelly just warm, but as little as possible so as not to be set; when quite cold, set the bowl in warm water, just to loosen the jelly, turn it out. Put the chicken into the jelly the day before it is wanted. *Cole*, 147.

Chickens after the Scotch manner.

Singe the chickens, wash and then dry them in a clean cloth; cut them into quarters, and put them into a sauce-pan with just water enough to cover them; put in a little bunch of parsley, a little chopped parsley, and a blade or two of mace, cover them close down; beat up five or six eggs with the whites, and when the liquor boils, pour the eggs into it. When the chickens are enough, take out the bunch of parsley, and send them to table with the liquor in a deep dish. They must be well skimmed while they are doing. *Mason*, 267.

Chickens roasted with Force-meat and Cucumbers.

Take two chickens, dress them very neatly, break the breast-bone, and make force-meat thus:—Take the flesh of a fowl, and of two pigeons, with some slices of ham or bacon; chop them all well together, take the crumb of a penny-loaf soaked in milk and boiled, then set to cool. When it is cold, mix it all together; season it with beaten mace, nutmeg, pepper, and a little salt, a very little thyme, some parsley, and a little lemon-

I 3

peel,

peel, with the yolks of two eggs; then fill your fowls, fplit them, and tie them at both ends. After you have papered the breaft, take four cucumbers, cut them in two, and lay them in falt and water two or three hours before; then dry them, and fill them with fome of the force-meat (which you muft take care to fave) and tie them with a packthread; flour them, and fry them of a fine brown. When your chickens are enough, lay them in the difh, and untie your cucumbers, but take care the meat does not come out; then lay them round the chickens. with the flat fide downwards, and the narrow end upwards, You muft have fome rich fried gravy, and pour into the difh; then garnifh with lemon.

Note.—One large fowl done this way, with the cucumbers laid round it, looks pretty, and is a very good difh. *Glaffe*, 77.

A Currey the Indian way.

Take two fmall chickens, fkin them, and cut them as for a fricaffee, wafh them clean, and ftew them in about a quart of water for about five minutes, then ftrain off the liquor, and put the chickens in a clean difh; take three large onions, chop them fmall, and fry them in about two ounces of butter; then put in the chickens, and fry them together till they are brown; take a quarter of an ounce of turmerick, a large fpoonful of ginger and beaten pepper together, and a little falt to your pa-late; ftrew all thefe ingredients over the chickens, whilft fry-ing, then pour in the liquor, and let it ftew about half an hour; then put in a quarter of a pint of cream, and the juice of two lemons, and ferve it up. The ginger, pepper, and turmerick, muft be beat very fine. *Cole*, 148.

To ftew Chickens.

Take two fine chickens, and half boil them. Then take them up in a pewter difh, and cut them up, feparating every joint one from the other, and taking out the breaft bones. If the fowls do not produce liquor fufficient, add a few fpoonfuls of the water in which they were boiled, and put in a blade of mace and a little falt. Cover it clofe with another difh, and fet it over a ftove or chafing-difh of coals. Let it ftew till the chickens are enough, and then fend them hot to the table. *Farley*, 69, from *Glaffe*, 79.

N. B. The above is a very pretty difh for any fick perfon, or for a lying-in lady. For change, it is better than butter, and the fauce is very agreeable and pretty.

** You may do rabbits, partridges, or moor-game, this way.

To force Chickens.

Roaft your chickens better than half, take off the fkin, then the meat, and chop it fmall with fhred parfley and crumbs of
bread,

bread, pepper and falt, and a little good cream ; then put in the
meat, and clofe the fkin ; brown it with a falamander, and ferve
it up with white fauce. *Raffald*, 126.

Stewed Chickens, or Matlot.

Cut a carp with the roe in pieces; alfo a chicken cut in
pieces, one dozen and an half of fmall onions, a flice of ham, a
faggot of parfley and green onions, thyme, laurel, bafil, and four
cloves; put all together in a ftew-pan with a piece of butter;
fimmer a little on a flow fire ; then add broth, cullis, a little
white wine, flour, pepper, and falt ; let it ftew till the chicken
is done, &c. and the fauce reduced ; take out the faggot and
ham, add a chopped anchovy and a few capers, and place the
chicken on the difh ; fkim the fauce, and ferve it with the
meat, Garnifh with fried bread. *Clermont*, 198.

Chickens Chiringrate.

Having cut off the feet of your chickens, beat the breaft-bone
flat with a rolling-pin, but take care you do not break the fkin.
Flour them, fry them of a fine brown in butter, and then drain
all the fat out of the pan, but leave the chickens in. Lay a
pound of gravy beef, cut very thin, over your chicken, and a
piece of veal cut very thin, a little mace, two or three cloves,
fome whole pepper, an onion, a little bunch of fweet herbs, and
a piece of carrot, Then pour in a quart of boiling water, cover
it clofe, and let it ftew for a quarter of an hour. Then take
out the chickens, and keep them hot ; let the gravy boil till it is
quite rich and good, and then ftrain it off and put it into your
pan again, with two fpoonfuls of red wine, and a few mufhrooms. Put in your chickens to heat, then take them up, lay
them into your difh, and pour the fauce over them. Garnifh
with lemon and a few flices of ham broiled. *Glaffe*, 79. *Farley*, 122.

Chickens in Afpic.

Put the pinions, livers, and gizzards into two fmall chickens,
with a piece of butter, fome pepper and falt ; cover them with
fat bacon, then with paper ; fpit them on a long fkewer, tie
them to a fpit, roaft them. When cold, cut them up, put them
into the following fauce, fhake them round in it, let them lie a
few minutes before they are difhed. Take what cullis is fufficient for fauce, heat it with fmall green onions chopped, or
fhallot, a little tarragon and green mint, pepper and falt. *Mafon*, 265.

Chickens Italian fafhion.

Trufs two chickens as for boiling, lard them with ham and
bacon, give them a fry in butter or oil, then put them into a
ftew-pan, with flices of veal and the butter they were fried in,
three cloves, a faggot, a clove of garlick, pepper, falt, and half

I 4

a lemon

a lemon peeled and fliced; cover with flices of bacon, foak it very flowly about half an hour, then add about a gill of white wine. When done, fkim and fift the fauce, add a piece of butter rolled in flour, and ferve it with the chickens. *Dalrymple*, 191.

Chickens and Tongues.

Boil fix fmall chickens very white; then take fix hogs'-tongues boiled and peeled, a cauliflower boiled whole in milk and water, and a good deal of fpinach boiled green. Then lay your cauliflower in the middle, the chickens clofe all round, and the tongues round them with the roots outwards, and the fpinach in little heaps between the tongues. Garnifh with little pieces of bacon toafted, and lay a little piece on each of the tongues. This is a good difh for a large company. *Glaffe*, 80. *Farley*, 122.

Chicken Pulled.

Take a chicken that has been roafted or boiled, if under-done the better, cut off the legs and the rump and fide-bones together; pull all the white part in little flakes, free from fkin; tofs it up with a little cream, thickened with a piece of butter mixed with flour; ftir it till the butter is melted, with pounded mace, whole pepper, and falt, a little lemon-juice. Put this into a difh, lay the rump in the middle, the legs at each end, peppered, falted, and broiled. *Cole*, 151.

To fry cold Chicken.

Quarter your chicken, rub the quarters with yolk of egg; ftrew on bread crumbs, pepper, falt, nutmeg, grated lemon-peel, and chopped parfley; fry them; thicken fome gravy with a little flour, add chyan, mufhroom powder, or catchup, a little lemon-juice; pour it into the difh with the chickens. *Mafon*, 265.

To broil Chickens.

Slit your chickens down the back, feafon them with pepper and falt, and lay them on the gridiron over a clear fire, and at a great diftance. Let the infide continue next the fire till it is nearly half done; then turn them, taking care that the flefhy fides do not burn, and let them broil till they are of a fine brown. Have good gravy-fauce, with fome mufhrooms, and garnifh them with lemon and the liver broiled, and the giz-zards cut, flafhed, and broiled, with pepper and falt; or you may ufe any other fauce you fancy. *Farley*, 50.

Another way.

Cut your chicken down the back, pepper and falt it, broil it; pour over it white mufhroom-fauce, or melted butter with pickled mufhrooms. *Mafon*, 265.

To

To mince a Chicken or Veal, for perfons who are fick or weak.

Mince a chicken, or fome veal, very fine, take off the fkin; juft boil as much water as will moiften it, and no more, with a little falt, grate a little nutmeg; then throw a little flour over it, and when the water boils, put in the meat. Keep fhaking it about over the fire a minute; then have ready two or three very thin fippets, toafted nice and brown, laid in the plate, and pour the mince-meat over it. *Glaffe*, 242.

Chickens' Feet with Force-meat.

When you make a fricaffee or any fuch thing, preferve the feet to make a difh of this fort; ftrip off the ftockings by fcalding, tie them up in a bundle, and ftew them in a braze; boil them very tender, with a little feafoning, dry them in a cloth, and prepare fuch a force-meat as you think proper; fill up the claws with it, dip them into fome beaten eggs, and crumb them well: do it a fecond time and prefs it well on, and fry them in plenty of lard, and ferve them up without any fauce in the difh, with a heap of fried parfley under them.

Fowls or chickens feet make a pretty fecond difh, done many different ways, either in a little brown fauce, with afparagus-tops, peas, artichoke bottoms, &c. or in a fricaffee, or white fauce of any kind. *Verral*, 166.

Ducks à-la-braze.

Drefs and finge your ducks, lard them quite through with bacon rolled in fhred parfley, thyme, onions, beaten mace, cloves, pepper, and falt; put in the bottom of a ftew pan a few flices of fat bacon, the fame of hafh or gammon of bacon, two or three flices of veal or beef; lay your ducks in with the breaft down, and cover the ducks with flices, the fame as put under them; cut in a carrot or two, a turnip, one onion, a head of celery, a blade of mace, four or five cloves, a little whole pepper; cover them clofe down, and let them fimmer a little over a gentle fire till the breaft is a light brown; then put in fome broth or water, cover them as clofe down, again as you can; ftew them gently between two or three hours till enough; then take parfley, onion, or fhallot, two anchovies, a few gerkins or capers; chop them all very fine, put them into a ftew-pan with part of the liquor from the ducks, a little browning, and the juice of half a lemon; boil it up, and cut the ends of the bacon even with the breaft of your ducks, lay them on your difh, pour the fauce hot upon them, and ferve them up. *Raffald*, 128. *Farley*, 118.

Another way.

Lard your duck, put a flice or two of beef at the bottom of the veffel, then the duck, a bit of bacon, and fome more beef fliced, a carrot, an onion, a flice of lemon, whole pepper, a
bunch

bunch of fweet herbs ; cover this clofe, fet it over the fire a few minutes, fhake in fome flour, pour in near a quart of beef-broth or boiling water, a little red wine heated ; ftew it about half an hour, ftrain the fauce, fkim it, put to it chyan, and more wine, if neceffary, fhallot and tarragon chopped, a very little juice of lemon. If agreeable, add artichoke-bottoms, boiled and quartered. *Mafon* 272.

Macedonian Ducks.

Cut four artichoke-bottoms, each into pieces, and put them into boiling water, with about a pint of garden beans, firft fcalded and hufked ; boil thefe together till almoft done, then drain them, and put the whole into the ftew-pan, with a good piece of butter, chopped mufhrooms, a little winter favoury, parfley, and fhallots, all finely chopped ; add a little flour, two fpoonfuls of veal gravy, and a glafs of white wine, and fimmer flowly till all is well done ; reduce the fauce to a proper confiftence, and when ready to ferve, add a little cullis, a lemon-fqueeze, falt, and pepper. Serve this ragoo under two ducks, cut into quarters, and brazed in a well-feafoned braze, with flices of veal and lard as ufual. *Clermont*, 258.

Ducks à-la-mode,

Slit two ducks down the back, and bone them carefully, make a force-meat of the crumb of a penny loaf, four ounces of fat bacon fcraped, a little parfley, thyme, lemon-peel, two fhallots or onions fhred very fine, with pepper, falt, and nutmeg to your tafte, and two eggs ; ftuff your ducks with it, and few them up, lard them down each fide of the breaft with bacon, dredge them well with flour, and put them in a Dutch oven to brown ; then put them into a ftew-pan, with three pints of gravy, a glafs of red wine, a tea-fpoonful of lemon-pickle, a large one of walnut and mufhroom catchup, one of browning, and one anchovy, with chyan pepper to your tafte ; ftew them gently over a flow fire for an hour. When enough, thicken your gravy, and put in a few truffles and morels ; ftrain your gravy, and pour it upon them. You may à-la-mode a goofe in the fame way, *Raffald*, 129.

To boil Ducks the French way.

Lard your ducks, and let them be half roafted ; then take them off the fpit, put them into a large earthen pipkin, with half a pint of red wine, and a pint of good gravy, fome chefnuts, firft roafted and peeled, half a pint of large oyfters, the liquor ftrained, and the beards taken off, two or three little onions minced fmall, a very little ftripped thyme, mace, pepper, and a little ginger beat fine ; cover it clofe, and let them ftew half an hour over a flow fire, and the cruft of a French roll grated when you put in your gravy and wine.—When they are enough, take them up, and pour the fauce over them.

To

To boil Ducks, with Onion Sauce.

Scald your ducks and draw them, put them in warm water for a few minutes, then take them out ; put them in an earthen pot, pour over them a pint of boiling milk, let them lie in it two or three hours. When you take them out, dredge them well with flour, put them in a copper of cold water, put on your cover, let them boil slowly twenty minutes, then take them out, and smother them with onion-sauce. *Raffald*, 59.

Wild Duck, Wigeon, or Easterling, in perfection.

Half roast them; when they come to table, slice the breast, strew on pepper and salt, pour on a little red wine, and squeeze the juice of an orange or a lemon over ; put some gravy to this, set the plate on a lamp, cut up the bird, let it remain over the lamp till enough, turning it. *Mason*, 273.

To boil a Duck à-la-Francoise.

Put a pint of rich beef gravy into two dozen roasted chesnuts peeled, with a few leaves of thyme, two small onions (if agreeable , a little whole pepper, and a race of ginger; then take a fine tame duck, lard it, and half roast it ; put it into the gravy, let it stew ten minutes, put in a quarter of a pint of red wine. When the duck is enough, take it out, boil up the gravy to a proper thickness; skim it very clean from fat, lay the duck in the dish, and pour the sauce over it. *Cole*, 155.

To dress a Duck with green Peas.

Put a deep stew-pan over the fire, with a piece of fresh butter; singe your duck and flour it, turn it in the pan two or three minutes, then pour out all the fat, but let the duck remain in the pan; put to it a pint of good gravy, a pint of peas, two lettuces cut small, a small bundle of sweet herbs, a little pepper and salt; cover them close, and let them stew for half an hour; now and then give the pan a shake. When they are just done, grate in a little nutmeg, and put in a very little beaten mace, and thicken it either with a piece of butter rolled in flour, or the yolk of an egg beat up with two or three spoonfuls of cream; shake it all together for three or four minutes, take out the sweet herbs, lay the duck in the dish, and pour the sauce over it. You may garnish with boiled mint chopped, or let it alone. *Glasse*, 82.

Another way.

Half roast your duck, put it into some good gravy, with a little mint, and three or four sage leaves chopped; stew this half an hour, thicken the gravy with a little flour, throw in half a pint of green peas boiled, or some celery, then take out the mint. *Cole*, 156.

T.

To haſh a Wild Duck.

Having cut up your duck as for eating, put it into a toſſing-pan, with a ſpoonful of good gravy, the ſame of red wine, and an onion ſliced exceedingly thin. When it has boiled two or three minutes, lay the duck in the diſh, and pour the gravy over it. You may add a tea-ſpoonful of caper liquor, or a little browning; but remember that the gravy muſt not be thickened. *Farley*, 70.

To haſh Ducks different ways.

Roaſt two ducks till three parts done, and let them cool; then cut the breaſt in thin ſlices, and take care to preſerve the gravy. The legs will ſerve for another diſh, which you may dreſs by wrapping them in a caul with a good force-meat, and ſerve with cullis ſauce. For the fillets, cut cucumbers, and marinade them about an hour, with a little vinegar, ſalt, and one onion ſliced; then take out the onion, ſqueeze the cucumbers in a cloth, and put them into a ſtew-pan with a bit of butter, a ſlice of ham, a little broth, flour, and veal gravy; boil ſlowly, ſkim it well, take out the ham, and add the meat to it, to warm, without boiling. You may alſo do the ſame with chopped truffles, or muſhrooms, or any thing elſe you think proper, according to ſeaſon. A cold roaſted duck will anſwer much the ſame end for this diſh. *Clermont*, 260.

Another way.

When cut to pieces, flour it; put into a ſtew-pan ſome gravy, a little red wine, ſhallot chopped, ſalt and pepper, a piece of lemon; boil this, put in the duck, toſs it up, take out the lemon.—Toaſted ſippets. *Maſon*, 273.

To dreſs a Wild Duck in perfection.

Half roaſt your duck, lay it in a diſh, carve it, but leave the joints hanging together: throw a little pepper and ſalt, and ſqueeze the juice of a lemon over it; turn it on the breaſt, and preſs it hard with a plate, and add to its own gravy two or three ſpoonfuls of good gravy; cover it cloſe with another diſh, and ſet it over a ſtove ten minutes; then ſend it to table hot in the diſh it was done in, and garniſh with lemon. You may add a little red wine, and a ſhallot cut ſmall, if you like it; but it is apt to make the duck eat hard, unleſs you firſt heat the wine, and pour it in juſt as it is done, *Cole*, 157.

To ſtew Ducks.

Lard three young ducks down each ſide the breaſt, duſt them with flour, and ſet them before the fire to brown; then put them in a ſtew-pan, with a quart of water, a pint of red wine, one ſpoonful of walnut catchup, the ſame browning, an anchovy, half a lemon, a clove of garlic, a bundle of ſweet herbs,

chyan

chyan pepper to your tafte; let them ftew flowly for half an
hour, or till they are tender; lay them on a difh and keep them
hot, fkim off the fat, ftrain the gravy through a hair fieve, add
to it a few morels and truffles, boil it quick till reduced to a little
more than half a pint, pour it over your ducks, and ferve it up.
It is proper for a fide-difh for dinner, or bottom for fupper.
Raffald, 127.

Duckling rolled.

Make a good force-meat with breafts of roafted poultry, as
ufual; cut a pretty large duckling in two, bone it thoroughly,
and lay on the force-meat; roll it up, tie flices of lard round it,
and boil it in a little broth, with a glafs of white wine, a faggot,
and two cloves.   When done, fqueeze the fat gently out, and
wipe the duck clean.   Serve with what fauce you pleafe.—
Small ducklings may be dreffed in the fame manner, obferving
only that they muft not be cut in two.   *Clermont*, 255.

Pigeons en Compote.

Take fix young pigeons, and fkewer them as for boiling;
make a force-meat thus:—grate the crumb of a penny loaf,
half a pound of fat bacon, fhred fome fweet herbs and parfley
fine, two fhallots, or a little onion, a little lemon-peel, a little
grated nutmeg; feafon it with pepper and falt, and mix it up
with the yolk of two eggs; put it into the craws and bellies,
lard them down the breaft, and fry them brown with a little
butter; then put them in a ftew-pan, with a pint of ftrong
brown gravy, a gill of white wine; ftew them three quarters of
an hour, thicken it with a little butter rolled in flour, feafon
with falt and chyan pepper, put the pigeons in the difh, and
ftrain the gravy over them.   Lay fome hot force-meat balls
round them, and fend them up hot.   *Glaffe*, 91.

Another way.

Trufs the pigeons with their legs in their bodies, but firft
ftuff them with good force-meat (made in the fame manner as
for pigeons à-la-daube); let them be parboiled, then lard them
with bits of bacon, feafoned with pepper, fpices, minced chives,
and parfley; let them ftew as gently as poffible.   While they
are ftewing, make a ragoo of cocks' combs, fowls' livers, truffles,
morels, and mufhrooms; melt a little bacon in a frying-pan,
and put them in, fhake the pan round two or three times; then
put in fome rich gravy, let it fimmer a little, then put in fome
cullis of veal and ham to thicken it.   Take the pigeons, drain
them, and put them into this ragoo.   Let them juft fimmer in
it, then take them up, put them into a difh, and pour the ragoo
over them.   *Mafon*, 278.

Pigeons à-la-duxelle.

Cut off the feet and pinions of four or five pigeons, and fplit
them

them down the breaſt; then take out the liver, and flat them
with a cleaver.   Make a hot marinade of ſome ſcraped bacon,
feaſoned with a muſhroom or two, green onions, pepper, ſalt,
thyme, and parſley, and a little nutmeg.   Fry all a few minutes,
and let the pigeons be heated through in it, and let them remain till you put them upon your gridiron.   Take a thin ſlice
of ham for each pigeon, and put them with the ham always at
top.   I mean, when you turn your pigeons, turn your ham upon them.   For your ſauce, take a ladle of gravy, ſome ſweet
baſil, a little thyme, parſley, and ſhallot, minced very fine, and
a few ſlices of muſhrooms, boiled all together a few minutes;
diſh up, your breaſt downwards, let your ham continue upon
them, and pour your ſauce over, with the juice of a lemon or
orange.   *Verral*, 138.

Pigeons à-la-daube.

Put a layer of bacon in a large ſauce-pan, then a layer of veal,
a layer of coarſe beef, and another little layer of veal, about a
pound of beef, and a pound of veal, cut very thin; a piece of
carrot, a bundle of ſweet herbs, an onion, ſome black and white
pepper, a blade or two of mace, and four or five cloves.   Cover
the ſauce-pan cloſe, ſet it over a ſlow fire, draw it till it is brown,
to make the gravy of a fine light brown.   Then put in a quart
of boiling water, and let it ſtew till the gravy is quite rich and
good.   Then ſtrain it off, and ſkim off all the fat.   In the mean
time, ſtuff the bellies of the pigeons with force-meat, made
thus:—Take a pound of veal, a pound of beef ſuet, and beat
both fine in a mortar; an equal quantity of crumbs of bread,
ſome pepper, ſalt, nutmeg, beaten mace, a little lemon-peel
cut ſmall, ſome parſley cut ſmall, and a very little thyme ſtripped.   Mix all together with the yolks of two eggs, fill the
pigeons, and flat the breaſt down.   Then flour them, and fry
them in freſh butter a little brown.   Then pour the fat clean
out of the pan, and put the gravy to the pigeons.   Cover them
cloſe, and let them ſtew a quarter of an hour, or till you think
they are quite enough.   Then take them up, lay them in a diſh,
and pour in your ſauce.   On each pigeon lay a bay-leaf, and on
the leaf a ſlice of bacon.   You may garniſh with a lemon
notched; but it will do without.   You may leave out the ſtuffing, as it will be rich enough without it.   *Farley*, 125.

Pigeons in diſguiſe.

Draw and truſs your pigeons, feaſon them with pepper and
ſalt; make a nice puff-paſte, and roll each pigeon in a piece of
it; tie them in a cloth, and take care the paſte does not break;
boil them in a great deal of water.   They will take an hour
and an half boiling.   Take great care when they are untied they
do not break.   Put them into a diſh, and pour a little good
gravy to them.   *Cole*, 159.

Pigeons

Pigeons à-la-charmante.

Scald five or six small pigeons, and braze them with a few slices of lard and peeled lemon, pepper, salt, a faggot of sweet herbs, and broth. Lard three or four sweetbreads as for frican-deaus, and put these last into a stew-pan by themselves, with some broth, a few thin slices of veal fillet, a faggot, a few chibols, two cloves, and a little basil. Braze slowly, and when done, sift and skim the braze, and reduce it to a glaze, to rub over the larded side of.the sweetbreads; add a little consommee, to gather the remainder of the glaze which may stick to the bottom of the pan; sift it again through a sieve, and add a little more pepper and salt (if necessary), and a good squeeze of lemon. Intermix the pigeons and sweetbreads upon the table-dish, and pour the sauce over the former, but not over the latter, as it would spoil the colour of the glaze. *Cole*, 160.

Pigeons in Fricandeau.

Pick, draw, and wash your pigeons very clean, stuff the craws, and lard them down the sides of the breast, fry them in butter a fine brown, and then put them into a tossing-pan with a quart of gravy. Stew them till they are tender, then take off the fat, and put in a tea-spoonful of lemon-pickle, a large spoonful of browning, the same of walnut catchup, a little chy-an, and salt. Thicken your gravy, and add half an ounce of morels, and four yolks of hard eggs. Lay the pigeons in your dish, and put the morels and eggs round them, and strain your sauce over them. Garnish with barberries and lemon-peel, and serve it up. *Raffald*, 132. *Farley*, 125.

Pigeons au Soleil.

Make a force-meat with half a pound of veal, a quarter of a pound of mutton, and two ounces of beef. Beat them in a mortar, with some pepper, salt, and mace, till they are a paste. Then take the yolks of three or four eggs, beat them up well, and put them into a plate. Mix also a quarter of a pound of grated bread, and two ounces of flour, put it into another plate. Put on a stew-pan with a little rich beef-gravy, tie up three or four cloves in a bit of muslin, and put into the gravy. Put in the pigeons, let them stew till they are almost enough, then take them up, and set them before a fire to keep warm; then set on a frying-pan with some good beef-dripping, enough to cover the pigeons. When it boils, take them, one at a time, roll them in the meat that was beat, then in the yolk of egg; roll them in it till they are quite wet, then strew over with the bread and flour, put them into the boiling dripping, and let them remain till they are of a fine brown. *Mason*, 277.

Pigeons Surtout.

Having forced your pigeons, lay a slice of bacon on the breast, and a slice of veal beat with the back of a knife, and seasoned
with

with mace, pepper, and falt.   Tie it on with a fmall packthread,
or two fmall fine fkewers are better.   Spit them on a fine bird
fpit, roaft them and bafte them with a piece of butter, then
with the yolk of an egg, and then bafte them again with the
crumbs of bread, a little nutmeg, and fweet herbs.   When
they are enough, lay them in your difh.   Have good gravy
ready with truffles, morels, and mufhrooms, to pour into your
difh ; and garnifh with lemon. *Farley*, 126.

Pigeons tranfmogrified.

Pick and clean fix fmall young pigeons, but do not cut off
their heads ; cut off their pinions, and boil them ten minutes, in
water, then cut off the ends of fix large cucumbers and fcrape
out the feeds ; put in your pigeons, but let the heads be out at
the ends of the cucumbers, and ftick a bunch of barberries in
their bills ; and then put them into a tolling-pan with a pint
veal gravy, a little anchovy, a glafs of red wine, a fpoonful of
browning, a little flice of lemon, chyan and falt to your tafte ;
ftew them feven minutes. take them out, thicken your gravy
with a little butter rolled in flour ; boil it up, and ftrain it over
your pigeons, and ferve them up.   *Raffald*, 150.

Pigeons à-la-braze.

Pick, draw, and truls fome large pigeons, then take a ftew-
pan, and lay at the bottom fome flices of bacon, veal, and
onions ; feafon the pigeons with pepper, falt, fome fpice beat
fine, and fome fweet herbs ; lay them into a ftew-pan, then lay
upon them fome more flices of veal and bacon ; let them ftew
very gently over a ftove, the top of the ftew-pan put down very
clofe.   When they are ftewed make a ragoo with veal fweetbreads, truffles, morels, champignons ; the fweet breads muft be
blanched, and put into a ftew-pan with a ladleful of gravy, a little cullis, the truffles, morels, &c.   Let them all ftew together
with the pigeons. When they are enough, put them into a difh,
and pour the ragoo over them. *Cole*, 161.

A pupton of Pigeons.

Take favoury force-meat, rolled out like a pafte, put it in
a butter difh, lay a layer of very thin bacon, fquab pigeons,
fliced fweet-bread, afparagus tops, mufhrooms, cocks' combs, a
palate boiled tender and cut in peices, and the yolks of hard
eggs.   Make another force-mea andlay over like a pie ; bake
it, and when enough, turn it into a difh, and pour gravy round
it. *Glaffe*, 91. *Farley*, 127.

Pigeons in Pimlico.

Take the livers, with fome fat and lean of ham or bacon,
mufhrooms, truffles, parfley, and fweet herbs; feafon with beaten
mace,

mace, pepper, and falt; beat all this together, with two raw eggs, put it into the bellies, roll them all in a thin flice of veal, over them a thin flice of bacon; wrap them up in white paper, fpit them on a fmall fpit, and roaft them. In the mean time make for them a ragoo of truffles and mufhrooms, chopped fmall, with parfley cut fmall; put to it half a pint of good veal gravy; thicken with a peice of butter rolled in flour. An hour will do your pigeons. Bafte them. When enough, lay them in your difh, take off the paper, and pour your fauce over them. Garnifh with patties made thus :—Take veal and cold ham, beef fuet, an equal quantity, fome mufhrooms, fweet herbs, and fpice; chop them fmall, fet them on the fire, and moiften with milk or cream; then make a little puff-pafte, roll it, and make little patties about an inch deep and two inches long; fill them with the above ingredients, cover them clofe, and bake them; lay fix of them round a difh. This makes a fine difh for a firft courfe. *Glaffe*, 93.

Pigeons Royal fafhion.

Singe what number you pleafe of pigeons that are of an equal bignefs, put a peeled truffle in each, and give them a fry in butter, with chopped mufhrooms, parfley, chibols, a flice of ham, pepper, and falt; then put them into a faucepan to braze, with a few flices of veal firft fcalded, and the firft feafoning over the pigeons; cover them with thin flices of bacon and a laurel leaf, and put a fheet of white paper over the whole. Stop the pan clofe, and fimmer on a flow fire till they are quite tender. Take out the pigeons, and wipe off the fat; fift the braze, boil a moment to fkim it very clean; and when ready, add a lemon-fqueeze, and ferve it upon the pigeons. *Clermont*, 243.

Boiled Pigeons and Bacon.

Take fix young pigeons, wafh them clean, turn their legs under their wings, boil them in milk and water by themfelves twenty minutes; have ready boiled a fquare piece of bacon, take off the fkin and brown it, put the bacon in the middle of your difh, and lay the pigeons round it, and lumps of ftewed fpinach; pour plain melted butter over them, and fend parfley and butter in a boat. *Raffald*, 133.

Pigeons à-la-fouffel.

Bone four pigeons, and make a force-meat as for pigeons compote. Stuff them, and put them into a ftew-pan with a pint of veal gravy. Stew them half an hour very gently, and then take them out. In the mean time, make a veal force-meat, and wrap it all round them. Rub it over with the yolk of an egg, and fry them of a nice brown in good dripping. Take the

K

gravy

gravy they were stewed in, skim off the fat, thicken with a little butter rolled in flour, the yolk of an egg, and a gill of cream, beat up. Season it with pepper and salt, mix all together, and keep it stirring one way till it is smooth. Strain it into your dish, and put the pigeons on. Garnish with plenty of fried parsley. You may leave out the egg and cream, and put in a spoonful of browning, and a little lemon-pickle and catchup. *Farley* 127.

To stew Pigeons.

Let your pigeons be seasoned with pepper and salt, a few cloves and mace, and some sweet herbs ; wrap this seasoning up in a piece of butter, and put it in their bellies ; then tie up the neck and vent, and half roast them. Put them in a stew-pan, with a quart of good gravy, a little white wine, a few pepper-corns, three or four blades of mace, a bit of lemon, a bunch of sweet herbs, and a small onion. Stew them gently till they are enough; then take the pigeons out, and strain the liquor through a sieve; skim it and thicken it in your stew-pan, put in the pigeons, with some pickled mushrooms and oysters; stew it five minutes, and put the pigeons in a dish, and the sauce over. *Cole*, 164.

Pigeons in savoury Jelly.

Roast your pigeons with the head and feet on, put a sprig of myrtle in their bills ; make a jelly for them the same way as for chickens ; pour a little into a bason. When it is set, lay in the pigeons with their breasts down; fill up your bowl with your jelly, and turn it out. *Raffald*, 283.

To bake Pigeons.

Season them with pepper and salt, put a bit of butter into each, pour over them the following batter—three eggs, two spoonfuls of flour, half a pint of milk, and a little salt. *Mason*, 281.

Pigeons in a hole.

Pick, draw, and wash four young pigeons, stick their legs in their bellies as you do boiled pigeons, season them with pepper, salt, and beaten mace. Put into the belly of every pigeon a lump of butter the size of a walnut. Lay your pigeons in a pie-dish, pour over them a batter made of three eggs, two spoonfuls of flour, and half a pint of good milk. Bake it in a moderate oven, and serve them to table in the same dish. *Raffald*. 130.

Pigeons boiled with rice.

Stuff the bellies of six pigeons with parsley, pepper and salt, rolled in a very little piece of butter ; put them into a quart of mutton broth, with a little beaten mace, a bundle of sweet herbs,
and

and an onion; cover them clofe, and let them boil a full
quarter of an hour ; then take out the onion and fweet herbs,
and take a good piece of butter rolled in flour, put it in, and
give it a fhake; feafon it within falt, if it wants it ; then have
ready half a pound of rice boiled tender in milk. When it
begins to be thick (but take great care it does not burn) take
the yolks of two or three eggs, beat up with two or three fpoonfuls of cream, and a little nutmeg. Stir it together till it is
quite thick ; then take up the pigeons and lay them in a difh.
Pour the gravy to the rice, ftir it all together, and pour over
the pigeons. Garnifh with hard eggs cut into quarters.
Glaffe, 91.

To broil Pigeons.

When you fet about to broil pigeons, take care that your
fire is clear. Take fome parfley fhred fine, a piece of butter
as big as a walnut, with a little pepper and falt, and put into
their bellies. Tie them at both ends, and put them on the
gridiron. Or you may fplit and broil them, having firft feafoned them with pepper and falt. Serve them with a little
parfley and butter in the difh. *Farley*, 50.

Partridges in Panes.

Take two roafted partridges, and the flefh of a large fowl, a
little parboiled bacon, a little marrow or fweet fuet chopped
fine, a few mufhrooms and morels chopped fine, truffles, and
artichoke bottoms. Seafon with beaten mace, pepper, a little
nutmeg, falt, fweet herbs chopped fine, and the crumb of a two-
penny loaf foaked in hot gravy. Mix all well together with
the yolks of two eggs, make your panes on paper, of a round
figure, and the thicknefs of an egg, at a proper diftance one
from another. Dip the point of a knife in the yolk of an egg,
in order to fhape them ; bread them neatly, and bake them a
quarter of an hour in a quick oven. Obferve that the truffles
and morels are boiled tender in the gravy you foak the bread
in. Serve them up for a fide difh ; or they will ferve to garnifh the above difh, which will be a very fine one for a firft
courfe.

Note.—When you have cold fowls in the houfe, this makes
a pretty addition in an entertainment. *Glaffe*, 96.

Partridges en Afpic.

Chop herbs, fuch as fhallots, parfley, tarragon, chives, gar-
den-creffes, a little bafil, one clove of garlic, and chopped anchovies. Mix thefe with muftard, oil, tarragon vinegar, pepper,
and falt. If you ferve the partridges whole, ferve the fauce
cold in a fauce-boat. If for hot, cut the partridges as for a

hafh ;

hafh; warm them in a little broth, then put them to the fauce; warm them together without boiling. You may alfo mix it the fame manner cold. If cold, it will be better to be mixed an hour or more before ufing. *Dalrymple*, 234.

Partridges in Ragoo, with Oranges.

Trufs your partridges, and roaft in the Englifh way, only ufe no flour. Mafte a fauce of the livers pounded, and add two or three of chickens; put it into a ftew-pan with a green onion or two, a mufhroom, pepper and falt, and parfley. Boil all in cullis a few minutes, and ftrain through your etamine; cut the partridges as for a fricaffee, and put to your fauce. Let it boil but juft long enough to make the meat hot through. Strip in a morfel or two of the peel, a bit of minced fhallot and parfley, fqueeze in a good deal of juice, and difh it up. Garnifh with oranges in quarters. *Verral*, 131.

Partridges à-la-braze.

Take two brace of patridges, trufs the legs into the bodies, lard them, feafon them with beaten mace, pepper, and falt; take a ftew-pan, lay flices of bacon at the bottom, then flices of beef, and then flices of veal, all cut thin, a piece of carrot, an onion cut fmall, a bundle of fweet herbs, and fome whole pepper. Lay the partridges with the breafts downward, lay fome thin flices of beef and veal over them, and fome parfley fhred fine. Cover them, and let them ftew eight or ten minutes over a flow fire, then give your pan a fhake, and pour in a pint of boiling water. Cover it clofe, and let it ftew half an hour over a little quicker fire: then take out your birds, keep them hot, pour into the pan a pint of thin gravy, let them boil till there is about half a pint, then ftrain it off, and fkim of all the fat. In the mean time have a veal fweetbread cut fmall, truffles and morels, cocks' combs, and fowl's livers ftewed in a pint of good gravy half an hour, fome artichoke bottoms, and afparagus tops, both blanched in warm water, and a few mufhrooms. Then add the other gravy to this, and put in your partridges to heat. If it is not thick enough, take a piece of butter rolled in flour, and tofs up in it. If you will be at the expence, thicken it with veal and ham cullis, but it will be full as good without. *Glaffe*, 96. *Farley*, 128.

To ftew Partridges.

Trufs your partridges as for roafting, ftuff the craws, and lard them down each fide of the breaft; then roll a lump of butter in pepper, falt, and beaten mace, and put into the bellies. Sew up the vents, dredge them well, and fry them a light brown. Then put them into a ftew-pan, with a quart of good gravy, a fpoonful of Madeira wine, the fame of mufhroom catchup,

catchup, a tea-fpoonful of lemon-pickle, and half the quantity
of mufhroom powder, one anchovy, half a lemon, a fprig of
fweet marjoram. Cover the pan clofe, and ftew them half an
hour; then take them out, and thicken the gravy. Boil it a
little, and pour it over the partridges, and lay round them
articloke bottoms, boiled and cut in quarters, and the yolks of
four hards eggs, if agreeable. *Raffald*, 134.

Partridges rolled.

Lard young partridges with ham or bacon; ftrew over
them fome pepper and falt, with fome beaten mace, fome fhred
lemon-peel, and fweet herbs cut fmall; then take fome thin
beef-fteaks (there muft be no holes in them); ftrew over thefe
fome of the feafoning, and fqueeze on them fome lemon juice;
lay a partridge upon each fteak, and roll it up; tie it round to
keep it together, and pepper the outfide. Set it on a ftew-pan
with fome flices of bacon, and an onion cut into pieces; lay
the partridges carefully in, put to them fome rich gravy, and
let them ftew gently till they are done; then take the partridges out of the beef, lay them in a difh, and pour over them
fome rich effence of ham. *Cole*, 167.

Partridges broiled with fweet herbs.

Trufs them as for boiling; fplit them down the back, and
marinade them about an hour in a little oil, with pepper and
falt, and all forts of fweet herbs chopped; then roll them in
paper, with all the feafoning; broil flowly. When done, take
off the paper, mix the herbs with a little good cullis, add the
fqueeze of a lemon, and ferve with the partridges. *Dalrymple*, 231.

Partridges with confommée fauce.

Trufs your partridges as for boiling; put them in a ftew-
pan, with flices of veal and bacon, above and below, a flice of
ham, a faggot, three cloves, fliced onions and carrots; braze
on a very flow fire. When done, fift and fkim the fauce, and
ferve upon the partridges. *Cole*, 168.

Partridges à-la-paifanne.

Pick, draw, and trufs your partridges, and put them upon an
iron fkewer; tie them to the fpit, lay them down to roaft; put
a piece of fat bacon upon a toafting-fork, and hold it over the
partridges, that as it melts it may drop upon them as they roaft.
When they are well bafted with this, duft over them fome
crumbs of bread and fome falt; cut fome fhallots very fine,
with a little gravy, falt, and pepper, and the juice of half a
lemon. Mix all thefe together over the fire, and thicken them
up. Pour them into a difh, and lay the partridges upon them.
Cole, 168.

K 3   Ti

To hash a Partridge or Woodcock.

Cut it up as for eating, work the entrails very fine with the back of a spoon, mix it with a spoonful of red wine, the same of water, half a spoonful of allegar; cut an onion in slices, and pull it into rings; roll a little butter in flour, put them all in your tossing-pan, and shake it over the fire till it boils; then put in your bird, and when it is thoroughly hot, lay it in your dish, with sippets round it; strain the sauce over the partridge, and lay the onion in rings. It is a pretty corner dish for dinner or supper. *Raffald*, 75.

Pheasants à-la-braise.

Having put a layer of beef all over your pan, a layer of veal, a little piece of bacon, a piece of carrot, an onion stuck with cloves, a blade or two of mace, a spoonful of pepper, black and white, and a bundle of sweet herbs, lay in the pheasant. Then lay a layer of beef, and a layer of veal, to cover it. Set it on the fire five or six minutes, and then pour in two quarts of boiling gravy. Cover it close, and let it stew very softly an hour and a half. Then take up your pheasant, and keep it hot. Let the gravy boil till it is reduced to about a pint, and then strain it off and put it in again. Put in a veal sweetbread, first being stewed with the pheasant. Then put in some truffles and morels, some livers of fowls, artichoke bottoms, and asparagus tops, if you have them. Let these simmer in the gravy about five or six minutes, and then add two spoonfuls of catchup, two of red wine, and a little piece of butter rolled in flour, with a spoonful of browning. Shake all together, put in your pheasant, let them stew all together, with a few mushrooms, about five or six minutes more; then take up your pheasant, and pour your ragoo all over, with a few forcemeat balls. Garnish with lemon. You may lard it, if you think proper so to do. *Glasse*, 98. *Mason*, 306 *Farley*, 129.

Pheasants a-la-Mongelas.

Provide a large pheasant, cut off the pinions as to roast, and make a good force-meat; put it into your pheasant and spit it, with some lards of bacon and paper; take care you roast it nicely, and prepare your sauce as follows:—take some fat livers of turkies or fowls, blanch them till thoroughly done, and pound them to a paste; put to some gravy and cullis, mix it well together, and pass it through an etamine; cut off the flesh of the pheasant, slice it very thin and put to it, and preserve the carcase hot; add to your sauce, which should be about the thickness of your cullis, a little pepper, salt, some minced parsley, and the juice of two or three oranges; and, if you approve of it, you may strip a few morsels of the orange-peel in, and

and ferve it up with the hafh poured over the breaft, and garnifh with fome oranges in quarters. *Verral*, 88.

To ftew a Pheafant.

Take a pheafant, and ftew it in veal gravy; take artichoke
bottoms parboiled, fome chefnuts roafted and blanched. When
your pheafant is enough (but it muft ftew till there is juft
enough for fauce, then fkim it) put in the chefnuts and artichoke bottoms, a little beaten mace, pepper, and falt enough to
feafon it, and a glafs of white wine. If you do not think it thick
enough, thicken it with a little piece of butter rolled in flour.
Squeeze in a little lemon, pour the fauce over the pheafant, and
have fome force-meat balls fried and put into the difh.

Note.—A good fowl will do full as well, truffed with the
head on like a pheafant. You may fry faufages inftead of force-
meat balls. *Glaffe*, 97.

Mrs. Mafon, page 306, has the fame receipt in different
words.

Pheafants à-l'-Italienne.

Cut the livers fmall. If only one pheafant is to be dreffed,
take but half a dozen oyfters, parboil them, and put them into
a ftew-pan, with the liver, a piece of butter, fome green onions,
and fome parfley, pepper and falt, fome fweet herbs. and a little
all-fpice; let them ftand a very little time over the fire, and ftuff
the pheafant with them; then put it into a ftew-pan, with fome
oil, green onions, parfley, fweet bafil, and lemon-juice, for a
few minutes; take them off, cover the pheafant with flices of
bacon, and put it upon a fpit; tie fome paper round it whilft it
is roafting. Take fome oyfters, ftew them a little in their own
liquor; take a ftew-pan, put into it the yolks of four eggs, half
a-lemon cut into fmall dice, a little beaten pepper, a little fcraped
nutmeg, a little parfley cut fmall, a rocombole, an anchovy cut
fmall, a little oil, a glafs of white wine, a piece of butter, and
a little ham cullis; put the fauce over the fire to thicken, take
care it does not burn; put in the oyfters, and make the fauce
relifhing. When the pheafant is done, lay it in the difh, and
pour the fauce over it. *Mafon*, 306.

Snipes or Woodcocks in furtout.

Take force meat made of veal, as much beef fuet, chopped
and beat in a mortar, with an equal quanitty of crumbs of bread;
mix in a little beaten mace, pepper and falt, fome parfley, and
a little fweet herbs; mix it with the yolk of an egg. Lay fome
of this meat round the difh, then lay in the fnipes, being firft
drawn and half roafted. Take care of the trail, chop it, and
throw it all over the difh.

Take fome good gravy, according to the bignefs of your furtout, fome-truffles and morels, a few mufhrooms, a fweetbread

cut into pieces, and artichoke-bottoms cut fmall; let all ftew together, fhake them, and take the yolks of two or three eggs, according as you want them; beat them up with a fpoonful or two of white wine, ftir all together one way. When it is thick, take it off, let it cool, and pour it into the furtout. Have the yolks of a few hard eggs put in here and there; feafon with beaten mace, pepper, and falt, to your tafte; cover it with the force-meat all over, rub the yolks of eggs all over to colour it, then fend it to the oven. Half an hour does it, and fend it hot to table. *Cole*, 171.

Snipes or Woodcocks in falmy.

Trufs them, and half roaft them, without flour; cut them in fricaffee pieces, and take care to fecure all the infide, except the gizzards and galls, which you muft be fure to take clean away; but the ropes, livers, &c. pound to a pafte, with a morfel of fhallot, green onion and parfley, pepper, falt, and nutmeg; put in a ladle of your cullis, a glafs of red wine, and pafs it through your etamine, pour it into a ftew-pan to your meat; let it ftew very gently for three quarters of an hour; fling in a little minced parfley, the juice of an orange, and ferve it up, garnifhed with fried bread, and fome bits in the difh.

Any forts of birds, fuch as fnipes, quails, &c. that are not drawn, make a pleafing difh done in the fame manner. *Verral*, 132.

Another way.

Half roaft them, and cut them in quarters, put them in a ftew-pan with a little gravy, two fhallots chopped fine, a glafs of red wine, a little falt and chyan pepper, the juice of half a lemon; ftew them gently for ten minutes, and put them on a toaft ferved the fame as for roafting, and fend them up hot. Garnifh with lemon. *Glaffe*, 98.

Snipes with Purflain leaves.

Draw your fnipes, and make a force-meat for the infide, but preferve your ropes for your fauce; fpit them acrofs upon a lark-fpit, covered with bacon and paper, and roaft them gently. For fauce, you muft take fome prime thick leaves of purflain, blanch them well in water, put them into a ladle of cullis and gravy, a bit of fhallot, pepper, falt, nutmeg, and parfley, and ftew all together for half an hour gently. Have the ropes ready blanched and put in. Difh up your fnipes upon thin flices of bread fried, fqueeze the juice of an orange into your fauce, and ferve it up. *Verral*, 142.

Snipes Duchefs fafhion.

Split the fnipes at the back; take the infide out, which you make a force-meat of, with a few chopped capers, parfley, fhallots,

lots, mushrooms, pepper, salt, two chopped anchovies, and a
piece of butter; stuff them with it, sew them up close, and braze
them. While brazing, add a little good cullis and red wine.
When done, skim and sift the sauce If not thick enough, add
a little butter and flour, and serve with the snipes. *Dalrymple,*
237.

Quails, Thrushes, Plovers, and Lapwings.

They are all done as chickens, and may be dressed in all the
different ways of any other birds. *Dalrymple.*

The general method of dressing Plovers.

Green plovers roast like a woodcock, without drawing; and
the trail to run upon a toast;—with good gravy for sauce.

Grey plovers should be stewed.—Make a force-meat with the
yolks of two hard eggs bruised, some marrow cut fine, artichoke
bottoms cut small, and sweet herbs, seasoned with pepper, salt,
and nutmeg. Stuff the birds, then put them into a sauce-pan
with some good gravy (just enough to cover them), a glass of
white wine, and a blade of mace. Cover them close, and let
them stew very softly till they are tender. Then take up the
plovers, lay them in a dish, keep them hot, put a piece of butter
rolled in flour to thicken the sauce; let it boil till smooth,
squeeze into it a little lemon, skim it clean, and pour it over
them. *Mason,* 285.

Plovers Perigord fashion.

Truss them as chickens or pigeons for stewing; braze them
in a good braze. When done, skim and sift the braze. When
ready to serve, add the squeeze of a lemon. You may also stuff
and ro st them as partridges, &c. Thrushes and lapwings may
be dressed in the same manner, served with a cullis sauce. *Dalrymple,* 235.

To dress Ortolans and Quails.

Spit them side-ways, with a vine-leaf between; baste them
with butter, and have fried crumbs of bread round the dish.
Glasse, 100.

To dress Ruffs and Reifs.

These birds are principally found in Lincolnshire They may
be fatted, like chickens, with bread, milk, and sugar. They
feed very fast, and will die with fat if not killed in time. Draw
and truss them crofs-legged like snipes; roast them. For sauce
—good gravy thickened with butter, and a toast under them.
Cole, 173.

Small Birds in savoury Jelly.

Put a good piece of butter into the bellies of eight small birds,
with their heads and feet on, and sew up their vents. Put them
in a jug, cover it close with a cloth, and set them in a kettle of
boiling

boiling water till they are enough. When it is fet, lay in three birds with their breafts down, and cover them with the jelly. When it is fet, put in the other five, with their heads in the middle, and proceed in the fame manner as before directed for chickens. *Farley*, 129.

To drefs Larks Pear fafbion.

Trufs them clofe, and cut off the legs; feafon them with falt, pepper, cloves, and mace; make a force-meat thus :—Take a veal fweetbread, as much beef fuet, a few morels and mufh-rooms; chop all fine together, fome crumbs of bread, and a few fweet herbs, a little lemon-peel cut fmall; mix all together with the yolk of an egg, wrap up the larks in force-meat, and fhape them like a pear; ftick one leg in the top like the ftalk of a pear, rub them over with the yolk of an egg and crumbs of bread; bake them in a gentle oven, ferve them without fauce; or they make a good garnifh to a very fine difh.

You may ufe veal if you have not a fweetbread. *Glaffe*, 101.

Mrs. Mafon gives the fame receipt in fubftance, though in other words, page 287.

Larks à-la-Françoife.

Trufs your larks with the legs acrofs, and put a fage-leaf over their breafts; put them upon a long thin fkewer; between every lark put a piece of thin bacon, then tie the fkewer to a fpit, and roaft them at a brifk clear fire; bafte them with butter, and ftrew over them fome crumbs of bread mixed with flour; fry fome bread-crumbs of a fine brown in butter. Lay the larks round the difh, the bread-crumbs in the middle. *Cole*, 174.

A ragoo of Larks.

Fry your larks with an onion ftuck with cloves, a few truf-fles and mufhrooms; pour off the fat; fhake over the larks, &c. a little flour; put to them fome good gravy; ftew them till they are enough. If there is any fat, fkim it off. Add chop-ped parfley, lemon-juice, pepper, and falt, if neceffary.

Other fmall birds may be dreffed in the fame manner, *Cole*, 174.

CHAP.

Chap. IX.—MADE DISHES OF HARES, RABBITS, &c.

To florendine a Hare.

TAKE a grown hare, and let her hang up four or five days, then cafe her, and leave on the ears; and take out all the bones except the head, which muft be left on whole; lay your hare flat on the table, and lay over the infide a force-meat, and then roll it up to the head; fkewer it with the head and ears leaning back, tie it with a packthread as you would a collar of veal, wrap it in a cloth, and boil it an hour and a half in a fauce-pan with a cover on it, with two quarts of water. When your liquor is reduced to one quart, put in a pint of red wine, a fpoonful of lemon-pickle, and one of catchup, the fame of browning, and ftew it till it is reduced to a pint; thicken it with butter rolled in flour, lay round your hare a few morels, and four flices of force-meat, boiled in a caul of a leg of veal. When you difh it up, draw the jaw-bones, and ftick them in the eyes for horns; let the ears lie back on the roll, and ftick a fprig of myrtle in the mouth; ftrain over your fauce, and ferve it up. Garnifh with barberries and parfley.—Force-meat for the hare:—take the crumb of a penny loaf, the liver fhred fine, half a pound of fat bacon fcraped, a glafs of red wine, one an-chovy, two eggs, a little winter favoury, fweet marjoram, lemon-thyme, pepper, falt, and nutmeg to your tafte. *Raffald*, 136.

Mr. Farley, page 130. has given the above in fubftance, with a little tranfpofition. The fact is, both *Mrs. Raffald*, and *Mr. Farley*, have taken from *Mrs. Glaffe*.—See her Art of Cookery, page 101.

To drefs a Hare.

When the hare is cafed. cut it in two juft below the ribs; cut the fore quarters into pieces, and put them into a clean ftew-pan, with a blade or two of mace, an onion ftuck with cloves, fome whole pepper, an anchovy, and a bunch of fweet herbs; cover them with water, and let them ftew gently; make a pudding and put into the belly of the other part; lard and roaft it, flour and bafte it well with butter or fmall beer. When the ftew is tender, take it out with a fork into a difh, and ftrain off the liquor; put into it a glafs of red wine, a fpoonful of good catchup, and a piece of butter rolled in flour; fhake all together over the fire till it is of a good thicknefs; take up the roafted hare, and lay it in the middle of the difh, with the ftew round, and fauce poured over it, and fome good gravy in a boat. *Mafon*, 300.

Hare

Hare à-la-daube.

Cut a hare in fix pieces; bone and lard them with bacon, feafoned with fpices, powder of laurel, chopped parfley, thyme, fhallots, and one clove of garlick; braze it with flices of lard, the bones, a little broth, as much of the blood as you can fave, a glafs of brandy, and a quarter of a pound of good butter; ftop the pan well, and ftew it on a very flow fire, or in the oven, about four hours; then take out the bones, put the hare in a tureen, and the flices of bacon upon it; fift the fauce, and put it in the tureen; let it cool before ufing. It ought to be like a pie. *Clermont,* 288.

To fcare a Hare.

Lard a hare, and put a pudding in the belly; put it into a pot or fifh kettle, then put to it two quarts of ftrong drawn gravy, one of red wine, a whole lemon cut, a faggot of fweet herbs, nutmeg, pepper, a little falt, and fix cloves; cover it it clofe, and ftew it over a flow fire till it is three parts done; then take it up, put it into a difh, and ftrew it over with crumbs of bread, fweet herbs chopped fine, fome lemon-peel grated, and half a nutmeg; fet it before the fire, and bafte it till it is of a fine light brown. In the mean time, take the fat off your gravy, and thicken it with the yolk of an egg. Take fix eggs, boiled hard and chopped fmall, fome pickled cucumbers cut very thin; mix thefe with a fauce, and pour it into the difh.

A fillet of mutton, or neck of venifon, may be done the fame way.

Note.—You may do rabbits the fame way, but it muft be veal gravy and white wine, adding mufhrooms for cucumbers. *Glaffe,* 102.

A Hare Civet.

Bone your hare, and take out all the finews; cut one half in thin flices, and the other half in pieces an inch thick, flour them, and fry them in a little frefh butter, as collops, quick, and have ready fome gravy made with the bones of the hare and beef; put a pint of it into the pan to the hare, fome muftard, and a little elder vinegar; cover it clofe, and let it do foftly till it is as thick as cream, then difh it up, with the head in the middle. *Cole,* 177.

To ftew a Hare.

When you have paunched and cafed your hare, cut her as for eating, put her into a large fauce-pan with three pints of beef gravy, a pint of red wine, a large onion ftuck with cloves, a bundle of winter favoury, a flice of horfe-radifh, two blades of beaten mace, one anchovy, a fpoonful of walnut or mum catchup, one of browning, half a lemon, chyan and falt to your tafte; put on a clofe cover, and fet it over a gentle fire, and
ftew

ftew it for two hours; then take it up into a foup-difh, and thicken your gravy with a lump of butter rolled in flour; boil it a little, and ftrain it over your hare. Garnifh with lemon-peel cut like ftraws, and ferve it up. *Raffald*, 135.

To Lodge-podge a Hare.

Take your hare and cut it in pieces, as if you intended it for ftewing, and put into the pitcher, with two or three onions, a little falt and pepper, a bunch of fweet herbs, and a piece of butter; ftop the pitcher very clofe to prevent the fteam from getting out, fet it in a kettle full of boiling water, keep the kettle filled up as the water waftes; let it ftew four or five hours at leaft. You may, when you firft put the hare into the kettle, put in lettuce, cucumbers, celery, and turnips, if you like it better. *Cole*, 177.

To jug a Hare.

Cut your hare into little pieces, and lard them here and there with little flips of bacon. Seafon them with a little pepper and falt, and pour them into an earthen jug with a blade or two of mace, an onion ftuck with cloves, and a bundle of fweet herbs. Cover the jug clofe, that nothing may get in; fet it in a pot of boiling water, and three hours will do it. Then turn it out into the difh, take out the onion and fweet herbs, and fend it hot to table. As to the larding, you may omit it if you pleafe. *Farley*, 71.

To hafh a Hare.

Cut your hare into fmall pieces; if any of the pudding is left, rub it fmall in fome gravy, to which put a glafs of red wine, a little pepper and falt, an onion, a flice of lemon; tofs it up till hot through, take out the onion and lemon. *Cole*, 178.

Another way.

Cut it in fmall pieces, and if you have any of the pudding left, rub it fmall, and put to it a gill of red wine, the fame quantity of water, half an anchovy chopped fine, an onion ftuck with four cloves, and a quarter of a pound of butter rolled in flour. Shake all thefe together over a flow fire till your hare is thoroughly hot, for it is a bad cuftom to let any kind of hafh boil longer, as it hardens the meat. Send your hare to table in a deep difh, but before you fend it up, take out the onion, and lay fippets round the difh. *Farley*, 70.

To collar a Hare.

Bone a hare, and lard it with thick pieces of bacon, feafoned with fpices and falt; put a good force-meat in it or not; roll it up very tight, and tie it well; braze it with flices of veal, half a pint of white wine, and a pint of broth; cover it over with flices of bacon. You may alfo put fuch meat and other feafon-

ing

ing to make a jelly of the braze after, and serve the hare cold with it, either whole or sliced. *Dalrymple*, 241.

Hare Cake.

Chop the flesh of a hare very fine, take some bacon in dice about half the quantity, season with pepper, a little salt, and spice, a green onion or two, and a morsel of shallot; mix all well together, and prepare a stew-pan just wide enough, that it may cut in slices about two inches thick; line your bottom with thin bacon, and cover with the same; pour in a ladle of broth, and a glass of red wine, some slices of carrot, onion and herbs; let it simmer gently for two or three hours, take off the cover, and let it cool; the next day take it out, and trim it nice and round; pound some of the bacon it was stewed in, and when you serve it to table, spread it upon the top like sugar upon a plumb cake, and serve it to table upon a napkin. If it is well done, it will keep a fortnight for slices.

Veal cake may be done in the same manner, only instead of red wine put white; and do not cover it so much but that every one at table may see what it is. *Verral*, 227.

Hare Cake in Jelly.

Having boned the hare, and picked out the sinews, add an equal quantity of beef; chop these and pound them; add fresh mushrooms, shallot (and garlick if agreeable), sweet herbs, pepper and salt, two or three eggs. Mix these with bacon and pickled cucumbers cut like dice, put it into a mould sheeted with slices of bacon; cover it, bake it in a moderate oven; when cold, turn it out. Lay over it the following jelly:—a pound and an half of scrag of veal, a slice of ham, two or three cloves, a little nutmeg, some sweet herbs, a carrot or two, some shallot, two bay leaves, an ounce of ising-glass, with some beef broth; stew this till it will jelly, pass it through a fine sieve, then through a bag; add some lemon-juice. *Mason*, 303.

Leveret Kid fashion.

Lard a large leveret, marinade it about three hours in a warm marinade, made of water, vinegar, butter, flour, pepper, and salt, chopped parsley, shallots, sliced onions, thyme, laurel, basil, lemon-peel, and cloves; then roast it, basting with some of the marinade; sift the remainder, mix it with a little cullis, and serve it in a sauce-boat. *Clermont*, 291.

To florendine Rabbits.

Skin three young rabbits, but leave on the ears; wash and dry them with a cloth, take out the bones carefully, leaving the head whole, then lay them flat; make a force-meat of a quarter of a pound of bacon scraped, it answers better than suet, it
makes

makes the rabbits eat tenderer, and look whiter; add to the bacon the crumb of a penny loaf, a little lemon thyme, or lemon-peel fhred fine, parfley chopped fmall, nutmeg, chyan, and falt to your palate; mix them up together with an egg, and fpread it over the rabbits, roll them up to the head, fkewer them ftraight, and clofe the ends, to prevent the force-meat from coming out; fkewer the ears back, and tie them in feparate cloths, and boil them half an hour. When you difh them up, take out the jaw-bones, and ftick them in the eyes for ears; put round them force-meat balls and mufhrooms. Have ready a white fauce made of veal gravy, a little anchovy, the juice of half a lemon, or a tea-fpoonful of lemon-pickle; ftrain it, take a quarter of a pound of butter rolled in flour, fo as to make the fauce pretty thick; keep ftirring it whilft the flour is diffolving, beat the yolk of an egg; put to it fome thick cream, nutmeg, and falt; mix it with the gravy, and let it fimmer a little over the fire, but not boil, for it will curdle the cream; pour it over the rabbits, and ferve it up. *Raffald*, 137. *Farley*, 130.

Rabbits Surprize.

Take two half grown rabbits, roaft them, cut off the heads clofe to the fhoulders and the firft joints; then take off all the lean meat from the back bones; cut it fmall, and tofs it up with fix or feven fpoonfuls of cream and milk, and a piece of butter as big as a walnut rolled in flour, a little nutmeg, and a little falt; fhake all well together till it is as thick as good cream, and fet it to cool; then make a force-meat with a pound of veal, a pound of fuet, as much crumbs of bread, two anchovies, a little piece of lemon-peel cut fine, a little fprig of thyme, and a little nutmeg grated; let the veal and fuet be chopped very fine, and beat in a mortar, then mix it altogether with the yolks of two raw eggs; place it all round the rabbits, leaving a long trough in the back-bone open, that you think will hold the meat you cut out for the fauce; pour it in, and cover it with the force-meat, fmooth it all over with your hand as well as you can with a raw egg, fquare at both ends; throw on a little grated bread, and butter a magazine or pan, and take them from the dreffer where you formed them, and place them on it very carefully. Bake them three quarters of an hour, till they are of a fine brown colour. Let your fauce be gravy thickened with butter, and the juice of a lemon; lay them in the difh, and pour in the fauce. Garnifh with orange cut into quarters, and ferve it up for a firft courfe. *Glaffe*, 103.

Rabbits in Cafferole.

Take a couple of rabbits, divide them into quarters, flour
them

them if they are not larded, and fry them in butter ; then put them in a stew-pan, with some good gravy and a glass of white wine ; season them with pepper and salt, and a bunch of sweet herbs ; cover them down close, and let them stew till tender ; then take up the rabbits, strain off the sauce. thicken it with butter and flour, and pour it over them. *Mason*, 295.

Another way.

Having divided your rabbits into quarters, you may lard them or not, just as you please. Shake some flour over them, and fry them in lard or butter. Then put them into an earthen pipkin, with a quart of good broth, a glass of white wine, a little pepper and salt, a bunch of sweet herbs, and a small piece of butter rolled in flour. Cover them close, and let them stew half an hour ; then dish them up, and pour the sauce over them. Garnish with Seville oranges cut into thin slices and notched. *Glasse*, 104. *Farley*, 131.

To roast a Rabbit Hare fashion.

Take your rabbit and lard it with bacon, and then roast it as you do a hare, with a stuffing in the belly. Make a gravy sauce ; but if you do not lard it, have white sauce made as follows :—take a little veal broth, boil it up with a little flour and butter to thicken it, and add a gill of cream. Keep it stirring one way till it is smooth, and then put it into a boat.

Portuguese Rabbits.

Get some rabbits, truss them chicken fashion, the head must be cut off, and the rabbit turned with the back upwards, and two of the legs stripped to the claw end, and so trussed with two skewers. Lard them and roast them with what sauce you please. If you want chickens, and they are appear as such, they must be dressed in this manner :—send them up hot with gravy in the dish, and garnish with lemon and beet-root. *Glasse*, 103.

Rabbits Pulled.

Half boil your rabbits, with an onion, a little whole pepper, a bunch of sweet herbs, and a piece of lemon-peel ; pull the flesh into flakes, put to it a little of the liquor, a piece of butter mixed with flour, pepper, salt, nutmeg, chopped parsley, and the liver boiled and bruised ; boil this up, shaking it round. *Mason*, 294.

A Scotch Rabbit.

Having toasted a piece of bread very nicely on both sides, butter it, and toast a slice of cheese about as big as the bread on both sides, and lay it on the bread. *Cole*, 182.

A Welch

A Welch Rabbit.

Toaft a piece of bread on both fides, then toaft the cheefe on one fide ; lay it on the toaft, and with a hot iron brown the other fide.   You may rub it over with muftard.

An Englifh Rabbit.

Toaft the bread brown on both fides, and lay it in a plate before the fire, then pour a glafs of red wine over it, and let it foak the wine up ; then cut fome cheefe very thin, and lay it pretty thick over the bread, and put it in a tin oven before the fire, and it will be prefently toafted and browned.   Serve it hot.   *Cole,* 182.

Chap. X —TURTLES AND MOCK TURTLES.

To dreſs a Turtle the Weſt India way.

TAKE the turtle out of the water the night before you dreſs it, and lay it on its back. In the morning cut its head off, and hang it up by its hind fins for it to bleed till the blood is all out ; then cut the callapee, which is the belly, round, and raiſe it up ; cut as much meat to it as you can ; throw it into ſpring water with a little ſalt, cut the fins off, and ſcald them with the head ; take off all the ſcales, cut all the white meat out, and throw it into ſpring water and ſalt ; the guts and lungs muſts be cut out. Waſh the lungs very clean from the blood, then take the guts and maw and ſlit them open, waſh them very clean, and put them on to boil in a large pot of water, and boil them till they are tender. Then take off the inſide ſkin, and cut them in pieces of two or three inches long. Have ready a good veal broth made as follows :—Take one large, or two ſmall knuckles of veal, and put them on in three gallons of water ; let it boil, ſkim it well, ſeaſon with turnips, onions, carrots, and celery, and a good large bundle of ſweet herbs ; boil it till it is half waſted, then ſtrain it off. Take the fins, and put them in a ſtew-pan, cover them with veal broth, ſeaſon with an onion chopped fine, all ſorts of ſweet herbs chopped very fine, half an ounce of cloves and mace, half a nutmeg beat very fine ; ſtew it very gently till tender ; then take the fins out, and put in a pint of Madeira wine, and ſtew it for fifteen minutes. Beat up the whites of ſix eggs with the juice of two lemons, put the liquor in and boil it up, run it through a flannel bag, make it very hot, waſh the fins very clean, and put them in. Take a piece of butter and put at the bottom of a ſtew-pan, put your white meat in, and ſweat it gently till it is almoſt tender. Take the lungs and heart, and cover them with veal broth, with an onion, herbs, and ſpice ; as for the fins, ſtew them till tender ; take out the lungs, ſtrain the liquor off, thicken it, and put in a bottle of Madeira wine, ſeaſon with chyan pepper and ſalt pretty high ; put in the lungs and white meat, ſtew them up gently for fifteen minutes ; have ſome force-meat balls made out of the white part inſtead of veal, as for Scotch collops. If any eggs, ſcald them ; if not, take twelve hard yolks of eggs, made into egg balls. Have your callapaſh, or deep ſhell, done round the edges with paſte, ſeaſon it in the inſide with chyan pepper and ſalt, and a little Madeira wine ; bake it half an hour, then put in the lungs and white meat, force meat, and eggs over, and bake it half an hour.

hour. Take the bones, and three quarts of veal broth, seasoned with an onion, a bundle of sweet herbs, two blades of mace; stew it an hour, strain it through a sieve, thicken it with butter and flour, put in half a pint of Madeira wine, stew it half an hour; season with chyan pepper and salt to your liking. This is the soup. Take the callapee, run your knife between the meat and shell, and fill it full of force-meat; season it all over with sweet herbs chopped fine, a shallot chopped, chyan pepper and salt, and a little Madeira wine; put a paste round the edge, and bake it an hour and an half. Take the guts and maw, put them in a stew-pan, with a little broth, a bundle of sweet herbs, and two blades of mace beat fine; thicken with a little butter rolled in flour, stew them gently for half an hour, season with chyan pepper and salt, beat up the yolks of two eggs in half a pint of cream, put it in, and keep stirring it one way till it boils up, then dish them up as follows:

CALLAPEE.

FRICASSEE.   SOUP.   FINS.

CALLAPASH.

The fins eat fine, when cold, put by in the liquor. *Glasse*, 344 to 346. *Farley*, 22 to 26.

To dress a Turtle of about thirty pounds weight.

When you kill the turtle, which must be done the night before, cut off the head, and let it bleed two or three hours; then cut off the fins, and the callapee from the callapash; take care you do not burst the gall; throw all the inwards into cold water, the guts and the tripe keep by themselves, and slip them open with a penknife, wash them very clean in scalding water, and scrape off all the inward skin; as you do them, throw them into cold water, wash them out of that and put them into fresh water, and let them lie all night, scalding the fins and edges of the callapash and callapee; cut the meat off the shoulders, and hack the bones, and set them over the fire with the fins in about a quart of water; put in a little mace, nutmeg, chyan, and salt; let it stew about three hours, then strain it, and put the fins by for use. The next morning take some of them eat you cut off the shoulders, and chop it small, as for sausages, with about a pound of beef or veal suet; season with mace, nutmeg, sweet marjoram, parsley, chyan, and salt to your taste, and three or four glasses of Madeira wine, so stuff it under the two fleshy parts of the meat; and if you have any left, lay it over to prevent the meat from burning; then cut the remainder of the meat and fins in pieces the size of an egg; season it pretty high with chyan, salt, and a little nutmeg, and put it into the callapash; take care that it be sewed or secured up at the end, to keep in the gravy; then boil up the gravy, and add more wine, if re-

I. 2 quired,

quired, and thicken it a little with butter and flour ; put some
of it to the turtle, and set it in the oven with a well buttered
paper over it to keep it from burning, and when it is about half
baked, squeeze in the juice of one or two lemons, and stir it
up. Callapash, or back, will take half an hour more baking
than the callapee, which two hours will do. The guts must
be cut in pieces two or three inches long, the tripes in less,
and put into a mug of clear water, and set in the oven with the
callapash, and when it is enough drained from the water, it is
to be mixed with the other parts, and sent up very hot. *Raffald*, 19. *Farley*, 22.

Another way.

I have seen, says Mr. Verral, many a turtle dressed ; but I
think not all as they should be. And as I have had the honour
of sending several to table myself, to some of the politest gentry
in the kingdom, with great applause, I shall give the following
receipt from experience, rather than from the general rule of
hodge-podging it together. To dissect it then—Let its head
be chopped off close to the shell, set it on that part that all the
blood may run away ; have plenty of water in pails or tubs ;
lay your fish upon the back, or callapash, cut off the under
shell, or callapee, in the first line or partition, from the edge of
the callapash ; take off that, and immediately put it into water.
Next cut off the four fins in the shoulder and aich-bone joints,
and put into water too, and with a cleaver chop out the bones
from the shoulders and hinder parts, and put to the rest. Take
out your guts and tripe clean, and the other entrails, and lay
your callapash in water while you prepare your callapee, which
should be done as follows :—cut off all superfluous bits for your
soup, and trim it neatly. Cut little holes in the thick flesh,
with the point of your knife ; lay it in a dish, and soak it well
in Madeira wine, and season with chyan pepper, (but not too
much), a little salt, plenty of shallot and parsley minced and
strewed upon it. Next take the callapash, and order in the
same manner ; first cutting off the shell to the crease on the
other side of the edge, and put a neat rim of paste quite round,
and adorn it well ; pour a little cullis round, and squeeze the
juice of some lemons or oranges ; and they are ready for your
oven. The common way is to put some of the flesh into the
callapash ; but, in my opinion, it is best to put none. The next
to be made ready is your fins and head ; blanch them till you
can take off the outer skin ; trim them, and put them into a
stew-pan with the head ; pour in some Madeira, a ladle of
broth, a pinch of chyan, a small bundle of onions, herbs, and
shallots, and stew them tender with a little salt, and 'tis ready ;
the two biggest fins for one dish, and the head and two smallest
for another. Now cut the side shells in pieces, and blanch
them

them fo that you may take out the griftles or jelly part whole. While this is doing, prepare the tripe or guts with a fharp knife; flit them from end to end, and care muft be taken that all is wafhed and fcraped clean; cut them into pieces about two inches in length, and blanch them. When your broth is made of the flefh, to the tripe in a ftew-pan put as much as will cover it; put in a bunch of herbs, with an onion or two, a couple of whole fhallots, fome mace, and a little falt; ftew all till pretty tender; take out the herbs, &c. and put butter and flour to thicken it; provide a liafon as for a fricaffee of chickens, and at your dinner-time tofs it up with the juice of orange or lemon, and it is ready. Next take the jellies of your fide fheils, and prepare for a difh done in the fame manner as the fins and head; fqueeze in fome juice of orange or lemon, and it is ready. And now four the foup :— Moft of which that I have feen or tafted has been poor infipid ftuff. To fay why it was, is faying lefs than nothing. The whole matter is, to fhew how it may be made good; thus, they cut all the flefh from the bones into fmall pieces, and to about a pound of meat put a quart of water, and to five or fix quarts, a pint of Madeira. Take care that it is well fkimmed. Tie up in a bit of linen three or four onions, fome bits of carrot, a leek, fome herbs and parfley, with two or three pinches of chyan, and let it boil with the meat, and falt according to your tafte. Let it fimmer an hour, or a little more, and fend it up in a tureen or foup-difh, only the meat and the broth.

Thefe feven difhes make a pretty firft courfe; the callapafh and callapee at top and bottom, foup in the middle, and the other four the corners. *Verral,* 235.

To drefs a Mock Turtle.

Take the largeft calf's head you can get, with the fkin on, put it in fcalding water till you find the hair will come off, clean it well, and wafh it in warm water, and boil it three quarters of an hour. Then take it out of the water, and flit it down the face, cut off all the meat along with the fkin as clean from the bone as you can, and be careful you do not break the ears off. Lay it on a flat difh, and ftuff the ears with force-meat, and tie them round with cloths. Take the eyes out, and pick all the reft of the meat clean from the bone, put it in a tofling-pan, with the niceft and fatteft part of another calf's head, without the fkin on, boiled as long as the above, and three quarts of veal gravy. Lay the fkin in the pan on the meat, with the flefh-fide up, cover the pan clofe, and let it ftew over a moderate fire one hour; then put in three fweetbreads, fried a little brown, one ounce of morels, the fame of truffles, five artichoke bottoms boiled, one anchovy boned and chopped fmall, a tea-fpoonful of chyan pepper, a little falt, half a lemon,

three

three pints of Madeira wine, two meat fpoonfuls of mufhroom
catchup, one of lemon-pickle, and half a pint of mufhrooms.
Let them ftew flowly half an hour longer, and thicken it with
flour and butter. Have ready the yolks of four eggs boiled
hard, and the brains of both heads boiled ; cut the brains the
fize of nutmegs, and make a rich force-meat, and fpread it on
the caul of a leg of veal, roll it up, and boil it in a cloth one
hour. When boiled, cut it in three parts, the middle largeft ;
then take up the meat into the difh, and lay the head over it with
the fkin fide up, and put the largeft piece of force-meat between
the ears, and make the top of the ears to meet round it, (this is
called the crown of the turtle) lay the other flices of the force-
meat oppofite to each other at the narrow end and lay a few
of the truffles, morels, brains, mufhrooms, eggs, and artichoke
bottoms upon the face, and round it ; ftrain the gravy boiling
hot upon it. Be as quick in difhing it up as poffible, for it foon
grows cold. *Glaffe*, 347. *Raffald*, 82.

Another way.

Take a calf's head, and fcald off the hair, as from a pig ;
then clean it, cut off the horny part in thin flices, with as little
of the lean as poffible ; chop the brains ; have ready between a
quart and three pints of ftrong mutton or veal gravy, with a
quart of Madeira wine, a large tea-fpoonful of chyan, a large
onion cut very fmall, half the peel of a large lemon fhred as fine
as poffible, a little falt, the juice of four lemons, and fome fweet
herbs cut fmall. Stew all thefe together till the head is very
tender. Let them ftew about an hour and an half. Then have
ready the back fhell of a turtle, lined with a pafte made of flour
and water, which muft firft be fet in the oven to harden, then
put in the ingredients, and fet it in the oven to brown. When
that is done, lay the yolks of eggs boiled hard, and force-meat
balls round the top.

Some parboil the head the day before, take out the bones,
and then cut it into flices. *Mafon*, 155.

Mock Turtle from Calf's Feet.

Provide two calves feet and one chicken ; cut them into
pieces of a proper fize for a fricaffee ; make the feafoning with
three large onions, a large handful of parfley, and a few fweet
herbs ; chop them all together, then feafon the meat. Let the
feet ftew two hours and an half in three quarts of water ; then
put in the chicken ; let it ftew half an hour. Then take the
juice of two lemons, a tea-cupful of Madeira wine, fome chyan
pepper ; put that in laft. Let it ftew altogether half an hour,
and ferve it up in a foup-difh.

Force-meat balls of veal may be laid at top, and hard eggs.
Cole, 188.

CHAP.

Obſervations on Soups.

GREAT care is neceſſary to be taken that the pots, or ſauce-pans, and covers, be very clean, and free from all greaſe and ſand, and that they are well tinned, for fear of giving the broth or ſoups any braſſy taſte, or of injuring the health of thoſe who partake of the ſeveral diſhes. When you make any kind of ſoups, particularly portable, vermicelli, or brown gravy ſoup, or any other that has roots or herbs in it, always obſerve to lay the meat in the bottom of your pan, with a good lump of butter; cut the herbs and roots ſmall, lay them over your meat, cover it cloſe, ſet it over a very ſlow fire; it will draw all the virtue out of the roots or herbs, and turn it to a good gravy, and give the ſoup a very different flavor from putting water in at the firſt. When your gravy is almoſt dried up, fill your pan with water. When it begins to boil, take off the fat, and follow the directions of your receipt for what ſort of ſoup you are making. When you make old peas ſoup, take ſoft water; for green peas hard is preferable; it keeps the peas of a better colour. When you make any white ſoup, do not put in cream till you take it off the fire. Always diſh up your ſoups the laſt thing. If it be a gravy ſoup, it will ſkim over if you let it ſtand. If it be a peas-ſoup, it often ſettles, and the top looks thin. You muſt ob-ſerve in all broths and ſoups, that one thing does not taſte more than another, but that the taſte be equal, and that it has a fine agreeable reliſh, according to what you deſign it for; and you muſt be ſure that all the greens and herbs you put in are clean waſhed and picked. *Cole*, 189.

Rich Vermicelli Soup.

Put four ounces of butter into a large toſſing-pan; cut a knuckle of veal and a ſcrag of mutton into ſmall pieces about the ſize of walnuts; ſlice in the meat of a ſhank of ham, with three or four blades of mace, two or three carrots, two parſnips, two large onions, with a clove ſtuck in at each end. Cut in four or five heads of celery waſhed clean, a bunch of ſweet herbs, eight or ten morels, and an anchovy. Cover the pan cloſe, and ſet it over a ſlow fire, without any water, till the gravy is drawn out of the meat; then pour the gravy into a pot or baſon; let the meat brown in the ſame pan, and take care it does not burn. Then pour in four quarts of water, let it boil gently till it is waſted to three pints. Then ſtrain it, and put the gravy to it; ſet it on the fire, add to it two ounces of vermicelli, cut the niceſt part of a head of celery, chyan pep-pepper, and ſalt to your taſte, and let it boil for four minutes.

If

If not a good colour, put in a little browning, lay a fmall French roll in the foup-difh, pour in the foup upon it, and lay fome of the vermicelli over it. *Mafon*, 197. *Raffald*, 4. *Farley*, 155.

Another way.

Take three quarts of the broth, and fome of the gravy mixed together, a quarter of a pound of vermicelli, blanched in two quarts of water ; put it into the foup, boil it up for ten minutes, and feafon with falt, if it wants any. Put it in your turceen, with-the cruft of a French roll baked. *Glaffe*, 126.

Vermicelli Soup, with Meat or Fifh.

For a middling difh, take about a quarter of a pound of vermicelli, which you fcald a moment in boiling water ; then drain it, and boil in good broth or gravy, and a bit of bacon. When boiled tender, take out the bacon, feafon it with falt, and fkim off the fat very clean ; it muft be ferved of a middling confiftence. If you would make it of a crawfifh cullis, or any other, you will only mix it a moment before you ferve. If it is for meagre, fcald your vermicelli as above, and boil it with fifh broth and butter ; adding a liafon of yolks of eggs made with the fame broth and gravy. *Dalrymple*, 20.

Hare Soup.

This being a rich foup, it is proper for a large entertainment, and may be placed at the bottom of the table, where two foups are required, and almond or onion foup be at the top. Hare foup is made thus :—Cut a large old hare into fmall pieces, and put it in a mug, with three blades of mace, a little falt, two large onions, a red herring, fix morels, half a pint of red wine, and three quarts of water. Bake it three hours in a quick oven, and then ftrain it into a tofling-pan. Have ready boiled three ounces of French barley, or fago, in water. Then put the liver of the hare two minutes in fcalding water, and rub it through a hair fieve, with the back of a wooden fpoon. Put it into the foup with the barley or fago, and a quarter of a pound of butter. Set it over the fire, and keep it ftirring, but do not let it boil. If you difapprove of the liver, you may put in crifped bread, fteeped in red wine. *Farley*, 156.

Soup à-la-Reine.

Take a knuckle of veal, and three or four pounds of lean beef, put to it fix quarts of water with a little falt. When it boils, fkim it well, then put in fix large onions, two carrots, a head or two of celery, a parfnip, one leek, and a little thyme. Boil them all together till the meat is boiled quite down, then ftrain it through a hair fieve, and let it ftand about half an hour ; then fkim it well, and clear it off gently from the fettlings into a clear pan. Boil half a pint of cream, and pour it

on

on the crumb of a halfpenny loaf, and let it foak well. Take half a pound of almonds, blanch and beat them as fine as pof-ble, putting in now and then a little cream to prevent them from oiling. Then take the yolks of fix hard eggs, and the roll that is foaked in the cream, and beat them all together quite fine. Then make your broth hot, and pour it to your almonds. Strain it through a fine hair fieve, rubbing it with a fpoon till all the goodnefs is gone through into a ftew-pan, and add more cream to make it white. Set it over the fire, keep ftirring it till it boils, fkim off the froth as it rifes, foak the tops of two French rolls in melted butter, in a ftew pan, till they are crifp, but not brown; then take them out of the butter, and lay them on a plate before the fire; and a quarter of an hour be-fore you fend it to the table, take a little of the foup hot, and put it to the roll in the bottom of the tureen; put your foup on the fire, keep ftirring it till ready to boil, then put it into your tureen, and ferve it up hot. Be fure you take all the fat off the broth before you put it to the almonds, or it will fpoil it; and take care it does not curdle. *Raffald*, 7. *Farley*, 149.

Soup Creffy.

Take a pound of lean ham, and cut it into fmall bits, and put at the bottom of a ftew-pan, then cut a French roll and put over the ham. Take two dozen heads of celery cut fmall, fix onions, two turnips, one carrot, cut and wafhed very clean, fix cloves, four blades of mace, two handfuls of water-creffes. Put them all into a ftew-pan, with a pint of good broth. Cover them clofe, and fweat it gently for twenty minutes; then fill it up with veal broth, and ftew it for four hours. Rub it through a fine fieve, or cloth, put it in your pan again; feafon it with falt and a little chyan pepper. Give it a fimmer up, and fend it to table hot, with fome French roll toafted hard in it. Boil a handful of creffes till tender, in water, and put it over the bread. *Glaffe*, 126. *Mafon*, 196. *Farley*, 156.

Another way.

Slice all forts of roots, ftew them in good butter, with flices of ham and veal; let them ftew in the butter as long as you poffibly can without letting them burn; then add fome good broth; let it boil till your roots are become like a marmalade, then prefs it through a cullis-cloth; add as much broth as ne-ceffary for your quantity of foup. If for meagre, inftead of veal and ham, ufe carps or pike, and meagre broth. *Clermont*, 25.

Almond Soup.

Blanch a quart of almonds, and beat them in a marble mor-tar, with the yolks of fix hard eggs, till they are a fine pafte; mix them by degrees with two quarts of new milk, a quart of

cream,

cream, and a quarter of a pound of double refined fugar, beat
fine; ftir all well together. When it is well mixed, fet it over
a flow fire, and keep it ftirring quick all the while, till you find
it is thick enough; then pour it into your difh, and fend it to
table. If you are not very careful, it will curdle. *Mafon*, 205.
from *Glaffe*, 156.

Another way.

Chop a neck of veal, and the fcrag end of a neck of mutton
into fmall pieces, put them in a large tolling-pan; cut in a
turnip, with a blade or two of mace, and five quarts of water;
fet it over the fire, and let it boil gently till it is reduced to two
quarts; ftrain it through a hair fieve into a clear pot, then put
in fix ounces of almonds blanched and beat fine, half a pint of
thick cream, and chyan pepper to your tafte. Have ready three
fmall French rolls, made for that purpofe, the fize of a fmall
tea-cup; if they are larger, they will not look well, and drink
up too much of the foup; blanch a few Jordan almonds, and
cut them lengthways, ftick them round the edge of the rolls
flankways, then ftick them all over the top of the rolls, and put
them in the tureen. When difhed up, pour the foup upon the
rolls. Thefe rolls look like a hedge-hog. Some French cooks
give this foup the name of Hedge-hog Soup. *Raffald*, 6. *Far-*
ley, 157.

Soup Santé, or Gravy Soup.

Put fix good rafhers of lean ham in the bottom of a ftew-
pan; then put over it three pounds of lean beef, and over the
beef three pounds of lean veal, fix onions cut in flices, two carrots, and two turnips fliced, two heads of celery, and a bundle
of fweet herbs. fix cloves, and two blades of mace; put a little
water at the bottom, draw it very gently till it fticks, then put
in a gallon of boiling water; let it ftew for two hours, feafon
with falt, and ftrain it off; then have ready a carrot cut in fmall
pieces of two inches long, and about as thick as a goofe-quill, a
turnip, two heads of leeks, two heads of celery, two heads of
endive cut acrofs, two cabbage lettuces cut acrofs, a very little
forrel, and chervil; put them in a ftew pan, and fweat them
for fifteen minutes gently; then put them in your foup, boil it
up gently for ten minutes; put it in your tureen, with a cruft
of French roll.

N. B. You may boil the herbs in two quarts of water for ten
minutes, if you like them beft fo; your foup will be the clearer.
Glaffe, 128. *Farley*, 161.

Soup Santé, with Herbs.

Of herbs or vegetables, you muft make fhift with celery and
endives in the winter, but add a lettuce, if you can get it; provide a duckling, or a chicken neatly blanched, and boil it in
                                                            your

your foup, which is nothing more than broth or gravy. With the celery, &c. cut in bits about an inch long ; let it boil gently for an hour or fo; and, when it is almoft your time of dining, add a little fpinach, forrel, and chervil, chopped, but not fmall, and boil it about five minutes ; prepare your crufts in a ftew-pan, and lay at the bottom of your difh ; lay your duckling in the middle, and pour your foup over it ; and ferve it up with fome thin bits of celery for garnifh, or without, as you like beft.

For the fummer feafon, you may add a handful of young peas, heads of afparagus, nice little firm bits of cauliflower, bottoms of artichokes, and many other things that the feafon affords. *Verral,* 9.

Soup Santé the Englifh way.

Provide about ten or twelve pounds of gravy-beef, a knuckle of veal, and the knuckle part of a leg of mutton, a couple of fowls (or two old cocks will do as well) and a gallon of water ; let thefe ftew very foftly till reduced to one half fet them on to ftew the night before) ; add to them fome crufts of bread ; put in a bunch of fweet herbs, fome celery, forrel, chervil and purflain if agreeable ; or any of them may be left out. When it is ftrong and good, ftrain it ; fend it to table, with either a roaft or boiled fowl, or a piece of roafted or boiled neck of veal, in the middle, and fome fried bread in a plate. *Cole,* 194.

Craw-fifh Soup.

Boil about fifty frefh craw-fifh; pick out all the meat, which you muft fave ; pick out all the meat of a frefh lobfter, which you muft likewife fave; pound the fhells of the craw fifh and lobfter fine in a marble mortar, and boil them in four quarts of water, with four pounds of mutton, a pint of green fplit peas, nicely picked and wafhed, a large turnip carrot, onion, mace, cloves, anchovy, a little thyme pepper, and falt. Stew them on a flow fire till all the goodnefs is out of the mutton and fhells, then ftrain it through a fieve, and put in the tails of your craw-fifh and the lobfter-meat, but in very fmall pieces, with the red coral of the lobfter, if it has any ; boil it half an hour, and juft before you ferve it up, add a little butter melted thick and fmooth ; ftir it round feveral times when you put it in ; ferve it very hot; but do not put too much fpice in it.

N. B. Pick out all the bags and the woolly part of your craw-fifh, before you pound them. *Raffald.* 13. *Farley,* 165.

Prawns make an excellent foup, done juft in the fame man-ner; but you muft obferve, that there is a fmall bag in the car-cafe, full of gravel, which muft be always taken out before you pound them for your ftock. *Verral,* 21.

Plumb

Plumb Porridge for Chriſtmas.

Put a leg and ſhin of beef into eight gallons of water, and boil them till they are very tender. When the broth is ſtrong, ſtrain it out. Then wipe the pots, and put in the broth again. Slice ſix penny loaves thin, cut off the tops and bottoms, put ſome of the liquor to them, and cover them up, and let them ſtand for a quarter of an hour. Then boil and ſtrain it, and put it into your pot. Let them boil a little, and then put in five pounds of ſtewed raiſins of the ſun, and two pounds of prunes. Let it boil a quarter of an hour, then put in five pounds of currants clean waſhed and picked. Let theſe boil till they ſwell, and then put in three quarters of an ounce of mace, half an ounce of cloves, and two nutmegs, all beat fine. Before you put theſe into the pot, mix them with a little cold liquor, and do not put them in but a little while before you take off the pot. When you take off the pot, put in three pounds of ſugar, a little ſalt, a quart of ſack, a quart of claret, and the juice of two or three lemons. You may thicken with ſago inſtead of bread, if you pleaſe. Pour your porridge into earthen pans, and keep it for uſe. *Farley*, 162.

Soup and Bouillie.

For the bouillie, roll five pounds of briſket of beef tight with a tape. Put it into a ſtew-pan, with four pounds of the leg of mutton piece of beef, and about ſeven or eight quarts of water. Boil theſe up as quick as poſſible, ſkim it very clean; add one large onion, ſix or ſeven cloves, ſome whole pepper, two or three carrots, a turnip or two, a leek, and two heads of celery. Stew this very gently, cloſe covered, for ſix or ſeven hours. About an hour before dinner, ſtrain the ſoup through a piece of dimity that has been dipped in cold water. Put the rough ſide upwards. Have ready boiled carrots cut like little wheels, turnips cut in balls, ſpinach, a little chervil and ſorrel, two heads of endive, one or two of celery cut in pieces. Put theſe into a tureen, with a Dutch loaf, or a French roll dried, after the crumb is taken out. Pour the ſoup to theſe boiling hot. Add a little ſalt and chyan. Take the tape from the bouillie; ſerve it in a ſeparate diſh; maſhed turnips, and ſliced carrots, in two little diſhes. The turnips and carrots ſhould be cut with an inſtrument that may be bought for that purpoſe. *Maſon*, 187.

A Tranſparent Soup.

Cut the meat from a leg of veal in ſmall pieces, and when you have taken all the meat from the bone, break the bone in ſmall pieces. Put the meat in a large jug, and the bones at top, with a bunch of ſweet herbs, a quarter of an ounce of mace,

half

half a pound of Jordan almonds, blanched and beat fine. Pour on it four quarts of boiling water; let it stand all night by the fire, covered close. The next day put it into a well-tinned sauce-pan, and let it boil slowly till it is reduced to two quarts. Be sure you take the scum and fat off as it rises, all the time it is boiling. Strain it into a punch-bowl, let it settle for two hours, pour it into a clean sauce-pan, clear from the sediments, if any, at the bottom. Have ready three ounces of rice, boiled in water. If you like vermicelli better, boil two ounces. When enough, put it in, and serve it up. *Cole*, 195.

Green Peas Soup.

Cut a knuckle of veal, and one pound of lean ham into thin slices; lay the ham at the bottom of a soup-pot, the veal upon the ham; then cut six onions in slices, and put on two or three turnips, two carrots, three heads of celery cut small, a little thyme, four cloves, and four blades of mace. Put a little water at the bottom, cover the pot close, and draw it gently, but do not let it stick; then put in six quarts of boiling water, let it stew gently for four hours, and skim it well. Take two quarts of green peas, and stew them in some of the broth till tender; then strain them off, and put them in a marble mortar, and beat them fine. Put the liquor in and mix them up, (if you have no mortar, you must bruise them in the best manner you can). Take a tammy, or fine cloth, and rub them through till you have rubbed all the pulp out, and then put your soup into a clean pot, with half a pint of spinach juice, and boil it up for fifteen minutes. Season with salt and a little pepper. If your soup is not thick enough, take the crumb of a French roll, and boil it in a little of the soup, beat it in the mortar, and rub it through your tammy or cloth; then put in your soup and boil it up. Then put it in your tureen, with dice of bread toasted very hard. *Glasse*, 129.

Another way.

Provide a peck of peas, shell them, and boil them in spring-water till they are soft; then work them through a hair sieve; take the water that your peas were boiled in, and put in a knuckle of veal, three slices of ham, and cut two carrots, a turnip, and a few beet leaves, shred small; add a little more water to the meat, set it over the fire, and let it boil one hour and a half; then strain the gravy into a bowl, and mix it with the pulp, and put in a little juice of spinach, which must be beat and squeezed through a cloth; put in as much as will make it look a pretty colour, then give it a gentle boil, which will take off the taste of the spinach: slice in the whitest part of a head of celery, put in a lump of sugar the size of a walnut, take a slice of bread, and cut it in little square pieces; cut a little bacon
the

the same way, fry them a light brown, in fresh butter; cut a large cabbage lettuce in slices, fry it after the other, put it in the tureen with the fried bread and bacon: have ready boiled, as for eating, a pint of young peas, and put them in the soup, with a little chopped mint, if you like it, and pour it into your tureen. *Raffald*, 9.

Soup à-la-Mousquetaire.

Take a pint of green peas, and a handful of sorrel; boil in your broth and gravy on a slow fire, a neck of mutton; which, when done, glaze it as a fricandeau, and serve it all together. *Dalrymple*, 26.

A Common Peas Soup.

Take a quart of split peas, put to them a gallon of soft water, a little lean bacon, or roast-beef bones; wash one head of celery, cut it, and put it in with a turnip, boil it till reduced to two quarts. then work it through a cullender, with a wooden spoon: mix a little flour and water, and boil it well in the soup, and slice in another head of celery, chyan pepper, and salt to your taste; cut a slice of bread in small dice, fry them a light brown, and put them in your dish; then pour the soup over it. *Farley*, 160.

Another way.

Cut two large onions, or three or four small ones, two carrots, some spinach, celery, endive, and a turnip, into a stew-pan; fry them with a bit of butter, so as to be as little greasy as possible. Put them into a stew-pan with four quarts of water, (if the soup is to be very rich, as much beef-broth), some roast-beef bones, if they are to be had, a red herring, or a bit of lean bacon, and a quart of split peas. Let this stew gently till the peas are very soft; pulp them through a fine cullender, or a coarse sieve. When cold, take off the top, heat the soup with celery boiled and cut to pieces, spinach, endive, and a little chyan. Cut some bread like dice, fry it very dry, put it into a tureen, and pour in the soup; add a little dried mint rubbed very fine; or if preferred, the herbs may be fried after they are boiled. Some gravy that has run from a piece of meat is a great addition. If the soup does not appear quite thick enough, mix a little flour very smooth, and add to it; but be sure to let it boil a few minutes, or the flour will taste raw. The liquor of a leg of pork makes good peas-soup in a common way, or any boiled bones, *Mason*, 194.

Peas Soup without Meat.

A British herring, with a pint of peas, celery, &c. makes good peas-soup. *Cole*, 198.

White

White Peas Soup.

Put four or five pounds of lean beef into fix quarts of water, with a little falt, and as foon as it boils, take off the fcum. Put in three quarts of old green peas, two heads of celery, a little thyme, three onions, and two carrots. Boil them till the meat is quite tender, then ftrain it through a hair fieve, and rub the pulp of the peas through the fieve. Split the blanched part of three cofs-lettuces into four quarters, and cut them about an inch long, with a little mint cut fmall. Then put half a pound of butter in a ftew-pan large enough to hold your foup, and put the lettuce and mint into the butter, with a leek fliced very thin, and a pint of green peas. Stew them a quarter of an hour, and fhake them frequently. Then put in a little of the foup, and ftew them a quarter of an hour longer. Then put in your foup, as much thick cream as will make it white, and keep ftirring it till it boils. Fry a French roll a little crifp in butter, put it at the bottom of your tureen, and pour over it your foup. *Farley*, 159.

Partridge Soup.

Skin two old partridges, and cut them into fmall pieces, with three flices of ham, two or three onions fliced, and fome celery; fry them in butter till they are as brown as they can be made without burning; then put them into three quarts of water with a few pepper-corns. Boil it flowly till a little more than a pint is confumed, then ftrain it, put in fome ftewed celery and fried bread. *Glaffe*, 133. *Mafon*, 198. *Raffald*, 14. *Farley*, 155.

Soup à la Chartre.

Take three or four fweetbreads well cleaned in warm water, and fcalded in boiling; put them in your pot with fcalded cocks'-combs, a faggot of parfley, green fhallots, three cloves, and a few mufhrooms; ftew all with good broth on a flow fire; have crufts of rolls well foaked in broth in the foup-difh, then put upon this the fweetbreads, mufhrooms, and cocks'-combs. *Clermont*, 19.

Portable Soup for Travellers.

Cut into fmall pieces three large legs of veal, one of beef, and the lean part of half a ham. Put a quarter of a pound of butter at the bottom of a large cauldron, then lay in the meat and bones, with four ounces of anchovies, and two ounces of mace. Cut off the green leaves of five or fix heads of celery, wafh the heads quite clean, cut them fmall, put them in with three large carrots cut thin, cover the cauldron clofe, and fet it over a mo-derate fire. When you find the gravy begins to draw, keep taking it up till you have got it all out, then put water in to cover the meat; fet it on the fire again, and let it boil flowly for four hours,

hours, then ſtrain it through a hair ſieve into a clean pan, and
let it boil three parts away; then ſtrain the gravy that you drew
from the meat, into the pan, let it boil gently (obſerving to ſkim
the fat off as it riſes) till it looks thick like glue. You muſt take
great care, when it is near enough, that it does not burn; put in
chyan pepper to your taſte, then pour it on flat earthen diſhes
a quarter of an inch thick, and let it ſtand till the next day, and
cut it out with round tins a little larger than a crown piece; lay
the cakes on diſhes, and ſet them in the ſun to dry. This ſoup
will anſwer beſt to be made in froſty weather. When the cakes
are dry, put them in a tin box, with writing-paper between
every cake, and keep them in a dry place. This is a very
uſeful ſoup to be kept in gentlemens' families, for by pouring
a pint of boiling water on one cake, and a little ſalt, it will
make a good baſon of broth. A little boiling water poured on
it will make gravy for a turkey or fowls. The longer it is kept
the better.

N. B. It will be neceſſary to keep turning the cakes, as they
dry. *Raffald*, 2. *Farley* 150.

Macaroni Soup.

Mix three quarts of ſtrong broth, and one of gravy. Take
half a pound of ſmall pipe-macaroni, and boil it in three quarts
of water, with a little butter in it, till it is tender. Then ſtrain
it through a ſieve. Cut it in pieces of about two inches in
length, put it into your ſoup, and boil it up for ten minutes.
Send it to table in a tureen, with the cruſt of a French roll
toaſted. *Glaſſe*, 126. *Maſon*, 121.

Soup au Bourgeois.

Cut ten or a dozen heads of endive, and four or five bunches
of celery into ſmall bits; waſh them, let them be well drained
from the water, and put into a large pan; pour upon them four
quarts of boiling water; ſet on three quarts of beef gravy made
for ſoup, in a large ſauce-pan, ſtrain the herbs from the water
very dry. When the gravy boils, put them in. Cut off the
cruſts of two French rolls, break them, and put into the reſt.
When the herbs are tender, the ſoup is enough. A boiled
fowl may be put into the middle, but it is very good without.

If a white ſoup is liked better, it ſhould be veal gravy. *Cole*,
199.

Onion Soup.

Boil eight or ten large Spaniſh onions in milk and water;
change it three times. When they are quite ſoft, rub them
through a hair ſieve. Cut an old cock into pieces, and boil it
for gravy, with one blade of mace. Strain it, and pour it
upon the pulp of the onions; boil it gently with the crumb of
an old penny loaf, grated into half a pint of cream. Add
chyan

chyan pepper and falt to your tafte. A few heads of afparagus, or boiled fpinach, both make it eat well and look very pretty. Grate a cruft of brown bread round the edge of the diſh. *Raf-fald, 8.*

Ox-Cheek Soup.

Break the bones of an ox-cheek, and waſh them till they are perfectly clean. Then lay them in warm water, and throw in a little falt, which will fetch out the ſlime. Then take a large ftew-pan, and put two ounces of butter at the bottom of it, and lay the fleſhy ſide of the cheek-bone in it. Add to it half a pound of ſhank of ham cut in ſlices, and four heads of celery, with the leaves pulled off, and the heads waſhed clean. Cut them into the foup with three large onions, two carrots, a parſ-nip ſliced, a few beets cut fmall, and three blades of mace. Set it over a moderate fire for a quarter of an hour, which will draw the virtue from the roots, and give to the gravy an agree-able ſtrength. A very good gravy may be made by this me-thod, with roots and butter, adding only a little browning to give it a good colour. When the head has ſimmered a quarter of an hour, put to it fix quarts of water, and let it ftew till it is reduced to two quarts. If you would have it eat like foup, ſtrain and take out the meat and the other ingredients, and put in the white part of a head of celery cut in fmall pieces, with a little browning to make it of a fine colour. Take two ounces of vermicelli, give it a fcald in the foup, and put it into the tureen, with the top of a French roll in the middle of it. If you would have it eat like a ftew, take up the face as whole as poſſible, and have ready a boiled turnip and carrot cut in fquare pieces, and a ſlice of bread toaſted and cut in fmall dice. Put in a little chyan pepper, and ſtrain the foup through a hair fieve upon the meat, bread, turnip, and carrot. *Farley, 198.*

Soup Lorraine.

Take a pound of fweet almonds, blanch and beat them in a mortar, with a very little water to keep them from oiling; put to them all the white part of a large roaft fowl, and the yolks of four poached eggs; pound all together as fine as poſſible. Take three quarts of ſtrong veal broth; let it be very white, and ſkim off all the fat. Put it into a ſtew-pan with the other ingredients, and mix them well together. Boil them foftly over a ſtove, or on a clear fire. Mix the white part of another roaft fowl very fine; feafon with pepper, falt, nutmeg, and a little beaten mace. Put in a bit of butter as big as an egg, and a fpoonful or two of the foup ſtrained, and fet it over the ſtove to be quite hot. Cut two French rolls in thin ſlices, and fet them before the fire to crifp. Take one of the hollow rolls, which are made for oyfter loaves, and fill it with the mince;

M   lay

lay on the top as clofe as poffible, and keep it hot. Strain the foup through a piece of dimity into a clean fauce-pan, and let it ftew till it is the thickneſs of cream. Put the crifped bread in the diſh or tureen, pour the fauce over it, and place the roll with the minced meat in the middle. *Mafon*, 191.

Dauphin Soup.

Put a few flices of lard in the bottom of your fauce-pan, fliced ham and veal, three onions fliced, a carrot and parfnip. Soak over the fire till it catches, then add weak broth or boiling water; boil it on a flow fire till the meat is done. Pound the breaſt of a roaſted fowl, fix yolks of hard eggs, as many fweet almonds. Sift your broth, and add enough to your pounded compound as will fift it with a ftamine. Soak your bread till tender, in broth; warm your cullis without boiling, and mix it with as much broth as gives it a pretty thick confiſtence. You may garniſh this foup with a fowl, or knuckle of veal, as in all white foups. *Clermont*, 21.

Afparagus Soup.

Provide four or five pounds of beef, cut it into pieces; fet it over a fire, with an onion or two, a few cloves, and fome whole black pepper, a calf's foot or two, a head or two of celery, and a very little bit of butter. Let it draw at a diſtance from the fire. Put in a quart of warm beer three quarts of warm beef broth, or water. Let thefe ftew till enough. Strain it, take off the fat very clean, put in fome afparagus heads, cut fmall, (palates may be added, boiled very tender) and a toaſted French roll, the crumb taken out. *Cole*, 201.

Calf's Head Soup.

After waſhing a calf's head clean, ftew it with a bunch of fweet herbs, an onion ftuck with cloves, mace, pearl barley, and Jamaica pepper. When it is very tender, put to it fome ftewed celery. Seafon it with pepper, and ferve it with the head in the middle. *Cole*, 202.

Gravy Soup thickened with yellow Peas.

Put in fix quarts of water, a ſhin of beef, a pint of peas, and fix onions. Set them over the fire, and let them boil gently till all the juice is out of the meat. Then ftrain it through a fieve; add to the ftrained liquor one quart of ftrong gravy to make it brown; put in pepper and falt to your taſte. Then put in a little celery and beet-leaves, and boil it till they are tender. *Raffald*, 11.

Giblet Soup.

Provide about two pounds of fcrag of mutton, the fame quantity of fcrag of veal, and four pounds of gravy beef. Put this

this meat into two gallons of water, and let it ftew very foftly till it is a ftrong broth. Let it ftand till it be cold, and fkim off the fat. Take two pair of giblets, fcalded and cleaned, put them into the broth, and let them fimmer till they are very tender. Take out the giblets and ftrain the foup through a cloth. Put a piece of butter rolled in flour into a ftew-pan, make it of a light brown. Have ready, chopped fmall, fome parfley, chives, a little pennyroyal, and a little fweet marjoram. Put the foup over a very flow fire. Put in the giblets, fried butter, herbs, a little Madeira wine, fome falt, and fome chyan pepper. Let them fimmer till the herbs are tender, then fend the foup to table with the giblets in it. *Cole,* 202.

Soup Maigre.

PUT half a pound of butter into a deep stew-pan, shake it about, and let it stand till it has done making a noise; then have ready six middling onions peeled and cut small, throw them in, and shake them about. Take a bunch of celery, clean washed and picked, cut it in pieces half as long as your finger, a large handful of spinach clean washed and picked, a good lettuce clean washed (if you have it) and cut small, a little bundle of parsley chopped fine; shake all this well together in the pan for a quarter of an hour, then shake in a little flour; stir all together, and pour into the stew-pan two quarts of boiling water. Take a handful of dry hardcrust, throw in a tea-spoonful of beaten pepper, three blades of mace beat fine; stir all together, and let it boil softly for half an hour; then take it off the fire, and beat up the yolks of two eggs, and stir in, and one spoonful of vinegar; pour it into the soup-dish, and send it to table. If you have any green peas, boil half a pint in the soup for change. *Glasse*, 153. *Mason*, with little variation, 203. *Farley*, 152.

Queen's Rice Soup Maigre.

Take half a pound of rice, well washed in warm water, boil it tender in broth and butter; make a gravy without colouring, with carp, onions, carrots, and parsnips. When it is ready to catch, add broth, and boil it some time, then sift it; pound a dozen sweet almonds with six hard yolks of eggs, a few bits of boiled fish, crumbs of bread soaked in milk or cream; mix all together with the gravy and sift it. Warm it without boiling, and serve this cullis upon the rice. *Dalrymple*, 30.

Rice Soup.

Put a pound of rice and a little cinnamon to two quarts of water; cover it close, and let it simmer very softly till the rice is quite tender. Take out the cinnamon, then sweeten it to your palate; grate half a nutmeg, and let it stand till it is cold; then beat up the yolks of three eggs with half a pint of white wine. Mix them very well, and stir them into the rice, set them on a slow fire, and keep stirring all the time for fear of curdling. When it is of a good thickness, and boils, take it up. Keep stirring it till you put it into your dish. *Glasse*, 156. *Farley*, 164.

Oyster Soup.

Take a proper quantity of fish stock; then take two quarts of of oyfters without the beards ; beat the hard part in a mortar, with the yolks of ten hard eggs; put them to the fifh ftock, fet it over the fire ; feafon it with pepper, falt, and grated nut-meg. When it boils, put in the eggs ; let it boil till it is of a good thicknefs, and like a fine cream. *Mafon*, 202. *Farley*, 166.

Another way.

Make your ftock of any fort of fifh the place affords ; let there be about two quarts : take a pint of oyfters, beard them, put them into a fauce-pan, ftrain the liquor, let them ftew two or three minutes in their own liquor ; then take the hard parts of the oyfters, and beat them in a mortar with the yolks of four hard eggs ; mix them with fome of the foup ; put them with the other part of the oyfters and liquor into a fauce-pan, a little nutmeg, pepper and falt ; ftir them well together, and let it boil a quarter of an hour. Difh it up, and fend it to table. *Cole*, 204.

Green Peas Soup.

In fhelling your peas, feparate the old ones from the young, and boil the old ones foft enough to ftrain through a cullen-der ; then put the liquor, and what you ftrained through, to the young peas. which muft be whole, and fome whole pepper, mint, and a little onion fhred fmall ; put them in a large fauce-pan, with near a pound of butter ; as they boil up, fhake in fome flour ; then put in a French roll fried in butter, to the foup ; you muft feafon it to your tafte with falt and herbs. When you have done fo, add the young peas to it, which muft be half boiled firft. You may leave out the flour, if you think proper, and inftead of it, put in a little fpinach and cabbage lettuce, cut fmall, which muft be fried in butter, and well mixed with the broth. *Raffald*, 12.

Another way.

Boil a quart of old green peas in a quart of water, till they are as tender as pap, then ftrain them through a fieve, and boil a quart of young peas in that water. In the mean time put the old peas into a fieve, pour half a pound of melted butter over them, and ftrain them through a fieve with the back of a fpoon, till you have got all the pulp. When the young peas are boiled enough, add the pulp and butter to the young peas and liquor ; ftir them together till they are fmooth, and feafon with pepper and falt. You may fry a French roll, and let it fwim in the difh. If you like it, boil a bundle of mint in the peas. *Glaffe*, 153.

Mrs. Mafon, page 204, has the fame receipt in different words.

Onion

Onion Soup.

Brown half a pound of butter with a little flour; take care
it does not burn. When it has done hiffing, flice a dozen of
large white onions, fry them very gently till they are tender;
then pour to them, by degrees, two quarts of boiling water,
fhaking the pan well round as it is poured in; add alfo a cruft
of bread. Let it boil gently for half an hour; feafon it with
pepper and falt. Take the top of a French roll, and dry it at
the fire; put it into a fauce-pan with fome of the foup to foak
it; then put it into the tureen. Let the foup boil fome time
after the onions are tender, as it gives the foup a great rich-
nefs; ftrain it off, and pour it upon the French roll. *Mafon*,
203.

Eel Soup.

Take a pound of eels, which will make a pint of good foup,
or any greater quantity of eels, in proportion to the quantity of
foup you intend to make. To every pound of eels, put a quart
of water, a cruft of bread, two or three blades of mace, a little
whole pepper, an onion, and a bundle of fweet herbs. Cover
them clofe, and let them boil till half the liquor is wafted; then
ftrain it, and toaft fome bread; cut it fmall, lay the bread into
your difh, and pour in the foup. If you have a ftew-hole, fet
the difh over it for a minute, and fend it to table. If you find
your foup not rich enough, you may let it boil till it is as thick
as you would have it. You may add a piece of carrot to brown
it. *Farley*, 167.

Peas Soup.

Put a quart of fplit peas into a gallon of water to boil.
When they are qutte foft, put in half a red herring, or two
anchovies, a good deal of whole pepper, black and white, two
or three blades of mace, four or five cloves, a bundle of fweet
herbs, a large onion, the green tops of a bunch of celery, and
a good bundle of dried mint; cover them clofe, and let them
boil foftly till there is about two quarts; then ftrain it off, and
have ready the white part of the celery wafhed clean, and cut
fmall and ftewed tender in a quart of water, fome fpinach
picked and wafhed clean, put to the celery; let them ftew till
the water is quite wafted, and put it to your foup.

Take out the crumb of a French roll, fry the cruft brown in
a little frefh butter; take fome fpinach, ftew it in a little butter,
after it is boiled, and fill the roll; take the crumb, cut it in
piece, beat it in a mortar with a raw egg, a little fpinach, and a
little forrel a little beaten mace, a little nutmeg, and an anchovy; then mix it up with your hand, and roll them into balls
with a little flour, and cut fome bread into dice, and fry them
crifp; pour your foup into your difh, put in the balls and bread,
and

and the roll in the middle. Garnifh your difh with fpinach.
If it want falt, you muft feafon it to your palate ; rub in fome
dried mint. *Glaffe*, 152.

Muffel Soup.

Wafh a hundred muffels very clean, and put them into a
fauce-pan till they open, then take them from the fhells, beard
them, and ftrain the liquor through a lawn fieve ; beat a dozen
craw-fifh very fine, with as many almonds blanched in a mortar ; then take a carrot and a fmall parfnip fcraped, and cut in
flices, fry them in butter ; take the muffel liquor, with a fmall
bunch of fweet herbs, a little parfley and horfe radifh, with the
craw-fifh and almonds, a little pepper and falt, and half the
muffels, with a quart of water or more ; let it boil till all the
goodnefs is out of the ingredients, then ftrain it off to two
quarts of the white fifh-ftock ; put it into a fauce-pan ; put in
the reft of the muffels, a few mufhrooms and truffles, a leek
wafhed and cut fmall ; take two French rolls, cut out the
crumb, fry it brown, cut it into little pieces, and put it into the
foup ; let it boil together for a quarter of an hour, with the fried
carrot and parfnip ; at the fame time, take the cruft of the roll,
and fry them crifp. Take the other half of the muffels, a
quarter of a pound of butter, a fpoonful of water ; fhake in a
little flour, fet them on the fire till the butter is melted ; feafon
it with pepper and falt, then beat the yolks of three eggs, put
them in, ftir them all the time for fear of curdling ; grate a
little nutmeg. When it is thick and fine, fill the rolls, pour
the foup into the tureen, and fet the rolls in the middle. *Cole,*
206.

Barley Soup.

To a gallon of water put half a pound of barley, a blade or
two of mace, a large cruft of bread, and a little lemon-peel.
Let it boil till it comes to two quarts ; then add half a pint of
white wine, and fweeten to your palate. *Cole,* 207.

Scate Soup.

Having fkinned and wafhed two pounds of fcate, boil it in fix
quarts of water. When it is boiled, take the meat from the
bones ; take two pounds of flounders, wafh them clean, put
them into the water the fcate was boiled in, with fome lemon-
peel, a bunch of fweet herbs, a few blades of mace, fome horfe-
radifh, the cruft of a penny loaf, a little parfley, and the bones
of the fcate ; cover it very clofe, and let it fimmer till it is
reduced to two quarts ; then ftrain it off, and put to it an
ounce of vermicelli ; fet it on the fire, and let it boil very foftly. Take one of the hollow rolls which are made for oyfters,
and fry it in butter. Take the meat of the fcate, pull it into
little flices, put it into a fauce-pan, with two or three fpoonfuls

of

of the foup; fhake into it a little flour and a piece of butter, fome pepper and falt; fhake them together in a fauce-pan till it is thick, then fill the roll with it; pour the foup into the tureen, put the roll into it, and fend it to table. *Mafon,* 201.

Mr. Farley, page 168, has the fame receipt in fubftance, though expreffed in different words.

Mrs. Glaffe, page 155, has alfo the fame receipt; to whom *Mrs. Mafon* and *Mr. Farley* appear to be indebted.

Egg Soup.

Beat the yolks of two eggs in a difh, with a piece of butter, as big as a hen's egg; take a tea-kettle of boiling water in one hand, and a fpoon in the other. Pour in about a quart, by degrees, then keep ftirring it well all the time, till the eggs are well mixed, and the butter melted. Then pour it into a fauce-pan, and keep ftirring it all the time till it begins to fimmer. Take it off the fire, and pour it between two veffels, out of one into another, till it is quite fmooth, and has a great froth. Set it on the fire again, keep ftirring it till it is quite hot, then pour it into your foup-difh, and fend it hot to table. *Farley,* 165.

Milk Soup.

Put into two quarts of milk, two fticks of cinnamon, two bay leaves, a very little bafket falt, and a very little fugar; then blanch half a pound of fweet almonds while the milk is heating; beat them up to a pafte in a marble mortar, mix with them, by degrees, fome milk. While they are beating, grate the peel of a lemon with the almonds and a little of the juice; then ftrain it through a coarfe fieve, and mix it with the milk that is heating in the ftew-pan, and let it boil up.

Cut fome flices of French bread, dry them before the fire, foak them a little in the milk, lay them at the bottom of the tureen, and pour in the foup. *Cole,* 208.

Milk Soup the Dutch way.

Boil a quart of milk with cinnamon and moift fugar; put fippets in the difh, pour the milk over it, and fet it over a charcoal fire to fimmer till the bread is foft. Take the yolks of two eggs, beat them up, and mix it with a little of the milk, and throw it in. Mix it all together, and fend it up to table. *Cole,* 208.

Turnip Soup Italian fashion.

Cut turnips in what fhape you pleafe, colour them with butter in a ftew-pan, and two fpoonfuls of oil; add flices of roots, &c. and boil them in good fifh gravy; give it a confiftence with any fort of porridge. *Clermont,* 25.

CHAP.

Brown Gravy without Meat.

MELT a piece of butter as big as a walnut in a saucepan; stir it round, and when the broth sinks, dust some flour in it. Then take half a pint of small beer that is not bitter, and half a pint of water, a spoonful of walnut-liquor, or catchup, the same quantity of mushroom liquor, one anchovy, a little blade of mace, some whole pepper, and a bit of carrot. Let it simmer for a quarter of an hour, and then strain it off. Use it for fish or fowl. *Mason*, 327.

Good brown Gravy.

To half a pint of beer or ale that is not bitter, put half a pint of water, an onion cut small, a little bit of lemon-peel cut small, three cloves, a blade of mace, some whole pepper, a spoonful of mushroom-pickle, a spoonful of walnut-pickle, a spoonful of catchup, and an anchovy. First put a piece of butter into a sauce-pan, as big as an hen's egg; when it is melted, shake in a little flour, and let it be a little brown; then by degrees stir in the above ingredients, and let it boil a quarter of an hour, then strain it, and it is fit for fish or roots. *Cole*, 209.

Gravy for a Turkey, Fowl, or Ragoo.

Take a pound of lean beef, cut and hack it well, then flour it well. Put a piece of butter, as big as an hen's egg, in a stew-pan; when it is melted, put in your beef, fry it on all sides a little brown; then pour in three pints of boiling water, and a bundle of sweet herbs, two or three blades of mace, three or four cloves, twelve whole pepper-corns, a little bit of carrot, a little piece of crust of bread-toasted brown; cover it close, and let it boil till there is about a pint or less. Then season it with salt, and strain it off. *Glasse*, 125.

To make Gravy.

As gravy is not always to be procured, especially by those who live remote from large towns, in such cases the following directions may be useful: When your meat comes from the butcher's, take a piece of beef, veal and mutton, and cut them into small pieces. Take a large deep sauce-pan, with a cover, lay your beef at bottom, then your mutton, then a very little piece of bacon, a slice or two of carrot, some mace, cloves, whole black and white pepper, a large onion cut in slices, a bundle of sweet herbs, and then lay in your veal. Cover it close over a slow fire for six or seven minutes, and shake the sauce-pan often; then dust some flour into it, and pour in boiling

ing water till the meat is fomething more than covered. Cover
it clofe again, and let it ftew till it is rich and good. Then feafon it to your tafte with falt, and ftrain it off; when you will
have a gravy that will anfwer moft purpofes. *Farley,* 137.

Gravy for a Fowl, when you have neither Meat nor Gravy ready.

Boil the neck, liver, and gizzard of the fowl in half a pint
of water, with a little piece of bread toafted brown, a little pepper and falt, and a little bit of thyme. Let them boil till there
is a quarter of a pint; then pour in half a glafs of red wine,
boil it, and ftrain it, then bruife the liver well in, and ftrain it
again, thicken it with a little piece of butter rolled in flour,
and it will be very good.

An ox's kidney makes good gravy, cut all to pieces, and
boiled with fpices, &c. *Cole,* 210.

Beef Gravy.

Take fome lean beef, according to the quantity of gravy
that is wanted, cut it into pieces; put it into a ftew-pan, with
an onion or two fliced, and a little carrot; cover it clofe, fet
it over a gentle fire; pour off the gravy as it draws from it,
then let the meat brown, turning it that it may not burn.
Pour over it boiling water; add a few cloves, pepper-corns, a
bit of lemon-peel, a bunch of fweet herbs. Let this fimmer
gently; ftrain it with the gravy that was drawn from the meat.
Add a fpoonful of catchup and fome falt.

A pound of meat will make a pint of gravy. *Mafon,* 328.

Mutton or Veal Gravy.

Take your mutton or veal, cut and hack it very well, fet it
on the fire with water, fweet herbs, mace and pepper. Let it
boil till it is as good as you would have it, then ftrain it off.
Your great cooks always. if they can, chop a partridge or two
and put into gravies. *Cole,* 210.

A ftrong Fifh Gravy.

Take two or three eels, or any other fifh you may have;
fkin or fcale them, gut them and wafh them from grit, cut
them in little pieces, put them into a ftew-pan, cover them
with water, a little cruft of bread toafted brown, a blade or two
of mace, and fome whole pepper, a few fweet herbs. and a very
little bit of lemon-peel. Let it boil till it is rich and good; then
have ready a piece of butter, according to your gravy. If a
pint, as big as a walnut. Melt it in the fauce-pan, then fhake
in a little flour, tofs it about till it is brown, and then ftrain
in the gravy to it. Let it boil a few minutes, and it will be
good. *Glaffe,* 127.

Mutton

Mutton Broth.

Cut a neck of mutton, of about six pounds, into two, and boil the scrag in about four quarts of water. Skim it well, and put in a little bundle of sweet herbs, an onion, and a good crust of bread. Having boiled this an hour, put in the other part of the mutton, a turnip or two, some dried marigolds, a few chives chopped fine, and a little parsley chopped small. Put these in about a quarter of an hour before your broth is enough, and season it with salt You may, if you choose it put in a quarter of a pound of barley or rice at first. Some like it thickened with oatmeal, and some with bread, and some have it seasoned with mace, instead of sweet herbs and onion; but these are mere matters of fancy, on which the difference of palates must determine. If you use turnips for sauce, do not boil them all in the pot with the meat, but some in the sauce pan, by themselves, otherwise the broth will taste too strong of them. *Farley*, 150. From *Glasse*, 132.

Another way.

Boil a scrag of mutton in between three and four quarts of water; skim it as soon as it boils, and put to it a carrot, a turnip, a crust of bread, an onion, and a small bundle of herbs; let these stew. Put in the other part of the neck, that it may be boiled tender; when enough, take out the mutton, and strain the broth. Put in the mutton again, with a few dried marigolds, chives, or young onions, and a little parsley chopped; boil these about a quarter of an hour. The broth and mutton may be served together in a tureen ; or the meat in a separate dish. Do not send up the scrag, unless particularly liked. Some do not like herbs : the broth must then be strained off. Send up mashed turnips in a little dish. The broth may be thickened either with crumbs of bread or oatmeal. *Mason.*

Veal Broth.

Take a knuckle of veal, stew it in about a gallon of water, two ounces of rice or vermicelli, a little salt, and a blade of mace. *Cole*, 211.

Scotch Barley Broth.

Chop a leg of beef all to pieces, boil it in three gallons of water, with a piece of carrot, and a crust of bread, till it is half boiled away; then strain it off, and put it into the pot again with half a pound of barley, four or five heads of celery washed clean and cut small, a large onion, a bundle of sweet herbs, a little parsley chopped small, and a few marigolds. Let it boil an hour. Take an old cock, or a large fowl, clean picked and washed, and put it into the pot, boil it till the broth is
quite

quite good; then feafon it with falt, and fend to table, with
the fowl in the middle. This broth is very good without the
fowl. Take out the onion and fweet herbs before you fend it
to table.

This broth is very good, when made with a fheep's head
inftead of a leg of beef; but you muft chop the head all to
pieces. *Cole, 211.*

Beef Broth.

Break the bone of a leg of beef in two or three places, put
it into a gallon of water, two or three blades of mace, a little
parfley, and a cruft of bread; boil the beef very tender, ftrain
the broth, and pour it into a tureen; if agreeable, the meat may
be put in with it. Toaft fome bread, cut it into fquares, and
put it in a plate. *Cole, 212.*

Strong Beef Broth to keep for use.

Take part of a leg of beef, and the fcrag end of a neck of
mutton, break the bones in pieces, and put to it as much water
as will cover it, and a little falt; and when it boils, fkim it
clean, and put into it a whole onion ftuck with cloves, a bunch
of fweet herbs, fome pepper, and a nutmeg quartered. Let
thefe boil till the meat is boiled in pieces, and the ftrength
boiled out of it. Strain it out, and keep it for ufe. *Glaffe, 206.*
Mafon, 128.

Jelly Broth

Put in your pot or ftew-pan flices of beef, a fillet of veal, a
fowl, one or two partridges, according to the quantity required;
put it on the fire till it catches a little, and turn the meat now
and then to give it a proper colour; then add fome good clear
boiling broth, and fcalded roots, as carrots, turnips, parfnips,
parfley-roots, celery, large onions, a few cloves, a fmall bit of
nutmeg, and fome whole pepper; boil it upon a flow fire about
four or five hours with attention, and add a few cloves of garlic
or fhallot, a fmall faggot or bunch of parfley and thyme tied together; when it is of a good colour, lift it; it ferves for fauces,
and to add ftrength to your foups, particularly thofe made of
herbs. *Clermont, 3.*

Chicken Broth.

Take an old cock, or large fowl, and flay it; pick off all
the fat, and break it to pieces with a rolling pin; put it into
two quarts of water, with a good cruft of bread and a blade
of mace; let it boil foftly till it is as good as you would have
it; it will take five or fix hours doing. Then pour it off, put
a quart more boiling water to it, and cover it clofe; let it boil
foftly till it is good, and then ftrain it off; feafon with a very
little

little falt. When you boil the chicken, fave the liquor ; and when the meat is eat take the bones, break them, and put them to the liquor you boiled the chicken in, with a blade of mace, and a cruft of bread, *Cole,* 212.

Broth to fweeten the fharpnefs of the blood.

Slice half a pound of veal ; boil it in three pints of water, with five or fix craw-fifh, pounded ; add to it white endives, a fmall handful of chervil, and as much purflain, three or four lettuces, all coarfely chopped ; reduce the liquid to half, and ftrain it through a cloth or ftamine, without fkimming it. *Clermont,* 5.

CHAP.

To fricassee Chickens.

SKIN your chickens, and cut them in small pieces, wash them in warm water, and then dry them very clean with a cloth ; season them with pepper and salt, and then put them into a stew-pan with a little fair water, and a good piece of butter, a little lemon-pickle, or half a lemon, a glass of white wine, one anchovy, a little mace and nutmeg, an onion stuck with cloves, a bunch of lemon-thyme, and sweet marjoram; let these stew together till your chickens are tender, and then lay them on your dish ; thicken the gravy with flour and butter, strain it, then beat the yolks of three eggs a little, and mix them with a large tea-cupful of rich cream, and put it in your gravy, and shake it over the fire, but do not let it boil, and pour it over your chickens. *Raffald*, 125.

A brown fricassee of Chickens or Rabbits.

Take your rabbits or chickens, and skin the rabbits but not the chickens, then cut them into small pieces, and rub them over with the yolks of eggs. Have ready some grated bread, a little beaten mace, and a little grated nutmeg mixed together, and then roll them in it ; put a little butter into a stew-pan, and when it is melted, put in your meat. Fry it of a fine brown, and take care they do not stick to the bottom of the pan ; then pour the gravy from them, and pour in half a pint of brown gravy, a glass of white wine, a few mushrooms, or two spoonfuls of the pickle, a little salt (if wanted) and a piece of butter rolled in flour. When it is of a fine thickness, dish it up, and send it to table. You may add truffles and morels, and cocks' combs. *Glasse*, 22. .

A white fricassee of Chickens or Rabbits.

Skin them, cut them to pieces, lay them in warm water; stew them in a little water, with a piece of lemon-peel, a little white wine, an anchovy, an onion, two or three cloves, a bunch of sweet herbs. When tender, take them out, strain the liquor, put a very little of it into a quarter of a pint of thick cream, with four ounces of butter, and a little flour ; keep it constantly stirring till the butter is melted; put in the chickens, a little grated lemon-peel and pounded mace, a little lemon-juice and mushroom-powder ; shake all together over the fire. If agreeable, put in pickled mushrooms, and omit the lemon-juice. *Mason*, 266.

N. B. You may fricassee lamb, veal, and tripe, in the same manner.

To

To fricaſſee Rabbits brown

Cut them up as for eating, fry them in butter a light brown, put them in a toſſing pan, with a pint of water, a tea-ſpoonful of lemon-pickle, a large ſpoonful of muſhroom catchup, the ſame of browning, one anchovy, a ſlice of lemon chyan pepper and ſalt to your taſte; ſtew them over a ſlow fire till they are enough; thicken your gravy and ſtrain it, diſh up your rabbits, and pour the gravy over. *Cole*, 214.

To fricaſſee Rabbits white.

Having cut up your rabbits, put them into a toſſing-pan, with a pint of veal gravy, a tea-ſpoonful of lemon-pickle, one anchovy, a ſlice of lemon, a little beaten mace, chyan pepper and ſalt; ſtew them over a ſlow fire. When they are enough, thicken your gravy with flour and butter; ſtrain it, then add the yolks of two eggs mixed with a large tea-cupful of thick cream, and a little nutmeg grated in it; do not let it boil, and ſerve it up. *Cole*, 214.

To fricaſſee Tripe.

Cut a piece of double tripe in pieces of about two inches; put them in a ſauce-pan of water, with an onion, and a bundle of ſweet herbs; boil it till it is quite tender, then have ready a biſhamel made thus: Take ſome lean ham, cut it in thin pieces, and put it in a ſtew-pan, and ſome veal, having firſt cut off the fat, put it over the ham; cut an onion in ſlices, ſome carrot and turnip, a little thyme, cloves, and mace, and ſome freſh muſhrooms chopped; put a little milk at the bottom, and draw it gently over the fire. Be careful it does not ſcorch, then put in a quart of milk, and half a pint of cream; ſtew it gently for an hour, thicken it with a little flour and milk, ſeaſon it with ſalt, and a very little chyan pepper bruiſed fine; then ſtrain it off through a tammy; put your tripe into it, toſs it up, and add ſome force-meat balls, muſhrooms and oyſters blanched; then put it into your diſh, and garniſh with fried oyſters, or ſweet-breads, or lemons. *Glaſſe*, 24.

Another way.

Cut ſome nice white tripe into ſlips, put it into ſome boiled gravy with a little cream and a bit of butter mixed with flour; ſtir it till the butter is melted; add a little white wine, lemon-peel grated, chopped parſley, pepper and ſalt, pickled muſhrooms or lemon-juice; ſhake all together; ſtew it a little. *Maſon*, 135.

To fricaſſee Ox Palates.

Clean your palates very well, put them into a ſtew-pot, and cover them with water, ſet them in the oven for three or four hours. When they come from the oven, ſtrip off the ſkins,
and

and cut them in square pieces; season them with mace, nutmeg, chyan, and salt; mix a spoonful of flour with the yolks of
two eggs, dip in your palates, and fry them a light brown, then
put them in a sieve to drain. Have ready half a pint of veal
gravy, with a little caper liquor, a spoonful of browing, and a
few mushrooms; thicken it well with flour and butter, pour it
hot on your dish, and lay in your palates. Garnish with fried
parsley and barberries. *Raffald,* 120.

Another way.

Boil and peel your palates, and cut them in small fillets; put
them into a stew-pan with a little butter, a slice of ham, mushrooms, a nosegay*, two cloves, a little tarragon, a glass of white
wine, and broth; simmer them till they are quite tender; add
salt, pepper, and a little chopped parsley. When ready to
serve, add a liason made of three yolks of eggs, cream, and
some bits of good butter; and add the squeeze of a lemon
when ready. *Clermont,* 55.

To fricassee Calves Tongues.

Get two tongues, which are enough for a small dish; boil
them till the skin comes well off the ragged parts, and slice
them very thin, put them into a stew-pan with a ladle or two of
broth, and put in a bunch of onions and parsley, a blade of
mace, pepper and salt. Let all stew softly till very tender, and
liason, pour it in when boiling hot, cover it close, and let it remain so till your time of dining; move it upon a stove for a
minute or two, squeeze in a lemon or orange, and dish it up.
Verral, 122.

To fricassee Neats Tongues.

Boil your neats tongues till they are tender, peel them, cut
them into slices, and fry them in fresh butter; then pour out
the butter, put in as much gravy as you want for sauce, a bundle of sweet herbs, an onion, some pepper and salt, a blade or
two of mace, and a glass of white wine. Having simmered all
together about half an hour, take out the tongues, strain the
gravy, and put both that and the tongues into the stew-pan again.
Beat up the yolks of two eggs, a little nutmeg grated, and a
small piece of butter rolled in flour. Shake all together for
four or five minutes, and dish it up. *Farley,* 85.

To fricassee Calf's Feet.

Boil the feet, take out the long bones, split them, and put
them into a stew-pan, with some veal gravy, and a very little
white wine; beat the yolks of two or three eggs with a little
cream, and put to them a little grated nutmeg, some salt, and

---

* *A faggot of parsley, onions, shallots, &c.*

a piece

a piece of butter; ftir it till it is of a proper thicknefs. *Cole,* 216.

To fricaffee Pigeons.

Cut your pigeons as you would do chickens for fricaffee, fry them a light brown, then put them into fome good mutton gravy, and ftew them near half an hour; then put in half an ounce of morels, a fpoonful of browning, and a flice of lemon; take up your pigeons, and thicken your gravy; ftrain it over your pigeons, and lay round them force-meat balls, and garnifh with pickles. *Raffald,* 133. *Farley,* 84.

To fricaffee Lamb Cutlets.

Cut a leg of lamb into thin cutlets acrofs the grain, and put them into a ftew-pan; in the mean time make fome good broth with the bones, fhank, &c. enough to cover the collops; put it into the ftew-pan, and cover it with a bundle of fweet herbs, an onion, a little cloves and mace tied in a muflin rag, and ftew them gently for ten minutes; then take out the collops, fkim off the fat, and take out the fweet herbs and mace; thicken it with butter rolled in flour, feafon it with falt and a little chyan pepper, put in a few mufhrooms, truffles, and morels, clean wafhed, fome force-meat balls, three yolks of eggs beat up in half a pint of cream, and fome nutmeg grated. Keep ftirring it one way till it is thick and fmooth, and then put in your collops. Give them a tofs up, take them out with a fork, and lay them in a difh; pour the fauce over them, and garnifh with beet-root and lemon. *Mafon,* 171.

To fricaffee Sweetbreads brown.

Having fcalded two or three fweetbreads, flice them, and dip them in the yolk of an egg, mixed with pepper, falt, nutmeg, and a little flour; fry them a nice brown, thicken a little good gravy with fome flour; boil it well; add chyan, catchup, or mufhroom powder, a little juice of lemon; ftew the fweetbreads in this a few minutes; garnifh with lemon. *Cole,* 217.

To fricaffee Sweetbreads white.

Scald and flice your fweetbreads, put them into a toffing-pan with a pint of veal gravy, a fpoonful of white wine, the fame of mufhroom catchup, and a little beaten mace; ftew them a quarter of an hour, thicken your gravy with flour and butter a little before they are enough. When you are going to difh them up, mix the yolk of an egg with a tea-cupful of thick cream and a little grated nutmeg; put it into your toffing-pan, and fhake it well over the fire, but do not let it boil; lay your fweetbreads on your difh, and pour your fauce over them. Garnifh with pickled red beet-root and kidney beans. *Raffald,* 99.

N

To

To fricaſſee Eels.

Skin three or four large eels, and notch them from end to end, cut them into four or five pieces each, and lay them in ſome ſpring water for half an hour to crimp them; dry them in a cloth, and toſs them over the fire a few minutes in a bit of freſh butter, a green onion or two, and a little parſley minced; but take care the colour of neither is altered by burning your butter; pour in about a pint of white wine, and as much good broth, pepper, ſalt, and a blade of mace; ſtew all together about three quarters of an hour, and thicken it with a bit of butter and flour. Prepare your liaſon with the yolks of four or five eggs beat ſmooth, with two or three ſpoonfuls of broth; grate in a little nutmeg, a little minced parſley; towards your dinner time, let your eels be boiling hot, and pour in your eggs, &c. Toſs it over the fire for a moment, add the juice of a lemon, and ſerve it up. Be very cautious that you do not let it curdle, by keeping it too long upon the fire after the eggs are in.

Tench cut in pieces make a very good diſh done in the ſame manner. *Verral*, 70.

To fricaſſee Carp Roes.

Put a little good butter in a ſtew-pan, with a dozen ſmall muſhrooms, a ſlice of ham, the ſqueeze of a lemon, and a faggot of ſweet herbs; ſoak it on a ſlow fire a little while, then add a little flour, and as many carp roes as you think proper, with a little good broth; ſtew them about a quarter of an hour, ſeaſoning with pepper and ſalt. When ready to ſerve, thicken it with a liaſon made with the yolks of two or three eggs and cream, with a little chopped parſley. *Dalrymple*, 407.

To fricaſſee Flounders and Plaice.

After cleaning the fiſh, take off the black ſkin, but not the white; cut the fleſh from the bones into long ſlices, and dip them into yolk of egg; ſtrew over them ſome bread raſpings, and fry them in clarified butter. When they are enough, lay them upon a plate, and keep them hot. For ſauce—take the bones of the fiſh, boil them in ſome water; then put in an anchovy, ſome thyme, parſley, a little pepper, ſalt, cloves, and mace. Let theſe ſimmer till the anchovy is diſſolved, then take the butter the fiſh was fried in, put it into a pan over the fire; ſhake ſome flour into it, and keep ſtirring it while the flour is ſhaking in; then ſtrain the liquor into it, and let it boil till it is thick; ſqueeze ſome lemon-juice into it; put the fiſh into a diſh, and pour the ſauce over them.

To fricaſſee Scate, or Thornback.

Cut the meat from the bones, fins, &c. and make it very clean. Then cut it into thin pieces, about an inch broad, and

two

two inches long, and lay them in your ftew-pan. To one pound of the flefh, put a quarter of a pint of water, a little beaten mace, and grated nutmeg, a fmall bundle of fweet herbs, and a little falt. Cover it, and let it boil fifteen minutes. Take out the fweet herbs, put in a quarter of a pint of good cream, a piece of butter the fize of a walnut, rolled in flour, and a glafs of white wine. Keep fhaking the pan all the time one way, till it is thick and fmooth; then difh it up, and gar= nifh with lemon. *Farley*, 88.

To fricaffee Cod Sounds.

Having cleaned them very well, cut them into little pretty pieces, boil them tender in milk and water, then throw them into a cullender to drain; pour them into a clean faucepan, feafon them with a little beaten mace and grated nutmeg and a very little falt; pour to them juft cream enough for fauce, and a good piece of butter rolled in flour; keep fhaking your faucepan round all the time, till it is thick enough; then difh it up, and garnifh with lemon. *Glaffe*, 182.

To fricaffee Oyfters.

Put a little butter in a ftew-pan, with a flice of ham, a fag-got of parfley and fweet herbs, and one onion ftuck with two cloves; foak it a little on a flow fire, then add a little flour, fome good broth, and a piece of lemon-peel; then put fcalded oyfters to it, and fimmer them a little. When ready to ferve, thicken it with a liafon made of the yolks of two eggs, a little cream, and a bit of good butter; take out the ham, faggot, onion, and lemon-peel, and add the fqueeze of a lemon. *Dal-rymple*, 408.

To fricaffee Eggs.

Boil your eggs pretty hard and flice them; then take a little veal gravy, a little cream and flour, a bit of butter, nutmeg, falt, pepper, chopped parfley, and a few pickled mufhrooms; boil this up, pour it over the eggs; a hard yolk laid in the middle of the difh; toafted fippets. *Mafon*, 288.

To fricaffee Mufhrooms.

Peel your mufhrooms, and fcrape the infide of them, throw them into falt and water; if buttons, rub them with flannel; take them out and boil them with frefh falt and water When they are tender, put in a little fhred parfley, an onion ftuck with cloves; tofs them up with a good lump of butter rolled in a little flour. You may put in three fpoonfuls of thick cream, and a little nutmeg cut in pieces; but take care to take out the nutmeg and onion before you fend it to table. You may leave out the parfley, and ftew in a glafs of wine, if you like it. *Raffald*, 143. *Farley*, 86.

To fricassee Artichoke Bottoms.

Take artichoke bottoms, either dried or pickled; if dried, you muſt lay them in warm water for three or four hours, ſhifting the water two or three times; then have ready a little cream and a piece of freſh butter ſtirred together one way till it is melted; then put in the artichokes, and when they are hot, diſh them up. *Glaſſe*, 196.

To fricassee Skirrets.

Having waſhed the roots very well, and boiled them till they are tender, take the ſkin off the roots and cut them into ſlices. Have ready a little cream, a piece of butter rolled in flour, the yolk of an egg beat, a little nutmeg grated, two or three ſpoonfuls of white wine, a very little ſalt, and ſtir all together. Your roots being in the diſh, pour the ſauce over them. It is a pretty ſide diſh.

Turbot au Court Bouillon, with Capers.

WASH and dry a small turbot, then take some thyme, parsley, sweet herbs, and an onion sliced; put them into a stew-pan, then lay in the turbot (the stew-pan should be just large enough to hold the fish) strew over the fish the same herbs that are under it, with some chives and sweet basil; then pour in an equal quantity of white wine, and white wine vinegar till the fish is covered; then strew in a little bay-salt, with some whole pepper; set the stew-pan over a gentle stove increasing the heat by degrees till it is enough; then take it off the fire, but do not take the turbot out; set a saucepan on the fire with a pound of butter, two anchovies, split, boned, and washed, two large spoonfuls of capers cut small, some chives whole, and a little pepper, salt, some nutmeg grated, a little flour, a spoonful of vinegar, and a little water; set the sauce-pan over the stove, and keep shaking it round for some time, and set the turbot on to make it hot; put it in a dish, and pour some of the sauce over it; lay some horse-radish round it, and put what remains of the sauce in a boat

Soles, flounders, large plaice or dabs, are very good done this way. *Mason*, 212.

To fry a Turbot.

Take a small turbot and cut it across as if it were ribbed. When it is quite dry, flour it and put it into a large frying-pan, with boiling lard enough to cover it; fry it till it is brown, then drain it; clean the pan, put into it claret or white wine, almost enough to cover it, anchovy, salt, nutmeg, and a little ginger; put in the fish, and let it stew till half the liquor is wasted; then take it out, and put in a piece of butter rolled in flour, and a minced lemon; let them simmer till of a proper thickness, rub a hot dish with a piece of shallot, lay the turbot in the dish, and pour the sauce over it. *Cole*, 220.

To bake a Turbot.

Take a dish about the size of the turbot, rub butter thick all over it, throw a little salt, a little beaten pepper, and half a large nutmeg, some parsley minced fine, and throw all over; pour in a pint of white wine, cut off the head and tail, lay the turbot in the dish, pour another pint of white wine all over, grate the other half of the nutmeg over it, and a little pepper, some salt, and chopped parsley. Lay a piece of butter here and there all over, and throw a little flour all over, and then a good many crumbs of bread. Bake it, and be sure that it is a fine brown;

then

then lay it in your difh, ftir the fauce in your difh all together, pour it into a faucepan, fhake in a little flour, let it boil, then ftir in a piece of butter and two fpoonfuls of catchup, let it boil, and pour it into bafons. Garnifh your difh with lemon ; and you may add what you fancy to the fauce, as fhrimps, anchovies, mufhrooms, &c. If a fmall turbot, half the wine will do. It eats finely thus. Lay it in a difh. fkim off all the fat, and pour the reft over it. Let it ftand till cold, and it is good with vinegar, and a fine difh to fet out a cold table. *Glaffe*, 178.

Turbot with Pontiff Sauce.

Take a fifh kettle or ftew-pan much of the fize of the turbot, with a fifh-plate in it, and garnifh it with thin flices of ham and veal, fliced roots and onions, one clove of garlic, a little whole pepper, and three cloves; foak it on a flow fire near half an hour, then add a bottle of white wine, and as much broth, with falt fufficient; ftew it on a flow fire till the meat is done, then ftrain the fauce, put the turbot to it, and ftew it on a flow fire till it is done; then drain it, and ferve it with pontiff fauce; or you may ferve it with the fauce it was ftewed in, thickening it with flour and butter, and feafoning it according to tafte and judgment. *Dalrymple*, 304.

Salmon a-la-braife.

Make a force-meat thus : — take a large eel, flit it open, and take out the bone, and take the meat quite clean from it ; chop it fine, with two anchovies, fome lemon-peel cut fine, a little pepper and grated nutmeg, with fome parfley and thyme cut fine, a yolk of an egg boiled hard. Mix them all together, and roll them up in a piece of butter ; then take a large piece of fine falmon, or a falmon trout, put the force-meat into the belly of the fifh, few it up, and lay it in an oval ftew-pan that will juft hold it ; then take half a pound of frefh butter, put it into a ftew-pan. When it is melted fhake in a little flour ; ftir it till it is a little brown, then put to it a pint of fifh broth, with a pint of Madeira. Seafon it with falt, mace, cloves, and whole pepper tied in a muflin rag; put in an onion and a bunch of fweet herbs. Stir it all together, and put it to the fifh. Cover it down very clofe, and let it ftew When the fifh is almoft done, put in fome frefh or pickled mufhrooms, truffles, or morels, cut in pieces; let them ftew all together till the fifh is quite done. Take the falmon up carefully, lay it in a difh, and pour the fauce over it. *Mafon*, 215.

To roll Salmon.

Take a fide of falmon, when fplit and the bone taken out and fcalded, ftrew over the infide pepper, falt, nutmeg, and
mace,

mace, a few chopped oyſters, parſley, and crumbs of bread, roll it up tight, put it into a deep pot, and bake it in a quick oven; make the common fiſh ſauce and pour over it. Garniſh with fennel, lemon and horſe-radiſh. *Raffald*, 24, from *Maſon*, 215.

To broil Salmon.

Cut your freſh ſalmon into thick pieces, and flour and broil them. Lay them in your diſh, and ſerve them up with plain melted butter in a boat. *Farley*, 51.

Salmon in Caſes.

Cut your ſalmon into ſmall pieces, ſuch as will lay rolled in half ſheets of paper. Seaſon it with pepper, ſalt, and nutmeg; butter the inſide of the paper well. fold the paper ſo as nothing can come out, then lay them in a tin plate to be baked, pour a little melted butter over the papers, and then crumbs of bread over them. Do not let your oven be too hot, for fear of burning the paper. A tin oven before the fire does beſt. When you think they are enough, ſerve them up juſt as they are. There will be ſauce enough in the papers; or put the ſalmon in buttered papers only and broil them. *Glaſſe*, 183.

Salmon with Shrimp ſauce.

Of a ſalmon the jowl is preferred to any other part; notch it to the bone on both ſides about an inch apart, lay it in a marinade, put it into ſome long ſtew-pan juſt its bigneſs, if you can with a fiſh plate or napkin under it, that you may take it out without breaking; put to it a pint of white wine, a daſh of vinegar, ſome ſweet bazil and thyme, whole pepper, ſalt, and mace, two or three ſhallots, a bunch of parſley and green onions; pour in as much water as will juſt cover it, let your lid be ſhut cloſe upon it, and, about an hour before your dinner, put it over a ſlow ſtove to ſimmer, and prepare your ſauce as follows:—provide as many ſmall prawns or ſhrimps (the tails only) as you think neceſſary for your piece of ſalmon; put into your ſtew-pan to them a proportionate quantity of cullis; add to it a litttle baſil, pimpernel, thyme, and parſley, all minced very fine, with a daſh of white wine. Boil all about a quarter of an hour, ſqueeze in the juice of a lemon or two. Take care that the diſh is well drained, and put meat into your diſh. Pour your ſauce over, and ſerve it up. Garniſh with lemons cut in quarters.

Trouts may be done in the ſame manner. *Verral*, 35.

Haſlets of Salmon.

Cut the ſalmon in middling pieces; ſeaſon them with ſweet herbs, pepper, and ſalt, mixed with butter, and the yolk of a raw egg or two; ſkewer them like haſlets, with all the ſeaſon-

ing:

ing: ſtrew them with bread-crumbs, and either roaſt or boil
them, baſting with oil or butter. When they are done of a
good colour, ſerve dry, with what ſauce you think proper in a
boat. *Clermont*, 361.

Salmon with ſweet herbs.

Take a piece of butter, and mix it with chopped parſley,
ſhallots, ſweet herbs, muſhrooms, pepper and ſalt; put ſome
of this in the bottom of the diſh you intend for table, then
ſome thin ſlices of ſalmon upon it, and the remainder of the
butter and herbs upon the ſalmon; ſtrew it over with bread
crumbs, and baſte it with butter; bake it in the oven. When
it is done, drain the fat from it, and ſerve with a clear reliſhing ſauce. *Dalrymple*, 294.

To dreſs dried Salmon.

Lay your dried ſalmon in ſoak for two or three hours, then
lay it on the gridiron, and ſhake a little pepper over it.

To dreſs a Jowl of pickled Salmon.

Lay your ſalmon in freſh water all night, then lay it in a
fiſh-plate, put it into a large ſtew pan, ſeaſon it with a little
whole pepper, a blade or two of mace tied in a coarſe muſlin
rag, a whole onion, a nutmeg bruiſed, a bundle of ſweet herbs
and parſley, a little lemon-peel; put to it three large ſpoonfuls
of vinegar, a pint of white wine, and a quarter of a pound of
freſh butter rolled in flour. Cover it cloſe, and let it ſimmer
over a ſlow fire for a quarter of an hour, then carefully take up
your ſalmon, and lay it in your diſh; ſet it over hot water and
cover it. In the mean time let your ſauce boil till it is thick
and good. Take out the ſpice, onion, and ſweet herbs, and
pour it over the fiſh. Garniſh with lemon. *Glaſſe*, 178.

Mrs. Maſon, page 216, has the ſame receipt, differently ex-
preſſed.

To dreſs Sturgeon.

Waſh your ſturgeon clean, lay it all night in ſalt and water.
The next morning take it out, rub it well with allegar, and let
it lie in it for two hours. Then have ready a fiſh kettle full
of boiling water, with an ounce of bay-ſalt, two large onions,
and a few ſprigs of ſweet marjoram. Boil your ſturgeon till
the bones will leave the fiſh, then take it up, take the ſkin off,
and flour it well; ſet it before the fire, baſte it with freſh
butter, and let it ſtand till it is of a fine brown. Then diſh
it up, and pour into the diſh what ſauce you think proper.
Garniſh with criſp parſley and red pickles.

This is a proper diſh for the top or middle. *Raffald*, 29.
F..rley, 29.

Sturgeon broiled.

Take your sturgeon, stew it in as much liquid as will stew it, being half fish-broth or water, and half white wine, with a little vinegar, sliced roots, onions, sweet herbs, whole pepper, and salt. When done, serve upon a napkin. Garnish with green parsley, and serve with what sauces you please in sauce-boats, such as capers, anchovies, &c. *Clermont*, 365.

Sturgeon Mayence fashion, or à-la-Mayence.

Take a piece of sturgeon, of what size you think proper, and lard it with Westphalia ham, fat and lean cut together. Wrap it it paper and roast it, basting it with butter. Make a sauce as follows :—Put in a stew-pan a few slices of ham and veal, sliced carrots, onions, parsley roots, shallots, and three cloves. Soak it on the fire till it begins to catch at bottom, then add a little cullis, half a pint of white wine, some whole pepper and a little salt. Reduce it to a proper consistence, then skim and strain it. When done, add the juice of half a lemon, and serve it upon the sturgeon.

This is called *à-la-Mayence*, from being larded with Westphalia ham, termed by the French, *Jambon de Mayence*. *Cole*, 224.

To stew Cod.

Cut some slices of cod as for boiling; season them with grated nutmeg, pepper, salt, a bunch of sweet herbs, an onion stuck with cloves. Put them into a stew-pan, with half a pint of white wine, and a quarter of a pint of water. Cover them close, and let them simmer for five or six minutes. Then squeeze in the juice of a lemon, a few oysters, and their liquor strained, a piece of butter rolled in flour, and a blade or two of mace. Cover them close, and let them stew softly. Shake the pan often to prevent its burning. When the fish is enough, take out the onion and sweet herbs, lay the cod in a warm dish, and pour the sauce over it. *Mason*, 219.

To bake a Cod's Head.

Make the head very clean, butter the pan you intend to bake it in, put the head into the pan, put in a bundle of sweet herbs, an onion stuck with cloves, three or four blades of mace, half a large spoonful of black and white pepper, a nutmeg bruised, a quart of water, a little piece of lemon-peel, and a little piece of horse-radish. Flour your head, grate a little nutmeg over it, stick pieces of butter all over it, and throw raspings all over that. Send it to the oven to bake. When it is enough, take it out of that dish, and lay it carefully into the dish you intend to serve it up in. Set the dish over boiling water, and cover it up to keep it hot. In the mean time be quick, pour all the liquor out of the dish it was baked in into a sauce-pan; set it on the fire to boil three or four minutes, then strain it, and put

to

to it a gill of red wine, two fpoonfuls of catchup, a pint of
fhrimps, half a pint of oyfters or muffels, liquor and all, but
firft ftrain it; a fpoonful of mufhroom pickle, a quarter of a
pound of butter rolled in flour. Stir it all together till it is thick
and boils, then pour it into the difh. Have ready fome toaft
cut three-corner ways, and fried crifp. Stick pieces about the
head and mouth, and lay the reft round the head. Garnifh
with lemon notched, fcraped horfe-radifh, and parfley crifped
in a plate before the fire. Lay one flice of lemon on the head,
and ferve it up hot. *Glaffe,* 175.

To drefs a Cod's Head and Shoulders.

Having taken out the gills, and the blood clean from the
bone, wafh the head very clean, rub over it a little falt and a
glafs of allegar, then lay it on your fifh-plate. When your
water boils, throw in a good handful of falt, with a glafs of allegar, then put in your fifh, and let it boil gently for half an
hour; if it is a large one, three quarters. Take it up very
carefully, and ftrip the fkin nicely off. Set it before a brifk
fire, dredge it all over with flour, and bafte it well with butter.
When the froth begins to rife, throw over it fome very fine
white bread crumbs. You muft keep bafting it all the time to
make it froth well. When it is of a fine white brown, difh it
up, and garnifh it with a lemon cut in flices, fcraped horfe-
radifh, barberries, a few fmall fifh fried and laid round it, or
fried oyfters. Cut the roe and liver into flices, and lay over it
a little of the lobfter out of the fauce in lumps, and then ferve
it. *Raffald,* 20.

To broil Cod.

Having cut a cod into flices of about two inches thick, dry
and flour them well; make a good clear fire, rub the gridiron
with a piece of chalk, and fet it high from the fire. Turn them
often till they are quite enough, and of a fine brown. They
require great care to prevent them from breaking. Lobfter or
fhrimp fauce. *Cole,* 226.

To drefs Salt Cod.

Let your fifh lie in water all night, and if you put a glafs
of vinegar into the water, it will draw out the falt, and make it
eat frefh. The next day boil it, and when it is enough, break
it into flakes on the difh. Pour over it parfnips boiled, and
beat fine, with butter and cream; but egg fauce is more generally ufed. As it very foon grows cold, you muft fend it to
table on a water plate. *Farley,* 28.

Frefh Cod with fweet herbs.

Cut a fmall cod in five or fix pieces, bone it, and marinade
it in melted butter, the juice of a lemon, chopped parfley, fhallots, and fweet herbs; then lay it upon the difh you intend for
table,

table, with all the marinade both under and over, and ftrew it over with bread-crumbs. Bafte it with melted butter, bake it in the oven, and ferve it with what fauce you think proper. *Dalrymple*, 321.

To crimp Cod.

Cut a very frefh cod into flices, and throw it into pump water and falt; fet over a ftove a fifh-kettle, or ftew-pan, almoft full of fpring water, and falt enough to make it tafte brackifh. Make it boil very quick, and then put in the flices of cod, and keep them boiling; fkim them very clean; they will take about eight or nine minutes; then take out the fifh, and lay them on a fifh-plate. Shrimp or oyfter fauce. *Cole*, 226.

To drefs Cod Sounds.

Steep them as you do the falt cod, and boil them in a large quantity of milk and water. When they are very tender and white, take them up, and drain the water out; then pour the egg-fauce boiling hot over them, and ferve them up. *Cole*, 227.

To boil Cod Sounds.

Lay them a few minutes in hot water; then take them out, and rub them well with falt, and take off the fkin and black dirt, when they will look white. After this, put them into water, and give them a boil. Take them out, flour them well, pepper and falt them, and then put them on the gridiron. As foon as they are enough, lay them on your difh, and pour melted butter and muftard over them. *Cole*, 227.

To broil Crimp Cod.

Having put a gallon of pump-water into a pot, fet it on the fire, put in it a handful of falt; boil it up feveral times, and fkim it often. When it is well cleared from the fcum, take a midling cod, as frefh as you can get, throw it into a tub of frefh pump water; let it lie a few minutes, and then cut it into flices two inches thick; throw thefe into the boiling brine, and let it boil brifkly for a few minutes; then take out the flices; take great care not to break them, and lay them on a fieve to drain. When they are well dried, flour them, and lay them at a diftance upon a very good fire to broil. Lobfter or fhrimp fauce. *Mafon*, 220.

To drefs Herrings.

The moft general way of dreffing herrings is to broil or fry them, with melted butter. *Cole*, 227.

To fry Herrings.

Scale them, gut them, cut off their heads, wafh them clean, dry them in a cloth, flour them, and fry them in butter. Have ready a good may onions peeled and cut thin. Fry them

of

of a light brown with the herrings. Lay the herrings in your
diſh, and the onions round ; butter and muſtard in a cup. You
muſt do them with a quick fire *Glaſſe,* 180.

Another way.

Scale them, and dry them well ; lay them ſeparately on a
board, and ſet them to the fire two or three minutes before you
want them, it will keep the fiſh from ſticking to the pan ; duſt
them with flour. When your dripping, or butter, is boiling
hot, put in your fiſh, a few at a time, fry them over a briſk fire.
When you have fried them all, ſet the tails one up againſt
another in the middle of the diſh ; then fry a large handful of
parſley criſp, take it out before it loſes its colour, lay it round
them, and parſley ſauce in a boat ; or, if you like onions better,
fry them, lay ſome round your diſh, and make onion-ſauce for
them ; or you may cut off the heads, after they are fried, chop
them, and put them into a ſauce-pan, with ale, pepper, ſalt, and
an anchovy ; thicken it with flour and butter, ſtrain it, then put
it in a ſauce-boat. *Raffald,* 33. *Farley,* 59.

Herrings with Muſtard ſauce.

Gut and wipe the herrings very clean. Melt ſome butter.
Add chopped parſley, ſhallots, green onions, pepper, and ſalt.
Dip the herrings in this, and roll them in bread-crumbs. Then
broil them, and ſerve them with a ſauce made of melted butter,
flour, broth, a little vinegar, pepper, and ſalt. When ready to
ſerve, add muſtard according to judgment. *Clermont,* 384.

To bake Herrings.

Having well cleaned your herrings, lay them on a board,
take a little black and Jamaica pepper, a few cloves, and a good
deal of ſalt ; mix them together, then rub it all over the fiſh,
lay them ſtraight in a pot, cover them with allegar, tie ſtrong
paper over the pot, and bake them in a moderate oven. If your
allegar is good, they will keep two or three months. You may
eat them either hot or cold. *Cole,* 228.

Soals with force-meat.

Provide a pair of large ſoals, or three or four of a leſſer ſize,
take the ſkin off from both ſides, and ſoak them in a marinade
for an hour. Dry them upon a cloth, cut them down the
middle, and with the point of your knife raiſe up the fillets.
Make a little force-meat of the fleſh of a couple of plaice or
flounders, a morſel of ſuet, ſeaſon with a muſhroom or two, a
green onion and parſley minced, pepper and ſalt, and nutmeg.
Scrape a bit of bacon, and fry it very gently. Let it cool, and
pound it well with a bit of bread well ſoaked, and a couple of
eggs, taking away one white. Lift up the fleſh of the ſoals, and
croud in as much as you can. Bruſh ſome egg over them, and
ſtrew

ftrew crumbs of bread, a little oil, or oiled butter, poured upon it. Bake them about half an hour, of a fine colour, and fend them up, garnifhed with fome little pats of your force-meat fried, and fome parfley. For your fauce, take a little fweet bafil, pimpernel, thyme, and parfley, a fhallot or two minced fine, with a ladle of your clear gravy, and a dafh of white wine, pepper, and falt. Boil all together for a few minutes, fqueeze in a lemon or two, aud fend it up in a fifh fauce-boat.

Small prills are good done in this manner, or any other firm-flefhed fifh. *Verral*, 72.

Soals à-la-Francoife.

Put a quart of water and half a pint of vinegar into an earthen difh; fkin and clean a pair of foals, put them into the vinegar and water, let them lie two hours, then take them out and dry them with a cloth; then put them into a ftew-pan with a pint of white wine, a quarter of a pint of water, a very little thyme, a little fweet marjoram, winter favoury, and an onion ftuck with four cloves. Put in the foals, fprinkle a very little bay-falt, and cover them clofe; let them fimmer very gently till they are enough Take them out, lay them in a warm difh before the fire; put into the liquor, after it is ftrained, a piece of butter rolled in flour; let it boil till of a proper thicknefs. Lay the foals into a difh, and pour the fauce over them.

A fmall turbot, or any flat fifh, may be drefled in the fame manner. *Mafon*, 225.

To ftew Soals.

Having taken the flefh from the bones of your foals, cut each of them into eight pieces. Put into a ftew-pan a quart of boiled gravy, a quarter of a pint of Madeira, or white wine, fome white pepper pounded, grated nutmeg, a piece of lemon-peel; ftew thefe together for near an hour; add fome cream, a piece of butter mixed with flour. Keep the fauce ftirring till it boils, put in the fifh, ftew it for a quarter of an hour; take out the lemon-peel, fqueeze in fome lemon-juice. The fifh may be ftewed whole in the fame fauce, and, if more convenient, cut the fifh as before directed, and make a little gravy with the bones and head. *Cole*, 229.

To ftew Soals, Plaice, or Flounders.

Half fry them in three ounces of butter of a fine brown, then take up your fifh, and put to your butter a quart of water, and boil it flowly a quarter of an hour, with two anchovies and an onion fliced; then put in your fifh again, with an herring, and ftew them gently twenty minutes; then take out your fifh, and thicken the fauce with butter and flour, and give it a boil;
then

then strain it through a hair sieve over the fish, and send them up hot.

N. B. If you chuse cockle or oyster liquor, put it in just before you thicken the sauce, or you may send oysters, cockles, or shrimps, in a sauce-boat to table. *Raffald*, 31.

To fry Soals.

Having skinned them, rub them over with yolk of egg, strew on them very fine bread-crumbs, or flour them; fry them with a brisk fire.—Anchovy sauce. *Cole*, 230.

Another way.

Scale and trim the soals properly, and skin the black side; mix some bread-crumbs with a very little flour; baste the soals with beat eggs, and strew them over with the bread-crumbs; fry them in hogs'-lard of a good colour. Garnish with fried parsley, and serve with anchovy sauce, &c. in a sauce-boat. *Dalrymple*, 312.

To marinade Soals.

Boil them in salt and water, bone and drain them, and lay them on a dish with their belly upwards. Boil some spinach, and pound it in a mortar; then boil four eggs hard, chop the yolks and white separate, and lay green, white, and yellow among the soals, and serve them up with melted butter in a boat. *Farley*, 136.

To fry Whitings.

Gut the whitings by the gills, trim and dry them well, bathe them with beat eggs, and roll them in fine bread-crumbs, mixed with a very little flour; fry them with hogs'-lard of a good colour, and garnish with fried parsley. Serve with plain butter, or what sauce you think proper, in a sauce-boat. *Cole*, 230.

Another way.

Wash, gut, and skin them, turn the tails in their mouths, dry them in a cloth, and flour them well all over; fill the frying-pan with lard enough to cover them. When it boils, put them in, and fry them of a fine brown. Lay them on a coarse cloth to drain, then put them on a warm dish. Sauce—shrimp, oyster, or anchovy. They are proper garnish for salmon or cod. *Mason*, 227.

To broil Whitings or Haddocks.

Gut and wash them, dry them with a cloth, and rub a little vinegar over them, it will keep the skin on better. Dust them well with flour, rub your gridiron with butter, and let it be very hot when you lay the fish on, or they will stick; turn them two or three times on the gridiron. When enough, serve them up, and

and lay pickles round them, with plain melted butter, or cockle sauce. They are a pretty dish for supper. *Raffald*, 35.

Mackarel àl-a-Maitre-d'Hotel.

Take three mackarel, and wipe them very dry with a clean cloth; cut them down the back from head to tail, but not open them; flour them, and broil them nicely; chop an handful of parsley, and an handful of green onions very fine, mix them up with butter, pepper, and salt. Put your mackarel in the dish, and put your parsley, &c. into the cut in the back, and put them before the fire till the butter is melted. Squeeze the juice of two lemons over them, and send them up hot. *Glasse*, 179.

To broil Mackarel whole.

Clean your mackarel, split them down the back, and season them with pepper and salt, some mint, parsley, and fennel, chopped very fine. Flour them and fry them of a fine light brown, and put them on a dish and strainer. Let your sauce be fennel and butter, and garnish with parsley. *Farley*, 51.

Mackarel au Court Bouillon.

Put in a stew-pan some weak broth, half a pint of white wine, sliced roots, onions, sweet herbs, pepper, and salt; boil this together about half an hour, then boil the fish in it; make a sauce with a piece of butter, a little flour, one shallot chopped very fine, some scalded fennel chopped, and a little of the boiling liquid. When ready to serve, add the squeeze of a lemon. *Clermont*, 382.

To bake Mackarel.

Cut their heads off, wash and dry them in a cloth, cut them open, rub the bone with a little bay-salt beat fine; take some mace, black and white pepper, a few cloves, all beat fine; lay them in a long pan, and between every layer of fish, put two or three bay-leaves, cover them with vinegar; tie writing-paper over them first, and then thick brown paper doubled; they must be put into a very slow oven, and will take a long time doing. When they are enough, uncover them, let them stand till they are cold, then pour away all the vinegar they were baked in, cover them with some more vinegar, and put in an onion stuck with cloves. Send them to a very slow oven again, and let them stand two hours. They will keep a great while. Always take them out with a slice; the hands will spoil them. The great bones taken out are good boiled. *Cole*, 231.

To stew a Trout.

Stuff a small trout with grated bread, a piece of butter, parsley chopped, lemon-peel grated, pepper, salt, nutmeg, savoury herbs and yolk of egg, mixed; put it into a stew-pan, with a quart of good boiled gravy, some Madeira, an onion, a little whole

whole pepper, a few cloves, a piece of lemon-peel; stew it in
this gently till enough; add a little flour mixed in some cream,
a little catchup; boil it up; squeeze in some lemon-juice.
Mason, 231.

Trout à-la-Chartreuse.

Scale and clean the fish, and cut each in three pieces; stew
them in broth, with pepper, salt, and two or three sliced
lemons peeled. Make a sauce with a little butter rolled in
bread-crumbs, chopped parsley, shallots, mushrooms, a little
basil, pepper, and salt, a little fish broth, and a glass of white
wine. Put the fish upon the dish you intend for table; squeeze
the juice of a Seville orange upon them, then the sauce over,
and strew them over with a few fine bread-crumbs. *Dalrymple*, 289.

To fry Trout or Perch.

Scale, gut, and wash them, dry them well, then lay them
separately on a board before the fire; two minutes before you
fry them, dust them well with flour, and fry them a fine brown
in roast drippings or rendered suet. Serve them up with melted butter and crisped parsley. *Raffald*, 36.

To marinade Trout.

Fry them in a sufficient quantity of oil to cover them, put
them in when the oil is boiling hot. When they are crisp, lay
them to drain till they are cold; then take some white wine
and vinegar, of each an equal quantity, with some salt, whole
pepper, nutmeg, cloves, mace, sliced ginger, savoury, sweet
marjoram, thyme, rosemary, a bay-leaf, and two onions; let
these boil together for a quarter of an hour; put the fish into
a stew-pan, pour the marinade to them hot; put in as much
oil as white wine and vinegar, which must be according to the
quantity of fish that are done as the liquor must cover them,
and they will keep a month. Serve them with oil and vinegar.
Cole, 232.

Pike with force-meat.

Prepare your pike thus:—Gut it without cutting it open, but
take care it is well cleaned; cut a notch down the back, from
head to tail, turn it round, and fasten the tail in the mouth,
and lay it in a marinade. For your force-meat, take the udder
of a leg of veal, or the kidney part of a loin of lamb, some fat
bacon cut in dice, the spawn or melt of the fish, some green
onions, a mushroom or two, or truffles, parsley, and salt, a little
nutmeg and pepper; add a morsel of butter to fry it, chop it
all well, and the crumb of a French roll soaked in cream or
milk; pound all together in a large mortar, with three or four
eggs; try if it is seasoned to your mind, and fill the belly of
your fish, and close up that part that is cut in the back, make
it

It nice and even; take two or three eggs, daub it well over; and ftrew fome crumbs of bread upon it, and bake it in a gentle oven; the time, according to the bignefs of your pike. For your fauce, to two or three ladles of your cullis, add two or three large fpoonfuls of whole capers, fome parfley minced fine, the juice of two lemons, a little minced fhallot, and ferve it up in your hot difh, but not poured over.

As this difh is baked, garnifh with a large quantity of fried parfley. *Verral*, 37.

To ftew Pike.

Make a brown with butter and flour, then add a pint of red wine, a faggot, four cloves, two dozen fmall onions half boiled, pepper and falt, then the pike cut in pieces. Stew it flowly till the fifh is done. Take out the faggot, and add a piece of butter. When ready to ferve, add two chopped anchovies, and a fpoonful of capers; garnifh with fried bread, and ferve the fauce over all. You may alfo add artichoke bottoms, mufhrooms, carp-roes, &c. *Clermont*, 338.

To drefs a Brace of Carp.

Put a piece of butter into a ftew-pan, melt it, and put in a large fpoonful of flour, keep it ftirring till it is fmooth; then put in a pint of gravy, and a pint of red port or claret; a little horfe-radifh fcraped, eight cloves, four blades of mace, and a dozen corns of all-fpice; tie them in a little linen rag; a bundle of fweet herbs, half a lemon, three anchovies, a little onion chopped very fine; feafon with pepper, falt, and chyan pepper, to your liking; ftew it for half an hour, then ftrain it through a fieve into the pan you intend to put your fifh in. Let your carp be well cleaned and fcaled; then put the fifh in with the fauce, and ftew them very gently for half an hour; then turn them, and ftew them fifteen minutes longer. Put in along with your fifh fome truffles and morels fcalded, fome pickled mufhrooms; an artichoke bottom, and about a dozen large oyfters; fqueeze the juice of half a lemon, ftew it five minutes; then put your carp in the difh, and pour all the fauce over; garnifh with fried fippets, and the roe of the fifh done thus :— Beat the roe up well with the yolks of two eggs, a little flour, a little lemon-peel chopped fine; fome pepper, falt, and a little anchovy liquor. Have ready a pan of beef-dripping boiling; drop the roe in to be as big as a crown piece; fry it of a light brown, and put it round the difh, with fome oyfters fried in batter, and fome fcraped horfe-radifh. Stick your fried fippets in the difh.

N. B. If you are in a great hurry, while the fauce is making, you may boil the fifh with fpring water, half a pint of vinegar, a little horfe-radifh, and a bay-leaf. Put your fifh in the difh, and pour the fauce over it. *Glaffe*, 124.

To

To stew Carp white.

Scale, gut, and wash them; put them into a stew-pan, with two quarts of water, half a pint of white wine, a little mace, whole pepper, and salt, two onions, a bunch of sweet herbs, and a stick of horse-radish; cover the pan close, let it stand an hour and a half over a slow fire; then put a gill of white wine into a sauce-pan, with two anchovies chopped, an onion, a little lemon-peel, a quarter of a pound of butter rolled in flour, a little thick cream, and a large tea-cup of the liquor the carp was stewed in; boil them a few minutes, drain your carp, add to the sauce the yolks of two eggs mixed with a little cream; when it boils up, squeeze in the juice of half a lemon; dish up your carp, and pour your sauce hot upon it. *Raffald,* 26. *Farley,* 74.

To stew Carp brown.

Put a quart of good gravy into the stew-pan, add the blood of the carp, (if agreeable) half a pint of small beer, (if bitter, only a quarter of a pint) a quarter of a pint of red wine, a large onion, half a dozen cloves, a piece of lemon-peel, and horse-radish; let them stew gently till reduced to the quantity that is wanted. Strain the liquor; add to it catchup, lemon juice, some of the hard roe bruised, chyan, a little salt, if necessary. Simmer this; and, if not thick enough, mix a little flour smooth in some gravy, and boil it up in it, stirring it. Let the carp be boiled, and well drained in a cloth; put it into the sauce, simmer it two or three minutes. Let the remainder of the roe be mixed with egg, a little grated lemon-peel and nutmeg, fried in little cakes; garnish the dish with these sippets, cut with three corners, and fried dry, horse-radish and sliced lemon. *Mason,* 235.

To dress Carp the best way.

When you kill your carp, save the blood, scale and clean them well; have ready some rich gravy made of beef and mutton, seasoned with pepper, salt, mace, and onion; strain it off before you stew your fish in it; boil your carp first before you stew it in the gravy. Be careful not to boil them too much before you put in the carp; then let it stew on a slow fire about a quarter of an hour, thicken the sauce with a good lump of butter rolled in flour; garnish your dish with fried oysters, fried toast cut three-corner ways, pieces of lemon, scraped horse radish, and the roe of the carp cut in pieces, some fried and the other boiled; squeeze the juice of a lemon into the sauce just before you send it up. Dish it up handsomely, and very hot. *Cole,* 235.

Carp à-la-Jacobine.

Put two dozen of small onions blanched in a stew-pan, with a few sliced truffles, a piece of butter, and a faggot of parsley

and

and fweet herbs; fimmer this on a flow fire till it catches a little; then add three half pints of white wine, and put a carp to it cut in pieces, with a little broth, pepper, and falt; reduce the fauce; when ready to ferve, add a liafon made of three yolks of eggs and cream, and the juice of half a lemon. *Dalrymple*, 267.

To drefs Carp au Blue.

Take a brace of carp alive, and gut them, but neither wafh nor fcale them; tie them to a fifh-drainer, and put them into a fifh-kettle, and pour boiling vinegar over till they are blue; or you may hold them down in a fifh-kettle with two forks, and another perfon pour the vinegar over them. Put in a quart of boiling water, a handful of falt, fome horfe-radifh cut in flices; boil them gently twenty minutes. Put a fifh-plate in the difh, a napkin over that, and fend them up hot. Garnifh with horfe-radifh. Boil half a pint of cream, and fweeten it with fine fugar for fauce, in a boat or bafon. *Glaffe*, 124.

To fry Carp.

Take a brace of carp, fcale, gut, and clean them, dry them well in a cloth, flour them, and put them into a frying-pan of boiling lard; let them be of a fine brown. Fry the roes, and cut fome thin flices of bread with three corners; fry them. Lay the fifh on a coarfe cloth to drain; then put them into the difh, the roes on each, the toafts between. Anchovy fauce.

To ftew Tench or Carp.

Having gutted and fcaled your fifh, wafh them, and dry them well with a clean cloth; dredge them well with flour, fry them in dripping, or fweet rendered fuet, till they are a light brown; then put them in a ftew-pan, with a quart of water, and the fame quantity of red wine, a meat-fpoonful of lemon-pickle, another of browning, the fame of walnut or mum-catchup; a little mufhroom-powder, and chyan to your tafte; a large onion ftuck with cloves, and a ftick of horfe-radifh. Cover your pan clofe to keep in the fteam; let them ftew gently over a flow fire till your gravy is reduced to juft enough to cover your fifh in the difh. Then take the fifh out, and put them on the difh you intend for table; fet the gravy on the fire, and thicken it with flour and a large lump of butter; boil it a little, and ftrain it over your fifh. Garnifh them with pickled mufhrooms and fcraped horfe-radifh; put a bunch of pickled barberries, or a fprig of myrtle in their mouths, and fend them to table.

It is a top-difh for a grand entertainment. *Raffald*, 29.

To fry Tench.

Gut, wafh, and dry them well in a cloth; flit them down the back, fprinkle a little falt over them, and dredge them with flour; fry them of a fine brown in boiling lard. Sauce—anchovy, with mushrooms, truffles, and capers, all chopped small, and stewed in gravy, with the juice of a lemon, and a little fishcullis. *Cole*, 236.

To fry Perch.

Scale and gut your perch and wash them clean; score them at some distance on the sides, but not very deep; dry them well, and flour them all over; fry them in oiled butter. When they are of a fine brown, lay some crisped parsley round the fish. For sauce, take plain butter. Some make the following sauce: —Two ounces of browned butter; put it to some flour, a few chives chopped small, some parsley, a few fresh mushrooms cut small, and a little boiling water. Lay the perch in this liquor after they are fried, and let them stew gently for four or five minutes; then lay them in a warm dish; add two large spoonfuls of capers cut small; thicken it with butter and flour, and pour it over them. *Mason*, 239.

To dress Perch in Water Souchy.

Having scaled, gutted, and washed them, put some salt in your water; when it boils, put in your fish, with an onion cut in slices, and separated into round rings, and an handful of parsley; put as much milk as will turn the water white. The perch being enough, put them in a soup-dish, and pour a little of the water over them, with the parsley and the onions; serve it up with butter and parsley in a boat; onions may be omitted, if you think proper. Trout may be boiled the same way. *Cole*, 236.

Smelts à-la-St. Menekoult.

The smelts being well cleaned, put them in a stew-pan with a piece of butter, chopped parsley, shallots, green onions, sweet herbs, pepper and salt; give them a few turns in this over the fire; then take them out, and add two or three yolks of eggs to the butter; mix it well together, dip the smelts in it, and strew them over with bread-crumbs. Serve with melted butter and lemon juice, or verjuice; or a relishing sauce in a sauce-boat, and garnish with fried parsley. *Clermont*, 349.

Smelts in savoury Jelly.

Season your smelts with pepper and salt, bake them and drain them. When they are cold, pour the jelly over them; or break the jelly, and heap over them. *Cole*, 237.

To fry Smelts.

Draw the guts out at the gills, but leave in the melt or roe; dry them with a cloth, beat an egg, rub it over them with a feather, and strew crumbs of bread over them. Fry them with hogs'-lard or beef-suet, and put in your fish when it is boiling hot.

hot. Shake them a little, and fry them till they are of a fine brown. Drain them on a difh, or in a fieve ; and when you difh them up, put a bafon, bottom up, in the middle of your difh, and lay the tails of your fifh on it. *Farley*, 57.

To pitchcock Eels.

Take a large eel, and fcour it well with falt to clean off all the flime ; then flit it down the back, take out the bone, and cut it in three or four pieces ; take the yolk of an egg and put over the infide, fprinkle crumbs of bread, with fome fweet herbs and parfley chopped very fine, a little nutmeg grated, and fome pepper and falt mixed all together ; then put it on a gridiron over a clear fire, broil it of a fine light brown, difh it up, and garnifh with raw parfley and horfe-radifh ; or put a boiled eel in the middle, and the pitchcocked round. Garnifh with an-chovy fauce, and parfley and butter in a boat. *Glaffe*, 184.

Another way.

Skin your eels, gut them and wafh them, then dry them with a cloth ; fprinkle them with pepper, falt, and a little dried fage ; turn them backward and forward, and fkewer them ; rub your gridiron with beef-fuet, broil them a good brown, put them on your difh with good melted butter, and lay round fried parfley. *Raffald*, 37.

Eel à-la-Nivernois.

Skin and trim the eel, cut it in pieces about three inches long, and marinade it about two hours with oil, chopped parfley, fhal-lots, mufhrooms, pepper and falt ; make as much of the mari-nade ftick to it as poffible ; ftrew it with crumbs of bread, broil it on a flow fire, bafting with the remainder of the marinade ; when done of a good colour, ferve with a *Nivernois fauce*. *Dal-rymple*, 279.

To ftew Eels.

Skin, gut, and wafh your eels very clean in fix or eight wa-ters, to wafh away all the fand ; then cut them in pieces about as long as your finger ; put juft water enough for fauce ; put in a fmall onion ftuck with cloves, a little bundle of fweet herbs, a blade or two of mace, and fome whole pepper in a thin muflin rag. Cover it clofe, and let them ftew very foftly.

Take care to look at them now and then ; put in a little piece of butter rolled in flour, and a little chopped parfley. When you find they are quite tender, and well done, take out the onion, fpice, and fweet herbs. Put in falt enough to feafon it ; then difh them up with the fauce. *Cole*, 238.

To broil Eels.

Having fkinned and cleanfed your eels, rub them with the yolk of an egg, ftrew over them bread crumbs, chopped parfley,

fage,

fage, pepper, and falt; bafte them well with butter, and fet them in a dripping-pan; roaft or broil them, and ferve them up with parfley and butter. *Cole*, 238.

To broil or roaft Eels.

Having fkinned and cleaned a large eel, mix bread crumbs, grated lemon-peel, parfley chopped, pepper, falt, nutmeg, a few oyfters chopped, a bit of butter, and the yolk of an egg. Stuff the eel, few it up, turn it round, rub it with yolk of egg, ftrew over it fine bread-crumbs, ftick on it bits of butter, a little water in the difh. Bake it either in a common or Dutch oven. Serve it with white fifh fauce; add to it what gravy comes from the fifh, firft taking off the fat. The oyfters in the ftuffing may be omitted. Or, ftrip the fkin off the eel to the tail, fcotch it, rub it with pepper and falt; ftuff it with the above ingredients, draw the fkin over it, fkewer it round, hang it in the Dutch oven, roaft it; or put it on a gridiron, at a great diftance, over a clear fire. When it is near done, fet it lower to brown. Anchovy, or white fifh-fauce. *Mafon*, 244.

To fry Eels.

Cut one or two eels in pieces; cut out the back-bone, and fcore it on both fides; marinade it about an hour in vinegar, with parfley, fliced onions, fhallots, and four cloves; then drain it, bafte it with eggs and bread-crumbs, fry it of a good colour. Garnifh with fried parfley, and ferve with a relifhing fauce in a fauce-boat. *Clermont*, 344.

To bake Sprats.

Rub them with falt and pepper; and to every two pints of vinegar put one pint of red wine. Diffolve a penny-worth of cochineal; lay your fprats in a deep earthen difh; pour in as much red wine, vinegar, and cochineal, as will cover them; tie a paper over them, fet them in an oven all night. They will eat well, and keep for fome time. *Raffald*, 34.

Sauce Poivrade.

TAKE a little butter, sliced onions, bits of carrot, parsley-root, two cloves of garlick, two cloves, a laurel-leaf. Soak all together till it takes colour; then add some cullis, a little vinegar and broth, salt and pepper; boil it to the consistence of sauces; skim and sift it for use. *Dalrymple*, 43.

Sauce for a Cod's Head.

Pick out a good lobster; if it be alive, stick a skewer in the vent of the tail to keep out the water. Throw an handful of salt into the water, and, when it boils, put in the lobster, which must boil half an hour. If it has spawn, pick them off, and pound them exceedingly fine in a marble mortar. Put them into half a pound of melted butter, then take the meat out of your lobster, pull it in bits, and put it in your butter, with a large spoonful of lemon-pickle, the same quantity of walnut-catchup, a slice of an end of a lemon, one or two slices of horse-radish, as much beaten mace as will lie on a six-pence, and season to your taste with salt and chyan pepper. Boil them one minute, and then take out the horse-radish and lemon, and serve it in your sauce-boat. If lobsters cannot be had, you may make use of oysters or shrimps the same way. And if you can get no kind of shell fish, you may then add two anchovies cut small, a spoonful of walnut-liquor, and a large onion stuck with cloves. *Raffald*, 21. *Farley*, 144.

Parsley and Butter.

Tie up some parsley in a bunch, wash it, and put it into some boiling water with a little salt; after it has boiled up very quick two or three times, take it out and chop it very fine; then mix it with some melted butter. *Cole*, 240.

Poor Man's Sauce.

Cut some young onions into water, with some chopped parsley. It is very good with roasted mutton. *Cole*, 240.

Another way, called by the French, Sauce à Pauvre Homme.

Slice half a lemon, boil it in a little broth with two or three chopped shallots, pepper and salt, and a spoonful of oil; and serve it in a sauce-boat. *Clermont*, 37.

Lemon Sauce for boiled Fowls.

Take a lemon and pare off the rind, cut it into slices, and take the kernels out, cut it into square bits; blanch the liver of the fowl and chop it fine; mix the lemon and liver together in

O 4

aboat,

a boat, and pour fome hot melted butter on it, and ftir it up. Boiling it will make it go to oil. *Cole*, 240.

Muſhroom Sauce for white Fowls of all ſorts.

Take about a quart of freſh muſhrooms, well cleaned and waſhed, cut them in two, put them in a ftew-pan, with a little butter, a blade of mace, and a little falt; ftew it gently for half an hour, then add a pint of cream, and the yolks of two eggs beat very well, and keep ftirring it till it boils up; then fqueeze half a lemon, put it over your fowls or turkies, or in bafons, or in a diſh, with a piece of French bread, firſt butter-ed, then toaſted brown, and juſt dip it in boiling water; put it in the diſh, and muſhrooms over. *Glaſſe*, 70. *Farley*, 146.

Celery Sauce.

Waſh and clean ten heads of celery, cut off the green tops, and take out the outſide ſtalks, cut them into thin bits, and boil it in gravy till it is tender; thicken it with flour and butter, and pour it over your meat. A ſhoulder of mutton, or a ſhoulder of veal, roaſted, is very good with this fauce. *Raffald*, 104.

Caper Sauce.

Take fome capers, chop half of them, put the reſt in whole; chop alſo a little parſley very fine, with a little bread grated very fine, and fome falt; put thefe into butter melted very fmooth. Some only chop the capers a little, and put them into the butter. *Farley*, 139, from *Mafon*, 320.

Shallot Sauce.

Take five or fix ſhallots, chopped fine, put them into a ſauce-pan with a gill of gravy, a fpoonful of vinegar, and fome pep-per and falt; ftew them for a minute, then pour them into your diſh, or put it in fauce-boats. *Cole*, 241.

Egg Sauce.

Take two eggs and boil them hard. Firſt chop the whites, then the yolks, but neither of them very fine, and put them to-gether. Then put them into a quarter of a pound of good melted butter, and ftir them well together. *Cole*, 241.

Apple Sauce.

Pare, core, and ſlice your apples, then put a little water in the fauce-pan to keep them from burning, and a bit of lemon-peel. When they are enough, take out the peel, bruife the apples, add a lump of butter, and a little fugar. *Cole*, 241,

Onion Sauce.

Boil eight or ten large onions, change the water two or three times while they are boiling. When enough, chop them on a
board

board to keep them from growing of a bad colour; put them in a fauce-pan with a quarter of a pound of butter, and two fpoonfuls of thick cream; boil it a little, and pour it over your difh. *Raffald*, 59.

Another way.

Having peeled your onions, boil them in milk and water, put a turnip with them into the pot (it draws out the ftrength); change the water twice; pulp them through a cullender, or chop them; then put them in a fauce-pan with fome cream, a piece of butter, a little flour, fome pepper and falt. They muft be very fmooth. *Cole*, 241.

Goofeberry Sauce.

Put fome coddled goofeberries, a little juice of forrel, and a little ginger, into fome melted butter. *Cole*, 241.

Fennel Sauce.

Having boiled a bunch of fennel and parfley, chop it fmall, and ftir into it fome melted butter. *Cole*, 241.

Bread Sauce.

Put a pretty large piece of crumb of bread, that is not new, into half a pint of water, with an onion, a blade of mace, and a few pepper-corns in a bit of cloth; boil thefe a few minutes; take out the onions and fpice, mafh the bread very fmooth, add a piece of butter and a little falt.

Bread-fauce for a pig is made the fame, with the addition of a few currants picked, wafhed, and boiled in it. *Cole*, 241.

Mint Sauce.

Wafh your mint perfectly clean from grit and dirt, chop it very fine, and put to it vinegar and fugar. *Cole*, 242.

Sauce Robert.

Cut fome large onions into fquare pieces, cut fome fat bacon in the fame manner, put them together in a fauce-pan over the fire, fhake them round to prevent their burning. When they are brown, put in fome good veal gravy, with a little pepper and falt; let them ftew gently till the onions are tender, then put in a little falt, fome muftard and vinegar, and ferve it hot. *Mafon*, 323. *Farley*, 140.

Another way.

Slice feveral onions, fry them in butter, turning often till they take colour; then add a little cullis and good broth, pepper and falt; let them boil half an hour, and reduce to a fauce; when ready, add muftard. You may fift it for thofe who only like the flavour of onions. *Dalrymple*, 41.

Anchovy Sauce.

Put an anchovy into a pint of gravy, then take a quarter of a
pound

pound of butter rolled in flour, and ſtir all together till it boils. You may add a little juice of lemon, catchup, red wine, and walnut liquor, juſt as you think proper.

Plain butter melted thick, with a ſpoonful of walnut pickle, or catchup, is a good ſauce, or anchovy: in ſhort, you may put as many things as you pleaſe into ſauce. *Glaſſe*, 123.

Shrimp Sauce.

Waſh half a pint of ſhrimps very clean, and put them into a ſtew-pan, with a ſpoonful of anchovy liquor, and a pound of butter melted thick. Boil it up for five minutes, and ſqueeze in half a lemon. Toſs it up, and put it into your ſauce-boat. *Cole*, 242.

To criſp Parſley.

Having picked and waſhed your parſley, put it into a Dutch oven, or on a ſheet of paper; do not ſet it too near the fire; turn it till it is quite criſp. Lay little bits of butter on it, but not to be greaſy. It is a better method than that of frying it. *Cole*, 242.

Plain Sour Sauce.

Take ſome freſh ſorrel-leaves, pick off the ſtalks, bruiſe the leaves, and put them into a plate with their juice; ſtrew on ſome pepper and ſalt, ſtir it all together, and ſerve it cold. *Cole*, 242.

White Sauce for Fiſh.

Having waſhed two anchovies, put them into a ſauce-pan, with one glaſs of white wine, and two of water, half a nutmeg, and a little lemon-peel. When it has boiled five or ſix minutes, ſtrain it through a ſieve. Add to it a ſpoonful of white wine vinegar, thicken it a little, then put in near a pound of butter rolled in flour. Boil it well, and pour it hot upon your fiſh. *Raffald*, 27.

White Sauce for Fowls or Chickens.

Take a little ſtrong veal gravy, with a little white pepper, mace, and ſalt, boiled in it. Have it clear from any ſkin or fat. As much cream, with a little flour mixed in the cream, a little mountain wine to your liking. Boil it up gently for five minutes, then ſtrain it over your chickens or fowls, or in beats. *Cole*, 243.

A white Sauce for Veal.

To a pint of good veal gravy, put a ſpoonful of lemon-pickle, half an anchovy, a tea-ſpoonful of muſhroom powder, or a few pickled muſhrooms; give it a gentle boil; then put in half a pint of cream, the yolks of two eggs beat fine; ſhake it over the fire after the eggs and cream are in, but do not let it boil; as that would curdle the cream. *Cole*, 243.

Sauce

Sauce Ravigotte à-la-Bourgeoise

Provide fome fage, parfley, a little mint, thyme, and bafil; tie them in a bunch, and put them into a fauce-pan of boiling water; let them boil a minute, then take them out, and fqueeze the water from them; chop them very fine, and add to them a clove of garlick, and two large onions minced fine. Put them into a ftew-pan with half a pint of broth, fome pepper, and a little falt; boil them up, and put in a fpoonful of vinegar. *Mafon*, 324.

Sauce à la-Nivernois.

Put in a fmall ftew pan two flices of ham, a clove of garlick, a laurel-leaf, fliced onions and roots; let it catch, then add a little broth, two fpoonfuls of cullis, a fpoonful of tarragon vinegar; ftew it an hour on a flow fire; then fift it through a fieve, and ferve it for a relifhing fauce. *Clermont*, 31.

Sauce for Pheafants or Partridges.

Thefe birds are ufually ferved up with gravy-fauce in the difh, and bread-fauce in a boat. *Cole*, 243.

Sauce for Wild Duck, Teal, &c.

Take a proper quantity of veal-gravy, with fome pepper and falt; fqueeze in the juice of two Seville oranges; add a little red wine, and let the red wine boil fome time in the gravy. *Cole*, 244.

To make Force-meat Balls.

Force-meat balls are a great addition to all made-difhes, made thus:—Take half a pound of veal, and half a pound of fuet cut fine, and beat in a marble mortar or wooden bowl. Have a few fweet herbs and parfley fhred fine, a little mace dried and beat fine, a fmall nutmeg grated, or half a large one, a little lemon-peel cut very fine, a little pepper and falt, and the yolks of two eggs. Mix all thefe well together, then roll them in little round balls, and fome in little long balls; roll them in flour, and fry them brown. If they are for any thing of white fauce, put a little water in a fauce-pan, and when the water boils, put them in, and let them boil for a few minutes, but never fry them for white fauce. *Glaffe*, 21. *Farley*, 139.

Sauce for a boiled Salmon.

Having boiled a bunch of fennel and parfley, chop them fmall, and put it into fome good melted butter, and fend it to table in a fauce-boat; another with gravy-fauce.

To make the gravy-fauce, put a little brown gravy into a fauce-pan with one anchovy, a tea-fpoonful of lemon-pickle, a meat-fpoonful of liquor from your walnut-pickle; one or two fpoonfuls of the water that the fifh was boiled in; it gives it a

pleſant

pleafant flavour ; a ftick of horfe-radifh, a little browning and falt; boil them three or four minutes, thicken it with flour and a good lump of butter, and ftrain it through an hair fieve.

N. B. This is a good fauce for moft kinds of fifh.   *Raffald*, 242.

An excellent Sauce for moft kinds of Fifh.

Take fome mutton or veal gravy, put to it a little of the water that drains from your fifh ; when boiled enough, put it in a fauce-pan, and put in a whole onion, one anchovy, a fpoonful of catchup, and a glafs of white wine ; thicken it with a lump of butter rolled in flour, and a fpoonful of cream ; if you have oyfters, cockles, or fhrimps, put them in after you take it off the fire, but it is extremely good without.   You may ufe red wine inftead of white, by leaving out the cream.   *Cole*, 244.

To make Oyfter Sauce.

The oyfters being opened, wafh them out of the liquor, then ftrain it ; put that and the oyfters into a little boiled gravy ; juft fcald them ; add fome cream, a piece of butter mixed with flour, and fome catchup ; fhake all up ; let it boil, but not much, as it will make the oyfters grow hard and fhrink ; yet care fhould be taken that they are enough, as nothing is more difagreeable than for the oyfters to tafte raw.   Or melted butter only, with the oyfters and their liquor.   *Mafon*, 327.

Another way.

Take a pint of large oyfters, fcald them, and then ftrain them through a fieve, wafh the oyfters very clean in cold water, and take the beards off; put them in a ftew pan, pour the liquor over them, but be careful to pour the liquor gently out of the veffel you have ftrained it into, and you will leave all the fediment at the bottom, which you muft avoid putting into your ftew-pan ; then add a large fpoonful of anchovy liquor, two blades of mace, half a lemon ; enough butter rolled in flour to thicken it ; then put in half a pound of butter, boil it up till the butter is melted, then take out the mace and lemon, fqueeze the lemon-juice into the fauce, give it a boil up, ftir it all the time, and then put it into your boats or bafons.

N. B. You may put in a fpoonful of catchup, or the fame quantity of mountain wine.   *Glaffe*, 123.

Afpic Sauce.

Infufe chervil, tarragon, burnet, garden-crefs, and a little mint, in a little cullis for above half an hour ; then fift it, and add to it a fpoolful of garlick-vinegar, pepper and falt; ferve up in a fauce-boat.   *Clermont*, 38.

Lobfter

Bruiſe the body of a lobſter into thick melted butter, and cut the fleſh into it in ſmall pieces; ſtew all together, and give it a boil; ſeaſon with a little pepper, ſalt, and a very ſmall quantity of mace. *Cole*, 245.

Another way.

Procure a lobſter that has a good deal of ſpawn, pull the meat to pieces with a fork; do not chop it; bruiſe the body and the ſpawn with the back of a ſpoon; break the ſhell, boil it in a little water to give it a colour; ſtrain it off, melt ſome butter in it very ſmooth, with a little horſe-radiſh and a very little chyan; take out the horſe radiſh, mix the body of the lobſter well with the butter, then add the meat, and give it a boil, with a ſpoonful of catchup or gravy, if agreeable. Some people chooſe only plain butter. *Maſon*, 327.

[*Culliſſes are uſed for thickening all ſorts of ragoos, ſoups, &c. and to give them an agreeable flavour. I have given the following receipts for making ſeveral of them, as they may probably be agreeable to ſome of my readers; though I have found by long experience, that Lemon-pickle and Browning (which ſee) anſwers much better both for taſte and beauty. It is infinitely cheaper, and prevents a great deal of unneceſſary trouble.*]

A Cullis for all ſorts of Ragoos and rich Sauces.

Take two pounds of veal, two ounces of ham, two or three cloves, a little nutmeg, a blade of mace, ſome parſley-roots, two carrots cut to pieces, ſome ſhallots, two bay-leaves; ſet theſe over a ſtove in an earthen veſſel; let them do very gently for half an hour cloſe covered, obſerving they do not burn; put beef-broth to it, let it ſtew till it is as rich as it is required to be, and then ſtrain it. *Cole*, 246.

A Cullis for all ſorts of Butcher's Meat.

The quantity of your meat muſt be proportioned to your company. If ten or twelve, you cannot take leſs than a leg of veal and an ham, with all the fat, ſkin, and outſide cut off. Cut the leg of veal in pieces about the thickneſs of your fiſt; place them in your ſtew-pan, and then the ſlices of ham, two carrots, an onion cut in two; cover it cloſe, let it ſtew ſoftly at firſt, and as it begins to brown, take off the cover and turn it, to colour it on all ſides the ſame; but take care not to burn the meat. When it has a pretty brown colour, moiſten you cullis with broth made of beef, or other meat; ſeaſon your cullis with a little ſweet baſil, ſome cloves, with ſome garlick; pare a lemon, cut it in ſlices, and put it into your cullis, with ſome muſhrooms. Put into a ſtew-pan a good lump of butter, and ſet it over a ſlow fire; put into it two or three handfuls of

flour,

flour, ftir it with a wooden ladle, and let it take a colour. If your cullis be pretty brown, you muft put in fome flour. Your flour being brown with your cullis, pour it very foftly into your cullis, keeping it ftirring with a wooden ladle; then let your cullis ftew foftly, and fkim off all the fat; put in two glaffes of Champagne, or other white wine; but take care to keep your cullis very thin, fo that you may take the fat off and clarify it. To clarify it, you muft put it in a ftove that draws well, and cover it clofe, and let it boil without uncovering till it boils over; then uncover it, and take off the fat that is round the ftew-pan, then wipe it off the cover alfo, and cover it again. When your cullis is done, take out the meat, and ftrain your cullis through a ftrainer. This cullis is for all forts of ragoos, fowls, pies, and terrines. *Glaffe*, 108.

A Cullis for Fifh.

Gut a large pike, and lay it whole upon the gridiron; turn it often. When done, take it off; take off the fkin, and take the meat from the bones; boil fix hard eggs, and take out the yolks; blanch a few almonds, beat them to a pafte in a marble mortar, and then add the yolks of the eggs; mix thefe well with butter, and put in the fifh; beat them all to mafh; then take half a dozen onions, and cut them into flices, two parf-nips, three carrots; fet on a ftew-pan, put in a piece of butter to brown, and when it boils, put in the roots; turn them till they are brown, and then pour in a little pea broth to moiften them. When they have boiled a few minutes, ftrain it into another fauce-pan; put in a whole leek, fome parfley, and fweet bafil, half a dozen cloves, fome mufhrooms and truffles, and a few crumbs of bread; let it ftew gently a quarter of an hour, and then put in the fifh from the mortar; let it ftew fome time longer; it muft not boil up, becaufe that would make it brown. When it is done, ftrain it through a coarfe fieve.

It ferves to thicken all made-difhes, and foups for Lent. *Cole*, 247.

Ham Cullis.

This is done with flices of veal-fillet, and ham fufficient to give it a pretty ftrong tafte; add all forts of roots; then add broth without falt, a glafs of white wine, a nofegay of thyme and parfley, half a laurel-leaf, one clove of garlick, a few mufh-rooms, and fhallots. *Dalrymple*, 11.

A white Cullis.

Cut a piece of veal into fmall bits, take fome thin flices of ham, and two onions cut into four pieces; moiften it with broth, feafoned with mufhrooms, a bunch of parfley, green onions, and three cloves; let it ftew. Being ftewed, take out all your meat and roots with a fkimmer, put in a few crumbs of of bread, and let it stew softly; take the white of a fowl, or two chickens, and pound it in a mortar; when well pounded, mix it in your cullis, but it must not boil, and your cullis must be very white; but if it is not white enough, you must pound two dozen of sweet almonds blanched, and put into your cullis. Let it be of a good taste, and strain it off, then put it in a small kettle, and keep it warm. You may use it for white loaves, white crust of bread and biscuits. *Glasse*, 110.

A Family Cullis.

Take a piece of butter rolled in flour, stir it in your stew-pan till the flour takes a fine yellow colour; then add small broth, a little gravy, a glass of white wine, a bundle of parsley, thyme, laurel, and sweet basil, two cloves, a little nutmeg or mace, a few mushrooms, whole pepper, and salt; boil for an hour on a slow fire; sift it through a lawn sieve, well skimmed from fat. This cullis is made either with meat or fish broth, according to your fancy. *Clermont*, 9.

To make Lemon Pickle.

Take twenty-four lemons, grate off the out-rinds very thin, and cut them in four quarters, but leave the bottoms whole, rub on them equally half a pound of bay-salt, and spread them on a large pewter dish; either put them in a cool oven, or let them dry gradually by the fire, till all the juice is dried into the peels; then put them into a well-glazed pitcher, with an ounce of mace, and half an ounce of cloves beat fine, an ounce of nutmeg cut into thin slices, four ounces of garlick peeled, half a pint of mustard seed bruised a little, and tied in a muslin bag; pour two quarts of boiling white wine vinegar upon them, close the pitcher well up, and let it stand five or six days by the fire; shake it well up every day, then tie it up, and let it stand for three months to take off the bitter. When you bottle it, put the pickle and lemon in an hair sieve; press them well to get out the liquor and let it stand till another day, then pour off the fine, and bottle it. Let the other stand three or four days, and it will refine itself. Pour it off, and bottle it; let it stand again, and bottle it till the whole is refined. It may be put in any white sauce, and will not hurt the colour. It is very good for fish-sauce and made-dishes. A tea-spoonful is enough for white, and two for brown sauce, for a fowl. It is a most useful pickle, and gives a pleasant flavour. Always put it in before you thicken the sauce, or put any cream in, lest the sharpness should make it curdle. *Raffald*, 8.

Chap. XVII. ELEGANT SMALL SAVOURY DISHES OF VEGETABLES, FRUITS, &c.

Artichoke Bottoms with Eggs.

TAKE your artichoke bottoms, and boil them in hard water; if dry ones, in soft water; put a good lump of butter in the water; it will make them boil in half the time, and they will be white and plump. When you put them up, put the yolk of an hard egg in the middle of every bottom, and pour good melted butter upon them, and serve them up. You may lay asparagus or brocoli between every bottom. *Raffald*, 290.

To fry Artichoke Bottoms.

Having blanched them in water, flour them and fry them in fresh butter. Lay them in your dish, and pour melted butter over them. Or you may put a little red wine into the butter, and season with nutmeg, pepper, and salt. *Glasse*, 197. *Farley*, 56.

A ragoo of Artichoke Bottoms.

If dried, let them lie in warm water for two or three hours, changing the water; put to them some good gravy, mushroom catchup or powder, chyan and salt; thicken with a little flour. Boil these together. *Cole*, 249.

A ragoo of Celery.

Cut the white part of your celery into lengths, boil it till it is tender; fry and drain it, flour it, put into it some rich gravy, a very little red wine, salt, pepper, nutmeg, and catchup; boil it up. *Cole*, 249.

Another way.

Having taken off all the outsides of your heads of celery, cut them in pieces, put them in a tossing-pan, with a little veal-gravy or water; boil them till they are tender; put to it a spoonful of lemon pickle, a meat spoonful of white wine, and a little salt; thicken it with flour and butter, and serve them up with sippets. *Raffald*, 286.

To fry Celery.

When boiled, dip it in batter, fry it of a light brown in hogs'-lard; put it on a plate, and pour melted butter over it. *Cole*, 250.

Cucumbers stewed.

Having pared your cucumbers, slice them about the thickness of a crown piece; slice some onion. Fry them both; drain and shake a little flour over them. Put them into a stew-pan

pan with some good gravy, chyan, and salt; stew them till tender. Or they may be stewed in their own liquor, without being fried; chyan, and salt. Or take out the seeds, quarter
the cucumbers, stew them till clear in some boiled gravy; mix
a little flour with some cream, a very little white wine, and
white pepper pounded. Boil it up. *Mason*, 338.

To ragoo Cucumbers.

Slice two cucumbers and two onions, and fry them in a
little butter, then drain them in a sieve, put them into a sauce-
pan, add six spoonfuls of gravy, two of white wine, and a blade
of mace; let them stew five or six minutes. Then take a piece
of butter as big as a walnut rolled in flour, a little salt, and
chyan pepper; shake them together, and when it is thick, dish
them up. *Glasse*, 113.

Cucumbers with Eggs.

Pare six large young cucumbers, and cut them into squares
about the size of a dice; put them into boiling water; let
them boil up, and take them out of the water, and put them
into a stew-pan, with an onion stuck with cloves, a good slice
of ham, a quarter of a pound of butter, and a little salt; set it
over the fire a quarter of an hour, keep it close covered, skim
it well, and shake it often, as it is apt to burn; then dredge in
a little flour over them, and put in as much veal-gravy as will
just cover the cucumbers; stir it well together, and keep a
gentle fire under it till no scum will rise; then take out the
ham and onion, and put in the yolks of two eggs, beat up with
a tea-cupful of cream; stir it well for a minute, then take it off
the fire, and just before you put it in the dish, squeeze in a little lemon-juice. Have ready five or six poached eggs to lay
on the top. *Cole*, 250.

Cucumbers stuffed with Force-meat.

Peel as many cucumbers as you propose for a dish; take out
the middle with an apple corer, blanch them a little in boiling water, and fill them with a force-meat made of roasted
poultry; braze them with some thin slices of bacon, a little
broth, two or three onions, a faggot of parsley and sweet herbs,
one carrot sliced, three cloves, a little whole pepper and salt.
When done drain and wipe them, and serve with a good relishing cullis-sauce. *Cole*, 250.

To ragoo Mushrooms.

Peel some large mushrooms, and take out the inside. Broil
them on a gridiron, and when the outside is brown, put them
in a tossing-pan, with a quantity of water sufficient to cover
them. Let them stand ten minutes, then put to them a spoonful of white wine, as much of browning, and a very little alle-

P

gar. Thicken it with butter and flour, and boil it a little.
Serve it up with fippets round the difh. *Farley*, 80, from *Raffald*, 288.

Another way.

Scrape the infide of fome large mufhrooms, and broil them.
When a little brown, put them into fome gravy thickened with
ale, a little flour, a very little Madeira, falt, and chyan; a little
juice of lemon. Boil thefe together. *Cole*, 251.

To ftew Mufhrooms.

Firft put your mufhrooms in falt and water, then wipe them
with a flannel, and put them again in falt and water; then
throw them into a fauce-pan by themfelves, and let them boil
up as quick as poffible; then put in a little chyan pepper and
a little mace: let them ftew in this a quarter of an hour, then
add a tea-cupful of cream, with a little flour and butter the fize
of a walnut. Serve them up as foon as done. *Cole*, 251.

Mufhroom Loaves.

Take fmall buttons, and wafh them as for pickling; boil
them a few minutes in a little water; put to them a little
cream, a piece of butter rolled in flour, falt, and pepper; boil
this up, and fill fome fmall Dutch loaves. If they are not too
be had, fmall French rolls will do, the crumb taken out; but
not fo well as the loaves. *Mafon*, 339.

Stewed Peas and Lettuce.

Take a quart of green peas and two large cabbage lettuces,
cut fmall acrofs, and wafhed very clean; put them in a ftew-
pan with a quart of gravy, and ftew them till tender; put in
fome butter rolled in flour, feafon with pepper and falt.
When of a proper thicknefs, difh them up.

N. B. Some like them thickened with the yolks of four eggs;
others prefer an onion chopped very fine, and ftewed with
them, with two or three rafhers of lean ham. *Glaffe*, 116.

Another way.

Boil and drain the peas, flice and fry the lettuce; put them
into fome good gravy; fhake in a little flour; add chyan and
falt, and a very little fhred mint; boil this up, fhaking it.
Cole, 252.

Another way.

Having fhelled your peas, boil them in hard water, with falt
in it, drain them in a fieve; then flice your lettuces and fry
them in frefh butter; put your peas and lettuces into a toffing-
pan, with a little good gravy, pepper and falt; thicken it with
flour and butter, put in a little fhred mint, and ferve it up in a
foup-difh. *Raffald*, 289.

To

To ragoo Asparagus.

Scrape and clean one hundred grafs, and throw them in cold water; then cut as far as they are good and green, and take two heads of endive, clean picked and wafhed, and cut very fmall, a young lettuce clean wafhed and cut fmall, and a large onion peeled and cut fmall   Put a quarter of a pound of butter into a ftew-pan, and when it is melted, throw in the above ingredients. Tofs them about, and fry them ten minutes; then feafon them with a little pepper and falt, fh ke in a little flour, tofs them about, and pour in half a pint of gravy. Let them ftew till the fauce is very thick and good, and then pour all into your difh. Garnifh with a few of the little tops of the grafs. *Farley*, 80.

Asparagus and Eggs.

Toaft a piece of bread as large as you have occafion for, butter it, and lay it on your difh; butter fome eggs and lay over it. In the mean time, boil fome grafs tender, cut it fmall, and lay it over the eggs.

N. B. The eggs are buttered thus:—take as many as you want, beat them well, put them into a fauce-pan with a good piece of butter, a little falt; keep beating them with a fpoon till they are thick enough, then pour them on the toaft. *Cole*, 252.

An Amulet of Asparagus.

Beat up fix eggs with cream, boil fome fine afparagus, and when boiled, cut off all the green in fmall pieces; mix them with the eggs, and add pepper and falt. Make your pot hot, and put in a flice of butter; then put them in, and fend them up hot. They may be ferved on buttered toafts. *Cole*, 252.

To make an Amulet.

Beat fix eggs, ftrain them through a hair fieve, and put them into a frying-pan, in which is prepared a quarter of a pound of hot butter. Throw in a little boiled ham, fcraped fine, fome fhred parfley, and feafon them with pepper, falt, and nutmeg. Fry it brown on the under fide, and lay it on your difh, but do not turn it. Hold a hot falamander over it for half a minute, to take off the raw look of the eggs. Some put in clary and chives, and fome put in onions. Serve it with curled parfley ftuck in it. *Cole*, 253.

An Amulet with Onions.

Fry four fliced onions in butter, till they are quite done. Add the yolks of three eggs, and a little chopped parfley. Make two fmall amulets without falt, put the onions upon them, and a few fillets of anchovies; roll them lengthways. Have ready fome pieces of bread cut like toafts, and fried in butter. Cut the amulets the fame fize of the bread upon

which

which you put them. Pour a little melted butter over, and
ſtrew them with raſped Parmeſan cheeſe and bread crumbs.
Give them a colour in the oven, and ſerve with a reliſhing-ſauce
under. *Dalrymple*, 413.

To ragoo Cauliflowers.

Take a large cauliflower, or two ſmall ones, pick as if you
intended them for pickling : ſtew them till they are enough in
a rich brown cullis, ſeaſoned with pepper and ſalt ; put them
in a diſh, and pour the cullis over them. Boil ſome ſprigs of
the cauliflower very white, and lay round them. *Maſon*, 337.
Farley, 81.

To broil Potatoes.

Boil them, then peel them, cut them in two, and broil them
till they are brown on both ſides ; then lay them in the plate
or diſh, and pour melted butter over them. *Cole*, 253.

To fry Potatoes.

Cut your potatoes into thin ſlices, as large as a crown piece,
fry them brown, lay them in the plate or diſh, pour melted
butter and ſack and ſugar over them. Theſe make a pretty
corner plate. *Cole*, 253.

To maſh potatoes.

Boil them, peel them, and put them into a ſauce-pan ; maſh
them well, and put a pint of milk to two pounds of potatoes ;
add a little ſalt, ſtir them well together, and take care that
they do not ſtick to the bottom ; then take a quarter of a
pound of butter, ſtir it in, and ſerve it up. *Cole*, 253.

To ſcollop Potatoes.

Having firſt boiled your potatoes, beat them fine in a bowl
with good cream, and a lump of butter and ſalt ; put them into ſcollop ſhells, make them ſmooth on the top, ſcore them with
a knife, lay thin ſlices of butter on the top of them, put them
in a Dutch oven to brown before the fire. Three ſhells is ſufficient for a diſh. *Raffald*, 287.

To fry Chardoons.

Cut them about ſix inches long, and ſtring them, then boil
them till tender. Take them out, have ſome butter melted in
your ſtew-pan, flour them, and fry them brown. Send them
in a diſh, with melted butter in a cup. Or you may tie them
up in bundles, and boil them like aſparagus. Put a toaſt under
them, and pour a little melted butter over them ; or cut them
into dice, and boil them like peas. Toſs them up in butter,
and ſend them up hot. *Glaſſe*, 195.

Chardoons à-la-Fromage.

String them, cut them an inch long, ſtew them in a little red
wine

wine till they are tender; feafon with pepper and falt, and thicken it with a piece of butter rolled in flour; then pour them into your difh, fqueeze fome juice of orange over it, then fcrape Parmefan or Chefhire cheefe all over them; then brown it with a cheefe iron, and ferve it up quick and hot. *Cole,* 254.

To ftew Pears.

Take fix pears, pare them, and either quarter them or ftew them whole. Lay them in a deep earthen pan, with a few cloves, a piece of lemon peel, a gill of red wine, and a quarter of a pound of fine fugar. If the pears are very large, they will require half a pound of fugar, and half a pint of red wine. Cover them clofe with brown paper, and ftew them in an oven till they are enough. They may be ferved up hot or cold. They make a very pretty difh with one whole and they reft cut in quarters, and the cores taken out. *Farley,* 72.

To ftew Pears in a fauce-pan.

Put them into a fauce-pan with the ingredients mentioned in the preceding article, cover them, and do them over a flow fire. When they are enough, take them off; add a penny-worth of cochineal bruifed very fine. *Cole,* 254.

To bake Pears.

Pare them, cut them in halves, and core them; then put them into an earthen pan with a few cloves, a litttle water and red wine, and about half a pound of fugar to fix pears; bake them in an oven moderately hot, then fet them over a flow fire; let them ftew gently; cut in a lemon-peel in fmall fhreds. If the fyrup is not rich enough, add more fugar. *Mafon,* 433.

Eggs and Broccoli.

Boil your broccoli tender, obferving to fave a large bunch for the middle, and fix or eight little thick fprigs to ftick round. Toaft a bit of bread as large as you would have it for your difh or butter plate. Butter fome eggs thus :—take fix eggs, or as many as you have occafion for, beat them well, put them into a fauce-pan with a good piece of butter, a little falt; keep beating them with a fpoon till they are thick enough, then pour them on the toaft. Set the largeft bunch of broccoli in the middle, and the other little pieces round and about, and garnifh the difh with little fprigs of broccoli. This is a pretty fide-difh, or corner-plate. *Glaffe,* 197.

To broil Eggs.

Cut a toaft round a quartern loaf, brown it, lay it in your difh, butter it, and very carefully break fix or eight eggs on the toaft. Take a red-hot fhovel and hold it over them.

·When they are done, fqueeze a Seville orange over them, grate a little nutmeg over it, and ferve it up for a fide-plate. Or you may poach your eggs and lay them on a toaft; or toaft your bread crifp, and pour a little boiling water over it. Sea-·fon it with a little falt, and then lay your poached eggs upon it. *Cole,* 255.

Eggs Dutchefs fashion.

Boil a pint of cream and fugar, a little orange-flower water, and piece of lemon-peel; poach fix or eight eggs in it; take out the eggs, reduce the cream for fauce to ferve upon them. *Dalrymple,* 416.

Spinach and Eggs.

Pick and wafh your fpinach very clean in feveral waters, put it into a fauce-pan with a little falt; cover it clofe, and fhake the pan often. When it is juft tender, and whilft it is green, throw it into a fieve to drain; lay it in your difh. Have ready a ftew-pan of water boiling, and break as many eggs into cups as you would poach. When the water boils, put in the eggs; have an egg flice ready to take them out with, lay them on the fpinach, and garnifh the difh with orange cut into quarters, with melted butter in a cup. *Cole,* 255.

To force Eggs.

Scald two cabbage lettuces with a few mufhrooms, parfley, forrel, and chervil; then chop them very fmall, with the yolks of hard eggs, feafoned with falt and nutmeg; then ftew them in butter, and when they are enough, put in a little cream, then pour them into the bottom of a difh. Then chop the whites very fine, with parfley, nutmeg, and falt. Lay this round the brim of the difh, and run a red-hot fire-fhovel over it to brown it. *Cole,* 255.

To poach Eggs with Toafts.

Pour your water in a flat-bottomed pan, with a little falt. When it boils, break your eggs carefully in, and let them boil two minutes; then take them up with an egg-fpoon, and lay them on buttered toafts. *Raffald,* 289.

Eggs with Saufages.

Fry fome faufages, and then a flice of bread; lay the faufages on the bread, with a poached egg between each link. If the toaft is too ftrong fried, butter it a little.

The common way of drefling eggs is to poach them, and ferve them on a buttered toaft, or on ftewed fpinach or forrel. *Cole,* 256.

CHAP.

Preliminary Obfervations on Puddings.

IN boiled puddings, particular care is required that the cloth be clean, and remember to dip it in boiling water, let it be well floured, and give your cloth a fhake. If it is a bread pudding, tie it loofe; if a batter pudding, tie it clofe; and never put your pudding in till the water boils. If you boil it in a bafon, butter it, and boil it in plenty of water, without covering the pan, and turn it often. When it is enough, take it up in the bafon, let it ftand a few minutes to cool, then untie the ftring, wrap the cloth round the bafon, lay your difh over it, and turn the pudding out; then take off the bafon and cloth with great care, otherwife a light pudding is liable to be broken in turning out. When you make a batter pudding, firft mix the flour well with a little milk, then gradually put in the ingredients, by which means it will be perfectly fmooth and without lumps. But for a plain batter pudding, the beft method is to ftrain it through a coarfe hair fieve, that it may neither have lumps nor the treadles of the eggs; and for all other puddings, ftrain the eggs when you beat them. With refpect to baking, all bread and cuftard puddings require time, and a moderate oven, that will raife and not burn them. Batter and rice puddings, a quick oven. Be particularly careful to butter the pan or difh before you put in your pudding. *Cole,* 256.

A baked Almond Pudding.

Having boiled the fkins of two lemons very tender, beat them very fine; beat half a pound of almonds in rofe water, and a pound of fugar very fine; then melt half a pound of butter and let it ftand till it is quite cold; beat the yolks of eight eggs and the whites of four; mix them and beat them all together, with a little orange-flower water, and bake it in the oven. *Raffald,* 168. *Farley,* 184.

A boiled Almond Pudding.

Strain two eggs well beaten into a quart of cream, a penny-loaf grated, one nutmeg, fix fpoonfuls of flour, half a pound of almonds blanched and beat fine, half a dozen bitter almonds, fweeten with fine fugar; add a little brandy; boil it half an hour; pour round it melted butter and wine; ftick it with almonds blanched and flit. *Mafon,* 370.

Almond Hog's Puddings.

Take a pound of beef marrow chopped fine, half a pound of fweet almonds blanched and beat fine, with a little orange-

flower

flower or rofe water; half a pound of white bread grated fine, half a pound of currants clean wafhed and picked, a quarter of a pound of fine fugar, a quarter of an ounce of mace, nutmeg, and cinnamon together, of each an equal quantity, and half a pint of fack or mountain. Mix all well together, with half a pint of good cream, and the yolks of four eggs. Fill your guts half full, tie them up, and boil them a quarter of an hour, and prick them as they boil to keep the guts from breaking. For a change, you may leave out the currants, but you muft then add a quarter of a pound more fugar. *Cole,* 257.

A baked Apple Pudding.

Boil half a pound of apples and pound them well; take half a pound of butter beaten to a cream, mix it with the apples before they are cold; add fix eggs with the whites, well beaten and ftrained, half a pound of fugar pounded and fifted, the rinds of two lemons well boiled and beaten; fift the peel into clean water twice in the boiling; put a thin cruft in the bottom and rims of your difh. It will take half an hour to bake it. *Cole,* 257.

Another way.

Pare twelve large pippins, and take out the cores; put them into a fauce-pan, with four or five fpoonfuls of water, and boil them till they are foft and thick. Then beat them well, ftir in a pound of loaf fugar, the juice of three lemons, and the peels of two cut thin and beat fine in a mortar, and the yolks of eight eggs beaten. Mix all well together, and bake it in a flack oven. When nearly done, throw over it a little fine fugar. You may, if you pleafe, bake it in a puff pafte, at the bottom of the difh, and round the edges of it. *Glaffe,* 217. *Farley,* 198.

Apple Dumplings.

Having pared and taken out the core of your apples, fill the hole with quince, or orange marmalade, or fugar (which ever beft fuits); then take a piece of cold pafte, and make a hole in it, as if you was going to make a pie; lay in your apple, and put another piece of pafte in the fame form, and clofe it up round the fide of your apple. It is much preferable to the method of gathering it in a lump at one end. Tie it in a cloth, and boil it three quarters of an hour; pour melted butter over them and ferve them up. Five is fufficient for a difh. *Raffald,* 183. *Farley,* 198.

An Apricot Pudding.

Coddle fix large apricots very tender, break them very fmall, fweeten them to your tafte; when they are cold add fix eggs and only two whites, well beat; mix them all well together,
with

with a pint of good cream; lay a puff paste all over your difh, and pour in your ingredients. Bake it half an hour; but the oven fhould not be too hot. When it is enough, throw a little fine fugar all over it, and fend it to table. *Glaſſe*, 272. *Farley*, 189.

A Batter Pudding.

Take a quart of milk, beat up the yolks of fix eggs, and the whites of three, and mix them with a quarter of a pint of milk. Take fix fpoonfuls of flour, a tea-fpoonful of falt, and one of beaten ginger. Mix them all together, boil them an hour and a quarter, and pour melted butter over the pudding. You may, if you think proper, put in half a pound of pruens, or currants, and two or three more eggs. Or you may make it without eggs, in the following manner : take a quart of milk, mix fix fpoonfuls of the flour with a little of the milk firft, a tea-fpoonful of falt, two of beaten ginger, and two of the tinc- ture of faffron. Then mix all together, and boil it an hour. *Farley*, 200, from *Glaſſe*, 219.

Another.

A pint of milk, four eggs, four fpoonfuls of flour, half a grated nutmeg, and a little falt ; tie the cloth very clofe, and boil it three quarters of an hour. Sauce, melted butter. *Cole*, 259.

A Bread Pudding.

Slice all the crumb of a penny loaf thin into a quart of milk, fet it over a chafing-difh of coals till the bread has foaked up all the milk, then put in a piece of butter, ftir it round, and let it ftand till cool. Or you may boil your milk and pour over your bread, and cover it up clofe ; this method is as good as the other. Then take the yolks of fix eggs, and half the whites, and beat them up with a little rofe water and nutmeg, and a little falt and fugar, if you like it. Mix all well together, and boil it an hour. *Glaſſe*, 220. *Farley*, 192.

A nice Bread Pudding.

Take half a pint of milk, boil it with a bit of cinnamon, four eggs, and the whites well beaten, the rind of a lemon grated, half a pound of fuet chopped fine, and as much bread as may be thought requifite. Pour your milk on the bread and fuet, keep mixing it till cold, then put in the lemon-peel, eggs, a little fugar, and fome nutmeg grated fine. This pud- ding may be either boiled or baked. *Raffald*, 173.

A Calf's-foot Pudding.

Boil four feet tender ; pick the niceft of the meat from the bones, and chop it very fine ; add the crumb of a penny loaf grated, a pound of beef fuet fhred fmall, half a pint of cream,

seven

feven eggs, a pound of currants, four ounces of citron cut
fmall, two ounces of candied orange peel cut like ftraws, a nutmeg, and a large glafs of brandy. Butter the cloth and flour
it, tie it clofe, let it boil three hours. *Mafon*, 370.

Mrs. *Raffald*, page 172, gives the fame receipt, with this
addition: " When you take the pudding up, it is beft to put
" it in a bowl that will juft hold it, and let it ftand a quarter
" of an hour before you turn it out; lay your difh upon the
" top of the bafon, and turn it upfide down." *Cole*, 261.

A Carrot Pudding.

Scrape a raw carrot very clean and grate it. Take half a
pound of the grated carrot, and a pound of grated bread; beat
up eight eggs, leaving out half the whites, and mix the eggs
with half a pint of cream. Then ftir in the bread and carrot,
half a pound of frefh butter melted, half a pint of fack, three
fpoonfuls of orange flower-water, and a nutmeg grated.
Sweeten to your palate. Mix all well together, and if it is not
thin enough, ftir in a little new milk or cream. Let it be of a
moderate thicknefs, lay a puff pafte all over the difh, and pour
in the ingredients. It will take an hour's baking. If you
would boil it, you muft melt butter, and put in white wine and
fugar. *Cole*, 259.

Green Codling Pudding.

Green about a quart of codlings as for a pie, rub them
through a hair fieve, with as much of the juice of beets as will
green your pudding; put in the crumb of half a penny loaf,
half a pound of butter, and three eggs well beaten; beat them
all together with half a pound of fugar, and two fpoonfuls of
cyder. Lay a good pafte round the rim of the difh and pour
it in. *Raffald*, 178. From *Mafon*, 377, with very little alteration.

A Cuftard Pudding.

Put a piece of cinnamon in a pint of thick cream; boil it;
add a quarter of a pound of fugar; when cold, add the yolks of
five eggs well beaten; ftir this over the fire till pretty thick,
but you fhould not let it boil. When quite cold, butter a
cloth well, duft it with flour, tie the cuftard in it very clofe,
boil it three quarters of an hour. When taken up, put it into
a bafon to cool a little; untie the cloth, lay the difh on the
bafon, turn it up. If the cloth is not taken off carefully,
the pudding will break; grate over it a little fugar. Melted
butter, and a little wine in a boat. *Raffald*, 169, from *Mafon*,
369; with this difference, *Mrs. Mafon* recommends but *five*
eggs, *Mrs. Raffald*, *fix*.

Damafcene

Having made a good hot paſte cruſt, roll it pretty thin, lay it in a baſon, and put in a proper quantity of damaſcenes; wet the edge of the paſte, and cloſe it up; boil it in a cloth one hour and ſend it up whole; pour melted butter over it, and grate ſugar round the edge of the diſh.

N. B. Dumplings may be made from any kind of preſerved fruit, in the ſame manner. *Raffald,* 183.

Gooſeberry Pudding.

Scald a pint of green gooſeberries, and rub them through a ſieve; put to them half a pound of ſugar, and an equal quantity of butter, two or three Naples' biſcuits, and four eggs well beaten; mix it well, bake it half an hour. *Maſon,* 377. *Raffald,* 182. *Farley,* 198. The two laſt recommended *ſix* eggs; *Mrs. Maſon,* only *four.* In other reſpects they all agree.

A Grateful Pudding.

Take a pound of fine flour, and a pound of white bread grated; take eight eggs, with half the whites, beat them up, and mix with them a pint of milk; then ſtir in the bread and flour, a pound of raiſins ſtoned, a pound of currants, half a pound of ſugar, a little beaten ginger; mix all well together, and either bake or boil it. It will take three quarters of an hour baking. Put in cream, if you have it, inſtead of milk; the pudding will be much improved by it. *Glaſſe,* 219.

Hard Dumplings.

Put a little ſalt to ſome flour and water, and make it into a paſte. Roll them in balls as large as a turkey's egg; roll them in a little flour, throw them into boiling water, and half an hour will boil them. They are beſt boiled with a good piece of beef. For a change, you may add a few currants.

A Haſty Pudding.

Take a pint of cream and a pint of milk, a little ſalt, and ſweeten it with loaf-ſugar; make it boil; then put in ſome fine flour, and keep it continually ſtirring while the flour is put in, till it is thick enough, and boiled enough; pour it out, and ſtick the tops full of little bits of butter. It may be eaten with ſugar or ſalt. *Maſon,* 368.

Herb Pudding.

Of ſpinach, beet, parſley, and leeks, take each a handful; waſh them and ſcald them, then ſhred them very fine; have ready a quart of groats ſteeped in warm water half an hour, and a pound of hog's-lard cut in little bits, three large onions chopped ſmall, and three ſage leaves hacked fine; put in a little ſalt, mix all well together, and tie it cloſe up. It will require

quire to be taken up in boiling to loosen the string a little, *Raffald,* 182, from *Mason,* 372.

A Hunting Pudding.

Take the yolks of ten eggs, and the whites of six; beat them up well with half a pint of cream, six spoonfulls of flour, one pound of beef suet chopped small, a pound of currants well washed and picked, a pound of jar raisins stoned and chopped small, two ounces of candied citron, orange and lemon, shred fine; put two ounces of fine sugar, a spoonful of rose water, a glass of brandy, and half a nutmeg grated. Mix all well together, tie it up in a cloth, and boil it four hours; be sure to put it in when the water boils, and keep it boiling all the time; turn it into a dish, and garnish with powder sugar. *Cole,* 261.

An Italian Pudding.

Take a pint of cream, and slice in some French rolls, as much as you think will make it thick enough; beat ten eggs fine, grate a nutmeg, butter the bottom of the dish, slice twelve pippins into it, throw some orange-peel and sugar over, and half a pint of red wine; then pour your cream, bread, and eggs over it; first lay a puff paste at the bottom of the dish, and round the edges, and bake it half an hour. *Glasse,* 217.

A Lemon Pudding.

Take three lemons and grate the rinds off, beat up twelve yolks and six whites of eggs, put in half a pint of cream, half a pound of fine sugar, a little orange flower water, a quarter of a pound of butter melted. Mix all well together, squeeze in the juice of two lemons; put it over the stove, and keep stirring it till it is thick; put a puff paste round the rim of the dish, put in pudding-stuff, with some candied sweetmeats cut small over it, and bake it three quarters of an hour. *Cole,* 262.

A Marrow Pudding.

Grate a penny loaf into crumbs, and pour on them a pint of boiling hot cream. Cut very thin a pound of beef marrow, beat four eggs well, and then add a glass of brandy, with sugar and nutmeg to your taste. Mix them all well together, and either boil or bake it. Three quarters of an hour will do it. Cut two ounces of citron very thin; and when you dish it up, stick them all over it. *Cole,* 262.

Another.

Take a quarter of a pound of rice, half boil it, half a pound of marrow shred very fine, a quarter of a pound of raisins stoned and chopped small, with two ounces of currants; beat four eggs a quarter of an hour, mix it all together, with a pint

of

of good cream, a fpoonful of brandy, and fugar and nutmeg to
your tafte. You may either bake it or put it into fkins for
hog's-puddings. *Cole*, 262.

A Millet Pudding.

Spread a quarter of a pound of butter at the bottom of a
difh; lay into it fix ounces of millet, and a quarter of a pound
of fugar. When going to the oven, pour over it three pints
of milk. *Mafon*, 377.

Norfolk Dumplings.

To half a pint of milk put two eggs, and a little falt, and
make them into a good thick batter with flour. Have ready a
clean faucepan of water boiling, and drop your batter into it,
and two or three minutes will boil them. Be particularly
careful that the water boils faft when you put the batter in.
Then throw them into a fieve to drain, turn them into a difh,
and ftir a lump of frefh butter into them. If eaten hot, they
are very good. *Cole*, 263.

An Oat Pudding.

Take two pounds of oats fkinned, and new milk enough to
drown it; eight ounces of raifins of the fun ftoned, the fame
quantity of currants neatly picked; a pound of fweet fuet
finely fhred, fix new laid eggs well beat; feafon with nutmeg,
beaten ginger, and falt; mix it all well together, it will make
an excellent pudding. *Cole*, 263.

An Oatmeal Pudding.

Boil a pint of fine oatmeal in three pints of new milk, ftirring it till it is as thick as hafty pudding; take it off, and ftir
in half a pound of frefh butter, a little beaten mace and nutmeg, and a gill of fack; then beat up eight eggs, half
the whites, ftir all well together, lay puff pafte all over the
difh, pour in the pudding, and bake it half an hour. Or you
may boil it with a few currants. *Cole*, 263.

An Orange Pudding.

Take the rind of a Sevelle orange, boil it very foft, beat it
in a marble mortar, with the juice; put to it two Naples' bifcuits grated very fine, half a pound of butter, a quarter of a
pound of fugar, and the yolks of fix eggs; mix them well together; lay a good puff pafte round the edge of your China
difh, bake it in a gentle oven half an hour. You may make a
lemon pudding the fame way, by putting in a lemon inftead
of the orange. *Raffald*, 171.

Peas Pudding.

Boil it till it is quite tender; then take it up, untie it, ftir in
a good

a good piece of butter, a little falt, and a good deal of beaten pepper; then tie it up tight again, boil it an hour longer, and it will eat fine. *Cole*, 263.

A Plain Pudding.

Put into a pint of milk three laurel leaves, a little grated lemon-peel, and a bit of mace; boil it, then ftrain it off, and with a little flour make it into a pretty thick hafty pudding; then ftir into it a quarter of a pound of butter, two ounces of fugar, half a fmall nutmeg grated, five yolks and three whites of eggs; beat them well up all together, pour it into a difh, and bake it. *Mafon*, 375.

Another.

Take the yolks and whites of three eggs, beat them together, with two large fpoonfuls of flour, a little falt, and half a pint of milk or cream; make it the thicknefs of a pancake batter, and beat all well together. It will take half an hour to boil it. *Cole*, 264.

An excellent Plum Pudding.

Take one pound of fuet, one pound of currants, and one pound of raifins ftoned; the yolks of eight eggs, and the whites of four; the crumb of a penny loaf grated, one pound of flour, half a nutmeg, a tea-fpoonful of grated ginger, a little falt, and a fmall glafs of brandy; beat the eggs firft, mix them with fome milk. By degrees add the flour and other ingredients, and what more milk may be neceffary; it muft be very thick and well ftirred. It will require five hours boiling. *Cole*, 264.

A Potatoe Pudding.

Boil a quarter of a pound of potatoes till they are foft, peel them, and mafh them with the back of a fpoon, and rub them through a fieve to have them fine and fmooth. Then take half a pound of frefh butter melted, half a pound of fine fugar, and beat them well together till they are fmooth. Beat fix eggs, both yolks and whites, and ftir them in with a glafs of fack or brandy. You may, if you pleafe, add half a pint of currants. Boil it half an hour. Melt fome butter, and put into it a glafs of white wine; fweeten with fugar, and pour it over it. *Farley*, 190.

A Quaking Pudding.

Take a quart of cream, boil it, and let it ftand till almoft cold, then beat four eggs a full quarter of an hour, with a fpoonful and a half of flour; then mix them with your cream, add fugar and nutmeg to your palate, tie it clofe up in a cloth well buttered; let it boil an hour, and turn it carefully. *Raffald*, 180.

A Rabbit

A Rabbit Pudding.

Take the meat of a large roasted rabbit, chop it very fine with the liver, soak the bones in a pint of cream about an hour; boil six onions in broth, with a faggot of parsley, shallots, two cloves, pepper and salt; boil it till the liquid is of a thick consistence, chop the onions very fine, mix them with the meat and bread crumbs soaked in cream, and the cream wherein you soaked the bones; add eight yolks of eggs, three quarters of a pound of lard cut in small pieces, salt, and spices to taste.

Puddings may thus be made of all sorts of poultry or game. They may be boiled in a cloth, as a common bread pudding, and served with a relishing sauce. *Dalrymple,* 150.

A Rice Pudding.

Put a quarter of a pound of rice into a saucepan, with a quart of new milk, and a stick of cinnamon; stir it often to keep it from sticking to the saucepan. When it has boiled thick, pour it into a pan, stir in a quarter of a pound of fresh butter, and sugar to your palate. Grate in half a nutmeg, add three or four spoonfuls of rose water, and stir it all well together. When it is cold, beat up eight eggs, with half the whites, beat it all well together, butter a dish, pour it in, and bake it. You may first lay a puff paste all over the dish. For a change, you may put in a few currants and sweet meats. *Glasse,* 217.

A Ground Rice Pudding.

Boil a quarter of a pound of ground rice in water till it is soft, then beat the yolks of four eggs, and put to them a pint of cream, a quarter of a pound of sugar, and a quarter of a pound of butter; mix them well together. You may either boil or bake it. *Cole,* 265.

A cheap plain Rice Pudding.

Take a quarter of a pound of rice, and half a pound of raisins stoned, and tie them in a cloth. Give the rice a great deal of room to swell. Boil it two hours. When it is enough, turn it into your dish, and pour melted butter and sugar over it, with a little nutmeg. *Cole,* 265.

Another Rice Pudding.

Take a quarter of a pound of rice, boil it in water till it is soft, and drain it through a hair sieve; beat it in a marble mortar, with the yolks of four eggs, four ounces of butter, and the same quantity of sugar; grate the rind of half a lemon, and half a nutmeg, work them well together for half an hour; then put in half a pound of currants well washed and cleaned, mix them
them

them well together, butter your cloth, and tie it up. Boil it an hour, and serve it up with white wine fauce. *Cole*, 265.

A Sago Pudding.

Take two ounces of fago, boil it with fome cinnamon and a bit of lemon-peel, till it is foft and thick. Grate the crumb of a halfpenny roll, put to it a glafs of red wine, four ounces of chopped marrow, the yolks of four eggs well beaten, and fugar to your tafte. When the fago is cold, put thefe ingredients to it. Mix it all well together. Bake it with a puff pafte. When it comes from the oven, ftick over it citron cut into pieces, and almonds blanched and cut into flips. *Raffald*, 175, from *Ma-fon*, 380.

A Spoonful Pudding.

Take a fpoonful of flour, a fpoonful of cream or milk, an egg, a little nutmeg, ginger, and falt; mix all together, and boil it in a little wooden difh half an hour. You may add a few currants. *Cole*, 266.

A Spinach Pudding.

Take a quarter of a peck of fpinach, picked and wafhed clean, put it into a fauce-pan with a little falt; cover it clofe, and when it has boiled juft tender, throw it into a fieve to drain; then chop it with a knife, beat up fix eggs, mix well with it half a pint of cream, and a ftale roll grated fine, a little nutmeg and a quarter of a pound of melted butter; ftir all well together, put it into the fauce-pan the fpinach was ftewed in, keeping it ftirring till it begins to be thick, then wet the pudding-cloth and flour it well; tie it up and boil it an hour; turn it into a difh, and pour over it melted butter, with a little Seville orange fqueezed in it, and fugar. You may bake it, but then you fhould put in a quarter of a pound of fugar. *Glaffe*, 225. *Mafon*, 372. *Farley*, 186.

A Suet Pudding.

Take a pound of fhred fuet, a quart of milk, four eggs, two tea-fpoonfuls of grated ginger, a little falt, and flour enough to make it a thick batter; boil it two hours. It may be made into dumplings, when half an hour will boil them. *Cole*, 266.

A Tanfey Pudding.

Put as much boiling cream to four Naples' bifcuits grated as will wet them, beat the yolks of four eggs. Have ready a few chopped tanfey-leaves, with as much fpinach as will make it a pretty green. Be careful not to put too much tanfey in, becaufe it will make it bitter. Mix all together when the cream is cold, with a little fugar, and fet it over a flow fire till it grows thick; then take it off, and, when cold, put it in a cloth well buttered and floured; tie it up clofe, and let it boil three quar-

ters

ters of an hour; take it up in a bafon, and let it ftand one quarter, then turn it carefully out, and put white-wine fauce round it.

The above receipt, with very inconfiderable alterations, appears in *Mafon,* 370; *Raffald,* 176; and *Farley,* 194.

A Tranfparent Pudding.

Beat eight eggs well, put them in a pan with half a pound of frefh butter, half a pound of fine powdered fugar, and half a nutmeg grated; fet it on the fire, and keep ftirring it till it is of the thicknefs of buttered eggs; then put it away to cool; put a thin puff pafte round the edge of your difh; pour in the ingredients, bake it half an hour in a moderate oven, and fend it up hot. It is a pretty pudding for a corner for dinner, and a middle for fupper. *Raffald,* 175, *Farley,* 189, from *Glaffe,* 222.

Vermicelli Pudding.

Boil a quarter of a pound of vermicelli in a pint of milk till it is foft, with a ftick of cinnamon; then take out the cinnamon, and put in half a pint of cream, a quarter of a pound of butter melted, and a quarter of a pound of fugar, with the yolks of four eggs well beaten. Bake it in an earthen difh without a pafte. *Cole,* 267.

Yeaft Dumplings.

Make a light dough, as for bread, with flour, water, yeaft, and falt; cover it with a cloth, and fet it before the fire for half an hour. Then have a fauce-pan of water on the fire, and when it boils, take the dough, and make it into little round balls, as big as a large hen's egg. Then flatten them with your hand, put them into the boiling water, and a few minutes will do them. Take care that they do not fall to the bottom of the pot or faucepan, for they will then be heavy, and be fure to keep the water boiling all the time. When they are enough, take them up, and lay them in your difh, with melted butter in a boat. To fave trouble, you may get your dough at the baker's, which will do as well. *Cole,* 267.

A Yorkfhire Pudding.

Take a quart of milk and five eggs, beat them well up together, and mix them with flour till it is of a good pancake batter, and very fmooth; put in a little falt, fome grated nutmeg and ginger; butter a dripping or frying-pan, and put it under a piece of beef, mutton, or a loin of veal, that is roafting, and then put in your batter; and when the top-fide is brown, cut it in fquare pieces, and turn it, and then let the underfide be brown. Put it in a hot difh, as clean from fat as you can, and fend it to table hot. *Cole,* 267.

Another way.

Take a quart of milk, three eggs, a little falt, fome grated ginger, and flour enough to make it as a batter pudding; put it into a fmall tin dripping-pan, of the fize for the purpofe; put it under beef, mutton, or veal, while roafting. When it is brown, cut it into four or five lengths, and turn it, that the other fide may become brown. *Cole*, 268.

White Puddings in fkins.

Boil half a pound of rice in milk till it is foft, having firft wafhed the rice well in warm water. Put it into a fieve to drain, and beat half a pound of Jordan almonds very fine with fome rofe water. Wafh and dry a pound of currants, cut a pound of hogs'-lard in fmall bits, beat up fix eggs well, half a pound of fugar, a large nutmeg grated, a ftick of cinnamon, a little mace, and a little falt. Mix them well together, fill your fkins, and boil them. *Farley*, 195.

To make Black Puddings.

Before you kill a hog, get a peck of groats, boil them half an hour in water, then drain them, and put them into a clean tub, or large pan; then kill your hog, and fave two quarts of the blood, and keep ftirring it till the blood is quite cold; then mix it with your groats, and ftir them well together. Seafon with a large fpoonful of falt, a quarter of an ounce of cloves, mace, and nutmeg together, an equal quantity of each; dry it, beat it well, and mix in. Take a little winter favoury, fweet marjoram and thyme, penny-royal ftripped of the ftalks and chopped very fine; juft enough to feafon them and give them a flavour, but no more. The next day take the leaf of the hog, and cut into dice, fcrape and wafh the guts very clean, then tie one end, and begin to fill them. Mix in the fat as you fill them; be fure to put in a good deal of fat, fill the fkins three parts full, tie the other end, and make your puddings what length you pleafe; prick them with a pin, and put them in a kettle of boiling water. Boil them very foftly an hour, then take them out, and lay them on clean ftraw. *Glaffe*, 256.

CHAP. XIX.—OF PIES.

Preliminary Obfervations on Pies.

IT may be neceffary to inform the reader, that raifed pies fhould have a quick oven, and be well clofed up, or they will fall in the fides. It fhould have no water put in till juft before you put it in the oven, as that will give the cruft a fodden appearance, and may probably occafion it to run. Light pafte requires a moderate oven, but not too flow, as it will make it look heavy, and a quick oven will catch and burn it, and not give it time to rife. Tarts that are iced, fhould be baked in a flow oven, or the icing will become brown before the pafte is properly baked. Tarts of this fort fhould be made of fugar pafte, and rolled very thin. *Cole,* 269.

Pafte for Tarts.

Take one pound of flour, three quarters of a pound of but-mix up together, and beat well with a rolling-pin. *Cole,* 269.

Crifp Pafte for Ta ts.

To one pound of fine flour, put one ounce of loaf-fugar, beat and fifted. Make it into a ftiff pafte with a gill of boiling cream, and three ounces of butter to it ; work it well, and roll it very thin. When you have made your tarts, beat the white of an egg a little, rub it over them with a feather, fift a little double-refined fugar over them, and bake them in a moderate oven. *Cole,* 296.

Another way.

Having beat the white of an egg to a ftrong froth, put in by degrees four ounces of double-refined fugar, with about as much gum as will lie upon a fix-pence, beat and fifted fine. Beat them half an hour, and then lay it thin on your tarts. *Cole,* 269.

Puff Pafte.

Take a quarter of a peck of flour, rub in a pound of butter very fine, make it up in a light pafte with cold water, juft ftiff enough to work it up ; then roll it out about as thick as a crown piece ; put a layer of butter all over ; fprinkle on a little flour, double it up, and roll it out again ; double it and roll three times, then it is fit for all pies and tarts that require a puff pafte. *Cole,* 269.

Short Cruft.

Rub fome flour and butter together, full fix ounces of butter to eight of flour ; mix it up with as little water as poffible, fo as to have it a ftiffifh pafte ; beat it well, and roll it thin. This is the beft cruft for all tarts that are to be eaten cold, and for

preferved

preferved fruit. A moderate oven. An ounce and a half of
fifted fugar may be had. *Cole,* 270.

A good Pafte for great Pies.

Put the yolks of three eggs to a peck of flour, pour in fome
bóiling water, then put in half a pound of fuet, and a pound
and a half of butter. Skim off the butter and fuet, and as much
of the liquor as will make it a light good cruft. Work it up
well, and roll it out. *Cole,* 270.

A Pafte for Cuftards.

Pour half a pound of boiling water on two pounds of flour,
with as much water as will make it into a good pafte. Work it
well, and when it has cooled a little, raife your cuftards, put a
paper round the infide of them, and when they are half baked,
fill them. *Cole,* 270.

Another way.

To half a pound of flour, put fix ounces of butter, the yolks
of two eggs, and three fpoonfuls of cream. Mix them together,
and let them ftand a quarter of an hour, then work it up and
down, and roll it very thin. *Cole,* 270.

An Apple Pie.

Make a good puff-pafte cruft, lay fome round the fides of the
difh, pare and quarter your apples, and take out the cores, lay
a row of apples thick, throw in half the fugar you intend for
your pie, mince a little lemon-peel fine, throw over, and fqueeze
a little lemon over them, then a few cloves, here and there one ;
then the reft of your apples, and the reft of your fugar. Sweeten
to your palate, and fqueeze in a little more lemon. Boil the
peeling of the apples and the cores in fome fair water, with a
blade of mace, till it is very good ; ftrain it, and boil the fyrup
with a little fugar, till there is but very little and good ; pour
it into your pie, put on your upper cruft, and bake it. You
may, if you pleafe, put in a little quince or marmalade.

Make a pear pie in the fame manner, but omit the quince.
You may butter them when they come out of the oven. Or,
beat up the yolks of two eggs, and half a pint of cream, with a
little nutmeg fweetened with fugar; put it over a flow fire, and
keep ftirring it till it juft boils up; take off the lid, and pour
in the cream. Cut the cruft into little three-corner pieces,
ftick about the pie, and fend it to table cold. *Glaffe,* 230.
Farley, 212.

An Apple Tart.

Take eight or ten large codlings, fcald them, and when cold,
fkin them ; beat the pulp as fine as you can with a filver fpoon,
then mix the yolks of fix eggs, and the whites of four ; beat all
together as fine as poffible, put in grated nutmeg, and fugar to
your tafte ; melt fome fine frefh butter, and beat it till it is like
a fine

a fine thick cream; then make a fine puff-paste, and cover a tin patty-pan with it, and pour in the ingredients, but do not cover it with the paste. Bake it a quarter of an hour, then flip it out of the patty-pan on a dish, and strew some sugar finely beat and sifted all over it. *Raffald*, 145.

A Beef-steak Pie.

Take four or five rump steaks, beat them very well with a paste pin, season them with pepper and salt, lay a good puff-paste round the dish, and put a little water in the bottom; then lay the steaks in, with a lump of butter upon every steak, and put on the lid. Cut a little paste in what form you please, and lay it on. *Cole*, 271.

A Bride's Pie.

Having boiled two calves' feet, take the meat from the bones, and chop it very small; take a pound of beef suet and a pound of apples, shred them small, wash and pick one pound of currants, dry them before the fire, stone and chop a quarter of a pound of jar raisins, a quarter of an ounce of cinnamon, the same quantity of mace and nutmeg, two ounces of candied citron, the same of lemon cut thin, a glass of brandy, and one of champagne; put them in a china dish, with a rich puff-paste over it; roll another lid, and cut it in leaves, flowers, figures, and put a glass ring in it. *Cole*, 271.

A Calf's-foot Pie.

Put your calf's feet into a sauce-pan, with three quarts of water, and three or four blades of mace; let them boil softly till there is about a pound and a half; then take out the feet, strain the liquor, and make a good crust. Cover your dish, then pick off the flesh from the bones, and lay half in the dish. Strew over it half a pound of currants, clean washed and picked, and half a pound of raisins stoned. Then lay on the rest of the meat, skim the liquor, sweeten it to your taste, and put in half a pint of white wine. Then pour all into the dish, put on your lid, and bake it an hour and an half. *Farley*, 205, from *Glasse*, 140.

A Calf's-head Pie.

Take a calf's head and parboil it; when it is cold, cut it in pieces, and season it well with pepper and salt. Put it in a raised crust, with half a pint of strong gravy; let it bake an hour and an half. When it comes out of the oven, cut off the lid, and chop the yolks of three hard eggs small; strew them over the top of the pie, and lay three or four slices of lemon, and pour on some melted butter. Send it to table without a lid. *Cole*, 272.

A Cherry

A Cherry Pie.

Make a good cruft, lay a little of it round the fides of your difh, and throw fugar at the bottom; then lay in your fruit, and fome fugar at the top. Some red currants added to the cherries are a great improvement. Then put on your lid, and bake it in a flack oven.

A plum pie, or a goofeberry pie, may be made in the fame manner. *Cole,* 272.

A favoury Chicken Pie.

Procure fome fmall chickens, feafon them with mace, pepper, and falt; put a lump of butter into each of them, lay them in the difh with the breafts up, and put a thin flice of bacon over them; it will give them a pleafant flavour; then put in a pint of ftrong gravy, and make a good puff-pafte; lid it, and bake it in a moderate oven. French cooks ufually add morels and yolks of eggs chopped fmall. *Raffald,* 151. *Farley,* 210.

A rich Chicken Pie.

Cover the bottom of the difh with a puff-pafte, and upon that, round the fide, lay a thin layer of force-meat; cut two fmall chickens into pieces, feafon them high with pepper and falt; put fome of the pieces into the difh, then a fweetbread or two, cut into pieces, and well feafoned, a few truffles and morels, fome artichoke bottoms cut each into four pieces, then the remainder of the chickens, fome force-meat balls, yolks of eggs boiled hard, chopped a little, and ftrewed over the top, a little water; cover the pie. When it comes from the oven, pour in a rich gravy, thickened with a little flour and butter. To make the pie ftill richer, frefh mufhrooms, afparagus tops, and cocks'-combs may be added.

The chickens are fometimes larded with bacon, and ftuffed with fweet herbs, pepper, nutmeg, and mace. You fhould then only flit them down, and lay them in the pie. *Cole,* 272.

A Codling Pie.

Put fome fmall codlings into a clean pan with fpring-water, lay vine-leaves on them, and cover them with a cloth, wrapped round the cover of the pan to keep in the fteam. As foon as they grow foft, peel them, and put them in the fame water as the vine leaves. Hang them a great height over the fire to green, and when you fee them of a fine colour, take them out of the water, and put them into a deep difh, with as much powder or loaf fugar as will fweeten them. Make the lid of a rich puff-pafte, and bake it. When it comes from the oven, take off the lid, and cut it in little pieces, like fippets, and ftick them round the infide of the pie, with the points upwards. Then make a good cuftard in the following manner, and pour

it

it over your pie. Boil a pint of cream with a ſtick of cinnamon, and ſugar enough to make it a little ſweet. As ſoon as it is cold, put in the yolks of four eggs well beaten, ſet it on the fire, and keep ſtirring it till it grows thick; but be careful not to let it boil, as that will curdle it. Pour this in your pie, pare a little lemon thin, cut the peel like ſtraws, and lay it on the top over your codlings. *Farley*, 214.

A Devonſhire Squab Pie.

Cover the diſh with a good cruſt, put at the bottom a layer of ſliced pippins, then a layer of mutton ſteaks cut from the loin, well ſeaſoned with pepper and ſalt, then another layer of pippins; peel ſome onions, and ſlice them thin, lay a layer all over the apples, then a layer of mutton, then pippins and onions; pour in a pint of water, cloſe your pie, and bake it. *Glaſſe*, 144.

A Duck Pie.

Take two ducks, ſcald them, and make them very clean; cut off the feet, the pinions, the neck, and head; pick them all clean, and ſcald them. Pick out the fat of the inſide, lay a good puff-paſte cruſt all over the diſh, ſeaſon the ducks both inſide and out with pepper and ſalt, and lay them in your diſh, with the giblets at each end properly ſeaſoned. Put in as much water as will almoſt fill the pie, and lay on the cruſt. *Cole*, 273.

Eel Pies.

After ſkinning and waſhing your eels, cut them in pieces of about an inch and an half long, ſeaſon them with pepper, ſalt, and a little dried ſage rubbed ſmall; raiſe your pies about the ſize of the inſide of a plate, fill your pies with eels, lay a lid over them, and bake them in a quick oven. They require to be well baked. *Raffald*, 155.

An Egg Pie.

Cover your diſh with a good cruſt, then have ready twelve eggs boiled hard, cut them in ſlices, and lay them in your pie, waſh and pick half a pound of currants, and throw all over the eggs; then beat up four eggs well, mixed with half a pint of white wine; grate in a ſmall nutmeg, and make it pretty ſweet with ſugar. Lay a quarter of a pound of butter between the eggs, then pour in your wine and eggs, and cover your pie. Bake it half an hour, or till the cruſt is done. *Cole*, 274.

A French Pie.

Lay a puff-paſte half an inch thick at the bottom of a deep diſh; lay a force-meat round the ſides of the diſh; cut ſome ſweetbreads in pieces, three or four, according to the ſize the pie is intended to be made; lay them in firſt, then ſome artichoke bottoms, cut into four pieces each, then ſome cocks'-

Q 4

combs,

combs, (or they may be omitted) a few truffles and morels, some asparagus tops, and fresh mushrooms, if to be had, yolks of eggs boiled hard, and force-meat balls; season with pepper and salt. Almost fill the pie with water, cover it, and bake it two hours. When it comes from the oven, pour in some rich veal gravy, thickened with a very little cream and flour. *Mason,* 357.

A plain Goose Pie.

Quarter your goose, season it well, and lay it in a raised crust; cut half a pound of butter into pieces, and put it on the top; lay on the lid, and bake it gently. *Cole,* 274.

A rich Goose Pie.

Take a goose and a fowl, bone them, and season them well; put the fowl into the goose, and some force-meat into the fowl; put these into a raised crust, and fill the corners with a little force-meat; lay half a pound of butter on the top, cut into pieces; cover it, and let it be well baked.

N. B. Goose pie is eaten cold. *Cole,* 274.

A Giblet Pie.

Let two pair of giblets be nicely cleaned, put all but the livers into a sauce pan, with two quarts of water, twenty corns of whole pepper, three blades of mace, a bundle of sweet herbs, and a large onion; cover them close, and let them stew very softly till they are quite tender; then have a good crust ready, cover your dish, lay a fine rump steak at the bottom, seasoned with pepper and salt; then lay in your giblets with the livers, and strain the liquor they were stewed in. Season it with salt, and put into your pie; put on the lid, and bake it an hour and an half. *Glasse,* 143.

A Ham Pie.

Bone the ham, and trim it properly; in the trimming, take care to cut off all the rusty fat or lean, till you come to the wholesome-looking flesh. If an old ham, soak it twenty-four hours; if fresh, six or eight hours; then braze it with slices of beef, slices of bacon, some butter, and hogs'-lard, a large faggot of sweet herbs, all sorts of roots, and whole pepper; braze it till three parts done; then let it cool, and put it in a raised paste, with the liquid, and a gill of brandy; bake it an hour, and let it cool before using. If it is to be served hot, skim off the fat very clean, and serve with a relishing cullis-sauce, without salt. *Clermont,* 401. *Dalrymple,* 332.

A Hare Pie.

Cut your hare in pieces, and season it well with pepper, salt, nutmeg, and mace; then put it in a jug with half a pound of butter; cover it close up with a paste or cloth, set it in a copper

of

of boiling water, and let it ftew an hour and an half; then take it out to cool, and make a rich force-meat, of a quarter of a pound of fcraped bacon, two onions. a glafs of red wine, the crumb of a penny loaf, a little winter favoury, the liver cut fmall, a little nutmeg; feafon it high with pepper and falt; mix it well up with the yolks of three eggs; raife the pie, and lay the force-meat in the bottom; lay in the hare, with the gravy that came out of it; lay the lid on, and put flowers or leaves on it. Bake it an hour and an half. It is a very hand-fide-difh for a large table. *Raffald,* 149.

An Herb Pie for Lent.

Take an equal quantity of fpinach, lettuce, leeks, beets, and parfley, about an handful of each; boil them, and chop them fmall. Have ready boiled in a cloth, a quart of groats, with two or three onions among them; put them and the herbs into a frying-pan, with a pretty large quantity of falt, a pound of butter, and fome apples cut thin; ftew them a few minutes over the fire, fill your difh or raifed cruft with it; bake it an hour, and ferve it up, *Cole,* 275.

A Lobfter Pie.

Boil two lobfters, and take the meat out of the fhells; feafon them with pepper, mace, and nutmeg, beat fine; bruife the bodies, and mix them with fome oyfters, if in feafon; cut fine a fmall onion, and a little parfley, and add a little grated bread: feafon with a little falt, pepper, fpice, and the yolks of two raw eggs; make this into balls, then make fome good puff-pafte, butter the difh, lay in the tails, claws, and balls; cover them with butter, pour in a little fifh gravy, and cover the pie. Have a little fifh gravy ready to put into it when it is taken out of the oven. *Mafon,* 364.

Mince Pies.

Shred three pounds of fuet very fine, and chop it as fmall as poffible; take two pounds of raifins ftoned and chopped very fine, the fame quantity of currants, nicely picked, wafhed, rubbed, and dried at the fire. Pare half an hundred fine pippins, core them, and chop them fmall; take half a pound of fine fugar, and pound it fine; a quarter of an ounce of mace, a quarter of an ounce of cloves, and two large nutmegs, all beat fine; put all together into a large pan, and mix it well together with half a pint of brandy and half a pint of fack; put it down clofe in a ftone pot, and it will keep good three or four months. When you make your pies, take a little difh, fomewhat larger than a foup-plate, lay a very thin cruft all over it; lay a thin layer of meat, and then a layer of citron, cut very thin, then a layer of mince meat, and a layer of orange-peel cut thin; over that a little meat, fqueeze half the juice of a

fine

fine Seville orange or lemon, lay on your cruſt, and bake it nicely. Theſe pies eat very fine cold. If you make them in little patties, mix your meat and ſweetmeats accordingly. If you chooſe meat in your pies, parboil a neat's tongue, peel it, chop the meat as fine as poſſible, and mix with the reſt; or two pounds of the inſide of a ſurloin of beef boiled. But when you uſe meat, the quantity of fruit muſt be doubled. *Glaſſe*, 148.

Another way.

Take a neat's tongue, and boil it two hours, then ſkin it, and chop it exceedingly ſmall. Chop very ſmall three pounds of beef ſuet, three pounds of good baking apples, four pounds of currants clean waſhed, picked, and well dried before the fire, a pound of jar raiſins ſtoned and chopped ſmall, and a pound of powder ſugar. Mix them all together with half an ounce of mace, as much nutmeg, a quarter of an ounce of cloves, a quarter of an ounce of cinnamon, and a pint of French brandy. Make a rich puff-paſte, and as you fill up the pie, put in a little candied citron and orange cut in little pieces. What mince-meat you have to ſpare, put cloſe down in a pot, and cover it up; but never put any citron or orange to it till you uſe it. *Farley*, 216.

Mutton and Lamb Pie.

Take off the ſkin and inſide fat of a loin of mutton, cut it into ſteaks, ſeaſon them well with pepper and ſalt; almoſt fill the diſh with water; put puff-paſte top and bottom. Bake it well. *Cole*, 277.

An Olive Pie.

Take a fillet of veal, cut it in thin ſlices, rub the ſlices over with yolks of eggs; ſtrew over them a few crumbs of bread; ſhred a little lemon-peel very fine, and put it on them, with a little grated nutmeg, pepper, and ſalt; roll them up very tight, and lay them in a pewter diſh; pour over them half a pint of good gravy made of bones; put half a pound of butter over it, make a light paſte, and lay round the diſh; roll the lid half an inch thick, and lay it on.

A beef olive pie may be made the ſame way. *Raffald*, 158.

A Partridge Pie.

Singe, draw, and truſs your partridges as for boiling; flatten the breaſt bones, and make a force-meat with the livers, a piece of butter or ſcraped lard, pepper, ſalt, chopped parſley, ſhallots, winter ſavoury, thyme, and ſweet marjoram; ſtuff the partridges with this, and fry them a little in butter; then put them in a raiſed cruſt, upon ſlices of veal, well ſeaſoned; finiſh it as all others. When done, if it is to ſerve up hot, add a reliſhing ſauce, fauce; if cold, add fome good jelly broth before it is quite cold. *Clermont*, 403. *Dalrymple*, 336.

A Pigeon Pie.

Cover your difh with a puff-pafte cruft, let your pigeons be very nicely picked and cleaned, feafon them with pepper and falt, and put a good piece of frefh butter, with pepper and falt, in their bellies; lay them in your pan; the necks, gizzards, livers, pinions, and hearts, lay between, with the yolk of a hard egg, and beef-fteak in the middle; put in as much water as will almoft fill the difh, lay on the top cruft, and bake it well. This is a very good way to make a pigeon pie; but fome French cooks fill the pigeons with a very high force-meat, and lay force-meat balls round the infide, with afparagus-tops, arti-choke-bottoms, mufhrooms, truffles, and morels, and feafon high. *Cole*, 277.

A Chefhire Pork Pie.

Having fkinned a loin of pork, cut it into fteaks; feafon it with falt, nutmeg, and pepper; make a good cruft, lay a layer of pork, then a layer of pippins, pared and cored, and a little fugar, enough to fweeten the pie, and then a layer of pork; put in half a pint of white wine, lay fome butter on the top, and clofe your pie; if it be large, it will require a pint of white wine. *Glaffe*, 144. *Mafon*, 357. *Farley*, 211.

A Rook Pie.

Take half a dozen young rooks, fkin them and draw them, cut out the back bones, feafon them well with pepper and falt, and lay them in a deep difh, with a quarter of a pint of water; lay half a pound of butter over them, make a good puff-pafte, and cover the difh; lay a paper over. It requires to be well baked. *Cole*, 278.

A Rabbit Pie.

Cut a couple of young rabbits into quarters; take a quarter of a pound of bacon, and bruife it to pieces in a marble mor-tar, with the livers, fome pepper, falt, a little mace, and fome parfley cut fmall, fome chives, and a few leaves of fweet bafil; when thefe are all beaten fine, make the pafte, and cover the bottom of the pie with the feafoning, then put in the rabbits; pound fome more bacon in a mortar, mix with it fome frefh butter, and cover the rabbits with it, and over that lay fome thin flices of bacon; put on the lid, and fend it to the oven. It will require two hours baking. When done, take off the lid, take out the bacon, and fkim off the fat. If there is not gravy enough in the pie, pour in fome rich mutton or veal gravy, boiling hot. *Mafon*, 358.

A Salmon Pie.

Boil your falmon as if you intended it for eating; take the
fkin

ſkin off, and all the bones out; pound the meat in a mortar fine, with mace, nutmeg, pepper and ſalt, to your taſte; raiſe the pie, and put flowers or leaves on the walls; put in the ſalmon and lid it; let it bake an hour and an half. When done, take off the lid, and put in a quarter of a pound of rich melted butter; cut a lemon in ſlices, and lay over it; ſtick in two or three leaves of fennel, and ſend it to table without a lid. *Raffald*, 149.

A Soal Pie.

Make a good cruſt, cover your diſh, boil two pounds of eels tender, pick the fleſh from the bones, put the bones into the liquor the eels were boiled in, with a blade of mace and ſalt; let them boil till there is only a quarter of a pint of liquor, then ſtrain it; cut the fleſh of the eels very fine, with a little lemon-peel cut ſmall, a little ſalt, pepper, and nutmeg, a few crumbs of grated bread, parſley cut fine, and an anchovy. Mix a quarter of a pound of butter, and lay it in the diſh; cut the meat from a pair of large ſoals, and take off the fins, lay it on the force-meat, then pour in the liquor the eels were boiled in, and cloſe the pie.

Turbot-pie may be made in the ſame manner. *Glaſſe*, 232. *Maſon*, 363.

A Sucking-Pig Pie

Bone the pig thoroughly; lard the legs and ſhoulders with bacon ſeaſoned with ſpices, and ſweet herbs chopped; put it in a raiſed cruſt of its own length; ſeaſon it with ſpices, ſweet herbs chopped, and a pound of butter or ſcraped bacon; cover it over with thin ſlices of bacon. Finiſh the pie, and bake it about three hours. When near done, add two glaſſes of brandy; let it be cold before uſing. *Dalrymple*, 333.

A ſweet Veal, or Lamb Pie.

Cut your veal or lamb into little pieces, ſeaſon it with pepper, ſalt, cloves, mace, and nutmeg, beat fine. Make a good puff paſte cruſt, lay it in your diſh, then lay in your meat, and ſtrew on it ſome ſtoned raiſins and currants clean waſhed, and ſome ſugar. Then lay on ſome force-meat balls made ſweet, and in the ſummer ſome artichoke-bottoms boiled; and in the winter ſcalded grapes. Boil Spaniſh potatoes cut into pieces, candied citron, candied orange, lemon-peel, and three or four blades of mace. Put butter on the top, cloſe up your pie, and bake it; have ready, when it comes from the oven, a caudle made as follows :—Take a pint of white wine, and mix in the yolks of three eggs. Stir it well together over the fire one way all the time, till it is thick; then take it off, ſtir in ſugar enough to ſweeten it, and ſqueeze in the juice of a lemon. Put it hot into your pie, and cloſe it up again. Send your pie hot to table. *Farley*, 203.

A ſavoury

A favoury Veal Pie.

Seafon the fteaks of a loin of veal with pepper, falt, beaten mace, and nutmeg ; put the meat in a difh with fweetbreads feafoned with the meat, and the yolks of fix hard eggs, a pint of oyfters, and half that quantity of good gravy ; lay a puff-pafte, of half an inch thick, round your difh, and cover it with a lid of the fame thicknefs ; bake it an hour and a quarter in a quick oven ; when done, cut off the lid, cut the lid into eight or ten pieces, and ftick it round the infide of the rim ; cover the meat with flices of lemon, and ferve it up. *Cole,* 279.

A Venifon Pafty.

Take a neck and breaft of venifon, bone them, and feafon them well with pepper and falt, put them into a deep pan, with the beft part of a neck of mutton fliced and laid over them ; pour in a glafs of red wine. put a coarfe pafte over it, and bake it two hours in an oven ; then lay the venifon in a difh, and pour the gravy over it. and put one pound of butter over it ; make a good puff-pafte, and lay it near half an inch thick round the edge of the difh ; roll out the lid, which muft be a little thicker than the pafte on the edge of the difh, and lay it on ; then roll out another lid pretty thin, and cut in flowers, leaves, or whatever form you pleafe, and lay it on the lid. If you do not want it, it will keep in the pot it was baked in eight or ten days ; but let the cruft be kept on that the air may not get to it. A breaft and a fhoulder of venifon is the moft proper for a pafty. *Raffald,* 154. *Farley,* 205.

A Vermicelli Pie.

Seafon four pigeons with a little pepper and falt, ftuff them with a piece of butter, a few crumbs of bread, and a little parfley cut fmall ; butter a deep earthen difh well, and then cover the botton of it with two ounces of vermicelli. Make a puff-pafte, roll it pretty thick, and lay it on the difh ; then lay in the pigeons, the breafts downwards; put a thick lid on the pie, and bake it in a moderate oven. When it is enough, take a difh proper for it to be fent to table in, and turn the pie on it. The vermicelli is then on the top, and looks very pretty. *Mafon,* 360.

Cream Pancakes.

TAKE a quart of milk, beat in six or eight eggs, leaving half the whites out; mix it well till your batter is of a fine thickness. You must observe to mix your flour first with a little milk, then add the rest by degrees; put in two spoonfuls of beaten ginger, a glass of brandy, and a little salt; stir all together, make your stew pan very clean, put in a piece of butter as large as a walnut, then pour in a ladleful of batter, which will make a pancake, moving the pan round that the batter may be all over the pan; shake the pan, and when you think that side is enough, toss it, if you cannot turn it cleverly; and when both sides are done, lay it in a dish before the fire, and so do the rest. You must take care that they are dry. When you send them to table, strew a little sugar over them. *Glasse*, 165.

Common Pancakes.

Take a pint of milk or cream, a pound of flour, and three eggs; put the milk by degrees into the flour; add a little salt, and grated ginger; fry them in lard, and grate sugar over them. *Cole*, 281.

Batter Pancakes.

Take a pound of flour and three eggs, beat them well together; put to it a pint of milk, and a little salt; fry them in lard or butter; grate sugar over them, cut them in quarters, and serve them up. *Raffald*, 166.

Fine Pancakes.

To a pint of cream add the yolks of eight eggs, but no whites, three spoonfuls of sack, or orange-flower water, a little sugar, and a grated nutmeg; the butter and cream must be melted over the fire; mix all well together with three spoonfuls of flour; butter the frying-pan for the first, let them run as thin as you can in the pan, fry them quick, and send them up hot. *Cole*, 281.

Rice Pancakes.

Wash and pick clean half a pound of rice, boil it till it is tender, and all the water boiled away; put it into a tin cullender, cover it close, and let it stand all night; then break it very small; take fourteen eggs, beat and strain them, and put them to the rice, with a quart of cream, a nutmeg grated; beat it well together, then shake in as much flour as will hold them together, and stir in as much butter as will fry them. *Cole*, 281.

Pancakes called a Quire of Paper.

Take a pint of cream, six eggs, three spoonfuls of fine flour, three spoonfuls of sack, one of orange-flower water, a little sugar, half a nutmeg grated, and half a pound of melted butter almost cold ; mingle all together, and butter the pan for the first pancake. Let them run as thin as possible. When they are just coloured, they are enough ; and so do with all the fine pancakes. *Glasse*, 165.

Cream Pancakes,

Mix the yolks of two eggs with half a pint of cream, and two ounces of sugar ; rub your pan with lard, and fry them as thin as you possibly can. Grate sugar over them, and let them be served up hot. *Cole*, 282.

Pink-coloured Pancakes.

Boil a large beet-root tender, and beat it fine in a marble mortar ; then add the yolks of four eggs, two spoonfuls of flour, and three spoonfuls of cream ; sweeten it to your taste, and grate in half a nutmeg, and add a glass of brandy ; beat them all together half an hour, fry them in butter, and garnish them with green sweetmeats, preserved apricots, or green sprigs of myrtle. It is a pretty corner dish for either dinner or supper. *Raffald*, 167.

Clary Pancakes,

Take three eggs, three spoonfuls of fine flour, and a little salt, beat them well, and mix them well with a pint of milk ; put lard into your pan ; when it is hot, pour in your batter as thin as possible, then lay in some clary leaves, washed and dried, and pour a little more batter thin over them ; fry them a fine brown, and serve them up. *Cole*, 282.

Common Fritters.

Get some large baking apples, pare them, and take out the core ; cut them in round slices, and dip them in batter made as follows :—Take half a pint of ale, and two eggs. and beat them in as much flour as will make it rather thicker than a common pudding, with nutmeg and sugar to your taste. Let it stand three or four minutes to rise. Having dipping your apples into this batter, fry them crisp, and serve them up with sugar grated over them, and wine sauce in a boat. *Farley*, 226.

Strawberry Fritters.

Make a batter with flour ; a spoonful of oil, white wine, a little rasped lemon-peel. and the whites of two or three eggs ; make it pretty soft, just fit to drop with a spoon. Mix some large strawberries with it, and drop them with a spoon, the bigness of a nutmeg, into the hot fritter. When of a good colour,

colour, take them out, and drain them on a fieve; when ready to ferve, ftrew fugar over, or glaze them. *Dalrymple,* 389.

Plain Fritters.

Grate the crumb of a penny loaf, and put it into a pint of milk; mix it very fmooth; when cold, add the yolks of five eggs, three ounces of fifted fugar, and fome grated nutmeg; fry them in hogs'-lard; pour melted butter, wine, and fugar, into the difh. Currants may be added, as an improvement. *Cole,* 283.

Tanfey Fritters.

Pour a pint of boiling milk on the crumb of a penny-loaf, let it ftand an hour, and then put as much juice of tanfey to it as will give it a flavour; (too much will make it bitter,) then, with the juice of fpinach, make it a pretty green. Put to it a fpoonful of ratafia-water, or brandy, fweeten it to your tafte, grate the rind of half a lemon, beat the yolks of four eggs, mix them all together; put them in a tofling-pan, with a quarter of a pound of butter; ftir it over a flow fire, till it is quite thick; take it off, and let it ftand two or three hours; then drop them into a pan full of boiling lard, a fpoonful is enough for a fritter; ferve them up with flices of orange round them, grate fugar over them, and ferve wine fauce in a boat. *Raffald,* 163.

Currant Fritters.

Take half a pint of ale that is not bitter, ftir a fufficient quantity of flour in it to make it pretty thick; add a few currants; beat this up quick, have the lard boiling, throw in a large fpoonful at a time. *Cole,* 283.

Royal Fritters.

Put a quart of new milk in a fauce-pan, and, as the milk boils up, pour in a glafs of fack. Let it boil up, then take it off, and let it ftand five or fix minutes; then fkim off all the curd and put it into a bafon; beat it up well with fix eggs, feafon it with nutmeg; then beat it with a whifk; add flour to make it as thick as batter ufually is, put in fome fine fugar, and fry them quick. *Glaffe,* 162.

Apple Fritters.

Pare, core, and flice fome fmall apples; make a batter with three eggs, a little grated ginger, and almoft a pint of cream; add a glafs of brandy, a little falt, and flour enough to make it thick; put in the apples, fry them in lard. *Mafon,* 382.

Hafty Fritters.

Heat fome butter in a ftew-pan. Stir a little flour by degrees into half a pint of ale; put in a few currants, or chopped apples;

apples; beat them up quick, and drop a large spoonful at a time all over the pan. Take care to prevent their sticking together, turn them with an egg-slice; and, when they are of a fine brown, lay them on a dish, and throw some sugar over them. You may cut an orange into quarters for garnish. *Farley*, 228.

Water Fritters.

For these fritters, the batter must be very thick. Take five or six spoonfuls of flour, a little salt, a quart of water, the yolks and whites of eight eggs well beat, with a little brandy; strain them through a hair sieve, and mix them with the other ingredients. The longer they are made before they are fried, the better. Just before they are fried, melt half a pound of butter, and beat it well in. The best thing to fry them in is lard. *Mason*, 381. *Raffald*, 163.

Fine Fritters.

Take some very fine flour, and dry it well before the fire. Mix it with a quart of milk, but be careful not to make it too thick; put to it six or eight eggs, a little salt, nutmeg, mace, and a quarter of a pint of sack, or ale, or a glass of brandy. Beat them well together, then make them pretty thick with pippins, and fry them dry. *Cole*, 284.

Apple Fraze.

Having cut your apples in thin slices, fry them of a fine light brown; take them up and lay them to drain, keep them as whole as you can, and either pare them or not, as you think proper; then make a batter as follows:—Take five eggs, leaving out two whites, beat them up with cream and flour, and a little sack, make it the thickness of a pancake-batter, pour in a little melted butter, nutmeg, and a little sugar. Let your batter be hot, and drop in your fritters, and on every one lay a slice of apple, and then more batter on them. Fry them of a fine light brown; take them up, and strew some double-refined sugar all over them. *Glasse*, 164.

Almond Fraze.

Blanch and beat half a pound of Jordan almonds, and about a dozen bitter; put to them a pint of cream, eight yolks and four whites of eggs, and a little grated bread. Fry them, as pancakes, in good lard; and when done, grate sugar over them. *Cole*, 285.

R

CHAP.

CHAP. XXI.—OF PICKLING.

General Observations on Pickling.

THE knowledge of pickling is very essential in a family, but it is to be lamented, that the health of individuals is often endangered, merely to gratify the age. Things known to be pernicious, are frequently made use of, in order to procure a brighter colour to the article meant to be pickled. It is indeed a common practice to make use of brass utensils, that the verdigrease extracted from it may give an additional tint to all pickles intended to be green; not considering that they are communicating an absolute poison to that which they are preparing for their food. Such inconsiderate proceedings, it is hoped, will hereafter be avoided, especially as there is no necessity for having recourse to such pernicious means, when these articles will become equally green, by keeping them of a proper heat upon the hearth, without the help of brass or verdigrease of any kind. It is therefore highly proper to be very particular in keeping the pickles from such things, and to follow strictly the directions of your receipts, given with respect to all kinds of pickles, which are greened only by pouring your vinegar hot upon them, and it will keep them a long time. Stone jars are the most proper for all sorts of pickles, for though they are expensive in the first purchase, yet they will, in the end, be found much cheaper than earthen vessels, through which, it has been found by experience, salt and vinegar will penetrate, especially when put in hot. Be careful never to put your fingers in to take the pickles out, as it will soon spoil them; but always make use of a spoon upon those occasions. *Cole*, 285.

To Pickle Cucumbers.

Let your cucumbers be as free from spots as possible, and take the smallest you can get. Put them into strong salt and water for nine or ten days, or till they become yellow; and stir them at least twice a day, or they will grow soft. Should they become perfectly yellow, pour the water from them, and cover them with plenty of vine-leaves. Set your water over the fire, and when it boils, pour it upon them, and set them upon the hearth to keep warm. When the water is almost cold, make it boiling hot again, and pour it upon them. Proceed in this manner till you perceive they are of a fine green, which they will be in four or five times. Be careful to keep them well covered with vine-leaves, with a cloth and dish over the top, to keep in the steam, which will help to green them the sooner. When they are greened, put them in an hair sieve to drain, and then make the following pickle for them:—To every two quarts of white wine vinegar, put half an ounce of mace, ten or twelve cloves,

cloves, an ounce of ginger cut into flices, an ounce of black pepper, and an handful of falt. Boil them all together for five minutes, pour it hot upon your pickles, and tie them down with a bladder for ufe. You may pickle them with ale, ale-vinegar, or diftilled vinegar; and you may add three or four cloves of garlic or fhallots. *Raffald,* 342. *Farley,* 236.

To pickle Cucumbers in flices.

Take fome large cucumbers before they are too ripe, flice them of the thicknefs of crown pieces in a pewter difh; to every twelve cucumbers, flice two large onions thin, and fo on till you have filled your difh, with a handful of falt between every row; then cover them with another pewter difh, and let them ftand twenty-four hours; then put them into a cullender, and let them drain very well. Put them in a jar, cover them over with white wine vinegar, and let them ftand four hours; pour the vinegar from them into a copper fauce-pan, and boil it with a little falt; put to the cucumbers a little mace, a little whole pepper, a large race of ginger fliced, and then pour the boiling vinegar on. Cover them clofe, and when they are cold, tie them down. They will be fit to eat in two or three days. *Glaffe,* 270.

To pickle Mangoes.

Cucumbers ufed for this purpofe muft be of the largeft fort, and taken from the vines before they are too ripe, or yellow at the ends. Cut a piece out of the fide, and take out the feeds with an apple fcraper or tea-fpoon. Then put them into very ftrong falt and water for eight or nine days, or till they are very yellow. Stir them well two or three times each day, and put them into a pan, with a large quantity of vine-leaves both over and under them. Beat a little roach-allum very fine, and put it into the falt and water they came out of. Pour it on your cucumbers, and fet it upon a very flow fire for four or five hours, till they are pretty green. Then take them out, and drain them in an hair fieve, and when they are cold, put to them a little horfe-radifh, then muftard-feed, two or three heads of garlic, a few pepper corns, a few green cucumbers fliced in fmall pieces, then horfe-radifh, and the fame as before-mentioned, till you have filled them. Then take the piece you cut out, and few it on with a large needle and thread, and do all the reft in the fame manner. Have ready the following pickle :— To every gallon of allegar, put an ounce of mace, the fame of cloves, two ounces of fliced ginger, the fame of long pepper, Jamaica pepper, and black pepper; three ounces of muftard-feed tied up in a bag, four ounces of garlic, and a ftick of horfe-radifh cut in flices. Boil them five minutes in the allegar, then pour it upon your pickles, tie them down, and keep them for ufe. *Farley,* 240.

To

To pickle Onions.

Take some small onions, peel them, and put them into salt
and water; shift them once a day for three days, then set them
over the fire in milk and water till ready to boil; dry them,
pour over them the following pickle when boiled and cold:
Double-distiled vinegar, salt, mace, and one or two bay leaves;
they will not look white with any other vinegar. *Cole*, 287.

Another way.

Take a sufficient number of the smallest onions you can get,
and put them into salt and water for nine days, observing to
change the water every day. Then put them into jars, and
pour fresh boiling salt and water over them. Let them stand
close covered till they are cold, then make some more salt and
water, and pour it boiling hot upon them. When it is cold,
put your onions into a hair sieve to drain, then put them into
wide-mouthed bottles, and fill them up with distilled vinegar.
Put into every bottle a slice or two of ginger, a blade of mace,
and a large tea-spoonful of eating oil, which will keep the
onions white. If you like the taste of bay-leaf, you may put
one or two into every bottle, and as much bay-salt as will lie
on a sixpence. Cork them well up. *Farley*, 249.

To pickle Walnuts black.

Your walnuts should be gathered when the sun is hot upon
them, and always before the shell is hard, which may be easily
known by running a pin into them; then put them into a strong
salt and water for nine days; stir them twice a day, and change
the salt and water every three days; then put them in a hair
sieve, and let them stand in the air till they turn black; then
put them into strong stone jars, and pour boiling allegar over
them; cover them up, and let them stand till they are cold,
then boil the allegar three times more, and let it stand till it is
cold between every time; tie them down with paper, and a
bladder over them, and let them stand two months; then take
them out of the allegar, and make a pickle for them. To
every two quarts of allegar, put half an ounce of mace, half an
ounce of cloves, one ounce of black pepper, the same of
Jamaica pepper, ginger, and long pepper, and two ounces of
common salt; boil it ten minutes, and pour it hot upon your
walnuts, and tie them down with a bladder, and paper over it.
Raffald, 347.

Another way.

Take large full-grown nuts, but before they are hard, and
lay them in salt and water; let them lie two days, then shift
them into fresh water; let them lie two days longer, then shift
them again, and let them lie three in your pickling jar. When
the

the jar is half full, put in a large onion ftuck with cloves. To a hundred walnuts, put in half a pint of muftard-feed, a quarter of an ounce of mace, half an ounce of black pepper, half an ounce of all-fpice, fix bay leaves, and a ftick of horfe-raddifh; then fill your jar, and pour boiling vinegar over them. Cover them with a plate, and when they are cold, tie them down with a bladder and leather, and they will be fit to eat in two or three months. The next year, if any remains, boil up your liquor again, and fkim it; when cold, pour it over your walnuts. This is by much the beft pickle for ufe, therefore you may add more vinegar to it; what quantity you pleafe. If you pickle a great many walnuts, and eat them faft, make your pickle for a hundred or two, the reft keep in ftrong brine of falt and water, boiled till it will bear an egg; and as your pot empties, fill them up with thofe in the falt and water. Take care that they are covered with pickle.

In the fame manner you may do a fmaller quantity; but if you can get rape vinegar, ufe that inftead of falt and water. Do them thus:—Put your nuts into the jar you intend to pickle them in, throw in a handful of falt and fill the pot with rape-vinegar. Cover it clofe, and let them ftand a fortnight; then pour them out of the pot, wipe it clean, and juft rub the nuts with a coarfe cloth, and then put them in the jar with the pickle as above. *Glaffe*, 270.

To pickle Walnuts green.

Take the largeft double, or French walnuts, before the fhells are hard, pare them very thin, and put them into a tub of fpring water as they are pared; put to them, if there are two or three hundred nuts, a pound of bay-falt; leave them in the water twenty-four hours, then put them into a ftone jar, a layer of vine-leaves, and a layer of walnuts; fill it up with cold vinegar, and when they have ftood all night, pour the vinegar from them into a copper, with a good quantity of bay-falt; fet it upon the fire, and let it boil, then pour it hot on the nuts; tie them over with a woollen cloth, and let them ftand a week; then pour that pickle from them, rub the nuts clean with a piece of flannel, and put them again into the jar, with vine-leaves, as before-mentioned; boil frefh vinegar; to every gallon of vinegar, four or five pieces of ginger, a quarter of an ounce of cloves, a nutmeg fliced, a quarter of an ounce of mace, and the fame quantity of whole black pepper; pour the vinegar boiling hot upon the walnuts, and cover them with a woollen cloth; let it ftand four or five days, and repeat the fame four or five times. When the vinegar is cold, put in half a pint of muftard-feed, a ftick of horfe radifh fliced; tie them down with a bladder, and then with leather; they will be fit to eat in three weeks. If they are intended to be kept, the vinegar muft not be boiled, but then they will not be ready under fix months. *Mafon*, 346.

To pickle French Beans.

Pour a boiling-hot wine over your French beans, and cover them clofe; the next day drain them and dry them; then pour over them a boiling-hot pickle of white wine vinegar, Jamaica pepper, black pepper, a little mace, and ginger. Repeat this for two or three days, or till the French beans look green. *Cole*, 289.

To pickle Red Cabbage.

Slice your cabbage crofs-ways, put it on an earthen difh, and fprinkle a handful of falt over it. Cover it with another difh, and let it ftand twenty-four hours; then put it into a cullender to drain, and lay it in your jar. Take white-wine vinegar enough to cover it, a little cloves, mace, and all-fpice. Put them in whole, with a little cochineal bruifed fine. Then boil it up, and pour it either hot or cold on your cabbage. Cover it clofe with a cloth till it is cold, if you pour on the pickle hot, and then tie it up clofe, as you do other pickles. *Glaffe*, 276. ' *Farley*, 246.

Another way.

Take a fine clofe red cabbage, and cut it thin; then take fome cold ale-allegar, and put to it two or three blades of mace and a few white pepper corns; make it pretty ftrong with falt, and put your cabbage into the allegar as you cut it; tie it clofe down with a bladder, and a paper over that. In a day or two it will be fit for ufe. *Cole*, 290.

To pickle Mufhrooms.

Take the fmalleft mufhrooms you can get, and put them into fpring water then rub them with a piece of new flannel dipped in falt, and put them into cold fpring water as you do them, to keep their colour; then put them into a fauce-pan, throw a handful of falt over them, cover them clofe, and fet them over the fire four or five minutes, or till you fee they are thoroughly hot, and the liquor is drawn out of them; then lay them between two clean cloths till they are cold, then put them into glafs bottles, and fill them up with diftilled vinegar; put a blade or two of mace, and a tea-fpoonful of good oil in every bottle; cork them up clofe, and fet them in a cool place.

If you have not any diftilled vinegar, you may ufe white wine vinegar, or even allegar, but it muft be boiled with a little mace, falt, and a few flices of ginger; it muft be cold before you pour it on your mufhrooms. If your vinegar, or allegar,

is

is too fharp, it will make your mufhrooms foft; neither will they keep fo long, or appear fo white. *Raffald*, 355.

To pickle Cauliflowers.

Take the largeft and clofeft you can get; pull them into fprigs, put them in an earthen difh, and fprinkle falt over them. Let them ftand twenty-four hours to draw out all the water, then put them in a jar, and pour falt and water boiling over them; cover them clofe, and let them ftand till the next day; then take them out, and lay them on a coarfe cloth to drain; put them into glafs jars, and put in a nutmeg fliced, and two or three blades of mace in each jar. Cover them with diftilled vinegar, and tie them down with a bladder, and over that a leather. They will be fit for ufe in a month. *Glaffe*, 272.

To pickle Capers.

Thefe are the flower-buds of a fmall fhrub, preferved in pickle. The tree which bears capers is called the caper-fhrub, or bufh. It is common in the Weftern part of Europe. We have them in fome gardens, but Toulon is the principal place for capers. We have fome from Lyons, but they are flatter, and lefs firm; and fome come from Majorca, but they are falt and difagreeable. The fineft flavoured are from Toulon. They gather the buds from the bloffoms before they are open, then fpread them upon a floor in the room, where no fun enters, and there let them lie till they begin to whither; they then throw them into a tub of fharp vinegar, and, after three days, they add a quantity of bay falt. When this is diffolved, they are fit for packing for fale, and are fent to all parts of Europe.

The fineft capers are thofe of a moderate fize, firm, and clofe, and fuch as have the pickle highly flavoured; thofe which are foft, flabby, and half open, are of little value. *Mafon*, 353.

To pickle Samphire.

Take the famphire that is green, put it into a clean pan, and throw over it two or three handfuls of falt; then cover it with fpring-water. Let it lie twenty-four hours, then put it into a clean fauce-pan, throw in a handful of falt, and cover it with good vinegar. Cover the pan clofe, and fet it over a flow fire. Let it ftand till it is juft green and crifp, and then take it off at that moment; for fhould it remain till it is foft, it will be fpoiled. Put it in your pickling-pot, and cover it clofe. As foon as it is cold, tie it down with a bladder and leather, and keep it for ufe. Or you may keep it all the year in a very ftrong brine of falt and water, and throw it into vinegar juft before you ufe it. *Glaffe*, 278. *Mafon*, 352. *Farley*, 251.

To

To pickle Beet Roots.

Beet-roots, which are a pretty garnifh for made dishes, are thus pickled :—Boil them tender, peel them, and, if agreeable, cut them into fhapes; pour over them a hot pickle of white-wine vinegar, a little pepper, ginger, and horfe-radifh fliced. *Cole,* 291.

To pickle Barberries.

Let your barberries be gathered before they are too ripe; take care to pick out the leaves and dead ftalks, and then put them into jars, with a large quantity of ftrong falt and water, and tie them down with a bladder.

N. B. When you fee a fcum over your barberries, put them into frefh falt and water; they require no vinegar, their own fharpnefs being fufficient to keep them. *Cole,* 291.

To pickle Codlings.

Gather your codlings when they are about the fize of a large French walnut, put a quantity of vine-leaves in the bottom of a brafs pan, then put in your codlings; cover them well with vine-leaves, and fet them over a very flow fire till you can peel the fkins off; then take them carefully up in a hair fieve, and peel them with a pen-knife, and put them into the fauce-pan again, with the vine-leaves and water as before; cover them clofe, and fet them over a flow fire till they are a fine green; then drain them through a hair fieve, and when they are cold, put them into diftilled vinegar; pour a little meat-oil on the top, and tie them down with a bladder. *Raffald,* 345.

Indian Pickle, or Peccadillo.

Quarter a white cabbage and cauliflower; take alfo cucumbers, melons, apples, French beans, plums, all or any of thefe; lay them on a hair fieve, ftrew over a large handful of falt, fet them in the fun for three or four days, or till very dry. Put them into a ftone jar with the following pickle:—Put a pound of rece ginger into falt and water, the next day fcrape and flice it, falt it, and dry it in the fun; flice, falt, and dry a pound of garlic; put thefe into a gallon of vinegar, with two ounces of long pepper, half an ounce of turmeric, and four ounces of muf-tard-feed bruifed; ftop the pickle clofe, then prepare the cabbage, &c. If the fruit is put in, it muft be green.

N. B. The jar need not ever be emptied, but put in the things as they come into feafon, adding frefh vinegar. *Mafon,* 351.

To pickle Artichoke-bottoms.

Take fome artichokes, and boil them till you can pull the leaves off, then take off the chokes, and cut them from the ftalk; take great care that you do not let the knife touch the

top;

top; throw them into falt and water for an hour, then take them out, and lay them on a cloth to drain; then put them into large wide-mouthed glaffes, put a little mace and fliced nutmeg between; fill them either with diftilled vinegar, or fugar, vinegar, and fpring water; cover them with mutton fat fried, and tie them down with a bladder and leather. *Cole*, 292.

To pickle Nafturtium Buds.

After the bloffoms are gone off, gather the little knobs, and put them into cold falt and water; fhift them once a day for three fucceffive days, then make a cold pickle of white-wine vinegar, a little white-wine, fhallot, pepper, cloves, mace, nutmeg quartered, and horfe radifh. Put in the buds. *Cole*, 292.

Chap. XXII.—OF POTTING.

General Observations on Potting.

ALL potted articles should be well covered with butter before they are sent to the oven; it is also very necessary to tie them over with strong paper, and to bake them well. When your meat is taken from the oven, pick out all the skins quite clean, and drain the meat from the gravy, otherwise the skins will appear as blemishes, and the gravy will soon turn it sour. Let your seasoning be well beat before you put in your meat, and put it in by degrees as you are beating. Press your meat well when you put it in your pots, and let it be quite cold before the clarified butter is poured over it. *Cole*, 293.

To pot Beef.

Take half a pound of brown sugar, and an ounce of salt-petre, and rub it into twelve pounds of beef. Let it lie twenty-four hours; then wash it clean, and dry it well with a cloth. Season it to your taste with pepper, salt, and mace, and cut it into five or six pieces. Put it into an eathen pot, with a pound of butter in lumps upon it, set it in an hot oven, and let it stand there three hours, then take it out, cut out the hard outsides, and beat it in a mortar. Add to it a little more pepper, salt, and mace. Then oil a pound of butter in the gravy and fat that came from your beef, and put it in as you find necessary; but beat the meat exceedingly fine. Then put it into your pots, press it close down, pour clarified butter over it, and keep it in a dry place. *Farley*, 262.

To pot Beef like Venison.

Cut the lean of a buttock of beef into pound pieces; for eight pounds of beef take four ounces of salt-petre, four ounces of petre-salt, a pint of white salt, and an ounce of sal prunella; beat the salts all very fine, mix them well together, rub the salts into the beef; then let it lie four days, turning it twice a day; then put it into a pan, cover it with pump water, and a little of its own brine; then bake it in an oven with houshold bread till it is as tender as a chicken, then take it from the gravy, and bruise it abroad, and take out all the skin and sinews; then pound it in a marble mortar, and lay it in a broad dish; mix in it an ounce of cloves and mace, three quarters of an ounce of pepper, and one nutmeg, all beat very fine. Mix it all very well with the meat, then clarify a little fresh butter, and mix with the meat, to make it a little moist; mix it very well together, press it down into pots very hard, set it at the oven's mouth just to settle, and cover it two inches thick with

clarified

clarified butter. When cold, cover it with white paper. *Glaſſe*, 261.

To pot Venison.

If your venison ſhould happen to be ſtale, rub it with vinegar, and let it lie one hour; then dry it clean with a cloth, and rub it all over with red wine; ſeaſon it with beaten mace, pepper, and ſalt; put it on an earthen diſh, and pour over it half a pint of red wine, and a pound of butter, and ſet it in the oven; if it be a ſhoulder, put a coarſe paſte over it and bake it all night in a baker's oven. When it comes out, pick it clean from the bones, and beat it in a marble mortar, with the fat from your gravy. If you find it not ſeaſoned enough, add more ſeaſoning and clarified butter and keep beating it till it is a fine paſte. Then preſs it hard down into your pots, and pour clarified butter over it; keep it in a dry place. *Raffald*, 295.

To pot a Hare.

Let your hare hang for ſome days, then cut it into pieces, bake it, with a little beer at the bottom of the pan, and ſome butter on the top; pick it from the bones and ſinews, and beat it with the butter from the top of the gravy, adding enough to make it very mellow; add ſalt, pepper, and pounded cloves; put it into pots, ſet it a few minutes in a ſlack oven, pour over clarified butter. *Maſon*, 302.

To pot Eels.

Take a large eel, ſkin it, cleanſe it, and waſh it very clean; dry it in a cloth, and cut it into pieces as long as your finger. Seaſon them with a little beaten mace and nutmeg, pepper, ſalt, and a little ſal prunella beat fine; lay them in a pan, then pour as much good butter over them as will cover them, and clarified as above. They muſt be baked half an hour in a quick oven, if a ſlow oven longer, till they are enough, but of that you muſt judge by the ſize of the eels. With a fork take them out, and lay them on a coarſe cloth to drain. When they are quite cold, ſeaſon them again with the ſame ſeaſoning, and lay them in the pot cloſe; then take off the butter they were baked in clear from the gravy of the fiſh, and ſet it in a diſh before the fire. When it is melted, pour the clear butter over the eels, and let them be covered with the butter.

N. B. In the ſame manner you may pot what you pleaſe. You may bone your eels, if you chuſe it, but then do not put in any ſal prunella. *Glaſſe*, 237. *Farley*, 265.

To pot Chars.

Cleanſe your chars, and cut off the heads, tails, and fins; lay them in rows in a long baking pan, and cover them with
butter.

butter. When they are enough, take them out with a fork, and lay them on a coarfe cloth to drain. When they are quite cold, feafon them well, and lay them clofe in the pot; then take off the butter they were baked in clear from the gravy of the fifh, and fet it in a difh before the fire. When it is melted, pour the clarified butter over the char, and let them be covered with it. *Cole, 295.*

To pot Veal.

Take a fillet of veal, cut it into three or four pieces, feafon it with pepper, falt, and a little mace; put it into pots with half a pound of butter; tie a paper over it, fet it in an hot oven, and bake it three hours. When you take it out, cut off all the outfides, then put the veal into a marble mortar, and beat it with the fat from your gravy; then oil a pound of frefh butter, and put it in, a little at a time, and keep beating it till you fee it is like a fine pafte; then put it clofe down into your potting-pots, put a paper upon it, and fet on a weight to prefs it hard. When your veal is cold and ftiff, pour over it clarified butter the thicknefs of a crown piece, and tie it down. *Raffald, 296.*

To pot Salmon.

Scale, wafh, and dry a falmon that is quite frefh; flit it up the back, and take out the bone; mix fome grated nutmeg, mace, pepper, and falt, and ftrew over the fifh; let it lie for two or three hours, then lay it in a large pot, and put to it half a pound of butter; put it in an oven, and let it bake an hour. When it is done, lay it on fomething flat, that the oil may run from it; then cut it to the fize of the pots it is to be put in, lay the pieces in layers till the pots are filled, with the fkin uppermoft · put a board over it, and lay on a weight to prefs it till cold; then take the board and weight off, and pour over it clarified butter. It may be fent to table in pieces, or cut in flices. *Mafon, 216.*

To pot Tongues.

Rub a neat's tongue with an ounce of falt-petre, and a quarter of a pound of brown fugar; let it lie two days, and then boil it till it is quite tender; then take off the fkin and fide bits, cut the tongue into very thin flices, and beat it in a marble mortar, with a pound of clarified butter, pepper, falt, and mace to your tafte. Beat the whole very fine, then put it clofe down into fmall potting-pots, and pour clarified butter over them. *Cole, 296.*

To pot Lampreys.

Skin them, cleanfe them with falt, and then wipe them dry; beat fome black pepper, mace, and cloves; mix them with falt
and

and feafon them. Lay them in a pan, and cover them with clarified butter. Bake them an hour. In other refpects, manage them as above directed for eels, and one will be enough for a pot. You muft feafon them well; let your butter be good, and they will keep a long time. *Glaffe*, 237.

To pot Pigeons.

Seafon your pigeons very high with pepper and falt, put them into a pot with butter in lumps; bake them, and pour off the fat and gravy. When it is cold, take the butter from the top, put more to it; clarify it, pour it over the pigeons, put fingly into a pot, with a little more feafoning added to them. *Cole*, 296.

To pot Woodcocks and Snipes.

Pot them as you do pigeons. *Cole*, 296.

To pot Moor Game.

Pick and draw them, wipe them clean, and let them be well feafoned with pepper, falt, and mace; put one leg through the other, roaft them till they are enough, and when cold, put them into potting pots, pour clarified butter over them, and keep them in a dry place. *Cole*, 296.

General Observations on Collaring.

IN collaring any kind of meat, &c. care is required in rolling it up properly, and binding it close. Always boil it till it is thoroughly done; and, when it is quite cold, put it into the pickle with the binding on. Take it off, however, the next day, and it will leave the skin clear. If you make fresh pickle often, your meat will continue good much longer. *Cole*, 297.

To Collar a Breast of Veal.

Bone your veal, and beat it a little, then rub it over with the yolk of an egg; strew over it a little beaten mace, nutmeg, pepper and salt, a large handful of parsley chopped small, with a few sprigs of sweet marjoram, a little lemon-peel cut extremely fine, one anchovy, washed, boned, and chopped very small, and mixed with a very few bread crumbs; then roll it up very tight, bind it hard with a fillet, and warp it in a clean cloth; then boil it two hours and an half in soft water; when it is enough, hang it up by one end, and make a pickle for it. To one pint of salt and water, put half a pint of vinegar; when you send it to table, cut a slice off one end. Garnish with pickles and parsley. *Raffald*, 300.

To Collar Beef.

Take a piece of thin flank of beef and bone it, cut the skin off and salt it with two ounces of salt-petre, two ounces of sal-prunella, the same quantity of bay-salt, half a pound of coarse sugar, and two pounds of white salt. Beat the hard salt fine, and mix all together. Turn it every day, and rub it well with the brine for eight days. Then take it out of the pickle, wash it, and wipe it dry. Take a quarter of an ounce of cloves, a quarter of an ounce of mace, twelve corns of all-spice, and a nutmeg beat very fine, with a spoonful of beaten pepper, a large quantity of chopped parsley, and some sweet herbs chopped fine. Sprinkle it on the beef, and roll it up very tight; put a coarse cloth round it, and tie it up very tight with a beggar's tape. Boil it in a large copper of water; and if it is a large collar, it will take six hours boiling, but a small one will be done in five. Take it out, and put it in a press till it is cold; but if you have no press, put it between two boards, and a large weight upon it till it is cold. Then take it out of the cloth, and cut it into slices. Garnish with raw parsley. *Glasse*, 262. *Farley*, 254.

To Collar flat Ribs of Beef.

Bone your beef, lay it flat upon a table, and beat it half an
hour

hour with a wooden mallet till it is quite foft ; then rub it with fix ounces of brown fugar, a quarter of a pound of common falt, and an ounce of falt-petre beat fine ; then let it lie ten days, turning it once every day ; then take it out, and put it in warm water for eight or ten hours ; then lay it flat upon a table, with the outward fkin down, and cut it in rows acrofs, about the breadth of your finger ; but be careful not to cut the outfide fkin ; then fill one nick with chopped parfley, the fecond with fat pork, the third with crumbs of bread, mace, nutmeg, pepper, and falt, then parfley again, and fo on till you have filled all your nicks ; then roll it up tight, and bind it round with coarfe broad tape ; wrap it in a cloth, and boil it four or five hours ; then take it up, and hang it by one end of the ftring to keep it round ; fave the liquor it was boiled in, the next day fkim it, and add to it half as much allegar as you have liqour, a little more mace, long pepper, and falt ; then put in your beef and keep it for ufe.

N. B. When you fend it to table, cut a little off at each end, and it will be in diamonds of different colours, and look very pretty ; fet it upon a difh as you do brawn. If you make a frefh pickle every week, it will keep a long time. *Raffald*, 303.

To Collar a Calf's Head.

Get a calf's head with the fkin on, fcald off the hair, parboil the head, and bone it ; the fore part muft be flit ; boil the tongue, peel it, and cut that and the palate into thin flices, put them and the eyes into the middle of the head ; take fome pepper, falt, cloves, and mace, and beat them ; add fome nutmeg grated, fcalded parfley, thyme, favory, and fweet marjoram, cut very fmall ; beat the yolks of three or four eggs, fpread them over the head, and then ftrew on the feafoning ; roll it up very tight, and tie it round with tape ; boil it gently for three hours in as much water as will cover it. When the head is taken out, feafon the pickle with falt, pepper, and fpice, and add to it a pint of white wine vinegar ; when it is cold put in the collar, and when fet to table, cut it in flices. *Cole*, 298.

To collar a Pig.

Your pig being killed, and the hair dreffed off, draw out the entrails, and wafh it clean ; rip it open with a fharp knife, and take out all the bones ; then rub it all over with pepper and falt beaten fine, a few fage-leaves, and fweet-herbs chopped fmall ; then roll up your pig tight, and bind it with a fillet. Fill your boiler with foft water, a pint of vinegar, a handful of falt, eight or ten cloves, a blade or two of mace, a few pepper-corns, and a bunch of fweet herbs. When it boils, put in your pig and boil it till it is tender, then take it up, and, when it is almoft

cold,

cold, bind it over again, and put it into an earthen pot; then pour the liquor your pig was boiled in upon it, keep it covered, and it is fit for use. *Mason*, 186.

To collar Venison.

Bone a fide of venison, and take away all the finews, and cut it into square collops of what fize you pleafe. It will make two or three collars. Lard it with fat clear bacon, and cut your lards as big as the top of your finger, and three or four inches long. Seafon your venifon with pepper, falt, cloves, and nutmeg. Roll up your collars, and tie them clofe with coarfe tape; then put them into deep pots, with feafonings at the bottoms, fome frefh butter, and three or four bay-leaves. Then put in the reft, with fome feafoning and butter on the top, and over that fome beef-fuet, finely fhred and beaten. Then cover up your pots with coarfe pafte, and bake them four or five hours. After that, take them out of the oven, and let them ftand a little; take out your venifon, and let it drain well from the gravy; add more butter to the fat, and fet it over a gentle fire to clarify. Then take it off, and let it ftand a little, and fkim it well. Make your pots clean, or have pots ready fit for each collar. Put a little feafoning, and fome of your clarified butter at the bottom; then put in your venifon, and fill up your pots with clarified butter, and be fure that your butter be an inch above the meat. When it is thoroughly cold, tie it down with double paper, and lay a tile on the top; they will keep fix or eight months; and you may, when you ufe a pot, put it for a minute into boiling water, and it will come out whole. Let it ftand till it is cold, ftick it round with bay-leaves, and a fprig at the top. *Farley*, 257.

To collar a Breaft of Mutton.

Bone your breaft of mutton, and rub it over with the yolk of an egg; grate over it a little lemon-peel and a nutmeg, with a little pepper and falt; then chop fmall one tea-cupful of capers, and two anchovies; fhred fine a handful of parfley, and a few fweet herbs. Mix them with the crumb of a penny loaf, and ftrew it over your mutton, and roll it up tight; boil it two hours, then take it up, and put it into a pickle like that for the calf's head. *Cole*, 300.

Mock Brawn.

Boil four ox-feet very tender, and pick the flefh entirely from the bones; take the belly piece of pork, boil it till it is almoft enough, then bone it, and roll the meat of the feet up in the pork very tight; then take a ftrong cloth, with fome coarfe tape, and roll it round very tight; tie it up in the cloth, boil it till it is fo tender that a ftraw may be run through it. Let it
be

be hung up in the cloth till it is quite cold; after which put it into cold falt and water, and it will be fit for ufe. *Mafon*, 179.

To collar Salmon.

Take a fide of falmon, cut off an handful of the tail, wafh your large piece very well; dry it with a clean cloth, wafh it over with the yolks of eggs, and then make force-meat with what you cut off the tail. But take off the fkin, and put to it a handful of parboiled oyfters, a tail or two of lobfters, the yolks of three or four eggs boiled hard; fix anchovies, an handful of fweet herbs chopped fmall, a little falt, cloves, mace, nutmeg, pepper beat fine, and grated bread. Work all thefe together into a body, with the yolks of eggs; lay it all over the flefhy part, and a little more pepper and falt over the falmon; fo roll it up into a collar, and bind it with broad tape, then boil it in water, falt, and vinegar but let the liquor boil firft; then put in your collars, a bunch of fweet herbs, fliced ginger, and nutmeg; let it boil, but not too faft. It will take near two hours boiling. When it is enough, take it up into your foucing pan, and when the pickle is cold, put it to your falmon, and let it ftand in till ufed, or otherwife you may pot it. Fill it up with clarified butter, as you pot fowls. That way will keep longeft. *Glaffe*, 235, and 262.

To collar Eels.

Cafe your eel, cut off the head, flit open the belly, take out the guts, cut off the fins, take out the bones, lay it flat on the back, grate over it a fmall nutmeg; add two or three blades of mace beat fine, a little pepper and falt; ftrew over it an handful of parfley fhred fine, with a few fage-leaves; roll it up tight in a cloth, and bind it well. If it is of a middle fize, boil it in falt and water three quarters of an hour, hang it up all night to drain; add to the pickle a pint of vinegar, a few peppercorns, and a fprig of fweet marjoram; boil it ten minutes, and let it ftand till the next day; take off the cloth, and put your eels into the pickle. You may fend them whole on a plate, or cut them in flices. Garnifh with green parfley. Lampreys are collared in the fame manner. *Raffald*, 46.

To collar Mackarel.

Gut your mackarel, and flit them down the belly; cut off the head, take out the bones, but take care not to cut it in holes; then lay it flat upon its back, feafon it with mace, nutmeg, pepper, and falt, and an handful of parfley fhred fine; ftrew it over them, roll them tight, and tie them well feparately

S

in cloths; boil them gently twenty minutes in vinegar, falt, and water; then take them out, put them into a pot, pour the liquor on them, or the cloth will ftick to the fifh; take the cloth off the fifh the next day, put a little more vinegar to the pickle, and keep them for ufe. When you fend them to table, garnifh with fennel and parfley, and put fome of the liquor under them. *Cole,* 301.

Chap. XXIV.—OF TARTS, CUSTARDS, AND CHEESECAKES.

Observations on Tarts, &c.

FOR tarts that are meant to be eaten cold, make the short cruft. An apple-tart is made the same as the pie, but if to be eaten cold, make the short cruft. If you use tin patties to bake in, butter them, and put a little cruft all over them, or you will not be able to take them out; but if you bake them in glaſs or china, only an upper cruft will be neceſſary, as you will not want to take them out when you fend them to table. Lay fine ſugar at the bottom, then your cherries, plums, or whatever you may want to put in them, and put ſugar at the top. Currants and raſpberries make an exceeding good tart. and do not require much baking. Cherries require but little baking; gooſeberries, to look red, muſt ſtand a good while in the oven. Apricots, if green, require more baking than when ripe: Quarter or halve ripe apricots, and put in ſome of the kernels. Preſerved fruit, as damaſcenes and bullace, require but little baking; fruit that is preſerved high ſhould not be baked at all; but the cruft ſhould firſt be baked upon a tin the ſize the tart is to be; cut it with a marking-iron, or not, and when cold, take it off, and lay it on the fruit. Apples and pears intended to be put into tarts muſt be pared, cut into quarters, and cored. Cut the quarters acroſs again, ſet them on in a ſauce-pan with as much water as will barely cover them, and let them ſimmer on a ſlow fire juſt till the fruit is tender. Put a good piece of lemon-peel into the water with the fruit, and then have your patties ready. Lay fine ſugar at bottom, then your fruit, and a little ſugar at top. Pour over each tart a tea-ſpoonful of lemon-juice, and three tea-ſpoonfuls of the liquor they were boiled in; then put on your lid, and bake them in a ſlack oven. Apricot tarts may be made in the ſame manner, obſerving that you muſt not put in any lemon-juice. *Cole*, 301.

A Raſpberry Tart with Cream.

Roll out ſome thin puff-paſte, and lay it in a patty-pan; lay in ſome raſpberries, and ſtrew over them ſome very fine ſugar; put on the lid and bake it; cut it open, and put in half a pint of cream, the yolks of two or three eggs well beat, and a little ſugar. Let it ſtand to be cold before it is ſent to bake. *Maſon*, 391.

To make Rhubarb Tarts.

Put the ſtalks of the rhubarb that grows in the garden, and cut them in pieces of the ſize of a gooſeberry, and make it as a gooſeberry-tart. *Cole*, 302.

S 2

A Spinach

A Spinach Tart.

Scald the spinach in boiling water, and drain it very well to chop, then strew it in butter and cream, with a little salt, sugar, a few pieces of dried comfit citron, and a few drops of orange flower water. *Clermont*, 422.

Tart de Moi.

Make some good puff-paste, and lay round your dish, put some biscuits at the bottom, then some marrow, and a little butter; then cover it with different kinds of sweetmeats, as many as you have, and so on till your dish is full; then boil a quart of cream, and thicken with four eggs and a spoonful of orange flower water. Sweeten it with sugar to your palate, and pour over the rest. Half an hour will bake it. *Glasse*, 149. *Mason*, 390. *Farley*, 221.

Almond Custards.

Put a pint of cream into a tossing-pan, a stick of cinnamon, a blade or two of mace, boil it, and set it to cool; blanch two ounces of almonds, beat them fine in a marble mortar with rose-water; if you like a ratafia taste, put in a few apricot kernels, or bitter almonds; mix them with your cream, sweeten it to your taste, set it on a slow fire, and keep stirring it till it is pretty thick. If you let it boil, it will curdle; pour it into cups, &c. *Raffald*, 256.

Another way.

Put a bit of cinnamon into a pint of cream, sweeten and boil it. When cold, put to it one ounce of sweet almonds (five or six bitter) blanched and beaten, with a little brandy. Stir this over the fire till near boiling; strain it into cups. *Mason*, 398.

Plain Custards.

Take a quart of new milk, sweeten it to your taste, grate in a little nutmeg, beat up eight eggs, with only four whites; beat them up well, stir them into the milk, and bake it in China basons, or put them in a deep China dish; have a kettle of water boiling, set the cup in, let the water come above half way, but do not let it boil too fast, for fear of its getting into the cups, and take a hot iron, and colour them at the top. You may add a little rose-water. *Glasse*, 289.

Another way.

Set a quart of good cream over a slow fire, with a little cinnamon and four ounces of sugar. When it has boiled, take it off the fire, beat the yolks of eight eggs, and put to them a spoonful of orange-flower water, to prevent the cream from cracking. Stir them in by degrees as your cream cools, put the pan

pan over a flow fire, stir it carefully one way till it is almost boiling, and pour it into cups. *Farley*, 305.

Baked Custards.

Boil a pint of cream with mace and cinnamon; when cold, take four eggs, leaving out two of the whites, a little rose and orange-flower water and sack, nutmeg and sugar to your palate; mix them well together, and bake them in China cups. *Cole*, 303.

Orange Custards.

Take half the rind of a Seville orange, and boil it tender; beat it very fine in a mortar, and put to it a spoonful of brandy, a quarter of a pound of loaf sugar, the juice of a Seville orange, and the yolks of four eggs; beat them all well together for ten minutes, and then pour in by degrees a pint of boiling cream; keep beating them till they are cold, then put them in custard cups, and set them in an earthen dish of hot water. Let them stand till they are set, then take them out, and stick preserved orange on the top. They may be served up either hot or cold. *Cole*, 304.

Lemon Custards.

Beat the yolks of ten eggs, strain them, beat them with a pint of cream; sweeten the juice of two lemons, boil it with the peel of one; strain it. When cold, stir it to the cream and eggs; stir it till it near boils; or put it into a dish, grate over the rind of a lemon, and brown with a salamander. *Mason*, 398.

Rice Custards.

Put a blade of mace and a quartered nutmeg into a quart of cream; boil it, then strain it, and add to it some whole rice boiled, and a little brandy; sweeten it, stir it over the fire till it thickens, and serve it up in cups or a dish. It may be eaten either hot or cold. *Cole*, 304.

Fine Cheesecakes.

Take a pint of cream, warm it, and put to it five quarts of milk warm from the cow; then put runnet to it, and give it a stir about. When it is come, put the curd in a linen bag or cloth, let it drain well away from the whey, but do not squeeze it much; then put it in a mortar, and break the curd as fine as butter; put to your curd half a pound of sweet almonds blanched, and beat exceedingly fine, and half a pound of mac-karoons beat very fine. If you have no mackaroons, get Naples' biscuits; then add to it the yolks of nine eggs beaten, a whole nutmeg grated, two perfumed plums dissolved in rose or orange-flower water, and half a pound of fine sugar; mix all well together, then melt a pound and a quarter of butter, and stir it well in it; then make your puff-paste thus:—take a pound of fine

flour,

flour, wet it with cold water, roll it out, put into it by degrees a pound of fresh butter, and shake a little flour over each coat as you roll it. Make it just as you use it.

You need not put in the perfumed plums, if you dislike them; and, for variety, when you make them of mackaroons, put in as much tincture of saffron as will give them a high colour, but no currants. This we call a Saffron Cheesecake. *Glasse*, 287.

Almond Cheesecakes.

Take four ounces of Jordan almonds, blanch them, and put them into cold water, beat them with rose-water in a marble mortar, or wooden bowl, with a wooden pestle; put to it four ounces of sugar, and the yolks of four eggs beat fine; work it in the mortar or bowl till it becomes white and frothy; then make a rich puff-paste as follows:—take half a pound of flour, a quarter of a pound of butter, rub a little of the butter into the flour, mix it stiff with a little cold water, then roll your paste straight out, strew over a little flour, and lay over it in thin bits one third of your butter; throw a little more flour over the butter; do so for three times, then put your paste in your tins, fill them, and grate sugar over them, and bake them in a gentle oven. *Raffald*, 258.

Common Cheesecakes.

Put a quart of milk on the fire, beat eight eggs well; when the milk boils, stir them upon the fire till it comes to a curd, then pour it out; when it is cold, put in a little salt, two spoonfuls of rose-water, and three quarters of a pound of currants; put it into puff-paste, and bake it. *Mason*, 395.

Lemon Cheesecakes.

Boil the peel of two large lemons very tender, then pound it well in a mortar with four or five ounces of loaf-sugar, the yolks of six eggs, half a pound of fresh butter, and a little curd beat fine; pound and mix all together, lay a puff-paste in your patty-pans, fill them half full, and bake them.

Orange Cheesecakes are done the same way, only you should boil the peel in two or three waters to take out the bitterness. *Cole*, 305.

Bread Cheesecakes.

Having sliced a penny loaf as thin as possible, pour on it a pint of boiling cream, and let it stand two hours. Then take eight eggs half a pound of butter, and a nutmeg grated. Beat them well together, and put in half a pound of currants well washed and dried before the fire, and a spoonful of white wine or brandy. Then bake them in patty-pans or raised crust. *Farley*, 308.

Cheese-

Cheesecakes the French way, called Ramequins.

Take good Parmesan, of Cheshire cheese, melt it in a stew-pan with a bit of butter, and one or two spoonfuls of water; then add as much flour as will make it pretty thick, and quit the sides of the pan; put it into another pan, and add eggs to it, one by one, mixing well with a wooden spoon till it becomes pretty light and clear; add one or two pounded anchovies, and a little pepper; bake the cases singly upon a baking-plate, or in paper cases, of what shape you please; they require but a short time, and a soft oven, and must be served quite hot. *Clermont*, 434.

Citron Cheesecakes.

Boil a quart of cream; when cold, mix it well with the yolks of four eggs well beaten; then set it on the fire, and let it boil till it curds; blanch some almonds, beat them with orange-flower water, put them into the cream, with a few Naples' biscuits and green citron shred fine; sweeten it to your taste, and bake them in tea-cups. *Cole,* 306.

Rice Cheesecakes.

Boil a quarter of a pound of rice till it is tender, drain it, put in four eggs well beaten, half a pound of butter, half a pint of cream, six ounces of sugar, a nutmeg grated, and a glass of ratafia water or brandy. Beat them all together, and bake them in raised crusts. *Cole,* 306.

Chap.

CHAP. XXV.—THE ART OF CONFEC-
TIONARY.

The Colours used in Confectionary.

To make the red Colour.

BOIL an ounce of cochineal in half a pint of water for about five minutes, then add half an ounce of cream of tartar, and half an ounce of pounded allum; boil on a slow fire about as long again. It is easily known to be done, by dipping a pen, or a wooden skewer, into it, and writing with it on white paper, for if it writes freely like ink, and keeps its colour, it is done; take it off the fire, add two ounces of sugar, and let it settle; pour the clear off, to keep in a bottle well stopped. *Cole*, 306.

The blue Colour.

This colour is only made for present use; put a little warm water into a plate, and rub an indigo stone in it till the colour is come to the tint you would have it, whether pale, or a deep blue. *Cole*, 307.

The yellow Colour.

This is done in the same manner, by pouring a little water into a plate, and rubbing it with a bit of gamboge. It is also done better with a yellow lilly: take the heart of the flower, infuse it in milk-warm water, and preserve it in a bottle well stopped. *Cole*, 307

The green Colour.

Trim the leaves of spinach, boil them a moment in water, and drain them very well to pound; sift the juice in a sieve for use.

Of these cardinal colours, you may make any alteration in imitation of painters, by mixing to what shade you please; but taste and fancy must be your guides upon those occasions. *Cole*, 307.

OF CAKES,

General Observations upon Cakes,

ALWAYS have every thing in readiness before you begin to make any kind of cakes, then beat your eggs well, and never leave them till they are finished, as by that means your cakes will not be so light. When you put butter in your cakes, be particularly careful in beating it to a fine cream before you put in your sugar, otherwise double the beating will not have so good an effect. Rice-cakes, seed-cakes, or plum-cakes, are best baked in wooden garths; for when they are baked in pots or tins, the outsides of the cakes are burned, and they are so confined that the heat cannot penetrate into the middle, which hinders its rising. *Cole*, 307.

A Bride Cake.

Take four pounds of fine flour well dried, four pounds of fresh butter, two pounds of loaf sugar; pound and sift fine a quarter of an ounce of mace, and the same quantity of nutmegs; to every pound of flour put eight eggs; wash and pick four pounds of currants, and dry them before the fire; blanch a pound of sweet almonds, and cut them lengthways very thin, a pound of citron, a pound of candied orange, a pound of candied lemon, and half a pint of brandy; first work the butter with your hand to a cream, then beat in your sugar a quarter of an hour, beat the whites of your eggs to a very strong froth, mix them with your sugar and butter; beat your yolks half an hour at least, and mix them with your cake; then put in your flour, mace, and nutmeg; keep beating it till your oven is ready, put in your brandy, and beat your currants and almonds lightly in; tie three sheets of paper round the bottom of your hoop, to keep it from running out; rub it well with butter, put in your cake, and lay your sweetmeats in three lays, with cake betwixt every lay; after it is risen and coloured, cover it with paper before your oven is stopped up; it will take three hours baking. *Raffald*, 265.

A pound Cake.

Take a pound of butter, beat it in an earthen pan with your hand one way, till it is like a fine thick cream; then have ready twelve eggs, but half the whites; beat them well, and beat them up with the butter, a pound of flour beat in it, a pound of sugar, and a few carraways. Beat it all well together for an hour with your hand, or a great wooden spoon; butter a pan and put it in, and then bake it an hour in a quick oven.

For change, you may put in a pound of currants, clean washed and picked. *Glasse*, 281. *Mason*, 400. *Farley*, 292.

A good

A good Plum Cake.

Take three pounds of flour, three pounds of currants, three quarters of a pound of almonds, blanched and beat grofsly, about half an ounce of them bitter, a quarter of a pound of fugar, feven yolks and fix whites of eggs, one pint of cream, two pounds of butter, half a pint of good ale yeaft; mix the eggs and the yeaft together, ftrain them; fet the cream on the fire, melt the butter in it; ftir in the almonds and half a pint of fack, part of which fhould be put to the almonds while beating; mix together the flour, currants, and fugar, what nutmeg, cloves, and mace, are liked; ftir thefe to the cream, put in the yeaft. *Mafon*, 400.

A common Seed Cake.

Take one pound and a quarter of flour, and three quarters of a pound of lump fugar pounded, the yolks of ten eggs, and the whites of four, one pound of butter beat to a cream with the hand. Mix thefe well; add almoft an ounce of carraway-feeds bruifed; butter the pan or hoop; fift fugar on the top. *Cole*, 308.

A rich Seed Cake.

Take a pound of flour well dried, a pound of butter, a pound of loaf fugar beat and fifted, eight eggs, two ounces of carraway-feeds, one nutmeg grated, and its weight of cinnamon. Firft beat your butter to a cream, then put in your fugar, beat the whites of your eggs half an hour, mix them with your fugar and butter, then beat the yolks half an hour, put to it the whites; beat in your flour, fpices, and feeds, a little before it goes to the oven; put it in the hoop and bake it two hours in a quick oven, and let it ftand two hours. It will take two hours beating. *Raffald*, 267.

A good common Cake.

Take fix ounces of rice-flour, and the fame quantity of wheat-flour, the yolks and whites of nine eggs, half a pound of lump fugar pounded and fifted, and half an ounce of carraway-feeds; beat this an hour, and bake it an hour in a quick oven. This cake is well calculated for children and delicate ftomachs, as it is very light, and has no butter in it. *Cole*, 309.

Portugal Cakes.

Mix into a pound of fine flour a pound of loaf-fugar beat and fifted, then rub it into a pound of pure fweet butter till it is thick like grated white bread; then put to it two fpoonfuls of rofe-water, two of fack, ten eggs; whip them very well with a whifk, then put into it eight ounces of currants, mixed all well together; butter the tin pans, fill them but half full, and bake them; if made without currants, they will keep half a year.

Add

Add a pound of almonds blanched, and beat with rofe-water, as above, and leave out the flour. Thefe are another fort, and better. *Glaffe*, 283.

A plain Cake.

Take two pounds and an half of flour, fifteen eggs, two pounds and an half of butter, beat to a cream; three quarters of a pound of pounded fugar; bake it in a hot but not a fcorching oven. *Cole*, 309.

An Almond Cake.

Take two ounces of bitter, and one pound of fweet almonds, blanched and beat, with a little rofe or orange-flower water, and the white of one egg; half a pound of fifted loaf-fugar, eight yolks and three whites of eggs, the juice of half a lemon, the rind grated; bake it either in one large pan, or fmall pans. *Mafon*, 401.

Queen Cakes.

Take a pound of fugar, beat and fift it, a pound of well-dried flour, a pound of butter, eight eggs, half a pound of currants wafhed and picked; grate a nutmeg, and the fame quantity of mace and cinnamon. Work your butter to a cream, and put in your fugar; beat the whites of your eggs near half an hour, and mix them with your fugar and butter. Then beat your yolks near half an hour, and put them to your butter. Beat them exceedingly well together, and when it is ready for the oven, put in your flour, fpices, and currants. Sift a little fugar over them, and bake them in tins. *Farley*, 303.

Shrewfbury Cakes.

Take half a pound of butter, beat it to a cream, then put in half a pound of flour, one egg, fix ounces of loaf-fugar, beat and fifted, half an ounce of carraway-feeds mixed into a pafte; roll them thin, and cut them round with a fmall glafs, or little tins; prick them, and lay them on fheets of tin, and bake them in a flow oven. *Raffald*, 270.

Bath Cakes.

Take half a pound of butter, and rub it into a pound of flour; add one fpoonful of good barm, warm fome cream, and make it a light pafte, and fet it to the fire to rife. When you make them up, take four ounces of carraway comfits, work part of them in, and ftrew the reft on the top. Make them into a round cake, about the fize of a French roll. bake them on fheet tins, and fend them in hot for breakfaft. *Cole*, 310.

Little Fine Cakes.

Take one pound of butter beaten to a cream, a pound and a quarter of flour, a pound of fine fugar beat fine, a pound of cur-

rants

rants clean wafhed and picked, fix eggs, two whites left out; beat them fine, mix the flour, fugar, and eggs, by degrees into the batter, beat it all well with both hands. Either make it into little cakes, or bake it in one. *Cole*, 310.

Orange Cakes.

Take what quantity you pleafe of Seville-oranges that have good rinds, quarter them, and boil them in two or three waters till they are tender, and the bitternefs is gone off. Skin them and then lay them on a clean napkin to dry. Take all the fkins and feeds out of the pulp with a knife, fhred the peels fine, put them to the pulp, weigh them, and put rather more than their weight of fine fugar into a tofling-pan, with juft as much water as will diffolve it. Boil it till it becomes a perfect fugar, and then by degrees put in your orange-peels and pulp. Stir them well before you fet them on the fire; boil it very gently till it looks clear and thick, and then put them into flat-bottomed glaffes. Set them in a ftove, and keep them in a conftant and moderate heat; and when they are candied on the top, turn them out upon glaffes. *Farley*, 299.

N. B. Lemon-cakes may be made the fame way.

Ginzerbread.

Take three quarts of fine flour, two ounces of beaten ginger, a quarter of an ounce of nutmeg, cloves, and mace, beat fine, but moft of the latter. Mix all together, three quarters of a pound of fine fugar, two pounds of treacle; fet it over the fire, but do not let it boil. Three quarters of a pound of butter melted in the treacle, and fome candied lemon and orange-peel cut fine; mix all thefe together. An hour will bake it in a quick oven. *Glaffe*, 283.

Little Currant Cakes.

Take a pound and an half of fine flour, dry it well before the fire, a pound of butter, half a pound of fine loaf fugar, well beat and fifted, four yolks of eggs, four fpoonfuls of rofe-water, four fpoonfuls of fack, a little mace, and one nutmeg grated. Beat the eggs very well, and put them to the rofe-water and fack; then put to it the fugar and butter; work them all together, ftrew in the currants and flour, being both made warm together before. This quantity will make fix or eight cakes; bake them pretty crifp, and of a fine brown. *Raffald*, 272.

Heart Cakes.

Take a pound of butter, and work it with the hand to a cream; put to it a dozen yolks of eggs, and half the whites, well beaten, a pound of flour dried, a pound of fifted fugar, four fpoonfuls of good brandy, and a pound of currants wafhed and dried before the fire. As the pans are filled, put in two

ounces

of candied orange and citron; continue beating the cakes till they go into the oven. This quantity will fill three dozen of middling pans. *Cole,* 311.

Naples' Bifcuit.

Put three quarters of a pound of very fine flour to a pound of fine fugar fifted; fift it three times, then add fix eggs well beat, and a fpoonful of rofe-water. When the oven is almoft hot, make them, but take care that they are not made up too wet. *Cole,* 311.

Common Bifcuit.

Take eight eggs, and beat them half an hour; put to them a pound of fugar, beat and fifted, with the rind of a lemon grated. Whifk it an hour, or till it looks light, and then put in a pound of flour, with a little rofe-water. Sugar them over, and bake them in tins, or on papers. *Cole,* 311.

French Bifcuits.

Having a pair of clean fcales ready, in one fcale put three new-laid eggs; in the other fcale as much dried flour, an equal weight with the eggs; take out the flour, and as much fine powdered fugar; firft beat the whites of the eggs up well with the whifk, till they are of a fine froth; then whip in half an ounce of candied lemon-peel cut very thin and fine, and beat well; then, by degrees, whip in the flour and fugar, then flip in the yolks, and with a fpoon temper it well together; then fhape your bifcuits on fine white paper with your fpoon, and throw powdered fugar over them. Bake them in a moderate oven, not too hot, giving them a fine colour on the top. When they are baked, with a fine knife cut them off from the paper, and lay them in boxes for ufe. *Glaffe,* 285.

Savoy Bifcuits.

Beat the whites of eight eggs till they are a ftrong froth, then put it to the yolks, with a pound of fugar; beat them altogether a quarter of an hour. When the oven is ready, put in one pound of fine flour to the other ingredients; ftir it till it is well mixed; lay the bifcuits upon the paper, and ice them. Let the oven be hot enough to bake them quick. *Cole,* 312.

Drop Bifcuit.

Beat the yolks of ten eggs, and the whites of fix, with one fpoonful of rofe water, half an hour, then put in ten ounces of loaf fugar beat and fifted; whifk them well for half an hour, then add one ounce of carraway-feeds crufhed a little, and fix ounces of fine flour; whifk in your flour gently, drop them on wafer-papers, and bake them in a moderate oven. *Raffald,* 276.

Almond

Almond Puffs.

Take two ounces of sweet almonds, blanch them, and beat them very fine, with orange-flower water; beat the whites of three eggs to a very high froth, and then strew in a little sifted sugar. Mix your almonds with your sugar and eggs, and then add more sugar till it is as thick as paste. Lay it in cakes, and bake it in a cool oven, on paper. *Farley*, 289.

Sugar Puffs.

Beat the whites of ten eggs till they rise to a high froth, put them into a stone mortar, or wooden bowl, add as much double-refined sugar as will make them thick; put in a little ambergris to give them a flavour, rub them round the mortar for half an hour; put in a few carraway-seeds. Take a sheet of wafers, lay them on as broad as a sixpence, and as high as they can be laid; put them in a moderate oven half a quarter of an hour, and they will look as white as snow. *Mason*, 407.

German Puffs.

Mix two spoonfuls of fine flour with two eggs well beat; half a pint of cream or milk, and two ounces of melted butter; stir it all well together, and add a little salt and nutmeg. Put them in tea-cups, or little deep tin moulds, half full, and bake them a quarter of an hour in a quick oven; but let it be hot enough to colour them at top or bottom. Turn them into a dish, and strew powder-sugar over them. *Cole*, 313.

Lemon Puffs.

Beat and sift a pound of double-refined sugar, put it in a bowl with the juice of two lemons, and beat them well together. Then, having beat the white of an egg to a very high froth, put it also in your bowl, and beat it half an hour; add three eggs, and two rinds of lemons grated; mix it well up, dust some sugar on your papers, drop on the puffs in small drops, and bake them in an oven moderately hot. *Cole*, 313.

To make Wafers.

Put the yolks of two eggs, well beat, to a pint of cream, mix it as thick as a pudding with flour well dried, and sugar and orange-flower water to the taste; put in warm water enough to make it as thin as fine pancakes; mix them very smooth, and bake them over a stove. Butter the irons when they stick. *Cole*, 313.

Icings for Cakes.

Take a pound of double-refined sugar, pounded and sifted fine, and mix it with the whites of twenty-four eggs in an earthen pan; whisk them well for two or three hours, till it looks white and thick, and then, with a thin broad board, or bunch

bunch of feathers, spread it all over the top and sides of the cake. Set it at a proper distance before a clear fire, and keep turning it continually that it may not turn colour; but a cool oven is best, where an hour will harden it. Or you may make your icing thus:—Beat the whites of three eggs to a strong froth, beat a pound of Jordan almonds very fine with rose-water, and mix your almonds with the eggs lightly together; then beat a pound of loaf sugar very fine, and put it in by degrees. When your cake is enough, take it out, lay on your icing, and proceed as above directed. *Farley*, 304,

CANDYING

CANDYING AND DRYING.

BEFORE you attempt to candy any kind of fruit, it must be first preserved, and dried in a stove, or before the fire, that none of the syrup may remain in it; then boil your sugar to the candy height, dip in your fruit, and lay them in dishes in your stove to dry. Then put them in boxes for use, and keep them in places that are neither moist nor hot. *Cole*, 314.

To boil Sugar, candy height.

Put a pound of sugar into a clean tossing-pan, with half a pint of water, set it over a very clear flow fire; take off the scum as it rises, boil it till it looks fine and clear, then take out a little with a silver spoon; when it is cold, if it will draw a thread from your spoon, it is boiled high enough for any kind of sweet-meat; then boil your syrup, and when it begins to candy round the edge of your pan, it is candy height.

N. B. It is a great fault to put any kind of sweet meats into too thick a syrup, especially at the first, for it withers your fruit, and takes off both the beauty and flavour. *Raffald*, 247.

To candy Cassia.

Take as much of the powder of brown cassia as will lie upon two broad shillings, with what musk and ambergris you think proper. The cassia and perfume must be powdered together. Then take a quarter of a pound of sugar, and boil it to a candy height; then put in your powder and mix it well together, and pour it into pewter saucers or plates, which must be buttered very thin, and when it is cold it will slip out. The cassia is to be bought in London; sometimes it is in powder, and sometimes in a hard lump. *Glasse*, 373.

To dry Greengages.

Slit them down the seam, just scald them in a thin syrup, with vine-leaves at the top; put them by till the next day, keeping them under the syrup; then put them into a thick syrup cold; scald them gently in this, set them by, repeat it the next day till they look clear; set them by for a few days. If there is occasion, boil them once more; take them from the syrup, and dry them. When they are set by in the syrup, let it be in something rather narrow at the top, as they must be covered, or they will be discoloured. *Mason*, 435.

Candied Orange-flowers.

Boil some sugar to a candy-height, put some orange-flowers to it, and take it off the fire for about a quarter of an hour, or till the flowers discharge their juice, as it refreshes the sugar; put it upon the fire again to bring it to the same degree; let it cool to half, put it into moulds, and dry it in a stove of a moderate

derate heat, kept as equal as poffible. It is known to be candied by thrufting a fmall fkewer into the corner of each mould to the bottom, and the top muft be fparkling like a diamond; put the moulds upon one fide to drain a good while before you take out the candy, turn it over upon white paper, and keep it always in a dry place. *Clermont*, 541.

To candy Ginger.

Grate an ounce of race-ginger very fine, and put it into a tofling-pan, with a pound of loaf-fugar beat fine, and as much water as will diffolve it. Put them over a flow fire, and ftir them well till the fugar begins to boil; then ftir in another pound of fine fugar beat fine, and continue ftirring it till it becomes thick. Then take it off the fire, and drop it in cakes upon earthen difhes; fet them to dry in a warm place, when they will be hard and brittle, and have a white appearance. *Cole*, 315.

To candy Lemon or Orange-peel.

Cut your lemons, or oranges, long ways; take out all the pulp, and put the rinds into a pretty ftrong falt and hard water fix days, then boil them in a large quantity of fpring water till they are tender; then take them out, and lay them on a hair fieve to drain; then make a thin fyrup of fine loaf-fugar, a pound to a quart of water; put in your peels and boil them half an hour, or till they look clear; have ready a thick fyrup made of fine loaf-fugar, with as much water as will diffolve it; put in your peels, and boil them over a flow fire till you fee the fyrup candy about the pan and peels; then take them out and grate fine fugar all over them; lay them on a hair fieve to drain, and fet them in a ftove, or before the fire to dry, and keep them in a dry place for ufe.

N. B. Do not cover your fauce-pan when you boil either lemons or oranges. *Raffald*, 246.

To candy Angelica.

Take it in April; boil it in water till it is tender, then take it up and drain it from the water very well; then fcrape the outfide of it, and dry it in a clean cloth, and lay it in the fyrup; and let it lie in three or four days, covered clofe; the fyrup muft be ftrong of fugar, and keep it hot a good while, but without boiling. After it is heated a good while, lay it upon a pie-plate, and fo let it dry; keep it near the fire left it diffolve. *Glaffe*, 372.

Orange Chips.

Pare fome of the beft Seville oranges aflant, about a quarter of an inch broad, and if you can keep the parings whole, they will have a prettier effect. When you have pared as many as you intend, put them into falt and fpring-water for a day or

T   two;

two; then boil them in a large quantity of fpring-water till they are tender, and drain them on a fieve. Have ready a thin fyrup, made of a quart of water and a pound of fine fugar; boil them, a few at a time, to keep them from breaking, till they look clear; then put them into a fyrup made of fine loaf-fugar, with as much water as will diffolve it, and boil them to a candy height. When you take them up, lay them on a fieve, and grate double-refined fugar over them. Then put them in a ftove, or before the fire, to dry. *Farley*, 346.

To dry Damafcenes.

Gather the Damafcenes when full ripe, lay them on a coarfe cloth, fet them in a very cool oven, let them ftand a day or two; they muft be as dry as a frefh prune; if they are not, put them in another cool oven for a day or two longer; then take them out; they will eat like frefh damafcenes in the winter. *Mafon*, 436. *Raffald*, 242. *Farley*, 347.

To candy Cinnamon.

Soak fome cinnamon bark in water about twenty-four hours, cut it into pieces of what length you pleafe, and boil a moment in fugar of candy height; drain it and dry it in the ftove upon rails till it comes to a proper fubftance to put in candy moulds; garnifh with fugar, and when it is half cold, put it to dry as the orange-flower candy. *Clermont*, 542.

To dry Apricots.

Pare and ftone a pound of apricots, and put them in your toffing-pan; then take a pound of double-refined fugar, pound and fift it, and ftrew a little among your apricots, and lay the reft over them. After letting them ftand twenty-four hours, turn three or four times in the fyrup, then boil them pretty quick till they feem clear. When cold, take them out, and lay them on glaffes; then turn them every half hour the firft day, the next day every hour, and afterwards as may appear to be neceffary. *Cole*, 316.

To dry Pear Plumbs.

Take two pounds of pear-plumbs to one pound of fugar; ftone them, and fill every one of them with fugar; lay them in an earthen pot, put to them as much water as will prevent burning them; then fet them in an oven after bread is drawn, let them ftand till they are tender; then put them into a fieve to drain well from the fyrup; then fet them in an oven again till they are a little dry; then fmooth the fkins as well as you can, and fo fill them; then fet them in the oven again to harden; then wafh them in water fcalding hot, and dry them very well; then put them in the oven again very cool, to blue them. Put them between two pewter difhes, and fet them in the oven. *Glaffe*, 372.

To

To dry Currants in Bunches.

Stone your currants, and tie them up in bunches; to every pound of currants put a pound and an half of fugar, and to every pound of fugar put half a pint of water; boil the fyrup very well, lay your currants in it, fet them on the fire, and let them juft boil; take them off, cover it clofe with a paper, let them ftand till the next day, then make them fcalding hot let them ftand for two or three days with paper clofe to them; then lay them on earthen plates, and fift them well over with fugar; put them in a ftove to dry; the next day lay them on fieves, but do not turn them till the upper fide is dry, then turn them and fift the other fide well with fugar; when they are quite dry, lay them between papers. *Raffald*, 244.

T 2 CREAMS.

CREAMS.

WHEN creams are made, ftrain the eggs, or they will be very apt to curdle.

Cream with Eggs.

Boil three parts cream, and one of milk, a fpoonful of orange-flower water, a bit of dried lemon peel, and a quarter of a pound of fugar to a quart; let it boil to reduce to three parts; then take it off the fire, and add four yolks of eggs, beat up; make a liafon over the fire without boiling, fift it with a fieve, and finifh it with rennet. Serve either with or without. cream. *Clermont*, 603.

Piftachio Cream.

Take half a pound of Piftachio nuts, break them, and take out the kernels; beat them in a mortar with a fpoonful of brandy, put them into a toffing-pan, with a pint of cream, and the yolks of two eggs beat very fine; ftir it gently over a flow fire till it is thick, but do not let it boil, then put it into a china foup-plate; when it is cold, ftick fome kernels, cut longways, all over it, and fend it to table. *Glaffe*, 292. *Raffald*, 248. *Farley*, 310.

Coffee Cream.

Roaft one ounce of coffee, put it hot into a pint and an half of boiling cream; boil thefe together a little; take it off. put in two dried gizzards; cover this clofe, let it ftand one hour, fweeten with double-refined fugar; pafs it two or three times through a fieve with a wooden fpoon; put it into a difh with a tin on the top, fet the difh on a gentle ftove, put fire upon the top upon the tin; when it has taken, fet it by. Serve it cold.

Tea-cream is made in the fame manner. *Mafon*, 444.

Barley Cream.

Boil a quantity of pearl-barley in milk and water till it is tender; then ftrain the liquor from it, put your barley into a quart of cream, and let it boil a little; then take the whites of five eggs, and the yolks of one, beaten with a fpoonful of fine flour, and two fpoonfuls of orange-flower water; then take the cream off the fire, and mix in the eggs by degrees, and fet it over the fire again to thicken. Sweeten it to your tafte, pour it into bafons, and, when cold, ferve it up. *Cole*, 318.

Codling Cream.

Pare and core twenty codlings, and beat them in a mortar, with a pint of cream; ftrain it into a difh, and put into it fome bread-crumbs, with a little white wine. Send it to table.

Goofeberries may be done in the fame manner. *Cole*, 318.

Ice

Ice Cream.

Take twelve ripe apricots, pare, ftone, and fcald them, and beat them fine in a marble mortar; put to them fix ounces of double-refined fugar, and a pint of fcalding cream, and work it through a hair fieve; put it into a tin that has a clofe cover, and fet it in a tub of ice broke fmall, and a large quantity of falt put among it. When you fee your cream grow thick round the edges of your tin, ftir it, and fet it in again till it grows quite thick. When your cream is all frozen up, take it out of the tin, and put it into the mould you intend it to be turned out of. Then put on the lid, and have ready another tub, with falt and ice in it as before. Put your mould in the middle, and lay your ice under and over it; let it ftand four or five hours, and dip your tin in warm water when you turn it out; but if it be fummer, remember not to turn it out till the moment you want it. If you have not apricots, any other fruit will anfwer the purpofe, provided you take care to work them very fine in your mortar. *Raffald*, 312.

Hartfhorn Cream.

Take four ounces of hartfhorn fhavings, and boil it in three pints of water till it is reduced to half a pint, and run it through a jelly-bag; put to it a pint of cream and four ounces of fine fugar, and juft boil it up; put it into cups or glaffes, and let it ftand till it is cold. Dip your cups or glaffes in fcalding water, and turn them out into your difh; ftick fliced almonds on them. It is generally eaten with white wine and fugar. *Glaffe*, 292.

Mrs. Raffald, page 250, and *Mr. Farley*, page 311, have the fame receipt, with this fingle alteration—they have left out the four ounces of fugar, which I fuppofe proceeded from a miftake, inftead of being meant as an improvement.

Blanched Cream.

Seafon a quart of very thick cream with fine fugar and orange-flower water; boil it and beat the whites of twenty eggs with a little cold cream; ftrain it, and when the cream is upon the boil, pour in the eggs, ftirring it very well till it comes to a thick curd; then take it up, and ftrain it again through a hair fieve; beat it well with a fpoon till it is cold, then put it into a difh. *Mafon*, 446.

Whipt Cream.

Mix a quart of thick cream, the whites of eight eggs beat well, and half a pint of fack; fweeten to your tafte with double-refined fugar. You may perfume it, if you pleafe, with a little mufk or ambergris, tied in a rag, and fteeped a little in the cream; whip it up with a whifk, and fome lemon-peel tied in the middle of the whifk; take the froth with a fpoon, and lay

T 3   it it in your glaffes or bafons. This does well over a tart. *Cole*, 319.

Orange Cream.

Take and pare the rind of a Seville orange very fine, and fqueeze the juice of four oranges; put them into a ftew-pan with half a pint of water, and half a pound of fine fugar; beat the whites of five eggs, and mix into it, and fet them on a flow fire; ftir it one way till it grows thick and white, ftrain it through a gauze, and ftir it till cold; then beat the yolks of five eggs very fine, and put into your pan with the cream; ftir it over a gentle fire till it is ready to boil, then put it in a bafon, and ftir it till it is cold, and then put it into your glaffes. *Glaffe*, 291.

Mrs. *Raffald*, page 252, has the fame receipt, except that inftead of " half a pint of water," and " half a pound of fine fugar," fhe fays, " One pint of water, and eight ounces of fugar." Mr. *Farley*, page 314, has followed her example.

Spanifh Cream.

Mix well together three fpoonfuls of flour of rice fifted very fine, the yolks of three eggs, three fpoonfuls of water, and two of orange-flower water; then put to them one pint of cream, and fet it upon a good fire, ftirring it till of a proper thicknefs, and pour it into cups. *Cole*, 320.

Steeple Cream.

Take five ounces of hartfhorn, and two ounces of ivory, and put them into a ftone bottle; fill it up with fair water to the neck; put in a fmall quantity of gum-arabic and gum-dragon; then tie up the bottle very clofe, and fet it into a pot of water, with hay at the bottom. Let it ftand fix hours, then take it out, and let it ftand an hour before you open it, left it fly in your face; then ftrain it, and it will be a ftrong jelly; then take a pound of blanched almonds, beat them very fine, mix it with a pint of thick cream, and let it ftand a little; then ftrain it out, and mix it with a pound of jelly; fet it over the fire till it is fcalding hot, fweeten it to your tafte with double-refined fugar; then take it off, put in a little amber, and pour it into fmall high gallipots, like a fugar-loaf at top; when it is cold, turn them, and lay cold whipt cream about them in heaps. Be fure it does not boil when the cream is in. *Glaffe*, 290.

Snow and Cream.

Having made a rich boiled cuftard, put it into a china or glafs difh. Then take the whites of eight eggs, beaten with rofe-water, and a fpoonful of treble-refined fugar, till it is of a ftrong froth. Put fome milk and water into a broad ftew-pan, and as foon as it boils, take the froth off the eggs, lay it on the milk and water, and let it boil once up; then take it off carefully,

carefully, and lay it on your cuſtard. This is a pretty ſupper-diſh. *Furley*, 315.

Burnt Cream.

Take a pint of cream, boil it with ſugar and a little lemon-peel ſhred fine ; then beat the yolks of ſix, and the whites of four eggs ſeparately. When your cream is cooled, put in your eggs, with a ſpoonful of orange-flower water, and one of fine flour ; ſet it over the fire, keep ſtirring it till it is thick, then put it into a diſh. When it is cold, ſift a quarter of a pound of ſugar all over it, hold a hot ſalamander over it till it is very brown, and looks like a glaſs plate put over your cream. *Raf-fald*, 253.

Lemon-peel with Cream.

Pare two lemons, ſqueeze to them the juice of one large one, or two ſmall ones ; let it ſtand ſome time, then ſtrain the juice to a pint of cream ; add the yolks of four eggs beaten and ſtrained ; ſweeten it, ſtir it over the fire till thick, and, if agree-able, add a little brandy. *Maſon*, 443.

Pompadour Cream.

Take the whites of five eggs, and after beating them into a ſtrong froth, put them into a toſſing-pan, with two ounces of ſugar, and two ſpoonfuls of orange-flower water ; ſtir it gently three or four minutes, then pour it into a diſh, and melted but-ter over it. Send it in hot. *Cole*, 321.

PRESERVING.

General Observations upon Preserving.

IN making jellies of any kind, avoid letting any feeds from the fruit fall into your jelly; and be careful not to fqueeze it too near, which would render your jelly lefs tranfparent. Pound your fugar, and let it diffolve in the fyrup before you fet it on the fire, the fcum will then rife better, and the jelly will be of a finer colour. Boiling jellies too high, gives them a darkifh hue, which fhould therefore be avoided. All wet fweet-meats fhould be kept in a dry cool place, to prevent their becoming mouldy, or loofing their virtue. Tie them well down with white paper, with two folds of thick cap-paper over them. Leaving the pots open, or negligently tied, is deftructive to them. *Cole,* 321.

Hartfhorn Jelly.

Boil half a pound of hartfhorn in three quarts of water over a gentle fire, till it becomes a jelly. If you take out a little to cool, and it hangs on the fpoon, it is enough. Strain it while it is hot, put it in a well-tinned fauce-pan, put to it a pint of Rhenifh wine, and a quarter of a pound of loaf fugar; beat the whites of four eggs, or more, to a froth, ftir it all together that the whites may mix well with the jelly, and pour it in as if you were cooling it. Let it boil two or three minutes, then put in the juice of three or four lemons; let it boil a minute or two longer. When it is finely curdled, and of a pure white colour, have ready a fwan-fkin jelly-bag over a china bafon, pour in your jelly, and pour back again till it is as clear as rock water; then fet a very clean china bafon under, have your glaffes as clean as poffible, and with a clean fpoon fill your glaffes. Have ready fome thin rind of the lemons, and when you have filled half your glaffes, throw your peel into the bafon; and when the jelly is all run out of the bag, with a clean fpoon fill the reft of the glaffes, and they will look of a fine amber colour. In putting in the ingredients, there is no certain rule. You muft put in lemon and fugar to your palate. Moft people love them fweet; and indeed they are good for nothing unlefs they are. *Glaffe,* 294.

Another way.

Put two quarts of water into a clean pan, with half a pound of hartfhorn fhavings, let it fimmer till near one half is reduced; ftrain it off, then put in the peel of four oranges and two lemons, pared very thin; boil them five minutes, put to it the juice of the before-mentioned lemons and oranges, with about ten ounces of double-refined fugar; beat the whites of fix eggs to a froth, mix them carefully with your jelly, that you

do

do not poach the eggs ; juſt let it boil up, and run it through a
jelly-bag till it is clear. *Raffald*, 210.

Calves'-feet Jelly.

To two calf's feet, put three quarts of water, boil it to one
quart ; when cold, take off the fat, and take the jelly from the
fediment ; put to it one pint of white wine, half a pound of fugar, the juice of three lemons, the peel of one. Whiſk the
whites of two eggs. Put all into a fauce pan, boil it a few minutes ; put it through a jelly-bag till it is fine. *Maſon*, 447.

Red or white Currant Jelly.

Boil your currants in a preferving pan till the juice will
eafily maſh through a fieve or cloth ; put in an equal quantity
of clarified fugar and juice, boil and fcum it till it will jelly.
When cold, put on paper dipped in brandy. *Cole*, 323.

Black Currant Jelly.

Gather your currants on a dry day when they are ripe ; pick
them from the ftalks, put them into a large ftew-pot, and put
a quart of water to every ten quarts of currants ; fet them in
a cool oven for two hours having firſt tied a paper over them ;
then fqueeze them through a very fine cloth, and to every
quart of juice add a pound and an half of loaf-fugar broken
into fmall pieces. Stir it gently till the fugar is melted, and
when it boils, ſkim it well. Let it boil pretty thick for half
an hour over a clear fire, then pour it into pots, and put brandy papers over them. *Raffald*, 211. *Farley*, 321.

Orange Jelly.

Take half a pound of hartſhorn ſhavings, or four ounces of
ifing-glafs, and boil it in fpring-water till it is of a ftrong jelly ;
take the juice of three Seville oranges, three lemons, and fix
China oranges, and the rind of one Seville orange and one lemon, pared very thin ; put them to your jelly, fweeten it with
loaf-fugar to your palate ; beat up the whites of eight eggs to
a froth, and mix well in, then boil it for ten minutes, then run
it through a jelly-bag till it is very clear, and put it in moulds
till cold, then dip your mould in warm water, and turn it out
into a China diſh, or a flat glafs, and garniſh with flowers.
Glaſſe, 295.

Raſpberry Jelly.

Make it in the fame manner as currant jelly, only put one
half currants, and the other half raſpberries. *Cole*, 323.

Ifing-glaſs Jelly.

Boil an ounce of ifing-glafs, and a quarter of an ounce of
cloves, in a quart of water, till it is reduced to a pint, then
ſtrain it over fome fugar. *Cole*, 323.

Ribband

Ribband Jelly.

Take four calf's feet, take out the great bones, and put the feet into a pot with ten quarts of water, three ounces of hartf-horn, three ounces of ifing-glafs, a nutmeg quartered, and four blades of mace; boil it till it comes to two quarts, ftrain it through a flannel bag, let it ftand twenty-four hours, then fcrape off all the fat from the top very clean, then flice it, put to it the whites of fix eggs beaten to a froth; boil it a little, and ftrain it through a flannel bag; then run the jelly into little high glaffes, run every colour as thick as your finger, one colour muft be thoroughly cold before you put another on, and that you put on muft be but blood warm, for fear it mix together. You muft colour red with cochineal, green with fpinach, yellow with faffron, blue with fyrup of violets, white with thick cream, and fometimes the jelly by itfelf. You may add orange-flower water, or wine and fugar, and lemon, if you pleafe; but this is all fancy. *Glaffe, 295. Farley, 322.*

Cherry Jam.

Stone fome cherries, boil them well, and break them; take them off the fire, let the juice run from them; to three pounds of cherries boil together half a pint of red currant juice, and half a pound of loaf-fugar; put in the cherries as they boil, fift in three quarters of a pound of fugar; boil the cherries very faft for more than half an hour. When cold, put on brandy paper. *Mafon, 420.*

Red Rafpberry Jam.

Gather your rafpberries when they are ripe and dry, pick them very carefully from the ftalks and dead ones, crufh them in a bowl with a filver or wooden fpoon, (pewter is apt to turn them a purple colour); as foon as you have crufhed them, ftrew in their own weight of loaf-fugar, and half their weight of currant-juice, baked and ftrained as for jelly; then fet them over a clear flow fire, boil them half an hour, fkim them well, and keep ftirring them at the time, then put them into pots or glaffes, with brandy papers over them, and keep them for ufe.

N. B. As foon as you have got your berries, ftrew in your fugar; do not let them ftand long before you boil them, it will preferve their flavour. *Raffald, 212.*

Apricot Jam.

Provide fome fine rich apricots, cut them in thin pieces, and infufe them in an earthen pot till they are tender and dry; put a pound of double-refined fugar, and three fpoonfuls of water to every pound and an half of apricots. Then boil your fugar to a candy height, and put it upon your apricots. Set them

over

over a flow fire, and ftir them till they appear clear and thick; but they muft only fimmer, not boil; then put them in your glaffes. *Cole*, 324.

Black Currant Jam.

Gather your currants when they are full ripe, and pick them clean from the ftalks, then bruife them well in a bowl, and to every pound of currants put a pound and an half of loaf-fugar, finely beaten. Put them into a preferving-pan, boil them half an hour, fkim and ftir them all the time, and then put them into pots. *Farley*, 318.

Green Goofeberry Jam.

Take fome large full-grown green goofeberries, but not too ripe; cut them in half, take out the feeds; put them in a pan of cold fpring water, lay fome vine-leaves at the bottom, then fome goofeberries, then vine-leaves, till all the fruit is in the pan; cover it very clofe that no fteam can evaporate, and fet them on a very flow fire. When they are fcalding hot, take them off; then fet them on again, and then take them off; they muft be done fo till they are of a good green; lay them on a fieve to drain, beat them in a marble mortar with their weight in fugar; then take a quart of water, and a quart of goofeberries, boil them to a mafh, fqueeze them; to every pint of this liquor, put a pound of fine loaf-fugar, boil and fkim it; then put in the green goofeberries, let them boil till they are thick and clear, and of a good green. *Mafon*, 424.

To preferve Goofeberries whole without ftoning.

Take the largeft preferving goofeberries, and pick off the black eye, but not the ftalk, then fet them over the fire in a pot of water to fcald, cover them very clofe, but not boil or break, and when they are tender, take them up into cold water; then take a pound and an half of double-refined fugar to a pound of goofeberries, and clarify the fugar with water, a pint to a pound of fugar, and when your fyrup is cold, put the goofeberries fingle in your preferving pan, put the fyrup to them, and fet them on a gentle fire; let them boil, but not too faft, left they break; and when they have boiled, and you per-cieve that the fugar has entered them, take them off, cover them with white paper, and fet them by till the next day. Then take them out of the fyrup, and boil the fugar till it begins to be ropy; fkim it, and put it to them again, then fet them on a gentle fire, and let them fimmer gently till you per-ceive the fyrup will rope; then take them off, fet them by till they are cold, cover them with paper; then boil fome goofeberries in fair water, and when the liquor is ftrong enough, ftrain it out. Let it ftand to fettle, and to every pint take a

pound

pound of double-refined fugar, then make a jelly of it, put the goofeberries in glaffes when they are cold; cover them with the jelly the next day, paper them wet, and then half dry the paper that goes in the infide, it clofes down better, and then white paper over the glafs, Set in your ftove, or a dry place. *Glaffe*, 317.

To preferve Apricots.

Peel ripe apricots, flice them, and boil to a marmalade, with a drop of water; reduce it pretty thick on the fire, mix a quarter of a pound of the marmalade to a pound of fugar made candy height, and work it well together when it begins to cool, *Clermont*, 549.

To preferve green Apricots.

Gather your apricots before the ftones are hard, put them into a pan of hard water, with plenty of vine-leaves, fet them over a flow fire till they are quite yellow, then take them out, and rub them with flannel and falt to take of the lint; put them into the pan to the fame water and leaves, cover them clofe, fet them a great diftance from the fire till they are a fine light green, then take them carefully up; pick out all the bad-coloured and broken ones; boil the beft gently for two or three times in a thin fyrup, let them be quite cold every time. When they look plump and clear, make a fyrup of double-refined fugar, but not too thick; give your apricots a gentle boil in it, then put them into pots or glaffes; dip paper in brandy, lay it over them, and keep them for ufe; then take out all the broken and bad-coloured ones and boil them in the firft fyrup for tarts. *Raffald*, 218.

Syrup of Quinces.

Grate your quinces, and pafs their pulp through a cloth to extract the juice; fet their juices in the fun to fettle, or before the fire, and by that means clarify it. For every four ounces of this juice, take a pound of fugar boiled brown. If the putting in the juice of the quinces fhould check the boiling of the fugar too much, give the fyrup fome boiling till it becomes pearled; then take it off the fire, and, when cold, put it into the bottles. *Cole*, 326.

To preferve Almonds dry.

Take a pound of Jordan almonds, half a pound of double-refined fugar (one half of the almonds blanched, the other half unblanched) beat the white of an egg very well, pour it on the almonds, and wet them well with it; then boil the fugar, dip in the almonds, ftir them all together that the fugar may hang well on them, then lay them on plates; put them in the

OVEN

oven after the bread is drawn, let them ftay all night, and they will keep the year round. *Mafon* 410.

To preferve Damafcenes.

Pick the damafcenes off the ftalks, and prick them with a pin; then put them into a deep pot, and with them half their weight of pounded loaf fugar; fet them in a moderate oven till they are foft, then take them off and give the fyrup a boil, and pour it upon them. Having done fo two or three times, take them carefully out, and put them into the jars you intend to keep them in; then pour over them rendered mutton fuet, tie a bladder over them, and keep them for ufe in a very cool place. *Cole*, 327.

A conferve of Cherries.

Stone your cherries, and boil them a moment; fift them, and reduce the juice on a flow fire till it comes to a pretty thick marmalade; add the proportion of a quarter of a pound to a pound of fugar. *Clermont*, 550.

Conferve of red Rofes, or any other flower.

Take rofe-buds, or any other flowers, and pick them; cut off the white part from the red, and put the red flowers and fift them through a fieve, to take out the feeds; then weigh them, and to every pound of flowers take two pounds and an half of loaf-fugar; beat the flowers pretty fine in a ftone mortar, then by degrees put the fugar to them, and beat it very well till it is well incorporated together; then put it into gallipots, tie it over with paper, and over that a leather, and it will keep feven years. *Glaffe*, 315.

To preferve Strawberries.

On a dry day, gather the fineft fcarlet ftrawberries, with their ftalks on, before they are too ripe. Lay them feparately on a china difh, beat and fift twice their weight of double-refined fugar, and ftrew it over them. Then take a few ripe fcarlet ftraw berries, crufh them, and put them into a jar, with their weight of double-refined fugar beat fmall. Cover them clofe, and let them ftand in a kettle of boiling water till they are foft, and the fyrup is come out of them. Then ftrain them through a muflin rag into a toffing-pan, boil and fkim it well, and when it is cold, put in your whole ftrawberries, and fet them over the fire fire till they are milk warm; then take them off, and let them ftand till they are quite cold; then fet them on again, and make them a little hotter, and repeat the fame till they look clear; but be careful not to let them boil, as that will bring off their ftalks. When the ftrawberries are cold, put them into jelly-glaffes, with the ftalk downwards, and

fill

fill up your glaſſes with the ſyrup. Put over them papers dipped in brandy, and tie them down cloſe. *Farley*, 399.

To preſerve Red Currants in bunches.

Having ſtoned your currants, tie ſix or ſeven bunches together with a thread to a piece of ſplit deal, about the length of your finger; put double-refined ſugar, equal in weight to your currants, into your preſerving pan, with a little water, and boil it till the ſugar flies; then put the currants in, and juſt give them a boil up, and cover them till next day; then take them out, and either dry them or put them in glaſſes, with the ſyrup boiled up with a little of the juice of red currants; put brandy-paper over them, and tie them cloſe down with another paper, and ſet them in a dry place. *Raffald*, 214.

Another way.

Stone your currants, tie the bunches to bits of ſticks, ſix or ſeven together; allow the weight of the currants in ſugar, which make into a ſyrup; boil it high, put in the currants, give them a boil, ſet them by; the next day take them out. When the ſyrup boils, put them in again, give them a boil or two, and take them out. Boil the ſyrup as much as is neceſſary. When cold, put it to the currants in glaſſes. Cover with brandy-paper. *Maſon*, 421.

Currants preſerved in Jelly.

Clip your currants from the ſtalks, cut off the black top, and ſtone them. To every pound of fruit, add two pounds of ſugar, and boil it till it blows very ſtrong. Put in the currants and let them boil. Take them from the fire, let them ſtand to ſettle, then let them boil again. Put in a pint of currant jelly, let it all ſimmer a little, then take it from the fire. Let it ſettle a little, ſkim it. When cold, put it into glaſſes. Take care to diſperſe the currants equally. *Cole*, 328.

To preſerve Cherries with the leaves and ſtalks green.

Dip the ſtalks and leaves in the beſt vinegar when it is boiling hot, ſtick the ſprig upright in a ſieve till they are dry. In the mean time boil ſome double-refined ſugar to ſyrup, and dip the cherries, ſtalks, and leaves, in the ſyrup, and juſt let them ſcald; lay them on a ſieve, and boil the ſugar to a candy height, then dip the cherries, ſtalks, leaves, and all; then ſtick the branches and ſieves, and dry them as you do other ſweatmeats. They look very pretty at candle light in a deſert. *Glaſſe*, 312.

Conſerve of Apricots.

Peel ripe apricots, ſlice them, and boil to a marmalade, with a drop of water; reduce it pretty thick on the fire, mix a quarter of a pound of the marmalade to a pound of ſugar properly prepared, and work it well together when it begins to cool.

Peaches

Peaches and nectarines are done after the fame manner. *Clermont*, 549.

To preferve Currants fo Tarts.

Put a pound of fugar into a preferving-pan, for every pound and a quarter of currants, with a fufficient quantity of juice of currants to diffolve the fugar. When it boils, fkim it, and put in your currants, and boil them till they are very clear. Put them into a jar, cover them with brandy-paper, and keep them in a dry place. *Cole*, 329.

To preferve Rafpberries.

If you intend to preferve the red fort of rafpberries, gather them on a dry day, when they are juft turning red, with the ftalks on about an inch long. Lay them fingly on a difh, beat and fift their weight of double-refined fugar, and ftrew it over them. To every quart of rafpberries take a quart of red currant jelly juice, and put to it its weight of double refined fugar. Boil and fkim it well, then put in your rafpberries, and give them a fcald. Take them off, and let them ftand for two hours; then fet them on again, and make them a little hotter; proceed in this manner two or three times till they look clear; but take care to prevent their boiling, as that will occafion the ftalks to come off. When they are tolerably cool, put them into jelly glaffes with the ftalks downwards. White rafpberries may be preferved in the fame manner, only ufing white currant jelly inftead of red. *Farley*, 332.

To preferve Grapes.

Take fome clofe bunches of red or white grapes, before they are too ripe, and put them them into a jar, with a quarter of a pound of fugar candy, and fill the jar with brandy. Tie it clofe, and fet them in a dry place.

Morel cherries may be done in the fame manner. *Cole*, 329.

To preferve Golden Pippins.

Pare and flice your pippins, and boil them in fome water to a mafh, run the liquor through a jelly bag; put two pounds of loaf-fugar into a pan, with almoft one pint of water; boil and fkim it; put in twelve pippins, pared and cored with a fcoop, and the peel of an orange cut thin; let them boil faft till the fyrup is thick, taking them off when they appear to part, putting them on the fire again when they have ftood a little time; then put in a pint of the pippin juice, boil them faft till they are clear, then take them out; boil the fyrup as much more as is neceffary, with the juice of a lemon. The orange-peel muft be firft put into water for a day, then boiled, to take out the bitternefs. *Mafon*, 413.

To preserve Cucumbers.

You may take small cucumbers and large ones that will cut into quarters, (let them be as green and as free from seed as you can get them) put them into a strong salt and water, in a narrow-mouthed jar, with a cabbage-leaf to keep them down; tie a paper over them, set them in a warm place till they are yellow, wash them out, and set them over the fire in fresh water; with a little salt in, and a fresh cabbage leaf over them; cover the pan very close, but take care they do not boil; if they are not of a fine green, change your water, which will help them; then make them hot, and cover them as before. When they are of a good green, take them off the fire, let them stand till they are cold, then cut the large ones in quarters, take out the seeds and soft part; then put them in cold water, and let them stand two days, but change the water twice each day to take out the salt; take a pound of single refined sugar, and half a pint of water, set it over the fire. When you have skimmed it clear, put in the rind of a lemon, and one ounce of ginger, with the outside scraped off. When your syrup is pretty thick, take it off, and when it is cold, wipe the cucumbers dry, and put them in; boil the syrup once in two or three days for three weeks, and strengthen the syrup, if required, for the greatest danger of spoiling them is at first. The syrup is to be quite cold when you put it to your cucumbers. *Raffald*, 215.

To preserve Walnuts white.

Pare your walnuts till only the white appears, and be careful in doing them that they do not turn black, and as fast as you do them throw them into salt and water, and let them lie till your sugar is ready. Take three pounds of good loaf sugar, put it into your preserving-pan, set it over a charcoal fire, and put as much water as will just wet the sugar. Let it boil; then have ready ten or twelve whites of eggs strained and beat up to a froth; cover your sugar with a froth as it boils, and skim it; then boil it, and skim it till it is as clear as chrystal, then throw in your walnuts; just give them a boil till they are tender, then take them out, and lay them in a dish to cool; when cool, put them in your preserving-pan, and when the sugar is as warm as milk, pour it over them. When quite cold, paper them down.

Thus clear your sugar for all preserves, apricots, peaches, gooseberries, currants, &c. *Glasse*, 318.

To preserve Walnuts black.

Take walnuts of the smaller kind, put them in salt and water, and change the water every day for nine days. Then put them in a sieve, and let them stand in the air till they begin to turn black. Then put them into a jug, pour boiling water over them, and let them stand till the next day. Then put them into a sieve

it

to drain, stick a clove in each end of your walnut, put them into a pan of boiling water, and let them boil five minutes. Then take them up, make a thin syrup, and scald them in it three or four times a day, till your walnuts are black and bright. Then make a thick syrup with a few cloves, and a little ginger cut in slices. Skim it well, pour in your walnuts, boil them five or six minutes, and then put them into your jars. Lay brandy paper over them, and tie them down close with a bladder. They will eat better the second year after their keeping than in the first, as their bitterness goes off with time. *Farley*, 335.

To preserve Walnuts green.

Gather your walnuts when they are not much larger than a good nutmeg, wipe them very clean, and lay them in strong salt and water twenty-four hours; then take them out, and wipe them very clean; have ready a stewpan of boiling water, throw them in, let them boil a minute; and take them out; lay them on a coarse cloth, and boil your sugar as directed for the white walnuts; then just give your walnuts a scald in the sugar, take them up, and lay them to cool. Put them in your preserving-pot, and pour on your syrup. *Cole*, 331.

To preserve Barberries for Tarts.

Take female barberries, and add to them their weight in sugar, put them into a jar, and set them in a kettle of boiling water till the sugar is melted, and the barberries are become quite soft; the next day put them into a preserving-pan, and boil them a quarter of an hour; then put them into jars, and keep them in a place that is dry and cool. *Cole*, 331.

To preserve Fruit green.

Take pippins, pears, plums, apricots, or peaches, while they are green; put them in a preserving-pan, cover them with vine leaves, and then with clear spring-water; put on the cover of the pan, set them over a very clear fire; when they begin to simmer, take them off the fire, and with the slice carefully take them out; peel and preserve them as other fruit. *Mason*, 441.

To preserve Oranges whole.

Get the best Bermuda or Seville oranges, pare them very thin with a penknife, and lay your oranges in water three or four days, shifting them every day; then put them in a kettle with fair water, and put a board on them to keep them down in the water, and have a skillet on the fire with water, that may be ready to supply the kettle with boiling water as it wastes; it must be filled up three or four times while the oranges are doing, for they will take seven or eight hours boiling; they must be boiled till a white straw will run through them, then take them up and scoop the seeds out of them very carefully, by making a little hole in the top; then weigh them, and to
U   every

every pound of oranges put a pound and three quarters of double refined fugar, beat well, and fifted through a clean lawn fieve; fill your oranges with fugar, and ftrew fome on them. Let them lie a little while, and make your jelly thus :—take two dozen pippins of John-apples and flice them into water, and when they are boiled tender, ftrain the liquor from the pulp, and to every pound of oranges you muft have a pint and an half of this liquor, and put to it three quarters of the fugar you left in filling the oranges; fet it on the fire, and let it boil; fkim it well, and put it in a clean earthen pan till it is cold, then put it in your fkillet; put in your oranges; with a fmall bodkin job your oranges as they are boiling, to let the fyrup into them; ftrew on the reft of your fugar while they are boiling, and when they look clear, take them up, and put them in your glaffes; put one in a glafs juft fit for them, and boil the fyrup till it is almoft a jelly, then fill up your glaffes. When they are cold paper them up and keep them in a dry place. *Glaffe*, 313.

To preferve Oranges carved.

Get fome fine Seville oranges, cut the rinds with a pen-knife in what form you pleafe, draw out the part of your peel as you cut them, and put them into falt and hard water; let them ftand for three days to take out the bitter, then boil them an hour in a large faucepan of frefh water, with falt in it, but do not cover them, as it will fpoil the colour; then take them out of the falt and water, and boil them ten minutes in a thin fyrup for four or five days together; then put them into a deep jar, let them ftand two months, and then make a thick fyrup, and juft give them a boil in it; let them ftand till the next day, then put them in your jar with brandy-papers over; tie them down with a bladder, and keep them for ufe.

N. B. You may preferve whole oranges, without carving, the fame way, only do not let them boil fo long, and keep them in a very thin fyrup at firft, or it will make them fhrink and wither. Always obferve to put falt in the water for either oranges preferved, or any kind of orange chips. *Raffald*, 232.

To preferve Morel Cherries.

Gather your cherries when they are full ripe, take off the ftalks, and prick them with a pin. To every pound of cherries, put a pound and an half of loaf-fugar. Beat part of your fugar, ftrew it over them, and let them ftand all night. Diffolve the reft of your fugar in half a pint of the juice of currants, fet it over a flow fire, and put in the cherries with the fugar, and give them a gentle fcald; then take them carefully out, boil your fyrup till it is thick, and pour it upon your cherries. *Farley*, 338.

To

To preserve Green-gage Plums.

Gather some of your finest plums just before they are ripe, and put them into a pan with a layer of vine leaves under them, then put a layer of vine leaves over them, and a layer of plums on them, and proceed in the same manner till your pan is almost full, then fill it with water, and set them on a slow fire. When they are hot, and the skins begin to rise, take them off, take the skins carefully off, and put them on a sieve as you do them; then lay them in the same water with a layer of leaves as before; cover them close, that no steam may get out, and hang them a considerable distance from the fire till they appear green, which will be five or six hours, or longer; then take them carefully up, lay them on a hair sieve to drain, make a good syrup, boil them gently in it twice a day for two days, then take them out and put them in a fine clean syrup; cover them with brandy-paper, and keep them for use. *Cole*, 333.

To preserve white Citrons.

Having cut some white citrons into pieces, put them into salt and water, and let them remain there four or five hours, then take them out, and wash them in clean water; boil them till they are tender, drain them, and cover them with clarified sugar; after letting them stand twenty-four hours, drain the syrup and boil it smooth. When cold, put in the citrons, and let them stand till the next day; then boil the syrup quite smooth, and pour it over the citrons; boil all together the next day, and put them into a pot to be candied, or into jellies. *Cole*, 333.

To preserve Lemons.

Prepare your lemons very thin, then make a round hole on the top, of the size of a shilling, and take out all the pulps and skins. Rub them with salt, and put them in spring water as you do them, which will prevent their turning black. Let them lie in it five or six days, and then boil them in fresh salt and water fifteen minutes. Have ready made a thin syrup, of a quart of water and a pound of loaf sugar. Boil them in it for five minutes once a day, for four or five days, and then put them in a large jar. Let them stand for six or eight weeks, and it will make them look clear and plump; then take them out of that syrup, or they will mould. Make a syrup of fine sugar, put as much water to it as will dissolve it, boil it and skim it; then put in your lemons and boil them gently till they are clear. Put them into a jar, with brandy-paper over them, and tie them down close. *Farley*, 338.

To preserve green Codlings to keep all the year.

Gather your codlings when they are about the size of a

U 2

walnut,

walnut, and let the ſtalk and a leaf or two remain on each. Put ſome vine-leaves into a braſs pan of ſpring water, and cover them with a layer of codlings, then another of vine-leaves, and proceed in the ſame manner till the pan is full. Cover it cloſe to keep the ſteam in, and ſet it on a ſlow fire. When they become ſoft, take off the ſkins with a penknife, then put them in the ſame water with the vine-leaves; it muſt be quite cold, or it perhaps may crack them. Put a little roach allum, and ſet them over a very ſlow fire till they are green, (which will be in about three or four hours) then take them out, and lay them on a ſieve to drain. Make a good ſyrup, and give them a gentle boil once a day for three days, then put them into ſmall jars. Put brandy-paper over them, and keep them for uſe. *Raffald*, 217.

To preſerve Eringo roots.

Parboil ſome eringo roots till they are tender, peel them, waſh them, and dry them with a cloth, and cover them with clarified ſugar; boil them gently till they are clear, and the ſyrup ſeems to be thickiſh; put them up when half cold. *Cole*, 334.

Marmalade of Oranges.

This is uſually made with China oranges; cut each into quarters, and ſqueeze out the juice; take off the hard parts at both ends, and boil in water till they are quite tender; ſqueeze them to extract the water, and pound them in the water to a marmalade to ſift, mix it with an equal weight of raw ſugar, and boil it till it turns to ſyrup; the proportions are, for keeping, two pounds of ſugar to one pound of marmalade. *Clermont*, 579.

Red Quince Marmalade.

Take quinces that are full ripe, pare them, cut them in quarters, and core them; put them in a ſaucepan, cover them with the parings, fill the ſaucepan almoſt full of ſpring water, cover it cloſe, and ſtew them gently till they are quite ſoft, and of a deep pink colour; then pick out the quince from the parings, and beat them to a pulp in a mortar; take their weight in loaf-ſugar, put in as much of the water they were boiled in as will diſſolve it, and boil and ſkim it well; put in your quinces, and boil them gently three quarters of an hour; keep ſtirring them all the time, or it will ſtick to the pan and burn; put it into flat pots, and when cold, tie it down cloſe. *Glaſſe*, 313.

White Quince Marmalade.

To a pound and an half of quinces take a pound of double refined ſugar, make it into a ſyrup, boil it high; pare and ſlice the fruit, and boil it quick. When it begins to look clear, pour in half a pint of juice of quince, or, if quinces are ſcarce,
pippins;

pippins; boil it till thick, take off the fcum with a paper. To make a juice, pare the quinces, or pippins, cut them from the core, beat them in a ftone mortar, ftrain the juice through a thin cloth; to every half pint, put more than a pound of fugar; let it ftand at leaft four hours before it is ufed. *Mafor*, 438.

Apricot Marmalade.

Take ripe apricots and boil them in the fyrup till they will mafh, then beat them in a marble mortar; add half their weight of fugar, and as much water as will diffolve it; boil and fkim it well, boil them till they look clear, and the fyrup like a fine jelly, then put them into your fweetmeat glaffes, and keep them for ufe. *Cole*, 335.

Tranfparent Marmalade.

Pick out fome very pale Seville oranges, cut them in quarters, take out the pulp, and put it into a bafon, pick the fkins and feeds out, put the peels in a little falt and water, let them ftand all night; then boil them in a good quantity of fpring water till they are tender, then cut them in very thin flices, and put them to the pulp; to every pound of marmalade put a pound and an half of double refined fugar beat fine; boil them together gently for twenty minutes. If it is not clear and tranf-parent, boil it five or fix minutes longer; keep ftirring it gently all the time, and take care you do not break the flices. When it is cold, put it into jelly or fweetmeat glaffes; tie them down with brandy-papers over them. They are pretty for a defert of any kind, *Raffald*, 224.

Apple Marmalade.

Scald fome apples in water, and when tender, drain them through a fieve; put three quarters of a pound of fugar to a pound of apples; put them into the preferving pan, and let them fimmer over a gentle fire, keep fkimming them all the time. When they are of a proper thicknefs, put them into pots or glaffes. *Cole*, 336.

SYLLABUBS, BLANC-MANGE, FLUMMERY, ORNAMENTS, &c.

A whipt Syllabub.

RUB a lump of sugar on the outside of a lemon, put it into a pint of thin cream, and sweeten it to your taste; then put in the juice of a lemon and a glass of Madeira wine, or French brandy; mill it to a froth with a chocolate mill, and take it off as it rises, and lay it in a hair sieve. Then fill one half of your posset glasses a little more than half full, with white wine, and the other half of your glasses a little more than half full with red wine; then lay on your froth as high as you can, but take care that it be well drained on your sieve, otherwise it will mix with your wine, and your syllabub will be spoiled. *Raffald,* 208. *Farley,* 327.

Another way.

Take a pint of cream, the whites of two eggs; a pint of white wine, and the juice and rind of a lemon; grate the rind into the wine, and then put in the cream; sweeten them, and whisk them up with a clean whisk. *Cole,* 336.

A Lemon Syllabub.

Take a pint of cream, a pint of white wine, the rind of two lemons grated, and the juice; sugar it to the taste; let it stand some time; mill or whip it; lay the froth on a sieve; put the remainder into glasses; lay on the froth; make them the day before they are wanted.

If they are to taste very strong of the lemon, put the juice of six lemons, and near a pound of sugar; they will keep four or five days. *Mason,* 448.

Solid Syllabub.

To a quart of rich cream, put a pint of white wine, the juice of two lemons, and the rind of one grated; sweeten it to your taste. Whip it up well, and take off the froth as it rises; put it upon a hair sieve, and let it stand in a cool place till the next day. More than half fill your glasses with the thin, and then heap up the froth as high as you can; the bottom will look clear, and keep for four or five days. *Cole,* 337.

Syllabub under the Cow.

Put into a punch-bowl a pint of cider, and a bottle of strong beer; grate in a small nutmeg, and sweeten it to your taste; then milk from the cow as much milk as will make a strong froth. Then let it stand an hour; strew over it a few currants

well

weil wafhed, picked, and plumped before the fire, and it will be fit for fervice. *Farley*, 327.

Everlafting Syllabub.

Take five half pints of thick cream, half a pint of rhenifh, half a pint of fack, and the juice of two large Seville oranges ; grate in juft the yellow rind of three lemons, and a pound of double-refined fugar well beat and fifted. Mix all together with a fpoonful of orange-flower water ; beat it well with a whifk half an hour, then with a fpoon take it off, and lay it on a fieve to drain ; then fill your glaffes. Thefe will keep above a week, and are better made the day before. The beft way to whip fyllabub is,—have a fine large chocalate mill, which you muft keep on purpofe, and a large deep bowl to mill them in ; it is quicker done, and the froth is ftronger. For the thin that is left at the bottom, have ready fome calf's foot jelly, boiled and clarified. There muft be nothing but the calf's foot boiled to a hard jelly. When cold, take off the fat, clear it with the whites of eggs, run it through a flannel bag, and mix it with the clear which you faved of the fyllabub. Sweeten it to your palate and, give it a boil ; then pour it into bafons, or what you pleafe. When cold, turn it out, and it is as a fine flummery. *Glaffe*, 293.

Blanc-mange with Ifing-glafs.

Put an ounce of picked ifing-glafs to a pint of water ; put to it a bit of cinnamon, and boil it till the ifing-glafs is melted ; put to it three quarters of a pint of cream, two ounces of fweet almonds, and fix bitter almonds, blancned and beaten, and a bit of lemon-peel ; fweeten it, ftir it over the fire, and let it boil ; ftrain it, ftir it till is cool, fquecze in the juice of a lemon, and put it into what moulds you pleafe. Turn it out, garnifh with currant-jelly and jam ; or marmalade, quinces, &c.

If you choofe to have your *blanc-mange* of a green colour, put in as much juice of fpinach as will be neceffary for that pur-pofe, and a fpoonful of brandy ; but it fhould not then retain the name of *blanc-mange*, (white food,) but *verde-mange*, (green food). If you would have it yellow, diffolve a little faffron in it ; you fhould then call it *jaune-mange* Or you may make it red, by putting a bit of cochineal into a little brandy, let it ftand half an hour, and ftrain it through a bit of cloth. It is then intitled to the appellation of *rouge-mange*.

Always wet the mould before you put in the blanc-mange. It may be ornamented, when turned out, by fticking about it blanched almonds fliced, or citron according to fancy. *Cole*, 338.

Clear Blanc-mange.

Take a quart of ftrong calf's foot jelly, fkim off the fat, and

ftrain

ftrain it, beat the whites of four eggs, and put it into a jelly-bag, and run it through feveral times till it is clear. Beat one ounce of fweet almonds, and one of bitter, to a pafte, with a fpoonful of rofe-water fqueezed through a cloth; then mix it with the jelly, and three fpoonfuls of very good cream; fet it over the fire again, and keep ftirring it till it is almoft boiling; then pour it into a bowl, and ftir very often till it is almoft cold; then wet your moulds and fill them. *Raffald*, 196.

Blanc-mange, with a preferved Orange.

Fill your orange with blanc-mange; and, when cold, ftick in it long flips of citron, like leaves; pour blanc-mange in the difh; when cold, fet the orange in the middle. Garnifh with preferved or dried fruits.

Or, you may pour blanc-mange into a mould like a Turk's cap, lay round it jelly a little broken; put a fprig of myrtle, or fmall preferved orange on the top. *Cole*, 338.

Flummery.

Take an ounce of bitter, and the fame quantity of fweet almonds, put them into a bafon, and pour over them fome boiling water to make the fkins come off. Then ftrip off the fkins, and throw the kernels into cold water; take them out, and beat them in a marble mortar, with a little rofe-water to keep them from oiling; and when they are beat, put them into a pint of calf's-feet ftock; fet it over the fire, and fweeten it to your tafte with loaf-fugar. As foon as it boils, ftrain it through a piece of muflin or gauze; and, when it is a little cold, put it into a pint of thick cream, and keep ftirring it often till it grows thick and cold. Wet your moulds in cold water, and pour in the flummery. Let them ftand about fix hours before you turn them out; and, if you make your flummery ftiff, and wet your moulds, it will turn out without putting them into warm water, which will be a great advantage to the look of the figures, as warm water gives a dulnefs to the flummery. *Farley*, 324.

Another way.

Boil an ounce of ifing-glafs in a little water, till it is melted; pour to it a pint of cream, a bit of lemon-peel, a little brandy, and fugar to the tafte; boil and ftrain it, put it into a mould, turn it out. *Mafon*, 451.

Hartfhorn Flummery.

Take half a pound of the fhavings of hartfhorn, boil them in three pints of water till it comes to a pint, then ftrain it through a fieve into a bafon, and fet it by to cool; then fet it over the fire, let it juft melt, and put to it half a pint of thick cream fcalded and grown cool again, a quarter of a pint of white wine, and two fpoonfuls of orange-flower water; fweeten it with fugar,

gar, and beat it for an hour and an half, or it will neither mix well nor look well; dip your cups in water before you put in the flummery, or it will not turn out well. It is beſt when it ſtands a day or two before you turn it out. When you ſerve it up, turn it out of the cups, and ſtick blanched almonds, cut in long narrow bits on the top. You may eat them either with wine or with cream. *Glaſſe*, 296.

Welch Flummery.

Put a little iſing-glaſs to a quart of ſtiff hartſhorn jelly; add to it a pint of cream, a little brandy, and ſome lemon-juice and ſugar; boil this till it is thick, then ſtrain it. You may, if you pleaſe, add three ounces of almonds, blanched and beaten; about ten bitter ones. *Cole*, 339.

Yellow Flummery.

Beat and open two ounces of iſinglaſs, put it into a bowl, and over it a pint of boiling water; cover it up till it is almoſt cold; then add a pint of white wine, the rind of one lemon, the juice of two lemons, the yolks of eight eggs, well beat, and ſweeten it to your taſte, then put it into a toſſing-pan, and continue ſtirring it. When it boils, ſtrain it; and, when almoſt cold, put it into moulds or cups. *Cole*, 340.

Solomon's Temple in Flummery.

Having made a quart of ſtiff flummery, divide it into three parts; make one part of a pretty thick colour, with a little co-chineal bruiſed fine, and ſteeped in French brandy; ſcrape one ounce of chocolate very fine, diſſolve it in a little ſtrong coffee, and mix it with another part of your flummery to make it a light ſtone-colour. The laſt part muſt be white. Then wet your temple mould, and fix it in a pot to ſtand even; then fill the top of the temple with red flummery, for the ſteps, and the four points with white; then fill it up with chocolate-flummery. Let it ſtand till the next day, then looſen it round with a pin, and ſhake it looſe very gently, but do not dip your mould in warm water, it will take off the gloſs, and ſpoil the colour. When you turn it out, ſtick a ſmall ſprig, or flower-ſtalk, down from the top of every point, it will ſtrengthen them, and make them look pretty. Lay round it rock candy ſweetmeats. It is proper for a corner diſh for a large table. *Raffald*, 204.

Oatmeal Flummery.

Put ſome oatmeal into a broad deep pan, then cover it with water; ſtir it together, and let it ſtand twelve hours; then pour off that water clear, and put on a good deal of freſh water; ſhift it again in twelve hours, and ſo on in twelve more; then pour off the water clear, and ſtrain the oatmeal through a coarſe hair ſieve, and pour it into a ſauce-pan, keeping it ſtirring all the

time

time with a stick till it boils, and is very thick; then pour it
into dishes. When cold, turn it into plates, and eat it with
what you please, either wine and sugar, or beer and sugar, or
milk. It eats very well with cider and sugar. *Cole*, 340.

French Flummery.

Take a quart of cream, and half an ounce of isinglass, beat it
fine, and stir it into the cream. Let it boil softly over a slow
fire a quarter of an hour, keep it stirring all the time; then
take it off, sweeten it to your palate, and put in a spoonful of
rose-water, and a spoonful of orange-flower water; strain it,
and pour it into a glass or bason, or what you please; and, when
it is cold, turn it out. It makes a fine side dish. You may eat
it with cream, or wine, or what you please. Lay round it
baked pears. It looks very pretty, and eats fine. *Glasse*, 298,
Farley, 324.

To make Colouring for Flummery or Jellies.

Bruise two pennyworth of cochineal with a knife, and put it
into half a tea-cupful of brandy; when it has stood a quarter of
an hour, filter it through a fine cloth, and put in as much as
will make the flummery, or jelly, of a fine pink colour. If
yellow, tie a little saffron in a rag, and dissolve it in cold water.
If green, boil some spinach, take off the froth, and mix it with
the jelly. If white, put in some cream. *Cole*, 341.

Chap. XXVI.—ORNAMENTS FOR GRAND ENTERTAINMENTS.

A Dish of Snow.

PUT twelve large apples into cold water, set them over a slow fire, and when they are soft, pour them upon a hair sieve. Take of the skins, and put the pulp into a bason; then beat the whites of twelve eggs to a very strong froth, beat and sift half a pound of double-refined sugar, and strew it on the eggs. Then beat the pulp of your apples to a strong froth; then beat them all together till they are like a stiff snow; lay it upon a china dish, and heap it up as high as you can. Set round it green knots of paste, in imitation of Chinese rails, and stick a sprig of myrtle in the middle of the dish. *Mason*, 450. *Raffald*, 205. *Farley*, 352.

Moonshine.

Take the shapes of half a moon, and five or seven stars; wet them, and fill them with flummery; let them stand till they are cold, then turn them into a deep China dish, and pour lemon-cream round them, made thus:—Take a pint of spring-water, put it to the juice of three lemons, and the yellow rind of one lemon; the whites of five eggs, well beaten, and four ounces of loaf-sugar; then set it over a slow fire, and stir one way till it looks white and thick. If you let it boil it will curdle. Then strain it through a hair sieve, and let it stand till it is cold; beat the yolks of five eggs, mix them with your whites, set them over the fire, and keep stirring it till it is almost ready to boil, then pour it into a bason. When it is cold, pour it among your moon and stars. Garnish with flowers. It is a proper dish for a second course, either for dinner or supper. *Raffald*, 201.

Floating Island of Apples.

Bake or scald eight or nine large apples; when cold, pare them, and pulp them through a sieve; beat this up with fine sugar; put to it the whites of four or five eggs that have been beaten, with a little rose-water; mix it a little at a time, beat it till it is light; heap it on a rich cold custard, or on jelly. *Mason*, 450.

Floating Island of Chocolate.

Take the whites of two eggs, and mix them up with two ounces of chocolate scraped; pile it on a thin custard or jelly. *Cole*, 342.

A Desert Island.

Form a lump of paste into a rock three inches broad at the top, then colour it, and set it in the middle of a deep China dish.

difh. Set a caft figure on it, with a crown on its head, and a knot of rock-candy at its feet; then make a roll of pafte an inch thick, and ftick it on the inner edge of the difh, two parts round. Cut eight pieces of eringo roots, about three inches long, and fix them upright to the roll of pafte on the edge. Make gravel walks of fhot comfits round the difh, and fet fmall figures in them. Roll out fome pafte, and cut it open like Chinefe rails. Bake it, and fix it on either fide of the gravel walks with gum, and form an entrance where the Chinefe rails are, with two pieces of eringo root, for pillars. *Farley*, 351.

A Floating Ifland.

Take a foup difh according to the fize and quantity you in-tend to make, but a pretty deep glafs is beft, and fet it on a China difh; take a quart of thick cream, make it pretty fweet with fine fugar, pour in a gill of fack, grate the yellow rind of a lemon in, and mill the cream till it is all of a thick froth; then carefully pour the thin from the froth into a difh; take a French roll, or as many as you want, cut it as thin as you can, lay a layer of that as light as poffible on the cream, then a layer of currant jelly, then a very thin layer of roll, and then hartf-horn-jelly, then French roll, and over that whip your froth which you faved off the cream very well milled up, and lay at the top as high as you can heap it; and as for the rim of the difh, fet it round with fruit or fweet-meats according to your fancy. This looks very pretty in the middle of a table, with candles round it, and you may make it of as many different co-lours as you fancy, and according to what jellies, and jams, or fweet-meats you may have; or at the bottom of the difh you may put the thickeft cream you can get; but that is as you fancy. *Glaffe*, 300.

A Hedge-Hog.

Blanch two pounds of almonds, beat them well in a mortar, with a little canary and orange-flower water to keep them from oiling. Make them into ftiff-pafte, then beat in the yolks of twelve eggs, leave out five of the whites, put to it a pint of cream, fweetened with fugar; put in half a pound of fweet butter melted, fet it on a furnace or flow fire, and keep it con-ftantly ftirring till it is ftiff enough to be made into the form of an hedge-hog; then ftick it full of blanched almonds, flit and ftuck up like the briftles of an hedge-hog. Then put it into a difh; take a pint of cream, and the yolks of four eggs beat up; fweeten with fugar to your palate. Stir them together over a flow fire till it is quite hot; then pour it round the hedge-hog in a difh, and let it ftand till it is cold, and ferve it up. Or a rich calf's-foot jelly made clear and good, poured into the difh
round

round the hedge-hog; when it is cold, it looks pretty, and makes a neat dish. Or it looks handsome in the middle of a table for supper. *Cole*, 343.

A Fish-pond.

Fill your large fish-moulds, and fix small ones with flummery; take a China bowl, and put in half a pint of stiff clear calf's-foot jelly; let it stand till cold; then lay two of the small fishes on the jelly, the right side down. Put in half a pint more jelly, let it stand till cold, then lay in the four small fishes across one another, that, when you turn the bowl upside down, the heads and tails may be seen. Then almost fill your bowl with jelly, and let it stand till cold; then lay in the jelly four large fishes, and fill the bason quite full with jelly, and let it stand till the next day. When you want to use it, set your bowl to the brim in hot water for one minute; take care that you do not let the water go into the bason. Lay your plate on the top of the bason, and turn it upside down. If you want it for the middle, turn it out upon a salver. Be sure you make your jelly very still and clear. *Raffald*, 194.

Sack Posset.

GRATE three Naples biscuits to one quart of cream or
new milk; let it boil a little, sweeten it, grate some nutmeg. When a little cool, pour it high from a tea-pot to a pint
of sack a little warmed, and put it into a bason or deep dish.
Mason, 452.

Another way.

Beat the yolks and whites of fifteen eggs very well, and strain
them; then put three quarters of a pound of white sugar into
a pint of canary, and mix it with your eggs in a bason; set it
over a chafing-dish of coals, and keep continually stirring it till
it is scalding hot. In the mean time grate some nutmeg in a
quart of milk, and boil it, then pour it into your eggs and wine,
they being scalding hot. Hold your hand very high as you
pour it, and let somebody stir it all the time you are pouring in
the milk; then take it off the chafing-dish, set it before the
fire half an hour, and serve it up. *Glasse*, 160.

An Orange Posset.

Put the crumb of a penny loaf, grated very fine, into a pint
of water, or rather more; and half the peel of a Seville orange
grated, or sugar rubbed upon it to take out the essence; boil all
together till it looks thick and clear, then beat it very well.
Then take a pint of mountain wine, the juice of half a Seville
orange, three ounces of Jordan almonds, and one ounce of bitter, beat fine, with a little French brandy and sugar to your
taste; mix it well, and put it in your posset, and serve it up.
Cole, 344.

A lemon posset is made in the same manner.

Wine Posset.

Boil the crumb of a penny loaf in a quart of milk till it is
soft, then take it off the fire, and grate in half a nutmeg; put
in sugar to your taste; then put it in a China bowl, and put in
by degrees a pint of Lisbon wine. Serve it up with toast and
butter upon a plate. *Cole*, 345.

Ale Posset.

Put a little white bread into a pint of milk, and set it over
the fire; then put some nutmeg and sugar into a pint of ale,
warm it, and when your milk boils, pour it upon the ale. Let
it stand a few minutes to clear, and the curd will rise to the top.
Cole, 345.

Panada

Panada.

Put a blade of mace, a large piece of the crumb of bread, and a quart of water into a fauce-pan. Let it boil two minutes, then take out the bread, and bruife it very fine in a bafon. Mix as much water as you think it will require, pour away the reft, and fweeten it to your palate. Put in a piece of butter as big as a walnut, but do not put in any wine, as that will fpoil it. Grate in a little nutmeg. *Farley*, 429, from *Glaffe*, 243.

A fweet Panada.

Slice the crumb of a penny loaf very thin, and put it into a fauce-pan with a pint of water; boil it till it is very foft and looks clear; then put in a glafs of Madeira wine, grate in a little nutmeg, and put in a lump of butter the fize of a walnut, and fugar to your tafte; beat it exceedingly fine, then put it in a deep foup-difh, and ferve it up.

N. B. You may leave out the wine and fugar, and put in a little cream and falt, if you like it better. *Raffald*, 316.

A White-pot.

Take two quarts of milk, eight eggs, and half the whites, beat up with a little rofe water, a nutmeg, and a quarter of a pound of fugar; cut a penny loaf in very thin flices, and pour milk and eggs over. Put a little piece of butter on the top. Bake it half an hour in a flow oven. *Cole*, 345.

A Rice White-pot.

Boil a pound of rice in two quarts of milk till it is tender and thick. Beat it in a mortar with a quarter of a pound of fweet almonds blanched. Then boil two quarts of cream, with a few crumbs of white bread, and two or three blades of mace. Mix it well with eight eggs, and a little rofe-water, and fweeten to to your tafte. Cut fome candied orange or citron-peels thin, and lay it in. It muft be put into a flow oven. *Glaffe*, 158. *Mafon*, 453.

White Caudle.

Take two quarts of water, and mix with it four fpoonfuls of oatmeal, a blade or two of mace, and a piece of lemon-peel. Let it boil, and keep ftirring it often. Let it boil about a quarter of an hour, and be careful not to let it boil over; then ftrain it through a coarfe fieve. When you ufe it, fweeten it to your tafte, grate in a little nutmeg, and what wine you think proper; and, if it is not for a fick perfon, fqueeze in the juice of a lemon. *Glaffe*, 243. *Farley*, 429.

Brown Caudle.

Make your gruel as above, with fix fpoonfuls of oatmeal, and ftrain it; then add a quart of ale that is not bitter; boil it, then

fweeten

sweeten it to your palate, and add half a pint of white wine or brandy. When you do not put in white wine or brandy, let it be half ale. *Cole*, 346.

Salop.

Salop is sold at the chemists. Take a large tea-spoonful of the powder, and put it into a pint of boiling water, keep stirring it till it is a fine jelly, and add wine and sugar to your taste. *Cole*, 346.

Beef Tea.

Cut a pound of lean beef into very thin slices, and put it in a jar; pour a quart of boiling water over it, and cover it close that the steam may not get out; let it stand by the fire. It is strongly recommended by physicians for those of a weak constitution. It should be drank milk warm. *Cole*, 346.

White-wine Whey.

Put a pint of skimmed milk, and half a pint of white wine into a bason. Let it stand a few minutes, then pour over it a pint of boiling water. Let it stand a little and the curd will gather in a lump, and settle to the bottom. Then pour your whey into a China bowl, and put in a lump of sugar, a sprig of balm, or a slice of lemon. *Raffald*, 313.

Water Gruel.

To a pint of water, put a large spoonful of oatmeal; then stir it well together, and let it boil up three or four times, stirring it often. Do not let it boil over. Then strain it through a sieve, salt it to your palate, put in a good piece of fresh butter, brew it with a spoon till the butter is all melted, and it will be fine and smooth. *Cole*, 346.

Barley Gruel.

Put a quarter of a pound of pearl barley, and a stick of cinnamon, into two quarts of water, and let it boil till it is reduced to one quart; add a pint of red wine, and sugar to your taste. You may add two or three ounces of currants. *Cole*, 347.

Sago.

To three quarters of a pint of water, put a large spoonful of sago, stir it, and boil it softly till it is as thick as you would have it; then put in wine and sugar, with a little nutmeg to your palate. *Cole*, 347.

Rice Milk.

Boil half a pound of rice in a quart of water, with a little cinnamon; let it boil till the water is wasted, but take care it does not burn; then add three pints of milk, and the yolk of an egg beat up; keep it stirring. When it boils, take it up and sweeten it. *Mason*, 452.

Barley

Barley Water.

Put a quarter of a pound of pearl barley into two quarts of water, let it boil, fkim it very clean, boil half away, and ftrain it off. Sweeten to your palate, but not too fweet, and put in two fpoonfuls of white wine. Drink it a little warm. *Glaffe*, 245. *Farley*, 427.

Another way.

Boil two ounces of barley in two quarts of water till it looks white, and the barley grows foft, then ftrain the water from the barley, and add to it a little currant jelly or lemon.

N. B. You may put a pint more water to your barley, and boil it over again. *Raffald*, 314.

Capillaire.

Take fourteen pounds of loaf-fugar, three pounds of coarfe fugar, fix eggs beat in with the fhells, and three quarts of water; boil it up twice, fkim it well, then add to it a quarter of a pint of orange flower water; ftrain it through a jelly-bag, and put it into bottles. When cold, mix a fpoonful or two of this fyrup, as it is liked for fweetnefs, in a draught of warm or cold water. *Mafon*, 454.

Orgeat.

Take two pounds of almonds, thirty bitter, and beat them to a pafte; mix it with three quarts of water, and ftrain it through a fine cloth; add orange and lemon-juice, with fome of the peel; fweeten to your palate. *Cole*, 347.

Lemonade.

Take two Seville oranges and fix lemons, pare them very thin, fteep the parings four hours in two quarts of water; put the juice of fix oranges and twelve lemons upon twelve ounces of fine fugar; when the fugar is melted, put the water to it. Add a little orange-flower water, and more fugar, if neceffary. Pafs it through a bag till it is fine. *Cole*, 348.

Goofeberry Fool.

Set two quarts of goofeberries on the fire in about a quart of water. When they begin to fimmer, turn yellow, and begin to plump, throw them into a cullender to drain the water out; then with the back of a fpoon carefully fqueeze the pulp through a fieve into a difh; make them pretty fweet, and let them ftand till they are cold. In the mean time, take two quarts of milk, and the yolks of four eggs, beat up with a little grated nutmeg; ftir it foftly over a flow fire. When it begins to fimmer, take it off, and by degrees ftir it into the goofeberries. Let it ftand till it is cold, and ferve it up. If you make it with cream, you need not put any eggs in. *Glaffe*, 159. *Mafon*, 452.

X

To mull Wine.

Grate half a nutmeg into a pint of wine, and sweeten it to your taste with loaf-sugar; set it over the fire, and when it boils, take it off to cool; take the yolks of four eggs well beaten, add to them a little cold wine; then mix them carefully with your hot wine, a little at a time; then pour it backwards and forwards several times, till it looks fine and bright; then set it on the fire, and beat it a little at a time for several times, till it is quite hot, and pretty thick, and pour it backwards and forwards several times; then send it in chocolate-cups, and serve it up with dry toast cut in long narrow pieces. *Raffald*, 311.

Syrup of Orange peel.

Cut two ounces of Seville orange-peel very small, put it in a pint and a quarter of white wine; strain it off, and boil it up with two pounds of double-refined sugar. *Cole*, 348.

Syrup of Maidenhair.

This plant is said to grow in Cornwall, but what is used in England comes principally from abroad; it is said the best comes from Canada. The proportion is one ounce of the dried leaves infused in half a pint of boiling water; keep it on an ashes-fire from one day to another, sift it in a napkin, and mix it with a pound and a quarter of sugar; keep it in a warm place some time, then bottle it. Observe the same proportion for a greater quantity. *Clermont*, 589.

Syrups may be made of any kind of fruits, seeds, or plants, only observing to regulate the quantities of sugar according to the sharpness and flavours of each kind. *Clermont*, 590.

Raisin Wine.

PUT two hundred weight of raisins, stalks and all, into a large hogshead; fill it with water, let them steep a fortnight, stirring them every day; then pour off the liquor, and press the raisins. Put both liquors together in a nice clean vessel that will just hold it, for it must be full; let it stand till it has done hissing, or making the least noise, then stop it close, and let it stand six months. Peg it, and if you find it quite clear, rack it off in another vessel; stop it close, and let it stand three months longer; then bottle it, and when you use it, rack it off into a decanter. *Glasse*, 391. *Farley*, 301.

Another way.

Take three hundred and an half of Malaga raisins, sixty-six gallons of water, in a large tub with a false bottom; let them stand for twenty-two or twenty-three days; stirring them once, or twice a day; then draw them off into a clean hogshead, and let them work as long as they will, filling the hogshead full every day for five or six months; then rack the liquor into another cask, and put to it two gallons of brandy. *Mason*, 465.

Elder Wine.

Pick your elder-berries when they are full ripe, put them into a stone jar, and set them in the oven, or in a kettle of boiling water till the jar is hot through; then take them out, and strain them through a coarse sieve, wringing the berries, and put the juice into a clean kettle. To every quart of juice put a pound of fine Lisbon sugar, let it boil, and skim it well. When it is clear and fine, pour it into a jar. When cold, cover it close, and keep it till you make raisin wine; then, when you tun your wine, to every gallon of wine put half a pint of elder syrup. *Cole*, 349.

Elder flower Wine.

Take the flowers of elder, but carefully reject the stalks. To every quart of flowers, put a gallon of water, and three pounds of loaf sugar. Boil the water and sugar a quarter of an hour, then pour it on the flowers, and let it work three days. Then strain the wine through a hair sieve, and put it into a cask. To every ten gallons of wine, add an ounce of ising-glass dissolved in cider, and six whole eggs. Close it up, let it stand six months, and then bottle it. *Farley*, 367.

Grape Wine.

Put a gallon of grapes to a gallon of water; bruise the

grapes

grapes and let them stand a week without stirring, then draw, it off fine. Put to a gallon of the wine three pounds of sugar and then put in a vessel, but do not stop it till it has done hissing. *Mason*, 465.

Orange Wine.

Put twelve pounds of the best powder sugar, with the whites of eight or ten eggs well beaten, into six gallons of spring water, and boil it three quarters of an hour. When cold, put into it six spoonfuls of yeast, and the juice of twelve lemons; which being pared, must stand with two pounds of white sugar in a tankard, and in the morning skim off the top, and then put it into the water; then add the juice and rinds of fifty oranges, but not the white parts of the rinds, and let it work all together, two days and two nights; then add two quarts of Rhenish or white wine, and put it into your vessel. *Glasse*, 301.

Another way.

Put twenty-four pounds of lump-sugar to ten gallons of water, beat the whites of six eggs very well, and mix them when the water is cold; then boil it an hour, and skim it well; take four dozen large rough Seville oranges, pare them very thin, put them into a tub, and put the liquor on boiling hot; and, when you think it is cold enough, add to it three or four spoonfuls of new yeast, with the juice of the oranges, and half an ounce of cochineal beat fine, and boiled in a pint of water; stir it all together, and let work four days, then put it in the casks, and in six weeks after bottle it for use. *Raffald*, 318.

Red Currant wine.

Gather the currants on a fine dry day, when the fruit is full ripe; strip them, and squeeze out the juice; put a gallon of cold water and two spoonfuls of yeast to a gallon of the juice. When it has worked two days, strain it through a hair sieve. In the mean time, put an ounce of ising-glass to steep in cider, and to every gallon of liquor put three pounds of loaf-sugar; then stir it well together, and put it in a cask. Put a quart of brandy to every five gallons of wine, mix them well in your cask, close it well up, and after letting it stand four months, bottle it. *Cole*, 350.

Another way.

Five quarts of currant juice, and fourteen pounds of sugar, will make a five gallon cask; fill it up with water, and let it all work together. When it has done working, put in a hop or two, and a quart of brandy. *Cole*, 351.

Birch Wine.

To a hogshead of birch water, take four hundred of Malaga raisins, raifins, pick them clean, and cut them fmall. Then boil the birch liquor for one hour at leaft, fkim it well, and let it ftand till it is no warmer than milk. Then put in the rafins, and let it ftand clofe covered, ftirring it well four or five times every day. Boil all the ftalks in a gallon or two of birch-water, which, added to the other when almoft cold, will give it an agreeable roughnefs. Let it ftand ten days, then put it in a cool cellar, and when it has done hifling in the veffel, ftop it up clofe. It muft ftand nine months, at leaft, before it is bottled. *Mafon*, 461. *Farley*, 366.

Rafpberry Wine.

Bruife fome rafpberries with the back of a fpoon, and ftrain them through a flannel bag into a ftone jar. Put a pound of double-refined fugar to every quart of juice, ftir it well together, and cover it clofe; after letting it ftand three days, pour it clear off. Put two quarts of white wine to one quart of juice, then bottle it off, and it will be fit to drink in about a week, Rafpberry brandy made thus is a very excellent dram. *Cole.* 351.

Turnip Wine.

Pare and flice a quantity of turnips, put them in a cider-prefs, and prefs out all the juice. To every gallon of juice, put three pounds of lump fugar. Have a veffel ready, juft large enough to hold the juice, put your fugar into a veffel, and half a pint of brandy to every gallon of juice. Pour in the juice, and lay fomething over the bung for a week, to fee if it works. If it does, you muft not bung it down till it has done working; then ftop it clofe for three months, and draw it off in another veffel, When it is fine, bottle it off. *Glaffe*, 305.

Goofeberry Wine.

Put three pounds of lump fugar to a gallon of water, boil it a quarter of an hour, and fkim it very well; then let it ftand till it is almoft cold, and take four quarts of full-ripe goofeberries, bruife them in a marble mortar, and put them in your veffel; then pour in the liquor, and let it ftand two days, and ftir it every four hours; fteep half an ounce of ifing-glafs two days in a pint of brandy, ftrain the wine through a flannel bag into the cafk, then beat the ifing-glafs in a marble mortar with five whites of eggs; then whifk them together half an hour, and put it in the wine, and beat them all together; clofe up your cafk, and put clay over it; let it ftand fix months, then bottle it off for ufe; put in each bottle a lump of fugar, and two raifins of the fun. This is a very rich wine, and when it has been kept in bottles two or three years, will drink like champaigne. *Raffald*, 321. X 4

Cherry

Cherry Wine.

Take fifty pounds of black cherries, picked clean from the stalks, let the stones remain, bruise them well with the hands; then take half a bushel of very ripe currants and get as much juice from them as possible, and also four quarts of raspberries squeezed in the same manner. To this quantity of fruit allow forty pounds of sugar; dissolve it in soft water, and when the sugar is melted, put it into a vessel with the bruised cherries and the juice of the currants and raspberries; then fill the vessel with soft water, only leaving room for the working; and, when all is in the vessel, stir it well together with a stick. It must not be bunged up in less three weeks; it may be bottled in five months. *Mason*, 466.

Cowslip Wine.

Take two pounds and an half of powder sugar, and two gallons of water; boil them half an hour, taking care to skim it as the scum rises; then pour it into a tub to cool, adding to it the rind of two lemons. When cold, put four quarts of the flowers of cowslips to the liquor, and with it the juice of two lemons. Let it stand in the tub two days, observing to stir it every two or three hours; then put it in the barrel, and after it has stood about three weeks, or a month, bottle it, not forgetting to put a lump of sugar into each bottle. *Cole*, 352.

Mead.

Take ten gallons of water, two gallons of honey, and an handful of raced ginger; then take two lemons, cut them in pieces, and put them into it; boil it very well, keep it skimming. Let it stand all night in the same vessel you boil it in; the next morning barrel it up, with two or three spoonfuls of good yeast. About three weeks or a month after you may bottle it. *Glasse*, 366.

Cowslip Mead.

Take fifteen gallons of water, and thirty pounds of honey, boil them together till one gallon is wasted; skim it, and take it off the fire. Have ready sixteen lemons cut in halves, put a gallon of the liquor to the lemons, and the rest into a tub with seven packs of cowslips; let them stand all night, then put in the liquor with the lemons, and eight spoonfuls of new yeast, and an handful of sweet-briar; stir them all well together, and let it work three or four days; then strain it, and put it in your cask, and in six months time you may bottle it. *Raffald*, 332. *Farley*, 370.

Smyrna Raisin Wine.

Put twenty-four gallons of water to a hundred pounds of raisins; after letting it stand about fourteen days, put it into your cask. When it has remained there six months, put a gallon of brandy to it. When it is fine, bottle it. *Cole*, 353.

CHAP.

CHAP. XXIX.—TO PREPARE BACON, HAMS, &c.

To make Bacon.

RUB the flitches very well with common falt; let them lie fo that the brine may run from them; in about a week put them into a tub for that purpofe, rubbing off all the falt. Rub the flitches with one pound of falt-petre, pounded and heated; the next day rub them well with falt, dry and hot; let them lie a week, often rubbing them; then turn them, add more hot falt, let them lie three weeks or a month in all, rubbing them well; then dry them. The hog may be either fcalded or finged; but finging is beft. *Mafon,* 178.

Another way.

Take off all the infide fat of a fide of pork, then lay it on a long board, or dreffer, that the blood may run away; rub it well with good falt on both fides; let it lie thus a day; then take a pint of bay-falt, and a quarter of a pound of falt-petre; beat them fine; two pounds of coarfe fugar, and a quarter of a peck of common falt. Lay your pork in fomething that will hold the pickle, and rub it well with the above ingredients. Lay the fkinny fide downwards and bafte it every day with the pickle for a fortnight; then hang it in a wood fmoke, and afterwards hang it in a dry place, but not hot. Obferve, that all hams and bacon fhould hang clear from every thing, and not againft a wall.

Obferve to wipe off all the old falt before you put it into this pickle, and never keep bacon or hams in a hot kitchen, or in a room where the fun comes; it makes them all rufty. *Glaffe,* 266. *Farley,* 269.

To cure Hams.

Rub a ham with a quarter of a pound of falt-petre, let it lie twenty-four hours; boil one quart of ftrong old beer with half a pound of bay-falt, half a pound of brown fugar, and a pound and an half of common falt; pour this on the ham boiling hot, rub and turn it every day for a fortnight, and bafte it with the liquor when there is opportunity. This is a very good receipt for curing a ham. *Mafon,* 176.

Another way.

Cut off a fine ham from a fat hind-quarter of pork. Take two ounces of falt-petre, a pound of coarfe fugar, a pound of common falt, and two ounces of fal prunella; mix all together, and rub it well. Let it lie a month in this pickle, turning and bafting it every day, then hang it in wood fmoke as you do

X 4

beef,

beef, in a dry place, fo as no heat comes to it; and, if you
keep them long, hang them a month or two in a damp place,
and it will make them cut fine and fhort. Never lay thefe
hams in water till you boil them, and then boil them in a copper, if you have one, or the largeft pot you have. Put them
in the cold water, and let them be four or five hours before
they boil. Skim the pot well and often till it boils. If it is a
very large one, three hours will boil it; if a fmall one, two
hours will do, provided it be a great while before the water
boils. Take it up half an hour before dinner, pull off the fkin,
and throw rafpings finely fifted all over. Hold a red-hot fire-
fhovel over; and when dinner is ready, take a few rafpings in
a fieve, and fift all over the difh; then lay in your ham, and
with your finger make fine figures round the edge of your difh.
Be fure to boil your ham in as much water as you can, and
keep it fkimming all the time it boils. It muft be at leaft four
hours before it boils.

This pickle does finely for tongues afterwards, to lie in it a
fortnight, and then hang in the wood fmoke a fortnight, or to
boil them out of the pickle.

Yorkfhire is famous for hams, and the reafon is this:—their
falt is much finer than ours in London; it is a large clear falt,
and gives the meat a fine flavour. I ufed to have it from Mal-
den, in Effex; and that falt will make any ham as fine as you
can defire. It is by much the beft falt for falting meat.

When you broil any of thefe hams in flices, or bacon, have
fome boiling water ready, and let the flices lie a minute or two
in water, then broil them; it takes out the falt, and makes
them eat finer. *Glaffe*, 265.

To falt Tongues.

Scrape them and dry them clean with a cloth and falt them
well with common falt, and half an ounce of falt-petere to
every tongue; lay them in a deep pot, and turn them every
day for a week or ten days; falt them again, and let them lie
a week longer; take them up, dry them with a cloth, flour
them, and hang them up. *Raffald*, 307.

To make Hung Beef.

Make a ftrong brine with bay-falt, falt-petre, and pump-
water, and put into it a rib of beef for nine days. Then hang
it up in a chimney where wood or faw duft is burnt. When
it is a little dry, wafh the outfide with blood two or three times
to make it look black; and when it is dried enough, boil it
for ufe. *Cole*, 355.

Another way.

Take the navel piece, and hang it up in your cellar as long
as it will keep good, and till it begins to be a little fappy.
Then

Then take it down and wafh it in fugar and water, one piece after another, for you muft cut it into three pieces. Then take a pound of falt-petre, and two pounds of bay-falt, dried and pounded fmall. Mix with them two or three fpoonfuls of brown fugar and rub your beef well with it in every part; then ftrew a fufficient quantity of common falt all over it, and let the beef lie clofe till the falt is diffolved, which will be in fix or feven days.   Then turn it every other day for a fortnight; and after that hang it up in a warm, but not a hot place. It may hang a fortnight in the kitchen; and, when you want it, boil it in bay-falt and pump water till it is tender It will keep, when boiled, two or three months, rubbing it with a greafy cloth, or putting it two or three minutes into boiling water to take off the mouldinefs. *Farley*, 273.

To pickle Pork.

Having cut your pork into pieces of a convenient fize to lie in your powdering tub, rub them all over with falt-petre; then make a mixture of two-thirds common falt, and one third bay-falt, and rub every piece well with it. Lay the pieces in your tub as clofe as poffible, and throw a little falt over them. *Cole*, 356.

To make very fine Saufages,

Take fix pounds of good pork, free from fkin, griftles, and fat; cut it very fmall, and beat it in a mortar till it is very fine; then fhred fix pounds of beef fuet very fine, and free from all fkin. Shred it as fine as poffible; then take a good deal of fage, wafh it very clean, pick off the leaves, and fhred it very fine. Spread your meat on a clean dreffer or table; then fhake the fage all over, about three large fpoonfuls; fhred the thin rind of a middling lemon very fine and throw over, with as many fweet herbs, when fhred fine, as will fill a large fpoon; grate two nutmegs over, throw over two tea-fpoofuls of pepper, and a large fpoonful of falt; then throw over the fuet and mix it all well together, Put it down clofe in a pot. When you ufe them, roll them up with as much egg as will make them roll fmooth.   Make them the fize of a faufage, and fry them in butter or good dripping. Be fure it be hot before you put them in, and keep them rolling about. When they are thoroughly hot, and of a fine light brown, they are enough. You may chop this meat very fine, if you do not like it beat. Veal eats well done thus; or veal and pork together. You may clean fome guts and fill them. *Glaffe*, 257.

Another way.

Take part of a leg of pork or veal, pick it clean from fkin or fat; to every pound, add two pounds of beef fuet.; fhred both feverally very fine; mix them well with fage-leaves chopped

fine,

fine, pepper, falt, nutmeg, and pounded cloves, and a little grated lemon-peel; put this clofe down in a pot. · When it is ufed, mix it with the yolk of an egg, and a few bread crumbs. Roll it into lengths. *Mafon*, 182.

Common Saufages.

Take three pounds of nice pork, fat and lean together, free from fkin or griftles, chop it very fine, feafon it with two tea-fpoonfuls of falt, and one of beaten pepper, fome fage fhred fine, about three tea-fpoonfuls; mix it well together, have the guts very nicely cleaned, and fill them, or put them down in a pot; fo roll them of what fize you pleafe, and fry them. *Cole*, 357.

Oxford Saufages.

Take a pound of young pork, fat and lean, without fkin or griftle, a pound of lean veal, and a pound of beef fuet chopped all fine together; put in half a pound of grated bread, half the peel of a lemon fhred fine, a nutmeg grated, fix fage leaves wafhed and chopped very fine, a tea-fpoonful of pepper, and two of falt, fome thyme, favoury, and marjoram fhred fine. Mix it all well together, and put it clofe down in a pan when you ufe it; roll it out the fize of a common faufage, and fry them in frefh butter of a fine brown, or broil them over a clear fire, and fend them to table as hot as poffible. *Glaffe*, 258.

CHAP. XXX.—VEGETABLES.

Observations on dressing Vegetables.

BE particularly careful in picking and washing greens of every kind, as dirt and insects are apt to lodge among the leaves; and always lay them in a clean pan, for fear of sand or dust, which frequently hang round wooden vessels. Boil all your greens in a well-tinned sauce-pan by themselves, with a great quantity of water; boil no kind of meat with them, as that will discolour them. All kinds of vegetables should have a little crispness; you must not therefore boil them too much. *Cole*, 357.

To dress Artichokes.

Twist off the stalks, put them into cold water, and wash them well; when the water boils, put them in with the top downwards, that all the dust and sand may boil out. An hour and an half, or two hours, will do them. Serve them with melted butter in little cups. *Cole*, 358.

To dress Asparagus.

Scrape your asparagus, and tie them in small bundles, cut them even, and throw them into water, and have ready a stew-pan boiling. Put in some salt, and tie the asparagus into little bundles. Let the water keep boiling, and when they are a little tender, take them up. Boiling them too much will make them lose their colour and flavour; lay them on a toast which has been dipped in the water the asparagus was boiled in; pour over them melted butter, or send them to table with butter in a bason. *Cole*, 358.

To dress Beans.

Boil them in plenty of water, with a good quantity of salt in it till they are tender. Boil and chop some parsley, put it into good melted butter, and serve them up with boiled bacon, and the butter and parsley in a boat. Never boil them with the bacon. *Cole*, 358.

To dress Broccoli.

Carefully strip off all the little branches till you come to the top one, and then with a knife peel off the hard outside skin that is on the stalks and little branches, and then throw them into water. Have ready a stew-pan of water, throw in a little salt, and when it boils, put in your broccoli. When the stalks are tender, it is enough. Put in a piece of toasted bread, soaked in the water the broccoli was boiled in, at the bottom of your dish, and put your broccoli on the top of it, as you do asparagus. Send them up to table laid in bunches, with butter in a boat. *Cole*, 358.

To

To drefs Cabbage, &c.

Quarter your cabbage, and boil it in plenty of water with an handful of falt. When it is tender, drain it on a fieve, but never prefs it. Savoys and greens are boiled in the fame manner, but always boil them by themfelves. *Cole*, 358.

To drefs Carrots.

Carrots require a great deal of boiling; when they are young, wipe them after they are boiled; when old, fcrape them before you boil them. Slice them into a plate, and pour melted butter over them. Young fpring carrots will be boiled in half an hour, large ones in an hour, and old Sandwich carrots will take two hours. *Cole*, 358.

To drefs Cauliflowers.

Cut the ftalks off, and leave a little green on; boil them in fpring water and falt; about fifteen minutes will do them. If it is boiled too foft, you will fpoil it. *Mrs. Mafon*, recommends boiling cauliflowers in plenty of milk and water, without falt. *Cole*, 359.

To drefs French Beans.

String them, and if not very fmall, fplit and quarter them, throw them into falt and water; boil them in a quantity of water, with fome falt. When they are tender, they are enough. They will be foon done.

N. B. Make all greens boil as quick as poffible, as it preferves their colour. *Cole*, 359.

To drefs Parfnips.

Parfnips fhould be boiled in a great deal of water, and when they are foft, which may be known by running a fork into them, they are enough. They either may be ferved whole with melted butter, or beat fmooth in a bowl, heated with a little cream, butter, and flour, and a little falt. *Cole*, 359.

To drefs Peas.

Your peas fhould not be fhelled till juft before you want them. Put them into boiling water with a little falt, and a lump of loaf fugar, and when they begin to dent in the middle, they are enough. Strain them into a fieve, put a good lump of butter into your difh, and ftir them till the butter is melted. Boil a fprig of mint by itfelf, chop it fine, and lay it round the edge of your difh in lumps. *Cole*, 359.

To drefs Potatoes.

Boil them in as little water as you can without burning the fauce-pan. Cover the fauce-pan clofe, and when the fkin begins to crack, they are enough. Drain all the water out, and let them ftand covered for a minute or two. *Cole*, 359.

To

To dress Spinach.

Pick it clean, and wash it in several waters; put it into a sauce-pan that will just hold it, throw a little salt over it and cover the pan close. Put no water in; shake the pan often. When the spinach is shrunk and fallen to the bottom, and the liquor which comes out of them boils up, they are enough. Throw it into a clean sieve to drain, and give it a squeeze between two plates. Put it on a plate, and send it up with butter in a boat, but never pour any over them.

Sorrel is stewed in the same manner. *Cole*, 359.

To dress Turnips.

Pare your turnips thick; when they are boiled, squeeze them, and mash them smooth; heat them with a little cream, a piece of butter; add pepper and salt, and serve them up; or the pepper and salt may be omitted, leaving the company at table to use what quantity of each they think proper. *Cole*, 360.

THE ART OF BREWING.

HAVING given ample inftructions for the preparations of wines, &c. malt liquors fhould not be paffed over unnoticed, as the houfe-keeper cannot be faid to be complete in her bufinefs, without a competent knowledge in the Art of Brewing.

Of Water proper for Brewing.

To fpeak in general terms, the beft water for brewing is river water; fuch as is foft, and has partook of the air and fun; for this eafily infinuates itfelf into the malt, and extracts its virtues. On the contrary, hard waters aftringe and bind the pores of the malt, and prevent the virtue of it from being freely communicated to the liquor. It is a rule adopted by many excellent brewers, that all water which will mix and lather with foap, is proper for brewing, and they wholly difapprove of any other. The experiment has been often tried, that where the fame quantity of malt has been ufed to a barrel of river water as to a barrel of fpring water, the former has excelled the latter in ftrength, in a degree almoft double. It may be neceffary to obferve likewife, that the malt was the fame in quality, as well as in quantity, for each barrel. The hops were the fame, both in quantity and quality, and the time of boiling was equal in each. They were worked in the fame manner, and tunned and kept in the fame cellar. Hence it is evident, that there could have been no difference but in the water, and yet one barrel was worth almoft two of the other.

But where foft water is not to be procured, that which is hard may be foftened, by expofing it to the air and fun, and putting into it fome pieces of foft chalk to infufe; or, before you begin to boil it, in order to be poured on the malt, put into it a quantity of bran, which will foften it a little. *Cole*, 361.

The neceffity of keeping the Veffels clean.

Obferve, the day before brewing, to have all your veffels very clean, and never ufe your tubs for any other ufe, except it be to make wines. Let your cafks be well cleaned with boiling water; and, if your bung is large enough, fcrub them well with a little birch broom, or brufh. If they are very bad, take out the heads, and let them be fcrubbed clean with a hand-brufh, fand, and fullers earth. Put on the head again, and fcald it well, then throw in a piece of unflacked lime, and ftop the bung clofe. *Cole*, 361.

General Rules for Brewing.

In the firft place, it is neceffary to have the malt clean, as it ought to ftand four or five days after it is ground.

Fine

Fine ſtrong October ſhould have five quarters of malt, and twenty-four pounds of hops, to three hogſheads. This will afterwards make two hogſheads of good keeping ſmall beer, with the addition of five pounds of hops.

For middling beer, a quarter of malt makes a hogſhead of ale, and another of ſmall beer; or it will make three hogſheads of good ſmall beer, allowing eight pounds of hops. This will keep all the year. Or it will make twenty gallons of ſtrong ale, and two hogſheads of ſmall beer, that will keep all the year.

Any one who intends to keep ale a great while, ſhould allow a pound of hops to every buſhel; if to keep only ſix months, five pounds to a hogſhead. If for preſent drinking, three pounds to a hogſhead, and the ſofteſt and cleareſt water you can get.

Pour the firſt copper of water, when it boils, into your maſh tub, and let it be cool enough to ſee your face in; then put in your malt, and let it be well maſhed. Have a copper of water boiling in the mean time, and when your malt is well maſhed, fill your maſhing tub; ſtir it well again, and cover it over with the ſacks. Let it ſtand three hours, ſet a broad ſhallow tub under the cock, let it run very ſoftly, and if it is thick, throw it up again till it runs fine; then throw an handful of hops in the under tub, let your maſh run into it, and fill your tubs till all is run off. Have water boiling in the copper, and lay as much more on as you have occaſion for, allowing one third for boiling and waſte. Let that ſtand an hour, boiling more water to fill the maſh-tub for ſmall beer; let the fire down a little, and put it into tubs enough to fill you maſh. Let the ſecond maſh be run off, and fill your copper with the firſt wort; put in part of your hops, and make it boil quick. About an hour is long enough. When it has boiled, throw in an handful of ſalt. Have a clean white wand, and dip it into the copper, and if the wort feels clammy, it is boiled enough; then ſlacken your fire, and take off your wort. Have ready a large tub, put two ſticks acroſs, and ſet your ſtraining baſkets over the tub on the ſticks, and ſtrain your wort through it. Put your other wort on to boil with the reſt of the hops; let your maſh be covered again with water, and thin your wort that is cooled in as many things as you can; for the thinner it lies, and the quicker it cools, the better. When quite cool, put it into the tunning-tub. Throw an handful of ſalt into every boil. When the maſh has ſtood an hour, draw it off; then fill your maſh with cold water, take off the wort in a copper, and order it as before. When cool, add to it the firſt in the tub. As ſoon as you empty one copper, fill the other, and boil your ſmall beer well. Let the laſt maſh run off, and when both are

boiled

boiled with fresh hops, order them as the two first boilings.
When cool, empty the mash-tub, and put the small beer to work
there. When cool enough, work it, set a wooden bowl full of
yeast in the beer, and it will work over with a little of the beer
in the boil. Stir your tun up every twelve hours; let it stand
two days, then tun it, taking off the yeast. Fill your vessels
full, and have some to fill your barrels; let it stand till it has
done working; then lay on your bung lightly for a fortnight,
after which stop it as close as you can. Take care to have a
vent-peg at the top of the vessel; in warm weather open it;
and if your drink hisses, as it often will, loosen it till it has
done, and then stop it close again. If you can boil your ale in
one boiling, it will be best, if the copper will admit of it; if
not, boil as conveniency serves.

If, when you come to draw your beer, you perceive it is not
fine, draw off a gallon, and set it on the fire, with two ounces
of ising-glass cut small and beat. Dissolve it in the beer over the
fire. When it is all melted, let it stand till it is cold, and pour
it in at the bung, which must lay loose on till it has done fer-
menting; then stop it close for a month.

Let me again repeat, that particular care is requisite that your
casks are not musty, nor have any ill taste. If they have, it will
be a difficult matter to sweeten them.

Wash your casks with cold water before you scald them, and
let them lie a day or two soaking; then clean them well, and
scald them. *Cole*, 362.

Of the proper time for Brewing.

The month of March is generally considered as a proper season for brewing malt liquor, which is intended for keeping; because the air at that time of the year is temperate, and contributes to the proper working or fermentation of the liquor,
which principally promotes its preservation and good keeping.
Very cold, or very hot weather, prevents the free fermentation,
or working of liquors; therefore, if you brew in very cold weather, unless you contrive some means to warm the cellar while
new liquor is working, it will never clear itself in the manner
you would wish. The same misfortune will arise if in very hot
weather you cannot put the cellar into a temperate state. The
consequence of which will be, that such liquor will be muddy
and sour, perhaps beyond all recovery. Such misfortunes indeed often happen, even in the proper season for brewing,
owing solely to the badness of a cellar; for when they are dug
in springy grounds, or are subject to damps in the winter, the
liquor will chill, and become vapid or flat. Where cellars are
of this kind, it will be advisable to brew in March, rather than
October; for you may be able to keep such cellars temperate
in

in fummer, but you cannot make them warm in water. The
beer therefore which is brewed in March, will have fufficient
time to fettle and adjuft itfelf before the cold can do it any material injury. *Cole*, 363.

The Country, or private Way of Bufinefs.

Several countries have their feveral methods of brewing, as
it is practifed in Wales, Dorchefter, Nottingham, Oundle, and
many other places ; but avoiding particulars, I fhall here recommend that which I think is the moft ferviceable both in the
country and London private families. And, firft, I fhall obferve, that the great brewer has fome advantages in brewing,
more than the fmall one ; and yet the latter has fome conve-
niences which the former has not ; for, 'tis certain, that the
great brewer can make more drink, and draw a greater length
in proportion to his malt, than a perfon can from a leffer quantity ; becaufe, the greater the body, the more is its united power
in receiving and difcharging ; and he can brew with lefs trouble
and expence; by means of his more convenient utenfils. But
then the private brewer is not without his advantages ; for he
can have his malt ground at pleafure, his tons and moveable
coolers fweeter and better cleaned than the great fixed tuns and
backs ; he can fkim off his top yeaft, and leave his bottom lees
behind, which is what the great brewer cannot fo well do. He
can, at difcretion, make additions of cold wort to his too forward ales and beers, which the great brewer cannot fo eafily do ;
he can brew how and when he pleafes, which the great ones are
in fome meafure hindered from. But, fuppofe a private family
fhould brew five bufhels of malt, whofe copper holds, brim-
full, thirty-fix gallons, or a barrel ; on this water we put half a
peck of bran or malt, when it is fomething hot, which will
much forward it, by keeping in the fteam, or fpirit of the water ; when it begins to boil, if the water is foul, fkim off the
bran or malt, and give it to the hogs, or lade both the water
and that into the mafh vat, where it is to remain till the fteam
is near fpent, and you can fee your face in it, which will be in
about a quarter of an hour in cold weather ; then let all but half
a bufhel of malt run very leifurely into it, ftirring it all the
while with an oar or paddle, that it may not ball, and when the
malt is nearly mixed with water, it is enough ; which I am fenfi-
ble is different from the old way, and the general prefent practice ; but I fhall here clear that point. For, by not ftirring or mafh-
ing the malt into a pudding confiftence, or thin mafh, the body
of it lies in a more loofe condition, that will eafier and fooner
admit of a quicker and more true paffage of the afterladings of
the feveral bowls or jets of hot water, which muft run through
it before the brewing is ended ; by which percolation, the wa-

Y   ter

ter has ready accefs to all the parts of the broken malt, fo that
the brewer is enabled to brew quicker or flower, and to make
more ale or fmall beer. If more ale, then hot boiling water
muft be laded over fo flow, that one boil muft run almoft off
before another is put over, which will occafion the whole brewing to laft about fixteen hours, efpecially if the *Oundle* way is
followed, of fpending it out of the tap as fmall as a ftraw, and
as fine as fack, and then it will be quickly fo in the barrel. Or
if lefs or weaker ale is to be made, and good fmall beer, then
the fecond copper of boiling water muft be put over expedi-
tioufly, and drawn out with a large and faft fteam. After the
firft ftirring of the malt is done, then put over the referve of
half a bufhel of frefh malt to the four bufhels and an half that
are already in the tub, which muft be fpread all over it, and
alfo cover the tubs with fome facks, or other cloths, to keep in
the fteam or fpirit of the malt ; then let it ftand for two or
three hours, at the end of which, put over now and then a
bowl of the boiling water in the copper, as is before directed,
and fo continue to do till as much is run off as will almoft fill
the copper. Then, in a canvafs, or other loofe woven cloth,
put in half a pound of hops, and boil them half an hour, when
they muft be taken out, and as many frefh ones put in their
room as are judged proper, to boil half an hour more, if for
ale. But if for keeping beer, half a pound of frefh ones ought to
be put in every half hour, and boil an hour and an half brifkly.
Now, while the firft copper of wort is boiling, there fhould be
fcalding water leifurely put over, bowl by bowl, and run off,
that the copper may be filled again immediately after the firft is
out, and boiled an hour, with nearly the fame quantity of frefh
hops, and in the fame manner as thofe in the firft copper of
ale-wort were. The reft for fmall beer may be all cold water
put over the the grains at once, or at twice, and boiled an hour
each copper, with the hops that have been boiled before. But
here I muft obferve, that fometimes I have not an opportunity
to get hot water for making all my fecond copper of wort,
which obliges me then to make ufe of cold to fupply what is
wanting. Out of five bufhels of malt, I generally make an
hogfhead of ale with the two firft coppers of wort, and an
hogfhead of fmall beer with the other two ; but this is more
or lefs, as it pleafes me, always taking care to let each copper of
wort be ftrained off through a fieve, and cool in four or five
tubs, to prevent its foxing. Thus I have brewed many hogf-
heads of middling ale, that, when the malt is good, has proved
ftrong enough for myfelf, and fatisfactory to my friends. But
for ftrong keeping beer, the firft copper of wort may be wholly
put to that ufe, and all the reft fmall beer. Or, when the firft
copper of wort is entirely made ufe of for ftrong beer, it may be
helped

helped with more fresh malt, according to the *London* fashion, and water, lukewarm, put over at first with the bowl; but soon after sharp, or boiling water, which may make a copper of good ale, and small beer after that. In some parts of the North, they take one or more cinders, red hot, and throw some salt on them to overcome the sulphur of the coal, and then directly thrust it into the fresh malt or goods, where it lies till all the water is laded over, and the brewing done; for there are only one or two mashings or stirrings, at most, necessary in a brewing. Others, who brew with wood, will quench one or more brand ends of ash in a copper of wort, to mellow the drink, as a burnt toast of bread does a pot of beer; but it must be observed, that this must not be done with oak, fir, or other strong scented wood, left it does more harm than good. *Cole*, 364.

Of bottling Malt Liquors.

Take care that your bottles are well cleaned and dried; for wet bottles will make the liquor turn watery or mouldy; and, by wet bottles, a great deal of good beer has been spoiled. Even though the bottles are clean and dry, if the corks are not new and found, the liquor will be still liable to be damaged; for if the air can get into the bottles, the liquor will grow flat, and will never rise. Many have plumed themselves on their saving knowledge, by using old corks on this occasion, and have spoiled as much liquor as cost them four or five pounds, to save the expence of three or four shillings. If bottles are corked properly, it will be difficult to pull out the cork without a screw; and, in order to be sure to draw the cork without breaking, the screw ought to go through the cork; of course, the air will find a passage where the screw has passed, and consequently the cork must have been spoiled. If a cork has once been in a bottle, though it has not been drawn with a screw, yet that cork will turn musty as soon as it is exposed to the air, and will communicate its ill flavour to the bottle in which it is next put, and spoil the liquor that way. In the choice of corks, prefer those that are soft and free from specks.

When you once begin to bottle a vessel of liquor, never leave it till it is completed, otherwise it will bear different tastes.

When a vessel of any liquor begins to grow flat, while it is in common draught, bottle it, and into every bottle put a piece of loaf sugar, of about the size of a walnut, which will make it rise and come to itself; and, to forward its ripening, you may set some bottles in hay in a warm place; but straw will not assist its ripening. *Cole*, 366.

To recover a Barrel of Beer that has turned sour.

To a kilderkin of beer, throw in at the bung a quart of oatmeal, lay the bung on loose two or three days, then stop it

down

down clofe, and let it ftand a month. Some throw in a piece
of chalk as large as a turkey's egg, and when it has done working, ftop it clofe for a month; then tap it. *Cole*, 367.

To recover a mufty Cafk.

Boil fome pepper in water, and fill the cafk with it fcalding
hot. *Cole*, 367.

An excellent Compofition for keeping Beer with.

Take a quart of French brandy, or as much Englifh, that is
free from any burnt flavour, or other ill tafte, and is full proof;
to this put as much wheat or bean flour, as will knead it into
dough, put it in long pieces into the bung-hole, as foon as the
beer has done working, or afterwards, and let it gently fall,
piece by piece, to the bottom of the butt. This will maintain
the drink in a mellow frefhnefs, keep ftalenefs off for fome time,
and caufe it to be ftronger as it grows aged. *Cole*, 357.

Another way.

Take a peck of egg-fhells, and dry them in an oven, break
and mix them with two pounds of fat chalk, and mix them with
water, wherein four pounds of coarfe fugar have been boiled,
and put into the butt. *Cole*, 367.

To ftop the Fret in malt Liquors.

Take a quart of black cherry brandy, and pour it in at the
bung-hole of the hogfhead, and ftop it clofe. *Cole*, 368.

To recover deadifh Beer.

When ftrong ale, or beer, grows flat, by the lofs of its fpirit,
take four or five gallons out of a hogfhead, and boil it with
five pounds of honey; fkim it, and, when cold, put it to the
reft, and ftop it clofe. This will make it pleafant, quick, and
ftrong. *Cole*, 368.

To fine malt Liquors.

Take a pint of water, and half an ounce of unflacked lime,
mix them well together; let it ftand three hours, and the lime
will fettle to the bottom, and the water be as clear as glafs. Pour
the water from the fediment, and put it into your ale or beer.
Mix it with half an ounce of ifing-glafs, firft cut fmall and boiled,
and in five hours time, or lefs, the beer in the barrel will fettle
and clear. *Cole*, 368.

To fine any fort of Drink.

Take the beft ftaple ifing-glafs; cut it fmall with fciffars, and
boil one ounce in three quarts of beer; let it lie all night to
cool. Thus diffolved, put it into your hogfhead the next morning, perfectly cold; for if it is but as warm as new milk, it will
jelly all the drink. The beer, or ale, in a week after, fhould be
tapped,

tapped, or it will be apt to flat; for this ingredient flats as well as fines. Remember to stir it well with a wooden paddle when the ising-glass is put into the cask. *Cole*, 368.

Another way.

Boil a pint of wheat in two quarts of water, then squeeze out the liquid part through a fine linen cloth. Put a pint of it into a kilderkin. It not only fines, but preserves. *Cole*, 368.

To cure cloudy Beer.

Rack off your butt, then boil two pounds of new hops in a sufficient quantity of water, with a due proportion of coarse sugar, and put all together into the cask when cold. Others have attempted this cure, by only soaking new hops in beer, which, when squeezed, they put into a cask of cloudy beer. *Cole*, 368.

To make Cyder.

After all your apples are bruised, take half your quantity and squeeze them, and the juice you press from them, pour upon the others half bruised, but not squeezed, in a tub for the purpose, having a tap at the bottom. Let the juice remain upon the apples three or four days. Then pull out your tap, and let the juice run into some other vessel set under the tub to receive it; and if it runs thick, as at the first it will, pour it upon the apples again till you see it runs clear; and, as you have a quantity, put it into your vessel; but do not force the cyder, but let it drop as long as it will of its own accord. Having done this, after you perceive that the sides begin to work, take a quantity of ising-glass, (an once will serve for forty gallons,) infuse this in some of the cyder till it is dissolved; put an ounce of isinglass to a quart of cyder, and when it is so dissolved, pour it into the vessel, and stop it close for two days, or something more; then draw off the cyder into another vessel. This do repeatedly, till you perceive your cyder to be free from all manner of sediment, that may make it ferment and fret itself. After Christmas you may boil it. You may, by pouring water on the apples, and pressing them, make a pretty small cyder; if it should be thick and muddy, by using ising-glass, you may make it as clear as the rest. You must dissolve the ising-glass over the fire till it be a jelly. *Cole*, 368.

For fining Cyder.

Take two quarts of skim-milk, for four ounces of ising-glass; cut the ising-glass in pieces, and work it luke-warm in the milk over the fire; and when it is dissolved, put it cold into the hogshead of cyder, and take a long stick and stir it well from top to bottom for half a quarter of an hour. *Cole*, 369.

After

After it has fined.

Take ten pounds of raifins of the fun, two ounces of turmeric, and half an ounce of ginger beaten; then take a quantity
of raifins, and grind them as you do muftard feed in a bowl,
with a little cyder, and fo the reft of the raifins; then fprinkle
the turmeric and ginger among it; then put all into a fine canvafs bag, and hang it in the middle of the hogfhead clofe, and
let lie. After the cyder has ftood thus a fortnight, or a month,
you may bottle it at your pleafure. *Cole*, 369.

THE FAMIAY PHYSICIAN;

O R,

The Country Lady's Benevolent Employment.

Want of Appetite.

IF want of appetite proceeds from errors in diet, or any other part of the patient's regimen, it ought to be changed. If naufea and reachings fhew that the ftomach is loaded with crudities, a vomit will be of fervice. After this, a gentle purge or two of rhubarb, or of any of the bitter purging falts, may be taken. The patient ought next to ufe fome of the ftomachic bitters infufed in wine. Though gentle evacuations be neceffary, yet ftrong purges and vomits are to be avoided, as they weaken the ftomach, and hurt digeftion.

Elixir of vitriol is an excellent medicine in moft cafes of indigeftion, weaknefs of the ftomach, or want of appetite. Twenty or thirty drops of it may be taken twice or thrice a day, in a glafs of wine or water. It may likewife be mixed with the tincture of the bark; one drachm of the former to an ounce of the latter, and two tea-fpoonfuls of it taken in wine or water, as above.

The chalybeate waters, if drank in moderation, are generally of confiderable fervice in this cafe. The falt water has likewife good effects, but it muft not be ufed too freely. The waters of Harrowgate, Scarborough, Moffat, and moft other fpas in Britain, may be ufed with advantage. We would advife all who are afflicted with indigeftion and want of appetite, to repair to thefe places of public rendezvous. The very change of air, and the cheerful company, will be of fervice; not to mention the exercife, diffipation, amufements, &c. *Tiffot. Buchan.*

The Afthma.

The paroxyfm of an afthma I muft leave to the phyfician; but as a palliative, nothing is of fo great importance in the afthma, as pure and moderately warm air. Afthmatic people can feldom bear either the clofe heavy air of a large town, or the fharp, keen atmofphere of a bleak hilly country: a medium, therefore, between thefe is to be chofen. The air near a large town is often better than at a diftance, provided the patient be removed fo far as not to be affected by the fmoke.

Y 4   Some

Some asthmatic patients indeed breathe easier in town than in the country; but this is seldom the case, especially in towns where much coal is burnt. Asthmatic persons who are obliged to be in town all day ought, at least, to sleep out of it. Even this will often prove of great service. Those who can afford it, ought to travel into a warmer climate. Many astmatic persons who cannot live in England, enjoy very good health in the south of France, Portugal, Spain, or Italy.

Exercise is likewise of very great importance in the asthma, as it promotes the digestion, preparation of the blood, &c. The blood of astmatic persons is seldom duly prepared, owing to the proper action of the lungs being impeded. For this reason, such people ought daily to take as much exercise, either on foot, horseback, or in a carriage, as they can bear. *Buchan.*

Dr. Mead's Prescription for the Bite of a Mad Dog.

Take ash-coloured ground liver-wort, cleaned, dried, and powdered, half an ounce; of black pepper, powdered, a quarter of an ounce. Mix these well together, and divide the powder into four doses; one of which must be taken every morning fasting, for four mornings successively, in half an English pint of cow's milk, warm.

After these four doses are taken, the patient must go into a cold bath, or cold spring or river, every morning fasting, for a month; he must be dipped all over, but not stay in (with his head above water) longer than half a minute, if the water be very cold. After this, he must go in three times a week for a fortnight longer.

The person must be bled before he begins to use the medicine Dr. Mead asserts, that he never knew this remedy fail, although he has tried it in a thousand instances. But Dr. Buchan, and some others, suspect the Doctor's veracity in this particular.

Burns.

In slight burns, which do not break the skin, it is customary to hold the part near the fire, for a competent time; to rub it with salt; or to lay a compress upon it dipped in spirits of wine or brandy. But when the burn has penetrated so deep as to blister or break the skin, it must be dressed with some of the following liniment:—

Take equal parts of Florence oil, or of fresh drawn linseed oil, and lime-water; shake them well together in a wide-mouthed bottle, so as to form a liniment. It may either be spread upon a cloth, or the parts affected may be anointed with it twice or thrice a day; or it may be dressed with the emollient and gently drying ointment, commonly called *Turner's cerate.* This may be mixed with an equal quantity of fresh olive oil,

and

and fpread upon a foft rag, and applied to the part affected.
When this ointment cannot be had, an egg may be beat up with
about an equal quantity of the fweeteft falad oil. This will
ferve very well till a proper ointment can be prepared. When
the burning is very deep, after the firft two or three days, it
fhould be dreffed with equal parts of yellow *bafilicum*, and *Turner's cerate*, mixed together.

When the burn is violent, or has occafioned a high degree
of inflammation, and there is reafon to fear a gangrene or mortification, the fame means muft be ufed to prevent it as are recommended in other violent inflammations. The patient, in
this cafe, muft live low, and drink freely of weak diluting
liquors. He muft likewife be bled, and have his body kept
open. But if the burnt parts become livid or black, with other
fymptoms of mortification, it will be neceffary to bathe them
frequently with warm camphorated fpirits of wine, tincture of
myrrh, or other antifeptics, mixed with a decoction of the bark.
In this cafe, the bark muft be taken internally, and the patient's
diet muft be more generous. *Buchan.*

Colds.

Colds are well known to be the effects of an obftructed perfpiration. We fhall not fpend our time in enumerating all the
various fymptoms of colds, as they are pretty generally known.
It may not, however, be amifs to obferve, that almoft every
cold is a kind of fever, which only differs in degree.

No age, fex, or conftitution, is exempted from this difeafe;
neither is it in the power of any medicine or regimen to prevent
it. The inhabitants of every climate are liable to catch cold,
nor can even the greateft circumfpection defend them at all
times from its attacks. Indeed, if the human body could be
kept conftantly in an uniform degree of warmth, fuch a thing
as catching cold would be impoffible; but as that cannot be
effected by any means, the perfpiration muft be liable to many
changes. Such changes, however, when fmall, do not affect
the health; but, when great, they muft prove hurtful.

When oppreffion of the breaft, a ftuffing of the nofe, unufual
wearinefs, pain of the head, &c. give ground to believe that
the perfpiration is obftructed, or, in other words, that the perfon has caught cold, he ought immediately to leffen his diet, at
leaft the ufual quantity of his folid food, and to abftain from
all ftrong liquors. Inftead of flefh, fifh, eggs, milk, and other
nourifhing diet, he may eat light bread pudding veal or chicken
broth, panada, gruels, and fuch like. His drink may be water
gruel fweetened with a little honey; an infufion of balm, or
linfeed fharpened with the juice of orange or lemon; a decoction of barley and liquorice with tamarinds, or any other c00,
diluting, acid liquor.

Abo

Above all, his fupper fhould be light; as fmall poffet, or water gruel fweetened with honey, and a little toafted bread in it.
If honey fhould difagree with the ftomach, the gruel may be
fweetened with treacle or coarfe fugar, and fharpened with the
jelly of currants. Thofe who have been accuftomed to generous liquors, may take wine whey inftead of gruel, which may
be fweetened as above.

The patient ought to be longer than ufual in bed, and to en-
courage a gentle fweat, which is eafily brought on towards
morning, by drinking tea, or any kind of warm diluting liquor.
I have often known this practice carry off a cold in one day,
which in all probability, had it been neglected, would have coft
the patient his life, or have confined him for fome months.
Would people facrifice a little time to eafe and warmth, and
practife a moderate degree of abftinence, when the firft fymptoms of a cold appear, we have reafon to believe, that moft of
the bad effects which flow from an obftructed perfpiration,
might be prevented. But after the difeafe has gathered
ftrength by delay, all attempts to remove it, often prove vain.
A pleurify, a peripneumony, or a fatal confumption of the
lungs, are the common effects of colds, which have either been
totally neglected, or treated improperly.

It is certain, however, that colds may be too much indulged.
When a perfon, for every flight cold, fhuts himfelf up in a
warm room, and drinks great quantities of warm liquor, it may
occafion fuch a general relaxation of the folids, as will not
eafily be removed. It will therefore be proper, when the difeafe will permit, and the weather is mild, to join to the regimen
mentioned above, gentle exercife; as walking, riding on horfeback, or in a carriage, &c. An obftinate cold, which no medicine can remove, will yield to gentle exercife, and a proper
regimen of the diet. *Tiffot. Buchan. Fothergil.*

The Cholic.

Cholics, which proceed from excefs and indigeftion, generally
cure themfelves, by occafioning vomiting or purging. Thefe
difcharges are by no means to be ftopped, but promoted by
drinking plentifully of warm water, or weak poffet. When
their violence is over, the patient may take a dofe of rhubarb,
or any other gentle purge, to carry off the dregs of his debauch.

Cholics which are occafioned by wet feet, or catching cold,
may generally be removed at the beginning, by bathing the feet
and legs in warm water, and drinking fuch warm diluting
liquors as will promote the perfpiration, as weak wine whey, or
water gruel with a fmall quantity of fpirits in it.

Thefe flatulent cholics, which prevail fo much among country

try people, might generally be prevented, were they careful to change their clothes when they get wet. They ought likewife to take a dram, or to drink fome kind of warm liquor, after eating any kind of green trafh. We do not mean to recommend the practice of dram-drinking, but in this cafe ardent fpirits prove a real medicine, and indeed the beft that can be adminiftered. A glafs of good peppermint-water will have nearly the fame effect as a glafs of brandy, and in fome cafes is rather to be preferred.

The bilious cholic is attended with very acute pains about the region of the navel. The patient complains of great thirft, and is generally coftive. He vomits a hot, bitter, yellow-coloured bile, which being difcharged, feems to afford fome relief, but is quickly followed by the fame violent pain as before. As the diftemper advances, the propenfity to vomit fometimes increafes fo as to become almoft continual, and the proper motion of the inteftines is fo far perverted, that there are all the fymptoms of an impending iliac paffion.

If the patient be young and ftrong, and the pulfe full and frequent, it will be proper to bleed; after which clyfters may be adminiftered. Clear whey or gruel, fharpened with the juice of lemon, or cream of tartar, muft be drank freely. Small chicken broth, with a little manna diffolved in it, or a flight decoction of tamarinds, are likewife very proper; or any other thin, acid, opening liquor.

In the bilious cholic, the vomiting is often very difficult to reftrain. When this happens, the patient may drink a decoction of toafted bread, or an infufion of garden mint in boiling water. Should thefe not have the defired effect, the faline draught, with a few drops of laudanum in it, may be given, and repeated according to the urgency of the fymptoms. A fmall quantity of Venice treacle may be fpread in form of a cataplafm, and applied to the pit of the ftomach. Clyfters, with a proper quantity of Venice treacle or liquid laudanum in them, may likewife be frequently adminiftered.

The general-treatment of the nervous cholic is fo nearly the fame with that of the iliac paffion, or inflammation of the guts, that we fhall not infift upon it. The body is to be opened by mild purgatives given in fmall dofes, and frequently repeated; and their operation muft be affifted by foft oily clyfters, fomentations, &c. The caftor oil is reckoned peculiarly proper in this difeafe. It may both be mixed with the clyfters, and given by the mouth. *Arbuthnot. Buchan.*

Confumption.

This difeafe generally begins with a dry cough, which often continues for fome months. If a difpofition to vomit after eating

ing

ing be excited by it, there is ftill greater reafon to fear an approaching confumption. The patient complains of a more than ufual degree of heat, a pain and oppreffion of the breaft, efpecially after motion ; his fpittle is of a faltifh tafte, and fometimes mixed with blood. He his apt to be fad : his appetite is bad, and his thirft great. There is generally a quick, foft, fmall pulfe ; though fometimes the pulfe is pretty full, and rather hard. Thefe are the common fymptoms of a begining confumption.

Next to proper air and exercife, we would recommend a due attention to diet. The patient fhould eat nothing that is either heating, or hard of digeftion ; and his drink muft be of a foft and cooling nature. All the diet ought to be calculated to leffen the acrimony of the humours, and to nourifh and fupport the patient. For this purpofe he muft keep chiefly to the ufe of vegetables and milk. Milk alone is of more value in this difeafe than the whole *materia medica.*

I have known very extraordinary effects from affes milk in obftinate coughs, which threatened a confumption of the lungs; and do verily believe, if ufed at this period, that it would feldom fail ; but if it be delayed till an ulcer is formed, which is generally the cafe, how can it be expected to fucceed ?

Some extraordinary cures in confumptive cafes have been performed by women's milk. Could this be obtained in fufficent quantity, I would recommend it in preference to any other. If the patient can fuck it from the breaft, it is better than to drink it afterwards. I knew a man who was reduced to fuch a degree of weaknefs in a confumption, as not to be able to turn himfelf in his bed. His wife was at that time giving fuck, and his child happening to die, he fucked her breafts, not with a view to reap any advantage from the milk, but to make her eafy. Finding himfelf, however, greatly benefited by it, he continued to fuck her till he became perfectly well, and is at prefent a ftrong and healthy man.

Cows milk is moft readily obtained of any ; and though it may not be fo eafily digefted as that of affes or mares, it may be rendered lighter, by adding to it an equal quantity of barleywater, or allowing it to ftand for fome hours, and afterwards taking off the cream. If it fhould, notwithftanding, prove heavy on the ftomach, a fmall quantity of brandy or rum, with a little fugar, may be added, which will render it both more light and nourifhing.

For the patient's drink, we would recommend infufions of the bitter plants, as ground-ivy, the leffer centaury, camomile flowers, or water trefoil. Thefe infufions may be drank at pleafure. They ftrengthen the ftomach, promote digeftion, rectify the blood, and at the fame time anfwer all the purpofes

of

of dilution ; and quench thirft much better than things that are lufcious or fweet. But if the patient fpits blood, he ought to ufe, for his ordinary drink, infufions or decoctions of the vulnerary roots, plants, &c. *Steevens. Tiffot. Buchan.*

Chilblains.

Chilblains often attack children in cold weather. They are generally occafioned by the feet or hands being kept wet or cold, and afterwards fuddenly heated. When children are cold, inftead of taking exercife to warm themfelves gradually they run to the fire. This occafions a fudden rarefaction of the humours, and an infraction of the veffels ; which being often repeated, the veffels are, at laft, over-diftended, and forced to give way.

To prevent it, violent cold and fudden heat muft be equally avoided. When the parts begin to look red and fwell the patient ought to be purged, and to have the affected parts rubbed frequen ly with muftard and brandy, or fomething of a warming nature. They ought likewife to be covered with flannel, and kept warm and dry. Some apply warm afhes betwixt cloth to the fwelled parts, which frequently help to reduce them. When there is a fore, it muft be dreffed with Turner's cerate, the ointment of tutty, the plafter of cerus, or fome other drying ointment. Thefe fores are indeed trublefome, but feldom dangerous. They generally heal as foon as the warm weather fets in. *Buchan.*

Coftivenefs.

Coftivenefs is increafed by keeping the body too warm, and by every thing that promotes the perfpiration ; as wearing flannel, lying too long in bed, &c. Intenfe thought, and a fedentary life, are likewife hurtful. All the fecretions and excretions are promoted by moderate excercife without doors, and by a gay, cheerful, fprightly temper of mind.

Thofe who are troubled with coftivenefs, ought, if poffible, to remedy it by diet, as the conftant ufe of medicines for that purpofe is attended with many inconveniencies, and often with bad confequences. I never knew any one get into a habit of taking medicine for keeping the body open, who could leave it off. In time, the cuftom becomes neceffary ; and generally ends in a total relaxation of the bowels, indigeftion, lofs of appetite, wafting of the ftrength, and death.

When the body cannot be kept open without medicine, I would recommend gentle dofes of rhubarb to be taken twice or thrice a week. This is not near fo injurious to the ftomach, as aloes, jalap, or the other draftic purgatives fo much in ufe. Infufions of fenna and manna may likewife be taken, or half an ounce of foluble tartar diffolved in water gruel.

About

About the fize of a nutmeg of lenitive electuary, taken twice or thrice a day, generally anfwers the purpofe very well. *Coles* 377.

Common Cough.

A cough is generally the effect of a cold, which has either been improperly treated, or entirely neglected. When it proves obftinate, there is always reafon to fear the confequences, as this fhews a weak ftate of the lungs, and is often the fore-runner of a confumption.

When the cough is not attended with any degree of fever, and the fpittle is vifcid and tough, fharp pectoral medicines are to be adminiftered ; as gum ammoniac, fquills, &c. Two table fpoonfuls of the folution of gum ammoniac may be taken three or four times a day, more or lefs, according to the age or conftitution of the patient. Squills may be given various ways ; two ounces of vinegar, the oxymel, or the fyrup, may be mixed with the fame quantity of fimple cinnamon water; to which may be added an ounce of common water, and an ounce of balfamic fyrup. Two table fpoonfuls of this mixture may be taken three or four times a day.

A fyrup made of equal parts of lemon-juice, honey, and fugar-candy, is likewife very proper in this kind of cough. A table fpoonful of it may be taken at pleafure.

In obftinate coughs, proceeding from a flux of humours upon the lungs, it will often be neceffary, befides expectorating medicines, to have recourfe to iffues, fetons, or fome other drain. In this cafe I have often obferved the moft happy effects from a Burgundy pitch plaifter applied between the fhoulders. I have ordered this fimple remedy in the moft obftinate coughs, in a great number of cafes, and in many different conftitutions, without ever knowing it fail to give relief, unlefs there were evident figns of an ulcer in the lungs.

But coughs proceed from many other caufes befides defluxions upon the lungs. In thefe cafes the cure is not to be attempted by pectoral medicines. Thus, in a cough proceeding from a foulnefs and debility of the ftomach, fyrups, oils, mucilages, and all kinds of balfamic medicines do hurt. The *ftomach cough* may be known from one that is owing to a fault in the lungs by this—that in the latter, the patient coughs whenever he infpires, or draws in his breath fully ; but in the former, that does no happen. *Tiffot. Buchan. Chambers.*

The Cramp.

Cramps are often prevented or cured by compreffion. Thus cramps in the legs are prevented, and fometimes removed, by tight bandages ; and when convulfions arife from a flatulent diftention of the inteftines, or from fpafms beginning in them,

they

they may be often leſſened or cured, by making a pretty ſtrong compreſſion upon the *abdomen*, by means of a broad belt. A roll of brimſtone held in the hands is frequently uſed as a remedy for cramps. Though this ſeems to owe its effects chiefly to imagination, yet, as it ſometimes ſucceeds, it merits a trial. When ſpaſms or convulſive motions ariſe from ſharp humours in the ſtomach and inteſtines, no laſting relief can be procured till theſe are either corrected or expelled. The Peruvian bark has ſometimes cured periodic convulſions after other medicines had failed. *Cole*, 378.

The Dropſy.

Take of broom-ſeed, well powdered and ſifted, one drachm; let it ſteep twelve hours in a glaſs and an half of good rich white-wine, and take it in the morning faſting, having firſt ſhaken it ſo, that the whole may be ſwallowed. Walk after it, if you are able, or uſe what excerciſe you can without fatigue, for an hour and an half*; after which you muſt be ſure to take two ounces of olive oil; and you muſt not eat or drink any thing in leſs than half an hour, or an hour, after taking the oil. Repeat this every other day, or once in three days, and not oftener, till cured; and do not let blood, or uſe any other remedy during the courſe.

Nothing can be more gentle and ſafe than the operation of this remedy, and it often has little or no ſenſible one. If the dropſy is in the body, it diſcharges it by urine, without any inconvenience; if it is between the ſkin and fleſh, it cauſes bliſters to ariſe on the legs, by which it will run off; but this does not happen to more than one in thirty; and in this caſe no plaſters muſt be uſed, for they would hinder the diſcharge; but you muſt apply red cabbage leaves. If the diſorder is cauſed by wind, it diſpels the phlegm that retains the wind. It cures the dropſy in pregnant women, without injury to the mother or the infant. It alſo cures the aſthma, conſumption, and diſorders of the liver. It is good for bleeding at the noſe, and for venomous bites and poiſons.

The efficacy of the above remedy has been proved by the cure of upwards of fifty dropſical women with child, and by that of more than three hundred other people of both ſexes.

Not

---

* *If the patient is too weak to uſe other exerciſe after taking the powder, the body and limbs may be rubbed with a flannel, from time to time, during the hour and an half, giving reſt at intervals, according to ſtrength; and indeed the practice of this exerciſe for ſome minutes, every night and morning, may be of great help.*

The quantities directed in the recipe have been given alike to men and to women; and there never has been found reaſon to think that they were too little for the one, or too much for the other.

Not long fince, this recipe was recommended to a lady, who feemed to be in, or nearly in, the laft ftage of a dropfy. She was fo much fwoln, that fhe appeared like a woman in the laft month of her pregnancy, and her diforder had refifted every thing that had been done for her by the faculty. She took the broom-feed, but could not take the whole of the oil; however, in a very few months, her hufband wrote a letter of thanks for her fpeedy and furpifing recovery.

Soon after, the report of this extraordinary cure induced another lady, who was afflicted with a dropfy, to make trial of the remedy. She was not fo much fwoln as the former lady, but fhe was exceedingly emaciated, and was fo weak, that fhe was carried like an infant into her carriage, when fhe went to take the air; and fhe had failed of relief from the advice of two of the moft eminent phyficians in London, who had pronounced it an afcites, with encyfted water. Happily they were too liberal minded to fet their faces againft the remedy, as fome others have fince done, becaufe it was not of their acquaintance. This lady followed the directions of the recipe very exactly, and was reftored to health in a few months.

Thefe fucceffes induced the lady, at whofe defire it is publifhed, to recommend the remedy with avidity whenever occafion offered; and it has pleafed God to crown her endeavours with fuch wonderful fuccefs, that fhe thinks fhe may venture to affirm, that fhe has never known it fail to cure, when taken according to the recipe and while there was any degree of ftrength remaining; and that it is almoft as certain a fpecific for the dropfy, as the bark is for the intermitting fever. *Cole,* 380.

The Gout.

As there are no medicines yet known that will cure the gout, we fhall confine our obfervations chiefly to regimen, both in and out of the fit.

In the fit, if the patient be young and ftrong, his diet ought to be thin and cooling, and his drink of a diluting nature; but when the conftitution is weak, and the patient has been accuftomed to live high, this is not a proper time to retrench. In this cafe, he muft keep nearly to his ufual diet, and fhould take frequently a cup of ftrong negus, or a glafs of generous wine. Wine whey is a very proper drink in this cafe, as it promotes the perfpiration without greatly heating the patient. It will anfwer this purpofe better, if a tea-fpoonful of *fal volatile oleofum,* or fpirits of hartfhorn, be put into a cup of it twice a day. It will likewife be proper to give at bed-time, a tea-fpoonful of the volatile tincture of *guaiacum,* in a large draught of warm
wine

wine whey. This will greatly promote perspiration through the night.

Many things will shorten a fit of the gout, and some will drive it off all together; but nothing has yet been found which will do this with safety to the patient. In pain, we eagerly grasp at any thing that promises immediate ease, and even hazard life itself for a temporary relief. This is the true reason why so many infallible remedies have been proposed for the gout, and why such numbers have lost their lives by the use of them. It would be as imprudent to stop the small-pox from rising, and to drive it into the blood, as to attempt to repel the gouty matter after it has been thrown upon the extremities. The latter is as much an effort of nature to free herself from an offending cause as the former, and ought equally to be promoted.

After the fit is over, the patient ought to take a gentle dose or two of the bitter tincture of rhubarb, or some other warm stomachic purge. He should also drink a weak infusion of stomachic bitters in small wine or ale, as the Peruvian bark, with cinnamon, Virginian snake-root, and orange-peel. The diet at this time should be light, but nourishing; and gentle exercise ought to be taken on horseback, or in a carriage. *Sydenham. Tissot. Buchan.*

The Gravel and Stone.

Persons afflicted with the gravel or stone, should avoid aliments of a windy or heating nature, as salt meats, sour fruits, &c. Their diet ought chiefly to consist of such things as tend to promote the secretion of urine, and to keep the body open. Artichokes, asparagus, spinach, lettuce, parsley, succory, purslane, turnips, potatoes, carrots, and radishes, may be safely eat. Onions, leeks, and celery, are, in this case, reckoned medicinal. The most proper drinks are whey, butter-milk, milk and water, barley-water, decoctions of the roots of marsh mallows, parsley, liquorice, or of other mild mucilaginous vegetables, as linseed, limetree-buds, or leaves, &c. If the patient has been accustomed to generous liquors, he may drink small gin punch without acid.

Dr. Whyte advises patients who are subject to frequent fits of the gravel in the kidnies, but have no stone in the bladder, to drink every morning, two or three hours before breakfast, an English pint of oyster or cockle-shell lime-water. The doctor very justly observes, that though this quantity might be too small to have any sensible effect in dissolving a stone in the bladder, yet it may very probably prevent its growth.

When a stone is formed in the bladder, the doctor recommends Alicant soap, oyster or cockle-shell lime-water, to be taken in the following manner:—The patient must swallow, every day, in any form that is least disagreeable, an ounce of

Z

the

the internal part of Alicant foap, and drink three or four English pints of oyfter or cockle-fhell lime-water. The foap is to be divided into three dofes; the largeft to be taken fafting in the morning early, the fecond at noon; and the third at feven in the evening; drinking after each dofe a large draugh of the lime water; the remainder of which he may take any time betwixt dinner and fupper, inftead of other liquors.

The patient fhould begin with a fmaller quantity of the lime-water and foap than that mentioned above; at firft, an English pint of the former, and three drachms of the latter, may be taken daily. This quantity, however, he may increafe by degrees, and ought to perfevere in the ufe of thefe medicines, efpecially if he finds any abatement of his complaints, for feveral months; nay, if the ftone be very large, for years. It may likewife be proper for the patient, if he be feverely pained, not only to begin with the foap and lime-water in fmall quantities, but to take the fecond or third lime-water inftead of the firft. However, after he has been accuftomed to thefe medicines, he may not only take the firft water, but, if he finds he can eafily bear it, heighten its diffolving power ftill more, by pouring it a fecond time on frefh calcined fhells.

The cauftic alkali, or foap-lees, is the medicine chiefly in vogue at prefent for the ftone. It is of a very acrid nature, and ought therefore to be given in fome gelatinous or mucilaginous liquor; as veal broth, new milk, linfeed-tea, a folution of gum arabic, or a decoction of marfh-mallow roots. The patient muft begin with fmall dofes of the lees, as thirty or forty drops, and increafe by degrees, as far as the ftomach will bear it.

The only other medicine which I fhall mention is the *uva urfi*. It has been greatly extolled of late both for the gravel and ftone. It feems, however, to be in all refpects inferior to the foap and lime-water; but it is lefs difagreeable, and has frequently, to my knowledge, relieved gravelly complaints. It is generall taken in powder from half a drachm to a whole drachm, two or three times a day. It may, however, be taken to the quantity of feven or eight drachms a day, with great fafety and good effect. *Buchan.*

The Gripes in Children.

When an infant is troubled with gripes, it ought not at firft to be dofed with brandy, fpiceries, and other hot things; but fhould have its body opened with an emollient clyfter, and, at the fame time, a little brandy may be rubbed on its belly with a warm hand before the fire. I have feldom feen this fail to eafe the gripes of infants. If it fhould happen, however, not to fucceed, a little brandy, or other fpirits, may be mixed with thrice the quantity of warm water, and a tea-fpoonful be given fre-

quently,

quently, till the infant be eafier. Sometimes a little pepper-
mint water will anfwer this purpofe very well.

The Hooping, or Chin Cough.

One of the moft effectual remedies in the chin-cough, is change
of air. This often removes the malady, even when the change
feems to be from a purer, to a lefs wholefome air. This may, in
fome meafure, depend on the patient's being removed from the
place where the infection prevails. Moft of the difeafes of children are infectious ; nor is it at all uncommon to find the chin-
cough prevailing in one town or village, when another, at a very
fmall diftance, is quite free from it. But whatever be the caufe,
we are fure of the fact. No time ought therefore to be loft in
removing the patient to fome diftance from the place where
he got the difeafe, and, if poffible, into a more pure and warm
air.

When the difeafe proves violent, and the patient is in danger
of being fuffocated by the cough, he ought to be bled, efpecially
if there be a fever, with a hard full pulfe. But as the chief intention of bleeding is to prevent an inflammation of the lungs,
and to render it more fafe to give vomits, it will feldom be neceffary to repeat the operation ; yet if there be fymptoms of an
inflammation of the lungs, a fecond, or even a third bleeding,
may be requifite.

The body ought to be kept gently open. The beft medicines
for this purpofe are rhubarb and its preparations, as the fyrup,
tincture, &c. Of thefe a tea-fpoonful or two may be given to
an infant twice or thrice a day, as there is occafion. To fuch
as are farther advanced, the dofe muft be proportionally increafed, and repeated till it has the defired effect. Thofe who cannot
be brought to take the bitter tincture, may have an infufion of
fenna and prunes, fweetened with manna, coarfe fugar, or honey ; or a few grains of rhubarb mixed with a tea-fpoonful or
two of fyrup, or currant jelly, fo as to difguife the tafte. Moft
children are fond of fyrups and jellies, and feldom refufe even a
difagreeable medicine when mixed with them.

The garlic ointment is a well-known remedy in North Britain for the chin-cough. It is made by beating in a mortar, garlic
with an equal quantity of hogs'-lard. With this the foles of the
feet may be rubbed twice or thrice a day ; but the beft method
is to fpread it upon a rag, and apply it in the form of a plafter.
It fhould be renewed every night and morning at leaft, as the
garlic foon loofes its virtue. This is an exceeding good medicine, both in the chin-cough, and in moft other coughs of
an obftinate nature. It ought not, however, to be ufed when
the patient is very hot and feverifh, left it fhould increafe thefe
fymptoms.

The

The feet fhould be bathed once in every two or three days in lukewarm water ; and a Burgundy-pitch plafter kept conftantly between the fhoulders. But when the difeafe proves very violent, it will be neceffary, inftead of it, to apply a blifteringplafter, and keep the part open for fome time with iffue ointment.

When the difeafe is prolonged, and the patient is free from a fever, the Peruvian bark, and other bitters, are the moft proper medicines. The bark may be either taken in fubftance, or in a decoction or infufion, as is moft agreeable. For a child, ten, fifteen, or twenty grains, according to the age of the patient, may be given three or four times a day. For an adult, half a drachm, or two fcruples, will be proper. Some give the extract of the bark with cantharides; but to manage this, requires a confiderable attention. It is more fafe to give a few grains of caftor along with the bark. A child of fix or feven years of age may take feven or eight grains of caftor, with fifteen grains of powdered bark, for a dofe. This may be made into a mixture with two or three ounces of fimple-diftilled water, and a little fyrup, and taken three or four times a day. *Buchan. Chambers.*

The Jaundice.

This difeafe is firft obfervable in the white of the eye, which appears yellow. Afterwards the whole fkin puts on a yellow appearance. The urine too is of a faffron colour, and dyes a white cloth of the fame colour. There is likewife a fpecies of this difeafe called the black jaundice.

If the patient be young, and the difeafe complicated with no other malady, it is feldom dangerous ; but in old people, where it continues long, returns frequently, or is complicated with the dropfy, or hypochondriac fymptoms, it generally proves fatal. The black jaundice is more dangerous than the yellow.

If the patient be young, of a full fanguine habit, and complains of pain in the right fide, about the region of the liver, bleeding will be neceffary. After this a vomit muft be adminiftered ; and if the difeafe proves obftinate, it may be repeated once or twice. No medicines are more beneficial in the jaundice than vomits, efpecially where it is not attended with inflammation. Half a drachm of ipecacuanha, in powder, will be a fufficient dofe for an adult. It may be wrought off with weak camomile tea, or lukewarm water. The body muft likewife be kept open, by taking a fufficient quantity of Caftile foap.

I have known Harrowgate fulphur-water cure the jaundice of very long ftanding. It fhould be ufed for fome weeks, and the patient muft drink and bathe.

The foluble tartar is a very proper medicine in the jaundice.

A dracham

A drachm of it may be taken every night and morning in a cup of tea or water-gruel. If it does not open the body, the dose may be increafed. A very obftinate jaundice has been cured by fwallowing raw eggs.

Perfons fubject to the jaundice, ought to take as much exercife as poffible, and to avoid all heating and aftringent aliments. *Buchan.*

The Itch.

The itch is feldom a dangerous difeafe, unlefs where it is rendered fo by neglect, or improper treatment. If it be fuffered to continue too long, it may vitiate the whole mafs of humours; and if it be fuddenly drove in, without proper evacuations, it may occafion fevers, inflammations of the vifcera, and other internal diforders.

The beft medicine yet known for the itch, is fulphur, which ought to be ufed both externally and internally. The parts moft affected may be rubbed with an ointment made of the flowers of fulphur, two ounces; crude fal ammoniac, finely powdered, two drachms; hog's lard or butter, four ounces; if a fcruple or half a drachm of the effence of lemon be added, it will entirely take away the difagreeable fmell. About the bulk of a nutmeg of this may be rubbed upon the extremities at bed-time, twice or thrice a week. It is feldom neceffary to rub the whole body; but when it is, it ought not to be done all at once, as it is dangerous to ftop too many pores at the fame time.

Before the patient begins to ufe the ointment, he ought, if he be of a full habit, to bleed, or to take a purge or two. It will likewife be proper, during the ufe of it, to take every morning as much of the flower of brimftone and cream of tartar, in a little treacle or new milk, as will keep the body gently open. He fhould beware of catching cold, fhould wear more clothes than ufual, and take every thing warm. The fame clothes, the linen excepted, ought to be worn all the time of ufing the ointment; and fuch clothes as have been worn while the patient was under the difeafe, are not to be ufed again, unlefs they have been fumigated with brimftone, and thoroughly cleaned, otherwife they will communicate the infection anew*. *Pringle.*

---

* Sir *John Pringle obferves, that, though this difeafe may feem trifling, there is no one in the army that is more troublefome to cure, as the infection often lurks in clothes, &c. and breaks out a fecond, or even a third time. The fame inconveniency occurs in private families, unlefs particular regard is paid to the changing or cleaning of their clothes, which laft is by no means an eafy operation.*

A Diar

A Diarrhœa, or Loofenefs.

A loofenefs, in many cafes, is not to be confidered as a difcafe, but rather as a falutary evacuation. It ought, therefore, never to be ftopped, unlefs when it continues too long, or evidently weakens the patient. As this, however, fometimes happens, I fhall point out the moft common caufes of a loofenefs, with the proper method of treatment.

When a loofenefs is occafioned by catching cold, or an obftructed perfpiration, the patient ought to keep warm, to drink freely of weak diluting liquors, to bathe his feet and legs frequently in lukewarm water, to wear flannel next his fkin, and to take every other method to reftore the perfpiration.

In a loofenefs which proceeds from excefs or repletion, a vomit is the proper medicine. Vomits not only cleanfe the ftomach, but promote all the fecretions, which render them of great importance in carrying off a debauch. Half a drachm of ipecacuanha, in powder, will anfwer this purpofe very well. A day or two after the vomit, the fame quantity of rhubarb may be taken, and repeated two or three times, if the loofenefs continues. The patient ought to live upon light vegetable food of eafy digeftion, and to drink whey, thin gruel, or barley water.

A loofenefs, occafioned by the obftruction of any cuftomary evacuation, generally requires bleeding. If that does not fucceed, other evacuations may be fubftituted in the room of thofe which are obftructed. At the fame time every method is to be taken to reftore the ufual difcharges, as not only the cure of the difeafe, but the patient's life may depend on this.

A periodical loofenefs ought never to be ftopped. It is always an effort of nature to carry off fome offending matter, which, if retained in the body, might have fatal effects. Children are very liable to this kind of loofenefs, efpecially while toothing. It is, however, fo far from being hurtful to them, that fuch children generally get their teeth with lefs trouble. If thefe loofe ftools fhould at any time prove four or griping, a tea-fpoonful of magnefia alba, with four or five grains of rhubarb, may be given to the child in a little panada, or any other food. This, if repeated three or four times, will generally correct the acidity, and carry off the griping ftools.

From whatever caufe a loofenefs proceeds, when it is found neceffary to check it, the diet ought to confift of rice boiled with milk, and flavoured with cinnamon; rice-jelly; fago, with red port; and the lighter forts of flefh meat roafted. The drink may be thin water-gruel, rice-water, or weak broth made from lean veal, or with a fheep's head, as being more gelatinous than mutton, beef, or chicken broth. *Buchan.*

Obftruc-

Obstructions in young Girls.

After a female has arrived at that period of life when the *menses* usually begin to flow, and they do not appear, but, on the contrary, her health and spirits begin to decline, I would advise, instead of shutting the poor girl up in the house, and dosing her with steel, asafœtida, and other nauseous drugs, to place her in a situation where she can enjoy the benefit of free air and agreeable company. There let her eat wholesome food, take sufficient exercise, and amuse herself in the most agreeable manner; and we have little reason to fear, but Nature, thus assisted, will do her proper work. Indeed she seldom fails, unless where the fault is on our side.

This discharge, in the beginning is seldom so instantaneous as to surprise females unawares. It is generally preceded by symptoms which foretel its approach; as a sense of heat, weight, and dull pain in the loins; distention and hardness of the breasts; head-ach; loss of appetite; lassitude; paleness of the countenance; and sometimes a slight degree of fever. When these symptoms appear about the age at which the menstrual flux usually begins, every thing should be carefully avoided which may obstruct that necessary and salutary evacuation; and all means used to promote it; as sitting frequently over the steam of warm water, drinking warm diluting liquors, &c.

After the *menses* have once begun to flow, the greatest care should be taken to avoid every thing that may tend to obstruct them. Females ought to be exceedingly cautious of what they eat or drink at the time they are out of order. Every thing that is cold, or apt to sour on the stomach, ought to be avoided; as fruit, butter milk, and such like. Fish, and all kinds of food that are hard of digestion, are also to be avoided. As it is impossible to mention every thing that may disagree with individuals at this time, I would recommend it to every female to be very attentive to what disagrees with herself, and carefully to avoid it.

From whatever cause this flux is obstructed, except in the state of pregnancy, proper means should be used to restore it. For this purpose I would recommend sufficient exercise in a dry, open, and rather cool air; wholesome diet, and if the body be weak and languid, generous liquors; also cheerful company, and all manner of amusements. If these fail, recourse must be had to medicine.

When obstructions proceed from a weak relaxed state of the solids, such medicines as tend to promote digestion, to brace the solids, and assist the body in preparing good blood, ought to be used. The principal of these are iron and the Peruvian bark, with all other bitter and astringent medicines. Filings of iron maybe infused in wine or ale, two or three ources to an Eng-

lish

lifh quart, and after it has ftood for two or three weeks, it may be filtered, and about half a wine glafs of it taken twice a day: or prepared fteel may be taken in the dofe of half a drachm, mixed with a little honey or treacle, three or four times a day. The bark, and other bitters, may be either taken in fubftance or infufion, as is moft agreeable to the patient.

But the menftrual flux may be too great as well as too fmall. When this happens, the patient becomes weak, the colour pale, the appetite and digeftion are bad, and œdematous fwellings of the feet, dropfies, and confumptions enfue. This frequently happens to women about the age of forty-five and fifty, and is very difficult to cure. It may proceed from a fedentary life, a full diet, confifting chiefly of falted, high feafoned, or acrid food; the ufe of fpirituous liquors; exceffive fatigue; relaxation; a diffolved ftate of the blood; violent paffions of the mind, &c.

The treatment of this difeafe muft be varied according to its caufe. When it is occafioned by any error in the patient's regimen. an oppofite courfe to that which induced the diforder, muft be purfued, and fuch medicines taken as have a tendency to reftrain the flux, and counteract the morbid affections of the fyftem from whence it proceeds. *Arbuthnot.*

The Bleeding and Blind Piles.

A difcharge of blood from the hœmorrhoidal veffels, is called the *bleeding piles.* When the veffels only fwell and difcharge no blood, but are exceeding painful, the difeafe is called the *blind piles.*

A flux of blood from the *anus* is not always to be treated as a difeafe. It is even more falutary than bleeding at the nofe, and often prevents or carries off difeafes. It is peculiarly beneficial in the gout, rheumatifm, afthma, and hypochondriacal complaints; and often proves critical in colics and inflammatory fevers.

In the management of the patient, regard muft be had to his habit of body, his age, ftrength, and manner of living. A difcharge which might be exceffive, and prove hurtful to one, may be very moderate, and even falutary to another. That only is to be efteemed dangerous which continues too long, and is in fuch quantity as to wafte the patient's ftrength, hurt digeftion, nutrition, and other functions neceffary to life.

When this is the cafe, the difcharge muft be checked by a proper regimen, and aftringent medicines. The diet muft be cool, but nourifhing, confifting chiefly of bread, milk, cooling vegetables, and broths. The drink may be chalybeate water, orange whey, decoctions or infufions of the aftringent and mucilaginous plants, as the tormentil root, biftort, the marfhmallow roots, &c.

The

The Peruvian bark is likewise proper in this cafe, both as a ſtrengthener and aſtringent : half a drachm of it may be taken in a glaſs of red wine, ſharpened with a few drops of the elixir of vitriol, three or four times a day.

The bleeding piles are ſometimes periodical, and return regularly once a month, or once in three weeks. In this cafe they are always to be conſidered as a ſalutary diſcharge, and by no means to be ſtopped. Some have entirely ruined their health by ſtopping a periodical diſcharge of blood from the hœmorrhoidal veins.

In the *blind piles*, bleeding is generally of uſe. The diet muſt be light and thin, and the drink cool and diluting. It is likewiſe neceſſary that the body be kept gently open. This may be done by ſmall doſes of the flowers of brimſtone and cream of tartar. They may be mixed in equal quantities, and a teaſpoonful taken two or three times a day, or oftener if neceſſary. Or an ounce of the flowers of brimſtone, and half an ounce of purified nitre, may be mixed with three or four ounces of the lenitive electuary, and a tea-ſpoonful of it taken three or four times a day.

Various ointments, and other external applications, are recommended in the piles ; but I do not remember to have ſeen any effects from theſe worth mentioning. Their principal uſe is to keep the part moiſt, which may be done as well by a ſoft poultice, or an emollient cataplaſm. When the pain, however, is very great, a liniment made of two ounces of emollient ointment, and half an ounce of liquid laudanum, beat up with the yolk of an egg, may be applied. *Tiſſot. Buchan.*

The *Quinſey, or Inflammation of the Throat,*

In general it proceeds from the ſame cauſes as other inflammatory diſorders, *viz.* an obſtructed perſpiration, or whatever heats or inflames the blood. An inflammation of the throat is often occaſioned by omitting ſome part of the covering uſually worn about the neck, by drinking cold liquor when the body is warm, by riding or walking againſt a cold northerly wind, or any thing that greatly cools the throat, and parts adjacent. It may likewiſe proceed from the neglect of bleeding, purging, or any other cuſtomary evacuation.

The inflammation of the throat is evident from inſpection, the parts appearing red and ſwelled ; beſides, the patient complains of pain in ſwallowing. His pulſe is quick and hard, with other ſymptoms of a fever. If blood be let, it is generally covered with a tough coat of a whitiſh colour, and the patient ſpits a tough phlegm. As the ſwelling and inflammation increaſe, the breathing and ſwallowing become more difficult ; the pain affects the ears ; the eyes generally appear red, and the face ſwells. The patient is often obliged to keep himſelf

in

in an erect posture, being in danger of suffocation; there is a constant nausea, or inclination to vomit, and the drink, instead of passing into the stomach is often returned by the nose. The patient is frequently starved at last, merely from an inability to swallow any kind of food.

When the breathing is laborious, with straitness of breast and anxiety, the danger is great. Though the pain in swallowing be very great, yet while the patient breathes easy, there is not so much danger. An external swelling is no unfavourable symptom; but if it suddenly falls, and the disease affects the breast, the danger is very great. When a quinsey is the consequence of some other disease, which has already weakened the patient, his situation is dangerous. A frothing at the mouth, with a swelled tongue, a pale, ghastly countenance, and coldness of the extremities, are fatal symptoms.

It is highly necessary that the patient be kept easy and quiet. Violent affections of the mind, or great efforts of the body, may prove fatal. He should never even attempt to speak but in a low voice. Such a degree of warmth as to promote a constant, gentle sweat, is proper. When the patient is in bed, his head ought to be raised a little higher than usual.

It is peculiarly necessary that the neck be kept warm; for which purpose several folds of soft flannel may be wrapped round it. That alone will often remove a slight complaint of the throat, especially if applied in due time. We cannot here omit observing the propriety of a custom which prevails among the peasants of this country:—when they feel any uneasiness of the throat, they wrap a stocking about it all night. So effectual is this remedy, that in many places it passes for a charm, and the stocking is applied with particular ceremonies. The custom, however, is undoubtedly a good one, and should never be neglected. When the throat has been thus wrapped up all night, it must not be exposed to the cold air through the day, but an handkerchief, or a piece of flannel, kept about it till the inflammation be removed.

The jelly of black currants is a medicine very much in esteem for complaints of the throat; and indeed it is of some use. It should be almost constantly kept in the mouth, and swallowed down leisurely. It may likewise be mixed in the patient's drink, or taken any other way. When it cannot be obtained, the jelly of red currants, or of mulberries, may be used in its stead.

Gargles for the throat are very beneficial. They may be made of sage tea, with a little vinegar and honey, or by adding to half an English pint of the pectoral decoction, two or three spoonfuls of honey, and the same quantity of currant jelly. This may be used three or four times a day; and if the patient

be

be troubled with tough vifcid phlegm, the gargle may be rendered more fharp and cleanfing, by adding to it a tea-fpoonful of the fpirit of *fal ammoniac*. Some recommend gargles made of a decoction of the leaves or bark of the blackberry bufh; but where the jelly can be had, this is unneceffary.

An inflammation of the throat being a moft acute and dangerous diftemper, which fometimes takes off the patient very fuddenly, it will be proper, as foon as the fymptoms appear, to bleed in the arm, or rather in the jugular vein, and to repeat the operation as circumftances require.

It fometimes happens, before the ulcer breaks, that the fwelling is fo great as entirely to prevent any thing from getting down into the ftomach. In this cafe, the patient muft inevitably perifh, unlefs he can be fupported in fome other way. This can only be done by nourifhing clyfters of broth, or gruel, with milk, &c. Patients have often been fupported by thefe for feveral days, till the tumour has broke; and afterwards they have recovered. *Huxham. Fothergill.*

The Rheumatifm.

The *acute* rheumatifm commonly begins with wearinefs, fhivering, a quick pulfe, reftlefsnefs, thirft, and other fymptoms of a fever. Afterwards the patient complains of flying pains, which are increafed by the leaft motion. Thefe at laft fix in the joints, which are often attended with fwelling and inflammation. If blood be let in this difeafe, it has generally the fame appearance as in the pleurify.

In this kind of rheumatifm, the treatment of the patient is nearly the fame as in an acute or inflammatory fever.

The chronic rheumatifm is feldom attended with any confiderable degree of fever, and is generally confined to fome particular part of the body, as the fhoulders, the back, or the loins. There is feldom any inflammation or fwelling in this cafe. Perfons in the decline of life are moft fubject to the chronic rheumatifm. In fuch patients it often proves extremely obftinate, and fometimes incurable.

In this kind of rheumatifm, the regimen fhould be nearly the fame as in the acute. Cool and diluting diet, confifting chiefly of vegetable fubftances, as ftewed prunes, coddled apples, currants or goofeberries boiled in milk, is moft proper. Arbuthnot fays, "If there be a fpecific in aliment for the rheumatifm, it is certainly whey;" and adds, "that he knew a perfon fubject to this difeafe, who could never be cured by any other method but a diet of whey and bread." He likewife fays, "that cream of tartar in water gruel, taken for feveral days, will eafe rheumatic pains confiderably. This I
have

have often experienced, but found it always more efficacious
when joined with gum guaiacum.

What I have generally found anfwer better than either of
thefe, in obftinate fixed rheumatic pains, is the *warm plafter*,
made as follows: " Take of gum plafter, one ounce; bliftering
" plafter, two drachms; melt them together over a gentle fire."
I have likewife known a plafter of Burgundy pitch, worn for
fome time on the part affected, give great relief in rheumatic
cafes. Dr. Alexander fays, " He has frequently cured many
" obftinate rheumatic pains, by rubbing the part affected with
" tincture of cantharides " When the common tincture did
not fucceed, he ufed it of a double or treble ftrength. Cupping upon the part affected is likewife very often beneficial,
and is greatly preferable to the application of leeches.

There are feveral of our own domeftic plants which may be
ufed with advantage in the rheumatifm. One of the beft, is
the white *muftard*. A table fpoonful of the feed of this plant
may be taken twice or thrice a day, in a glafs of water or fmall
wine. The water trefoil is likewife of great ufe in this complaint. It may be infufed in ale or wine, or drank in form of
tea. The ground-ivy, camomile, and feveral other bitters, are
alfo beneficial, and may be ufed in the fame manner. No benefit however is to be experienced from thefe, unlefs they be
taken for a confiderable time. *Tiffot. Arbuthnot.*

The Rickets.

As this difeafe is often attended with evident figns of weaknefs and relaxation, our chief aim in the cure muft be to brace
and ftrengthen the folids, and to promote digeftion and the
due preparation of the fluids. Thefe important ends will be
beft anfwered by wholefome nourifhing diet, fuited to the age
and ftrength of the patient, open dry air, and fufficient exercife. If the child has a bad nurfe, who either neglects her
duty or does not underftand it, fhe fhould be changed. If the
feafon be cold, the child ought to be kept warm; and when
the weather is hot, it ought to be kept cool; as fweating is
apt to weaken it, and too great a degree of cold has the fame
effect. The limbs fhould be rubbed frequently with a warm
hand, and the child kept as cheerful as poffible.

The diet ought to be dry and nourifhing, as good bread,
roafted flefh, &c. Bifcuit is generally reckoned the beft bread,
and pigeons, pullets, veal, rabbits, or mutton, roafted or minced, are the moft proper flefh. If the child be too young for
flefh meats, he may have rice, millet, or pearl barley, boiled
with raifins, to which may be added a little wine and fpice.
His drink may be good claret, mixed with an equal quantity of
water. Thofe who cannot afford claret, may give the child
now and then a wine-glafs of mild ale, or good porter.

Sometimes

Sometimes iffues have been found beneficial in this difeafe. They are peculiarly neceffary for children who abound with grofs humours. An infufion of the Peruvian bark, in wine or ale, would be of fervice, were it poffible to bring children to take it. I might here mention many other medicines which have been recommended for the rickets ; but as there is far more danger in trufting to thefe, than in neglecting them altogether, I chufe rather to pafs them over, and to recommend a proper regimen as the thing chiefly to be depended upon. *Buchan.*

The Scurvy.

This difeafe may be known by unufual wearinefs, heavinefs, and difficulty of breathing, efpecially after motion ; rottennefs of the gums, which are apt to bleed on the flighteft touch ; a ftinking breath ; frequent bleeding at the nofe ; crackling of the joints ; difficulty of walking ; fometimes a fwelling, and fometimes a falling away of the legs, on which there are livid, yellow or voilet-coloured fpots ; the face is generally of a pale or leaden colour. As the difeafe advances, other fymptoms come on ; as rottennefs of the teeth, hæmorrhages, or difcharges of blood from different parts of the body, foul obftinate ulcers, pains in various parts, efpecially about the breaft, dry fcaly eruptions all over the body, &c. At laft, a wafting or hectic fever comes on, and the miferable patient is often carried off by a dyfentry, a diarrhæa, a dropfy, the palfey, fainting fits, or a mortification of fome of the bowels.

I know no way of curing this difeafe, but by purfuing a plan directly oppofite to that which it brings on. It proceeds from a vitiated ftate of the humours, occafioned by errors in diet, air, exercife ; and thefe cannot be removed but by a proper attention to thefe important articles.

If the patient has been obliged to breathe a cold damp, or confined air, be fhould be removed, as foon as poffible, to a dry, open, and moderately warm one. If there is reafon to believe that the difeafe proceeds from a fedentary life, or depreffing paffions, as grief, fear, &c. the patient muft take daily as much exercife in the open air as he can bear, and his mind fhould be diverted by cheerful company, and other amufements. Nothing has a greater tendency either to prevent or remove this difeafe, than conftant cheerfulnefs and good humour. But this, alas ! is feldom the lot of perfons afflicted with the fcurvy ; they are generally furly, peevifh, and morofe.

When the fcurvy has been brought on by a long ufe of falted provifions, the proper medicine is a diet confifting of frefh vegetables ; as oranges, apples, lemons, limes, tamarinds, water creffes, fcurvy grafs, brook lime, &c. The ufe of thefe, with milk, pot herbs, new bread, and frefh beer or cyder, will feldom fail to remove a fcurvy of this kind, if taken before it be too far

advanced ;

advanced; but to have this effect, they must be persisted in for a considerable time.

I have often seen very extraordinay effects in the land-scurvy, from a milk diet. This preparation of nature, is a mixture of animal and vegetable properties, which of all others is the most fit for restoring a decayed constitution, and removing that particular acrimony of the humours which seems to constitute the very essence of the scurvy, and many other diseases. But people despise this wholesome and nourishing food because it is cheap; and devour with greediness flesh and fermented liquors, while milk is only deemed fit for their hogs.

The most proper drink in the scurvy is whey or butter-milk. When these cannot be had, sound cyder, perry, or spruce beer, may be used. Wort has likewise been found to be a proper drink in the scurvy, and may be used at sea, as malt will keep during the longest voyage. A decoction of the tops of the spruce fir, is likewise proper. It may be drank in the quantity of an English pint twice a-day. Tar water may be used for the same purpose, or decoctions of any of the mild mucilaginous vegetables; as sarsaparilla, marsh-mallow roots, &c. Infusions of the bitter plants, as ground-ivy, the lesser centaury, marsh trefoil, &c. are likewise beneficial. I have seen the peasants in some parts of Britain express the juice of the last-mentioned plant, and drink it with good effect in those foul scorbutic eruptions with which they are often troubled in the spring season

A flight degree of scurvy may be carried off by frequently sucking a little of the juice of a bitter orange, or a lemon. When the disease affects the gums only, this practice, if continued for some time, will generally carry it off. We would, however, recommend the bitter orange, as greatly preferable to lemon; it seems to be as good a medicine, and is not nearly so hurtful to the stomach. Perhaps our own sorrel may be little inferior to either of them.

All kinds of salad are good in the scurvy, and ought to be eat very plentifully, as spinach, lettuce, parsley, cellery, endive, radish, dandelion, &c. It is amazing to see how soon fresh vegetables in the spring cure the brute animals of any scab or foulness which is upon their skins. It is reasonable to suppose, that their effect would be as great upon the human species, were they used in proper quantity for a sufficient length of time. *Buchan. Chambers.*

Spitting of Blood, &c.

Spontaneous, or involuntary discharges of blood, often happen from various parts of body. These, however, are so far from being always dangerous, that they prove often salutary. When such discharges are critical, which is frequently the case in in fevers, they ought not to be ftopped. Nor indeed is it proper at any time to ftop them, unlefs they be fo great as to endanger the patient's life. Moft people, afraid of the fmalleft difcharge of blood from any part of the body, fly immediately to the ufe of ftyptic and aftringent medicines, by which means an inflammation of the brain, or fome other fatal difeafe is occafioned, which, had the difcharge been allowed to go on, might have been prevented.

In the early part of life, bleeding at the nofe is very common. Thofe who are further advanced in years, are more liable to hœmoptoe, or difcharge of blood from the lungs. After the middle period of life, hœmorrhoidal fluxes are moft common; and in the decline of life, difcharges of blood from the urinary paffages.

Involuntary fluxes of blood may proceed from very different, and often from quite oppofite caufes. Sometimes they are owing to a particular conftruction of the body, as a fanguine temperament, a laxity of the veffels, a plethoric habit, &c. At other times they proceed from a determination of the blood towards one particular part, as the head, the hœmorrhoidal veins, &c. They may likewife proceed from an inflammatory difpofition of the blood, in which cafe there is generally fome degree of fever; this likewife happens when the flux is occafioned by an obftructed perfpiration, or a ftricture upon the fkin, the bowels, or any particular part of the fyftem.

The cure of an hœmorrhage muft be adapted to its caufe. When it proceeds from too much blood, or a tendency to inflammation, bleeding, with gentle purges, and other evacuations, will be neceffary. It will likewife be proper for the patient in this cafe to live chiefly upon a vegetable diet, to avoid all ftrong liquors, and food that is of an acrid, hot, and ftimulating quality. The body fhould be kept cool, and the mind eafy.

When an hœmorrhage is owing to a putrid, or diffolved ftate of the blood, the patient ought to live chiefly upon acid fruits, with milk and vegetables of a nourifhing nature, as fago, falop, &c. His drink may be wine diluted with water, and fharpened with the juice of lemon, vinegar, or fpirits of vitriol. The beft medicine in this cafe is the Peruvian bark, which may be taken according to the urgency of the fymptoms.

When a flux of blood is the effect of acrid food, or of ftrong ftimulating medicines, the cure is to be effected by foft and mucilaginous diet. The patient may likewife take frequently about the bulk of a nutmeg of Locatelli's balfam, or the fame quantity of fperma-ceti.

When an obftructed perfpiration, or a ftricture upon any part of the fyftem is the caufe of an hœmorrhage, it may be

removed

removed by drinking warm diluting liquors, lying a-bed; bathing the extremities in warm water, &c. *Tiſſot.*

The Apthœ, or Thruſh.

The apthœ are little whitiſh ulcers affecting the whole in-ſide of the mouth, tongue, throat, and ſtomach of infants. Sometimes they reach through the whole inteſtinal canal ; in which caſe they are very dangerous, and often put at end to the infant's life.

If the apthœ are of a pale colour, pellucid, few in number, ſoft. ſuperficial, and fall eaſily off, they are not dangerous ; but if opaque, yellow, brown, black, thick, or running together, they ought to be dreaded.

The moſt proper medicines for the aphthœ, are vomits, and gentle laxatives. Five grains of rhubarb, and half a drachm of *magneſia alba*, may be rubbed together, and divided into ſix doſes. one of which may be given to the infant every four or five hours till they operate. Theſe powders may either be given in the child's food, or a little of the ſyrup of pale roſes, may be repeated as often as is found neceſſary to keep the body open. It is common in this caſe to adminiſter calomel ; but as that medicine ſometimes occaſions gripes, it ought al-ways to be given to infants with caution.

Many things have been recommended for gargling the mouth and throat in this diſeaſe ; but it is not eaſy to apply theſe in very young infants. I would, therefore, recommended it to the nurſe to rub the child's mouth frequently with a little bo-rax and honey ; or with the following mixture :—Take fine honey. an ounce ; borax, a drachm ; burnt allum, half a drachm ; roſe-water two drachms ; mix them together. A very proper application in this caſe, is a ſolution of ten or twelve grains of white vitroil in eight ounces of barley-water. Theſe may be applied with the finger, or by means of a bit of ſoft rag tied to the end of a probe. *Buchan.*

The Tooth-ach.

This diſeaſe is ſo well known, that it needs no deſcription. It has great affinity with the rheumatiſm, and often ſucceeds pains of the ſhoulders, and other parts of the body.

It may proceed from obſtructed perſpiration, or any of the other cauſes of inflammation. I have often known the tooth-ach occaſioned by neglecting ſome part of the uſual coverings of the head, by ſitting with the bare head near an open window, or expoſing it any how to a draught of cold air. Food or drink taken either too hot or too cold, is very hurtful to the teeth. Great quantities of ſugar, or other ſweetmeats, are like-wiſe hurtful. Nothing is more deſtructive to the teeth than cracking nuts, or chewing any kind of hard ſubſtances. Picking

ing the teeth with pins, needles, or any thing that may hurt the enamel with which they are covered, does great mischief, as the tooth is sure to be spoiled whenever any thing gets into it. Breeding women are very subject to the tooth-ach, especially during the first three or four months of pregnancy. The tooth ach often proceeds from scorbutic humours affecting the gums. In this case the teeth are sometimes wasted, and fall out without any considerable degree of pain. The more immediate cause of the tooth-ach is a rotten or *carious* tooth.

In order to relieve the tooth-ach, we must first endeavour to draw off the humours from the part affected. This may be done by mild purgatives, scarifying the gums, or applying leeches to them, and bathing the feet frequently with warm water. The perspiration ought likewise to be promoted, by drinking freely of weak wine whey, or other diluting liquors, with small doses of nitre. Vomits too, have often an exceeding good effect in the tooth-ach. It is seldom safe to administer opiates, or any kind of heating medicines, or even to draw a tooth till proper evacuations have been premised, and these alone will often effect the cure.

If this fails, and the pain and inflammation still increase, a suppuration may be expected, to promote which, a toasted fig should be held between the gums and the cheek; bags filled with boiled camomile flowers, flowers of elder, or the like, may be applied near the part affected, with as great a degree of warmth as the the patient can bear, and renewed as they grow cold. The patient may likewise receive the steam of warm water into his mouth, through an inverted funnel, or by holding his head over the mouth of a porringer filled with warm water, &c.

Such things as promote the discharge of saliva, or cause the patient to spit, are generally of service. For this purpose, bitter, hot, or pungent vegetables may be chewed; as gentian, calamus aromaticus, or pellitory of Spain.

Opiates often relieve the tooth-ach. For this purpose, a little cotton wet with laudanum may be held between the teeth; or a piece of sticking plaster, about the bigness of a shilling, with a bit of opium in the middle of it, of a size not to prevent the sticking of the other, may be laid on the temporal artery, where the pulsation is most sensible. *De la Motte* affirms, that there are few cases wherein this will not give relief. If there be a hollow tooth, a small pill made of equal parts of camphor and opium put into the hollow, is often beneficial. When this cannot be had the hollow tooth may be filled with gum mastich, wax, lead, or any substance that will stick in it, and keep out the external air.

Keeping the teeth clean has no doubt a tendency to prevent

A a

the

the tooth ach. The beſt method of doing this is to waſh them daily with ſalt and water, a decoction of the bark, or with cold water alone. All bruſhing and ſcraping of the teeth is dangerous, and unleſs it be performed with great care, does miſchief. *De la Motte. Buchan.*

The Bite of the Viper.

The greaſe of this animal rubbed into the wound, is ſaid to cure the bite. Though that is all the viper catchers generally do when bit, I ſhould not think it ſufficient for the bite of an enraged viper. It would be ſurely more ſafe to have the wound well ſucked*, and afterwards rubbed with warm ſalad oil. A poultice of bread and milk, ſoftened with ſalad oil, ſhould likewiſe be applied to the wound ; and the patient ought to drink freely of vinegar whey, or water-gruel with vinegar in it, to make him ſweat. Vinegar is one of the beſt medicines that can be uſed in any kind of poiſon, and ought to be taken very liberally. If the patient be ſick, he may take a vomit. This courſe will be ſufficient to cure the bite of any of the poiſonous animals of this country.

The Sting of Waſps, Hornets, Bees, &c.

The ſtings of theſe poiſonous inſects are ſeldom attended with danger, unleſs when a perſon happens to be ſtung by a great number of them at the ſame time ; in which caſe ſomething ſhould be done to abate the inflammation and ſwelling. Some, for this purpoſe, apply honey, others lay pounded parſley to the part. A mixture of vinegar and Venice treacle is likewiſe recommended ; but I have always found rubbing the part with warm ſalad oil ſucceed very well. Indeed, when the ſtings are ſo numerous as to endanger the patient's life, which is ſometimes the caſe, he muſt not only have oily poultices applied to the part, but muſt likewiſe be bled, and take ſome cooling medicines, as nitre, or cream of tartar, and ſhould drink plentifully of diluting liquors. *Buchan.*

Worms.

Though numberleſs medicines are extolled for killing and

---

* *The practice of ſucking out poiſons is very ancient, and indeed nothing can be more rational. When the bite cannot be cut out, this is the moſt likely way for extracting poiſon. There can be no danger in performing this office, as the poiſon does no harm unleſs it be taken into the body by a wound. The perſon who ſucks the wound ought, however, to waſh his mouth frequently with ſalad oil, which will ſave him from even the leaſt inconveniency. The Bſylli in Africa, and the Merſi in Italy, are famed for curing the bites of poiſonous animals by ſucking the wound ; and we are told that the Indians in North America practice the ſame at this day.*

expelling

expelling worms, yet no difeafe more frequently baffles the phyficians' fkill. In general, the moft proper medicines for their
expulfion, are ftrong purgatives; and to prevent their breeding, ftomachic bitters, with now and then a glafs of good wine.

The beft purge for an adult is jalap and calomel. Five and
twenty or thirty grains of the former, with fix or feven of the
latter, mixed in fyrup, may be taken early in the morning, for
a dofe. It will be proper that the patient keep the houfe all
day, and drink nothing cold. The dofe may be repeated once
or twice a week, for a fortnight or three weeks. On the inter-
mediate days, the patient may take a drachm of the powder of
tin, twice or thrice a day, mixed with fyrup, honey, or treacle.

Thofe who do not chufe to take calomel, may make ufe of
the bitter purgatives; as aloes, hiera picra, tincture of fenna,
and rhubarb, &c.   .

Oily medicines are fometimes found beneficial for expelling
worms. An ounce of falad oil and a table-fpoonful of common falt may be taken in a glafs of red port wine thrice a day,
or oftener if the ftomach will bear it. But the more common
form of ufing oil is in clyfters. Oily clyfters, fweetened with
fugar or honey, are very efficacious in bringing away the fhort
round worms called *afcardes*, and likewife the *teres*.

I have frequently known thofe big bellies, which in children
are commonly reckoned a fign of worms, quite removed by giving them white foap in their pottage, or other food. Tanfy,
garlic, and rue, are all good againft worms, and may be ufed
various ways. I might have mentioned many other plants,
both for external and internal ufe, as the cabbage-bark, &c. but
think the powder of tin, with Ethiops mineral, and the purges
of rhubarb and calomel, are more to be depended on.

Ball's purging vermifuge powder is a very powerful medicine.
It is made of equal parts of rhubarb, fcammony, and calomel,
with as much double refined fugar as is equal to the weight of
all the other ingredients. Thefe muft be well mixed together,
and reduced to a fine powder. The dofe for a child, is from
ten grains to twenty, one or twice a week. An adult may take
a drachm for a dofe.

Parents who would preferve their children from worms ought
to allow them plenty of exercife in the open air; to take care
that their food be wholefome and fufficiently folid; and, as far
as poffible, to prevent their eating raw herbs, roots, or green
trafhy fruits. It will not be amifs to allow a child who is fubject to worms, a glafs of red wine after meals; as every thing
that braces and ftrengthens the ftomach is good both for preventing and expelling thefe vermin. *Ball. Buchan.*

Of Vomiting.

Vomiting may proceed from various caufes; as excefs in eat-

ing

ing and drinking ; foulnefs of the ftomach; the acrimony of the aliments ; a tranflation of the morbific matter of ulcers, of the gout, the eryfipelas, or other difeafes of the ftomach. It may likewife proceed from a loofenefs having been too fuddenly ftopped; from the ftoppage of any cuftomary evacuation, as the bleeding piles, the *menfes*, &c. from a weaknefs of the ftomach, the cholic, the iliac paffion, a rupture, a fit of the gravel, worms, or from any kind of poifon taken into the ftomach. It is an ufual fymptom of injuries done to the brain; as contufions, compreffions, &c.

Vomiting may be occafioned by unufual motions ; as failing, being drawn backwards in a cart or coach, &c. It may likewife be excited by violent paffions, or by the idea of naufeous or difagreeable objects, efpecially of fuch things as have formerly produced vomiting. Sometimes it proceeds from a regurgitation of the bile into the ftomach ; in this cafe, what the patient vomits is generally of a yellow or greenifh colour, and has a bitter tafte. Perfons who are fubject to nervous affections are often fuddenly feized with violent fits of vomiting. Laftly, vomiting is a common fymptom of pregnancy. In this cafe it generally comes on about two weeks after the ftoppage of the *menfes*, and continues during the firft three or four months.

When vomiting proceeds from a foul ftomach or indigeftion, it is not to be confidered as a difeafe, but as the cure of a difeafe. It ought therefore to to be promoted by drinking lukewarm water, or thin gruel. If this does not put a ftop to the vomiting, a dofe of ipecacuanha may be taken, and worked off with weak camomile-tea.

When the obftruction of cuftomary evacuations occafion vomiting, all means muft be ufed to reftore thefe difcharges ; or, if that cannot be effected, their place muft be fupplied by others, as bleeding, purging, bathing the extremities in warm water, opening iffues, fetons, perpetual blifters, &c.

When vomiting is the effect of pregnancy, it may generally be mitigated by bleeding, and keeping the body gently open. The bleeding however ought to be in fmall quantities at a time, and the purgatives fhould be of the mildeft kind, as figs, ftewed prunes, manna, or fenna. Pregnant women are moft apt to vomit in the morning, immediately after getting out of bed, which is owing partly to the change of pofture, but more to the emptinefs of the ftomach. It may generally be prevented by taking a difh of coffee, tea, or fome light breakfaft in bed.

If vomiting proceeds from weaknefs of the ftomach, bitters will be of fervice. Peruvian bark infufed in wine or brandy, with as much rhubarb as will keep the body gently open, is an excellent medicine in this cafe. Habitual vomitings are fometimes alleviated by making oyfters a principal part of diet.

A vomit-

A vomiting which proceeds from acidities in the ftomach, is relieved by alkaline purges. The beft medicine of this kind is the magnefia alba, a tea-fpoonful of which may be taken in a difh of tea or a little milk, three or four times a day, or oftener if neceffary, to keep the body open.

When vomiting proceeds from violent paffions, or affections of the mind, all evacuants muft be carefully avoided, efpecially vomits. Thefe are exceedingly dangerous. The patient in this cafe ought to be kept perfectly eafy and quiet, to have the mind foothed, and to take fome gentle cordial, as negus, or a little brandy and water, to which a few drops of laudanum may occafionally be added.

Suppreffion of Urine.

Suppreffion of urine may proceed from various caufes; as an inflammation of the kidnies, or bladder; finall ftones or gravel lodging in the urinary paffages; hard *faces* lying in the *rectum*; pregnancy; a fpafm or contraction of the neck of the bladder; clotted blood in the bladder itfelf; a fwelling of the hæmorrhoidal veins, &c.

In thefe cafes a bougie may be ufed by any cautious hand, and will often fucceed.

In all obftructions of urine, the body ought to be kept open. This is not however to be attempted by ftrong purgatives, but by emollient clyfters, or gentle infufions of fenna and manna. Clyfters in this cafe not only open the body, but anfwer the purpofe of an internal fomentation, and greatly affift in removing the fpafms of the bladder and parts adjacent.

The food muft be light, and taken in fmall quantities. The drink may be weak broth, or decoctions and infufions of mucilaginous vegetables, as marfh-mallow roots, lime-tree buds, &c. A tea fpoonful of the fweet fpirits of nitre, or a drachm of Caftile foap, may be frequently put into the patient's drink; and, if there be no inflammation, he may drink fmall gin-punch.

Perfons fubject to a fuppreffion of urine ought to live very temperate. Their diet fhould be light, and their liquor diluting. They fhould avoid all acids and auftere wines, fhould take fufficient exercife, lie hard, and avoid ftudy and fedentary occupations.

Bleeding at the Nofe.

Bleeding at the nofe is commonly preceded by fome degree of quicknefs of the pulfe, flufhing in the face, pulfation of the temporal arteries, heavinefs in the head, dimnefs of the fight, heat and itching of the noftrils, &c.

To perfons who abound with blood, this difcharge is very falutary. It often cures a vertigo, the head-ach, a phrenzy, and even an epilepfy. In fevers, where there is a great determination

A a 3 mination

mination of blood towards the head, it is of the utmoſt ſervice. It is likewiſe beneficial in inflammations of the liver and ſpleen, and often in the gout and rheumatiſm. In all diſeaſes where bleeding is neceſſary, a ſpontaneous diſcharge of blood from the noſe is of much more ſervice than the ſame quantity let with a lancet.

In a diſcharge of blood from the noſe, the great point is to determine whether it ought to be ſtopped or not. It is a common practice to ſtop the bleeding, without conſidering whether it be a diſeaſe, or the cure of a diſeaſe. This conduct proceeds from fear; but it has often bad, and ſometimes fatal conſequences.

When a diſcharge of blood from the noſe happens in an inflammatory diſeaſe, there is always reaſon to believe that it may prove ſalutary; and therefore it ſhould be ſuffered to go on, at leaſt as long as the patient is not weakened by it.

When it happens to perſons in perfect health, who are full of blood, it ought not to be ſuddenly ſtopped. In this caſe, whenever bleeding at the noſe relieves any bad ſymptom, and does not proceed ſo far as to endanger the patient's life, it ought not to be ſtopped. But when it returns frequently, or continues till the pulſe becomes low, the extremities begin to grow cold, the lips pale, or the patient complains of being ſick or faint, it muſt immediately be ſtopped.

For this purpoſe, the patient ſhould be ſet nearly upright, with his head reclining a little, and his legs immerſed in water, about the warmth of new milk. His hands ought likewiſe to be put in lukewarm water, and his garters may be tied a little tighter than uſual.

Internal medicines can hardly be of uſe here, as they have ſeldom time to operate. It may not, however, be amiſs to give the patient half an ounce of Glauber's ſalt, and the ſame quantity of manna, diſſolved in four or five ounces of barley-water. This may be taken at a draught, and repeated, if it does not operate, in a few hours.

If the genitals be immerſed for ſome time in cold water, it will generally ſtop a bleeding at the noſe. This generally ſucceeds.

After the b'eeding is ſtopped, the patient ought to be kept as eaſy and quiet as poſſible. He ſhould not pick his noſe, nor take away the tents or clotted blood, till they fall off of their own accord, and ſhould not lie with his head low. *Buchan, Chambers.*

Head-Ach.

Sometimes the pain is internal, ſometimes external; ſometimes it is an original diſeaſe, and at other times only ſymptomatic. When the head-ach proceeds from a hot bilious habit,

habit, the pain is very acute and throbbing, with a considerable heat of the part affected. When from a cold phlegmatic habit, the patient complains of a dull heavy pain, and has a sense of coldness in the part. This kind of head-ach is sometimes attended with a degree of stupidity or folly.

In persons of a full habit, who abound with blood, or other humours, the head-ach often proceeds from the suppression of customary evacuations; as bleeding at the nose, sweating of the feet, &c. Also coldness of the extremities, or hanging down the head for a long time. Whatever prevents the return of the blood from the head, will likewise occasion a head-ach; as looking long obliquely at any object, or wearing any thing tight about the neck.

Sometimes the head-ach proceeds from the repulsion or retrocession of the gout, the erysipelas, the small-pox, measles, itch, or other eruptive diseases. Inanition, or emptiness, will also occasion head-achs. Nurses who give suck too long, or who do not take a sufficient quantity of solid food.

There is likewise a most violent, fixed, constant, and almost intolerable head-ach, which occasions great debility both of body and mind, prevents sleep, destroys the appetite, causes a *vertigo*, dimness of sight, a noise in the ears, convulsions, epileptic fits, and sometimes vomiting, costiveness, coldness of the extremities, &c.

When a head-ach attends an acute fever, with pale urine, it is an unfavourable symptom. In excessive head-achs, coldness of the extremities is a bad sign.

When the disease continues long, and is very violent, it often terminates in blindness, an apoplexy, deafness, a *vertigo*, the palsy, epilepsy, &c.

In this disease the cool regimen in general is to be observed. The diet ought to consist of such emollient substances as will correct the acrimony of the humours, and keep the body open; as apples boiled in milk, spinach, turnips, and such like. The drink ought to be diluting; such as barley-water. The patient ought as much as possible to keep in an erect posture, and not to lie with his head too low.

When the head-ach is owing to excess of blood, or an hot bilious constitution, bleeding is necessary. The patient may be be bled in the jugular vein, and the operation repeated if there be occasion. Cupping also, or the application of leeches to the temples, and behind the ears, will be of service. Afterwards a blistering-plaster may be applied to the neck, behind the ears, or to any part of the head that is most affected. In some cases it will be proper to blister the whole head. In persons of a gross habit, issues or perpetual blisters will be of service. The body ought likewise to be kept open by gentle laxatives.

When

When the head-ach is occasioned by the stoppage of a running at the nose, the patient should frequently smell to a bottle of volatile salts; he may likewise take snuff, or any thing that will irritate the nose, so as to promote a discharge from it; as the herb mastich, gound-ivy, &c.

A *hemicrania*, especially a periodical one, is generally owing to a foulness of the stomach, for which gentle vomits must be administered, as also purges of rhubarb.

When the patient cannot bear the loss of blood, his feet ought frequently to be bathed in lukewarm water, and well rubbed with a coarse cloth. Cataplasms with mustard or horse-radish ought likewise to be applied to them. This course is peculiarly necessary when the pain proceeds from a gouty humour affecting the head.

When the head-ach is occasioned by great heat, hard labour, or violent exercise of any kind, it may be allayed by cooling medicines, as the saline draughts with nitre, and the like.

A little of Ward's essence, dropped into the palm of the hand, and applied to the forehead, will sometimes remove a violent head-ach; and so will æther, when applied in the same manner.

The Ear-Ach.

This disorder is sometimes so violent, as to occasion great restlessness, anxiety, and even delirium.

It often proceeds from a sudden suppression of perspiration, or from the head being exposed to cold when covered with sweat. It may also be occasioned by worms, or other insects getting into the ear, or being bred there; or from any hard body sticking in the ear.

When the ear-ach proceeds from insects, or any hard body sticking in the ear, every method must be taken to remove them as soon as possible. The membranes may be relaxed by dropping into the ear oil of sweet almonds, or olive oil. Afterwards the patient should be made to sneeze, by taking snuff, or some strong sternutatory. If this should not force out the body, it must be extracted by art. Insects sometimes come out upon pouring in oil, which is a thing they cannot bear.

When the pain of the ear proceeds from inflammation, it may be fomented. An exceeding good method of fomenting the ear is to apply it close to the mouth of a jug filled with warm water, or a strong decoction of camomile-flowers.

The patient's feet should be frequently bathed in lukewarm water, and he ought to take small doses of nitre and rhubarb, *viz.* a scruple of the former, and ten grains of the latter, three times a day. His drink may be whey, or decoction of barley and liquorice with figs or raisins. The parts behind the ear ought frequently to be rubbed with camphorated oil, or a little of the volatile liniment.

Pains

Pains in the Stomach.

This may proceed from various caufes; as indigeftion; wind; the acrimony of the bile; fharp, acrid, or poifonous fubftances taken into the ftomach, &c. It may likewife be occafioned by worms; the ftoppage of cuftomary evacuations; a tranflation of gouty matter to the ftomach, the bowels, &c.

Women in the decline of life are very liable to pains of the ftomach and bowels, efpecially fuch as are afflicted with hyfteric complaints. It is likewife very common to hypochondriac men of a fedentary and luxurious life. In fuch perfons it often proves fo extremely obftinate as to baffle all the powers of medicine.

When the pain of the ftomach is moft violent after eating, there is reafon to fufpect that it proceeds from fome fault either in the digeftion or in the food. In this cafe the patient ought to change his diet till he finds what kind of food agrees beft with his ftomach, and fhould continue chiefly to ufe it. If a change of diet does not remove the complaint, the patient may take a gentle vomit, and afterwards a dofe or two of rhubarb. He ought likewife to take an infufion of camomile flowers, or fome other ftomachic bitter, either in wine or water. I have often known exercife remove this complaint, efpecially failing, or a long journey on horfeback, or in a carriage.

When a pain of the ftomach proceeds from flatulency, the patient is conftantly belching up wind, and feels an uneafy diftention of the ftomach after meals. This is a moft deplorable difeafe, and is feldom thoroughly cured. In general, the patient ought to avoid all windy diet, and every thing that fours on the ftomach, as greens, roots, &c.

If a pain of the ftomach proceed from the ftoppage of cuftomary evacuations, bleeding will be neceffary, efpecially in fanguine and very full habits. It will likewife be of ufe to keep the body gently open by mild purgatives, as rhubarb or fenna, &c. When this difeafe affects women, in the decline of life, after the ftoppage of the *menfes*, making an iffue in the leg or arm will be of peculiar fervice.

The Heart-burn.

What is commonly called the *heart-burn*, is not a difeafe of that organ, but an uneafy fenfation of heat or acrimony about the pit of the ftomach, which is fometimes attended with anxiety, naufea, and vomiting.

Perfons who are liable to this complaint ought to avoid ftale liquors, acids, windy or greafy aliments, and fhould never ufe violent exercife foon after a plentiful meal. I know many perfons who never fail to have the heart-burn if they ride foon after dinner, provided they have drank ale, wine, or any fermented

mented

mented liquor; but are never troubled with it when they have drank rum or brandy and water without any fugar or acid.

When the heart-burn proceeds from debility of the ftomach, or indigeftion, the patient ought to take a dofe or two of rhubarb; afterwards he may ufe infufions of the Peruvian bark, or any other of the ftomachic bitters, in wine or brandy. Exercife in the open air will likewife be of ufe, and every thing that promotes digeftion.

When bilious humours occafion the heart-burn, a tea-fpoonful of the fweet fpirit of nitre in a glafs of water, or a cup of tea, will generally give eafe. If it proceeds from the ufe of greafy aliments, a dram of brandy or rum may be taken.

If acidity or fournefs of the ftomach occafions the heartburn, abforbents are the proper medicines. In this cafe an ounce of powdered chalk, half an ounce of fine fugar, and a quarter of an ounce of gum-arabic, may be mixed in an Englifh quart of water, and a tea-cupful of it taken as often as is neceffary. Such as do not chufe chalk may take a tea-fpoonful of prepared oyfter fhells, or of the powder called crabs-eyes, in a glafs of cinnamon or peppermint-water. But the fafeft and beft abforbent is *magnefia alba*. This not only acts as an abforbent, but likewife as a purgative; whereas chalk, and other abforbents, of that kind, are apt to lie in the inteftines, and occafion obftructions. This powder is not difagreeable, and may be taken in a cup of tea, or a glafs of mint-water A large tea-fpoonful is the ufual dofe; but it may be taken in a much greater quantity when there is occafion. Thefe things are now generally made up into lozenges for the conveniency of being carried in the pocket, and taken at pleafure.

If wind be the caufe of this complaint, the moft proper medicines are thofe called carminatives; as annifeeds, juniper-berries, ginger, canella alba, cardamom feeds, &c. Thefe may either be chewed, or infufed in wine, brandy, or other fpirits. One of the fafeft medicines of this kind is the tincture made by infufing an ounce of rhubarb, and a quarter of an ounce of the leffer cardamon feeds, in an Englifh pint of brandy. After this has digefted for two or three days, it ought to be ftrained, and four ounces of white fugar candy added to it. It muft ftand to digeft a fecond time till the fugar be difolved. A table-fpoonful of it may be taken occafionally for a dofe.

The heart-burn has often been cured, particularly in pregnant women, by chewing green tea.

The Hiccup.

This may proceed from excefs in eating or drinking; from a hurt of the ftomach; poifons; inflammations or fchirrous tumours of the ftomach, inteftines, bladder, midriff, or the reft of

the

the *vifcera*. In gangrenes, acute and malignant fevers, a hiccup is often the forerunner of death.

When the hiccup proceeds from the ufe of ailment that is flatulent, or hard of digeftion, a draught of generous wine, or a drachm of any fpiritous liquor, will generally remove it. If poifon be the caufe, plenty of milk and oil muft be drank, as has been formerly recommended. When it proceeds from an inflammation of the ftomach, &c. it is very dangerous. In this cafe the cooling regimen ought to be ftrictly obferved. The patient muft be bled, and take frequently a few drops of the fweet fpirits of nitre in a cup of wine whey. His ftomach fhould likewife be fomented with cloths dipped in warm water, or have bladders filled with warm milk and water applied to it.

When the hiccup proceeds from a gangrene or mortification, the Peruvian bark, with other antifeptics, are the only medicines which have a chance to fucceed. When it is a primary difeafe, and proceeds from a foul ftomach, loaded either with a pituitous or a bilious humour, a gentle vomit and purge, if the patient be able to bear them, will be of fervice.

When the hiccup proves very obftinate, recourfe muft be had to the moft powerful aroma ic and antifpamodic medicines. The principal of thefe is mufk; fifteen or twenty grains of which may be made into a bolus, and repeated occafionally. Opiates are likewife of fervice; but they muft be ufed with caution. A bit of fugar dipped in compound fpirits of lavender, or the volatile aromatic tincture, may be taken frequently. External applications are fometimes alfo beneficial; as the ftomach plafter, or a cataplafm of the Venice treacle of the Edinburgh or London difpenfatory, applied to the region of the ftomach.

Diflocation; vulgarly called a Breaking of the Neck.

This may happen by falls, or violent blows. In this cafe, if the patient receives no affiftance, he foon dies, which makes people imagine the neck was broken: it is, however, for the moft part only partially diflocated, and may be reduced by almoft any perfon of refolution. A complete diflocation of the neck is inftantaneous death.

When the neck is diflocated, the patient is deprived of all fenfe and motion, his countenance is bloated, and his chin lies upon his breaft.

To reduce this diflocation, the patient fhould immediately be laid upon his back on the ground, and the operator muft place himfelf behind him fo as to be able to lay hold of his head with both hands, while he makes a refiftance by placing his knees againft the patient's fhoulder. In this pofture he muft

pull

pull the head with force, gently twisting it at the same time, if the face be turned to one side, till he perceives, that the joint is replaced, which may be known from the noise which the bones generally make when going in, the patient's begining to breathe, and the head continuing in its natural posture.

This is one of those operations which it is more easy to perform than describe It has been happily performed even by women, and often by men of no medical education. After the neck is reduced, the patient ought to be bled, and should be suffered to rest for some days, till the parts recover their proper tone.

Rickets.

This disease generally attacks children between the age of nine months and two years. It prevails most in towns where the inhabitants follow sedentary employments, neglecting either to take proper exercise themselves, or to give it to their children.

One cause of the rickets is diseased parents. Mothers of a weak relaxed habit, who neglect exercise, and live upon weak watery diet. Accordingly we find, that the children of such women generally die of the rickets, the scrophula, consumptions, or such like diseases. Children begotten by men in the decline of life, who are subject to the gout, the gravel, or other chronic diseases, are likewise very liable to the rickets.

Any disorder that weakens the constitution, as the small-pox, measles, teething, &c. disposes them to this disease. It may likewise be occasioned by improper diet, as food that is either too weak and watery.

Bad nursing is the chief cause of this disease. But children suffer oftener by want of care in nurses than want of food. Allowing an infant to lie or fit too much, or not keeping it thoroughly clean in its clothes, has the most pernicious effects.

The want of free air is likewise very hurtful to children in this respect. A healthy child should always be in motion, unless when asleep; if it be suffered to lie, or fit, instead of being tossed and dandled about, it will not thrive.

At the beginning of this disease the child's flesh grows soft and flabby; its strength is diminished; it looses its wonted cheerfulness, looks more grave and composed than is natural for its age, and does not chuse to be moved. The head and belly become too large in proportion to the other parts; the face appears full, and the complexion florid. Afterwards the bones begin to be affected, especially in the more soft and spongy parts. Hence the wrists and ancles become thicker than usual; the spine or back-bone puts on an unnatural shape; the breast is likewise often deformed.

As

As this difeafe is always attended with evident figns of weak-nefs and relaxation, our chief aim in the cure muft be to brace and ftrengthen the folids, and to promote digeftion and the due preparation of the fluids. Thefe important ends will be beft anfwered by wholefome nourifhing diet, fuited to the age and ftrength of the patient, open dry air, and fufficient exercife. The limbs fhould be rubbed frequently with a warm hand, and the child kept as cheerful as poffible.

The diet ought to be dry and nourifhing, as good bread, roafted flefh, &c. Bifcuits is generally reckoned the beft bread, and pigeons, pullets, veal, rabbits, or mutton roafted or minced, are the moft proper flefh. If the child be too young for flefh meats he may have rice, millet, or pearl-barley boiled with raifins, to which may be added a little wine and fpice. His drink may be good claret, mixed with an equal quantity of water. Thofe who cannot afford claret, may give the child now and then a wine-glafs of mild ale, or good porter.

Medicines are here of little avail. The difeafe may often be cured by the nurfe, but feldom by the phyfician. In children of a grofs habit, gentle vomits and repeated purges of rhubarb may fometimes be of ufe, but they will feldom carry off the difeafe; ufe the cold bath, efpecially in the warm feafon. It muft however, be done with prudence, as fome ricketty chil-dren cannot bear it. The beft time for ufing the cold bath is in the morning, and the child fhould be well rubbed with a dry cloth immediately after he comes out of it. If the child fhould be weakened by the cold bath, it muft be difconti-nued.

Sometimes iffues have been found beneficial in this difeafe. They are peculiarly neceffary for children who abound with grofs humours. An infufion of the Peruvian bark in wine or ale would be of great fervice.

Melancholy.

Melancholy is that ftate of alienation or weaknefs of mind which renders people incapable of enjoying the pleafures, or performing the duties of life. It is a degree of infanity, and often terminates in abfolute madnefs.

It may proceed from an hereditary difpofition; intenfe think-ing; violent paffions or affections of the mind, as love, fear, joy, grief, and fuch like; alfo from poifons, a fedentary life, folitude, the fuppreffion of cuftomary evacuations, acute fevers, or other difeafes. Violent anger will change melancholy into madnefs; and exceffive cold, efpecially of the lower extremities, will force the blood into the brain, and produce all the fymptoms of mad-nefs. To all which we may add gloomy or miftaken notions of religion.

When perfons begin to be melancholy, they are timorous,
watchful

watchful, fond of folitude, fretful, fickle, captious, and inquifi‑
tive, folicitous about trifles; fometimes niggardly, and at other
times prodigal. The body is generally bound; the urine thin,
and in fmall quantity; the ftomach and bowels inflated with
wind, the complexion pale, the pulfe flow and weak. The
functions of the mind are alfo greatly perverted, in fo much
that the patient often imagines himfelf dead, or changed into
fome other animal. Some have imagined their bodies were
made of glafs, or other brittle fubftances, and were afraid to
move, left they fhould be broken to pieces. The unhappy
patient, in this cafe, unlefs carefully watched, is apt to put an
end to his own miferable life.

When the difeafe is owing to an obftruction of cuftomary
evacuations, or any bodily diforder, it is eafier cured than when
it proceeds from affections of the mind, or an hereditary taint.
A difcharge of blood from the nofe, loofenefs, fcabby erup‑
tions, the bleeding piles, or the *menfes*, fometimes carry off
this difeafe.

The diet fhould confift chiefly of vegetables of a cooling and
opening quality. Animal food, efpecially falted or fmoke dried
fifh or flefh, ought to be avoided.

The moft proper drink is water, whey, or fmall beer. Tea
and coffee are improper. If honey agrees with the patient, it
may be eaten freely, or his drink may fweetened with it. In‑
fufions of balm-leaves, penny-royal, the roots of wild valerian,
or the flowers of the lime tree, may be drank freely, either by
themfelves, or fweetened with honey, as the patient fhall
chufe.

The patient ought to take as much exercife in the open air
as he can bear. This promotes the perfpiration, and all the other
fecretions. Every kind of madnefs is attended with a diminifh‑
ed perfpiration; all means ought therefore to be ufed to pro‑
mote that neceffary and falutary difcharge. Were he forced to
ride or walk a certain number of miles every day, it would tend
greatly to alleviate his diforder.

In the cure of this difeafe particular attention muft be paid
to the mind. When the patient is in a low ftate, his mind
ought to be foothed and diverted with a variety of amufements,
as entertaining ftories, paftimes, mufic, &c.

When the patient is high, evacuations are neceffary. In this
cafe he muft be bled, and have his body kept open by purging
medicines, as manna, rhubarb, cream of tartar, or the foluble
tartar. I have feen the laft have very happy effects. It may be
taken in the dofe of half an ounce, diffolved in water-gruel,
every day, for fundry weeks, or even for months, if neceffary.
More or lefs may be given according as it operates. Vomits
have

have likewife a good effect; but they muft be pretty ftrong, otherwife they will not operate.

Whatever increafes the evacuation of urine or promotes perfpiration, has a tendency to remove this difeafe. Both thefe fecretions may be promoted by the ufe of nitre and vinegar.

Wounds.

No part of medicine has been more miftaken than the treatment or cure of wounds. Mankind in general believe that certain herbs, ointments, and plafters are poffeffed of wonderful healing powers, and imagines that no wound can be cured without the application of them. It is however a fact, that no external application whatever contributes towards the cure of a wound, any other way than by keeping the parts foft, clean, and defending them from the external air, which may be as effectually done by dry lint, as by the moft pompous applications, while it is exempt from many of the bad confequences attending them.

The fame obfervation holds with refpect to internal applications. Thefe only promote the cure of wounds as far as they tend to prevent a fever, or to remove any caufe that might obftruct or impede the operations of Nature. It is Nature alone that cures wounds.

I fhall, however, confine myfelf to external wounds, recommending a fkilful furgeon for the cure of internal ones.

The firft thing to be done when a perfon has received a wound, is to examine whether any foreign body be lodged in it, as wood, ftone, iron, lead, glafs, dirt, bits of cloth, or the like. Thefe, if poffible, ought to be extracted, and the wound cleaned, before any dreffings be applied. When that cannot be affected with fafety, on account of the patient's weaknefs, or lofs of blood, they muft be fuffered to remain in the wound, and afterwards extracted when he is more able to bear it.

If the wound be in any of the limbs, and a copious bleeding follows, it may be ftopped by a bandage round the limb a little above the wound.

In flight wounds, which do not penetrate much deeper than the fkin, the beft application is a bit of the common black fticking plafter. This keeps the fides of the wound together, and prevents the air from hurting it, which is all that is neceffary. When a wound penetrates deep, it is not fafe to keep its lips quite clofe: this keeps in the matter, and is apt to make the wound fefter. In this cafe the beft way is to fill the wound with foft lint. It muft not be ftuffed in too hard, as it will do hurt. The lint may be covered with a cloth dipped in oil, and kept on by a proper bandage.

The

The firſt dreſſing ought to continue on for at leaſt two days; after which it may be removed, and freſh lint applied as before.

When a wound is greatly inflamed, the moſt proper application is a poultice of bread and milk, ſoftened with a little ſweet oil or freſh butter. This muſt be applied inſtead of a plaſter, and ſhould be changed twice a day.

If the wound be large, and there is reaſon to fear an inflammation, the patient ſhould be kept on a very low diet. He muſt abſtain from fleſh, ſtrong liquors, and every thing that is of a heating nature.

For broken ſhins, when the ſkin only is ſcraped off, a piece of brown paper moiſtened with brandy is generally ſufficient; moiſten the paper every day, but do not take it. off till the part is quite healed. Taking off the paper admits the air to it and retards the cure.

Bruiſes.

Theſe are generally productive of worſe conſequences than wounds. The danger does not appear immediately, by which means it often happens that they are neglected.

In ſlight bruiſes it will be ſufficient to bathe the part with warm vinegar, to which a little brandy or rum may occaſionally be added, and to keep cloths wet with this mixture conſtantly applied to it. This is more proper than rubbing it with brandy, ſpirits of wine, or other ardent ſpirits, which are commonly uſed in ſuch caſes.

In ſome parts of the country the peaſants apply to a recent bruiſe a cataplaſm of freſh cow-dung. I have often ſeen this cataplaſm applied to violent contuſions occaſioned by blows, falls, bruiſes, and ſuch like, and never knew it fail to have a good effect.

When a bruiſe is very violent, the patient ought immediately to be bled, and put upon a proper regimen. His food ſhould be light and cool, and his drink weak, and of an opening nature; as whey ſweetened with honey, decoctions of tamarinds, barley, cream-tartar-whey, and ſuch like. The bruiſed part muſt be bathed with vinegar and water, as directed above; and a poultice made by boiling crumb of bread, elder-flowers, and camomile-flowers, in equal quantities of vinegar and water, applied to it. This poultice is peculiarly proper when a wound is joined to the bruiſe. It may be renewed two or three times a-day.

GENERAL INSTRUCTIONS, WHICH WILL, IF FOLLOWED, INFALLIBLY PROLONG LIFE.

An attention to diet is not only neceſſary to the preſervation of health, but is likewiſe of importance in the cure of diſeaſes.
Every

Every intention in the cure of many difeafes, may be anfwered by diet alone. Its effects, indeed, are not always fo quick as thofe of medicine; but they are generally more lafting. Befides, it is neither fo difagreeable to the patient, nor fo dangerous as medicine, and is always more eafily obtained.

Though *moderation* be the chief rule with regard to the quantity, yet the quality of food merits a further confideration. Animal, as well as vegetable food, may be rendered unwholefome by being kept too long. All animal fubftances have a natural tendency to putrefaction; and, when that has proceeded too far, they not only become offenfive to the fenfes, but hurtful to health.

Animals which feed grofsly, as tame ducks, hogs, &c. are neither fo eafily digefted, nor afford fuch wholefome nourifhment as others. No animal can be wholefome that does not take fufficient exercife. Moft of our ftalled cattle are crammed with grofs food, but not allowed exercife nor free air; by which means they indeed grow fat, but their humours, not being properly prepared or affimilated, remain crude, and occafion indigeftions, grofs humours, and oppreffion of the fpirits, in thofe who feed upon them.

Animals are often rendered unwholfome by being overheated. Exceffive heat caufes a fever, exalts the animal falts, and mixes the blood fo intimately with the flefh, that it cannot be feparated. For this reafon, butchers fhould be feverely punifhed who overdrive their cattle. No perfon would chufe to eat the flefh of an animal who had died in a high fever; yet that is the cafe with all over-drove cattle; and the fever is often raifed even to the degree of madnefs.

But this is not the only way by which butchers render meat unwholefome. The abominable cuftom of filling the cellular membrane of animals with air, in order to make them appear fat, is every day practifed. This not only fpoils the meat, and renders it unfit for keeping, but is fuch a dirty trick; that the very idea of it is fufficient to difguft a perfon of any delicacy at every thing which comes from the fhambles. Who can bear the thought of eating meat which has been blown up with air from the lungs of a dirty fellow, perhaps labouring under the very worft of difeafes.

No people in the world eat fuch quantities of animal food as the Englifh, which is one reafon why they are fo generally tainted with the fcurvy, and its numerous train of confequences; low fpirits, hypochondriacifm, &c. Animal food was furely defigned for man, and, with a proper mixture of vegetables, it will be found the moft wholefome; but to gorge beef, mutton, pork, fifh, and fowl, twice or thrice a day, is certainly too much. All who value health ought to be contented with eating one

meal

meal of flesh in the twenty-four hours, and this ought to consist of one kind only.

Our aliment ought neither to be too moist nor too dry Moist aliments relax the solids, and render the body feeble. Thus we see females, who live much on tea, and other watery diet, generally become weak, and unable to digest solid food. Hence proceed hysterics, and all their dreadful consequences. On the other hand, food that is too dry, renders the solids in a manner rigid, and the humours viscid, which disposes the body to inflammatory fevers, scurvies, and the like.

Much has been said on the ill effects of tea in diet. They are, no doubt, numerous; but they proceed rather from the imprudent use of it, than from any bad qualities in the tea itself. Tea is now the universal breakfast in this part of the world; but the morning is surely the most improper time of the day for drinking it. Most delicate persons, who, by the bye, are the greatest tea drinkers, cannot eat any thing in the morning. If such persons, after fasting ten or twelve hours, drink four or five cups of tea, without eating almost any bread, it must hurt them. Good tea, taken in moderate quantity, not too strong, nor too hot, nor drank upon an empty stomach, will seldom do harm; but if it be bad, which is often the case, or substituted in the room of solid food, it must have many ill effects.

The liquid part of our aliment likewise claims our attention. Water is not only the basis of most liquors, but also composes a great part of our solid food. Good water must therefore be of the greatest importance in diet. The best water is that which is most pure, and free from any mixture of foreign bodies.

The common methods of rendering water pure by filtration, or soft by exposing it to the sun and air, &c. are so generally known, that it is unnecessary to expend time in explaining them. I shall only, in general, advise all to avoid waters which stagnate long in small ponds, or the like, as such waters often become putrid by the corruption of animal and vegetable bodies with which they abound. Even cattle frequently suffer by drinking, in dry seasons, water which has stood long in small reservoirs, without being supplied by springs, or freshened with showers. All wells ought to be kept clean, and to have a free communication with the air.

As fermented liquors, notwithstanding they have been exclaimed against by many writers, still continue to be the common drink of almost every person who can afford them, I shall rather endeavour to assist people in the choice of these liquors, than pretend to condemn what custom has so firmly established. It is not the moderate use of sound fermented liquors which hurts mankind: it is excess, or using such as are ill prepared, or vitiated.

All

All families who can, ought to prepare their own liquors. Since preparing and vending of liquors became one of the moft general branches of bufinefs, every method has been tried to adulterate them. The great object, both to the makers and venders of liquors, is to render it intoxicating. But it is well known that this may be done by other ingredients than thofe which ought to be ufed for making it ftrong. It would be imprudent even to name thofe things which are daily made ufe of to render liquors heady. Suffice it to fay, that the practice is very common, and that all the ingredients ufed for this purpofe are of a narcotic or ftupefactive nature. But as all opiates are of a poifonous quality, it is eafy to fee what muft be the confequences of their general ufe. Though they do not kill fuddenly, yet they hurt the nerves, relax and weaken the ftomach, and fpoil the digeftion.

I would recommend it to families, not only to prepare their own liquors, but likewife their bread. Bread is fo neceffary a part of diet, that too much care cannot be beftowed in order to have it found and wholefome. For the purpofe, it is not only neceffary that it be made of good grain, but likewife properly prepared, and kept free from all unwholefome ingredients. This, however, we have reafon to believe, is not always the cafe with bread prepared by thofe who make a trade of vending it. Their object is rather to pleafe the eye, than confult the health.

Perfons whofe folids are weak and relaxed, ought to avoid all vifcid food, or fuch things as are hard of digeftion. Their diet, however, ought to be nourifhing; and they fhould take plenty of exercife in the open air.

Such as abound with blood, fhould be fparing in the ufe of every thing that is highly nourifhing, as fat meat, rich wines, ftrong ale, and the like. Their food fhould confift moftly of bread and other vegetable fubftances; and their drink ought to be water, whey, or fmall beer.

Fat people fhould not eat freely of oily, nourifhing diet. They ought frequently to eat raddifh, garlic, fpices, or fuch things as are heating, and promote perfpiration and urine. Their drink fhould be water, coffee, tea, or the like; and they ought to take much exercife and little fleep.

Thofe who are too lean muft follow an oppofite courfe.

Such as are troubled with acidities, or whofe food is apt to four upon the ftomach, fhould live much on flefh meats; and thofe who are afflicted with hot, alkaline eructations, ought to ufe a diet confifting chiefly of acid vegetables.

People who are affected with the gout, low fpirits, hypochondriac, or hyfteric diforders, ought to avoid all flatulent food, every thing that is vifcid or hard of digeftion, all falted or fmoke dried provifions, and whatever is auftere, acid, or apt to four on the ftomach. Their food fhould be light, fpare, cool, and of an opening nature.

It is not only neceffary for health that our diet be whole-fome, but alfo that it be taken at regular periods. Some imagine long fafting will atone for excefs; but this, inftead of mend-ing the matter, generally makes it worfe. When the ftomach and inteftines are over diftended with food, they lofe their pro-per tone, and, by long fafting, they become weak, and inflated with wind. Thus either gluttony or fafting deftroys the powers of digeftion.

The frequent repetition of aliment is not only neceffary for repairing the continual wafte of our bodies, but likewife to keep the humours found and fweet. Our humours, even in the moft healthy ftate, have a conftant tendency to putrefaction, which can only be prevented by frequent fupplies of frefh nou-rifhment. When that is wanting too long, the putrefaction often proceeds fo far as to occafion very dangerous fevers. From hence we may learn the neceffity of regular meals. No perfon can enjoy a good ftate of health, whofe veffels are either frequently overcharged, or the humours long deprived of frefh fupplies of chyle.

Long fafting is extremely hurtful to young people; it not only vitiates their humours, but prevents their growth. Nor is it lefs injurious to the aged. Moft perfons, in the decline of life, are afflicted with wind. This complaint is not only in-creafed, but even rendered dangerous, and often fatal, by long fafting. Old people, when their ftomachs are empty, are fre-quently feized with giddinefs, head-achs, and faintnefs. Thefe complaints may generally be removed by a bit of bread and a glafs of wine, or tafting any other folid food, which plainly points out the method of preventing them.

It is a very common practice to eat a light breakfaft and a heavy fupper. This cuftom ought to be reverfed. When people fup late, their fupper fhould to be very light, but the breakfaft ought always to be folid. If any one eats a light fupper, goes foon to bed, and rifes betimes in the morning, he will be fure to find an appetite for his breakfaft, and he may freely in-dulge it.

The ftrong and healthy do not indeed fuffer fo much from fafting, as the weak and delicate; but they run great hazard from its oppofite, viz. repletion. Many difeafes, efpecially fevers, are the effect of a plethora, or too great fulnefs of the veffels. Strong people, in high health, have generally a great quantity of blood and other humours. When thefe are fud-denly increafed, by an overcharge of rich and nourifhing diet, the veffels become too much diftended, and obftructions and in-

flammations

flammations enfue. Hence fo many people are feized with inflammatory and eruptive fevers, after a feaft or debauch.

All great and fudden changes in diet are dangerous. What
the ftomach has been long accuftomed to digeft, although lefs
wholefome, will agree better with it than food of a more falutary nature which it has not been ufed to. When therefore a
change becomes neceffary, it ought always to be made gradually; a fudden tranfition from a poor and low, to a rich and
luxurious diet, or the contrary, might fo difturb the functions
of the body, as to endanger health, or even to occafion death
itfelf.

When I recommend regularity of diet, I would not be un-
derftood as condemning every fmall deviation from it. It is
next to impoffible for people at all times to avoid fome degree
of excefs; and living too much by rule might make even the
fmalleft deviation dangerous. It may therefore be prudent to
vary a little, fometimes taking more, fometimes lefs than the
ufual quantity of meat and drink, provided always that regard
be had to moderation. *Lemery. Arbuthnet. Tiffot. Buchan.*

ELECTUARIES.

Electuary for the Piles.

Take flowers of fulphur, one ounce; cream of tartar, half an
ounce; treacle, a fufficient quantity to form an electuary.

A tea-fpoonful of this may be taken three or four times a-
day.

Electuary for the Palfy.

Take of powdered muftard feed, and conferve of rofes, each
an ounce; fyrup of ginger, enough to make an electuary.

A tea-fpoonful of this may be taken three or four times a-
day.

Electuary for the Rheumatifm.

Take of conferve of rofes, two ounces; cinnabar of antimony, levigated, an ounce and an half; gum guaiacum, in
powder, an ounce; fyrup of ginger, a fufficient quantity to
make an electuary.

In obftinate rheumatifms, which are not accompanied with a
fever, a tea-fpoonful of this electuary, may be taken twice a-day
with confiderable advantage.

Lenitive Electuary.

Take of fenna, in fine powder, eight ounces; coriander feed,
alfo in powder, four ounces; pulp of tamarinds and of French
pruens, each a pound. Mix the pulps and powders together,
and with a fufficient quantity of fimple fyrup, reduce the whole
into an electuary.

A tea-

A tea-fpoonful of this electuary, taken two or three times a-day, generally proves an agreeable laxative.

Electuary for the Dysentery.

Take of the Japonic confection, two ounces; Locatelli's balfam, one ounce; rhubarb in powder, half an ounce; fyrup of marfh-mallows, enough to make an electuary.

It is often dangerous in dyfenteries to give opiates and aftringents, without interpofing purgatives. The purgative is here joined with thefe ingredients, which renders this a very fafe and ufeful medicine for the purpofes expreffed in the title.

About the bulk of a nutmeg fhould be taken twice or thrice a-day, as the fymptoms and conftitution may require.

OINTMENTS.

Yellow Bafilicum Ointment.

Take of yellow wax, white refin, and frankincenfe each a quarter of a pound; melt them together over a gentle fire; then add, of hog's lard prepared, one pound. Strain the ointment while warm.

This ointment is employed for cleanfing and healing wounds and ulcers.

Iffue Ointment.

Mix half an ounce of Spanifh flies, finely powdered, in fix ounces of yellow bafilicum ointment.

This ointment is chiefly intended for dreffing blifters, in order to keep them open during pleafure.

Ointment of Calamine.

Take of olive oil, a pint and an half; white wax, and calamine ftone, levigated, of each half a pound. Let the calamine ftone, reduced into a fine powder, be rubbed with fome part of the oil, and afterwards added to the reft of the oil and wax, previoufly melted together, continually ftirring them till quite cold.

This ointment, which is commonly known by the name of *Turner's Cerate*, is an exceeding good application in burns and excoriations, from whatever caufe.

Emollient Ointment.

Take of palm oil, two pounds; olive oil, a pint and an half; yellow wax, half a pound; Venice turpentine, a quarter of a pound. Melt the wax in the oils over a gentle fire; then mix in the turpentine, and ftrain the ointment.

This fupplies the place of *Althæa ointment*. It may be ufed for anointing inflamed parts, &c.

CLYSTERS.

CLYSTERS.

Laxative Clyfter.

Take of milk and water, each fix ounces; fweet oil or frefh butter, and brown fugar, of each two ounces. Mix them.

If an ounce of Glauber's falt, or two table-fpoonfuls of common falt, be added to this, it will be a *Purging Clyfter.*

Carminitive Clyfter.

Take of camomile flowers, an ounce; anifeeds, half an ounce. Boil in a pint and an half of water to one pint.

In hyfteric an hypochondraic complaints this may be adminiftered inftead of the *Fœtid Clyfter,* the fmell of which is fo difagreeable to moft patients.

Oily Clyfter.

To four ounces of the infufion of camomile flowers, add an equal quantity of Florence oil.

This clyfter is beneficial in bringing off the fmall worms lodged in the lower parts of the alimentary canal. When given to children, the quantity muft be proportionably leffened.

Turpentine Clyfter.

Take of common decoction, ten ounces; Venice turpentine, diffolved with the yolk of an egg, half an ounce; Florence oil, one ounce. Mix them,

This diuretic clyfter is proper in obftructions of the urinary paffages, and in cholicky complaints, proceeding from gravel

TINCTURES.

Sacred Tincture, or Tincture of Hiera Picra.

Take of fuccotorine aloes in powder, one ounce; Virginian fnake-root and ginger, of each two drachms. Infufe in a pint of mountain wine, and half a pint of brandy, for a week, frequently fhaking the bottle; then ftrain off the tincture.

This is a fafe and ufeful purge for perfons of a languid and phlegmatic habit; but is thought to have better effects, taken in fmall dofes as a laxative.

The dofe, as a purge, is from one to two ounces.

Volatile Tincture of Gum Guaiacum.

Take of gum guaiacum, four ounces; volatile aromatic fpirit, a pint. Infufe without heat, in a veffel well ftopped, for a few days; then ftrain off the tincture.

In rheumatic complaints, a tea fpoonful may be taken in a cup of the infufion water-trefoil, twice or thrice a-day.

Tincture of Black Hellebore.

Infufe two ounces of the roots of black hellebore, bruifed, in a pint of proof fpirit, for feven or eight days; then filter the

tincture

tincture through paper.　A scruple of cochineal may be infused along with the roots, to give the tincture a colour.

In obstructions of the *menses,* a tea-spoonful may be taken in a cup of camomile or penny-royal tea twice a-day.

Tincture of the Bark.

Take of Peruvian bark, two ounces ; Seville orange-peel and cinnamon, of each half an ounce.　Let the bark be powdered, and the other ingredients bruised ; then infuse the whole in a pint and an half of brandy, for five of six days, in a close vessel ; afterwards strain off the tincture.

This tincture is not only beneficial in intermitting fevers, but also in the slow, nervous, and putrid kinds, especially towards their decline.

The dose is from one drachm to three or four, every fifth or sixth hour.　It may be given in any suitable liquor, and occasionally sharpened with a few drops of the spirit of vitriol.

BOLUSSES.

Pectoral Bolus.

Take of sperma ceti, a scruple ; gum ammoniac, ten grains ; salt of hartshorn, six grains ; simple syrup, as much as will make them into a bolus.

This bolus is given in colds and coughs of long standing, asthmas, and beginning consumptions of the lungs.　It is generally proper to bleed the patient before he begins to use it.

Purging Bolus.

Take of jalap in powder, a scruple ; cream of tartar, two scruples.　Let them be rubbed together and formed into a bolus, with simple syrup.

Where a mild purge is wanted, this will answer the purpose very well.　If a stronger dose is necessary, the jalap may be increased to half a drachm or upwards.

Astringent Bolus

Take of alum, in powder, fifteen grains ; gum kino, five grains ; syrup, sufficient quantity to make a bolus.

In an excessive flow of the *menses,* and other violent discharges of blood, proceeding from relaxation, this bolus may be given every four or five hours, till the discharge abates.

Diaphoretic Bolus.

Take of gum guaiacum, in powder, ten grains ; flowers of sulphur and cream of tartar, of each one scruple ; simple syrup, a sufficient quantity.

In rheumatic complaints, and disorders of the skin, this bolus may be taken twice a-day.　It will also be of service in the inflammatory quinsey.

MIXTURES

Take ſimple cinnamon-water and common water, of each three ounces; ſpirituous cinnamon-water, an ounce and an half; Japonic confection, half an once. Mix them.

In dyſenteries which are not of long ſtanding, after the neceſſary evacuations a ſpoonful or two of this mixture may be taken every four hours, interpoſing every ſecond or third day a doſe of rhubarb.

Diuretic Mixture.

Take of mint-water, five ounces; vinegar of ſquills, ſix drachms; ſweet ſpirit of nitre, half an ounce; ſyrup of ginger, an ounce and an half. Mix them.

In obſtructions of the urinary paſſages, two ſpoonfuls of this mixture may be taken twice or thrice a-day.

ELIXIRS.

Stomachic Elixirs.

Take of gentian root, two ounces; Curaſſao oranges, one ounce; Virginian ſnake-root, half an ounce. Let the ingredients be bruiſed, and infuſed for three or four days in two pints of French brandy; afterwards ſtrain out the elixir.

This is an elegant ſtomachic bitter. In flatulencies, indigeſtion, want of appetite, and ſuch like complaints, a ſmall glaſs of it may be taken twice a-day. It likewiſe relieves the gout in the ſtomach, when taken in a large doſe.

Paregoric Elixir.

Take of flowers of benzoin, half an ounce; opium, two drachms. Infuſe in one pound of the volatile aromatic ſpirit, for four or five days, frequently ſhaking the bottle; afterwards ſtrain the elixir.

This is an agreeable and ſafe way of adminiſtering opium, It eaſes pain, allays tickling coughs, relieves difficult breathing, and is uſeful in many diſorders of children, particularly the hooping cough.

The doſe to an adult is from fifty to an hundred drops.

POWDERS.

Worm Powders.

Take of tin reduced into a fine powder, an ounce; Æthiop's mineral, two drachms. Mix them well together, and divide the whole into ſix doſes.

One of theſe powders may be taken in a little ſyrup, honey, or treacle, twice a day, After they have been all uſed, the following anthelmintic purge may be proper.

Purging

Purging Worm Powder.

Take of powdered rhubarb, a fcruple; fcammony and calomel, of each five grains. Rub them together in a mortar for one dofe.

For children, the above dofes muft be leffened according to their age.

If the powder of tin be given alone, its dofe may be confiderably increafed. The late Dr. Alfton gave it to the amount of two ounce in three days; and fays, when thus adminiftered, that it proved an egregious anthlemintic. He purged his patients both before they took the powder and afterwards.

Powder for the Tape Worm.

Early in the morning the patient is to take, in any liquid, two or three drachms, according to his age and conftitution, of the root of male fern reduced into a fine powder. About two hours afterwards, he is to take of calomel and refin of fcammony, each ten grains; gum gamboge, fix grains. Thefe ingredients muft be finely powdered and given in a little fyrup, honey, treacle, or any thing that is moft agreeable to the patient. He is then to walk gently about, now and then drinking a difh of weak green tea till the worm is paffed. If the powder of the fern produces naufea, or ficknefs, it may be removed by fucking the juice of an orange or lemon.

This medicine, which had been long kept a fecret abroad, for the cure of the tape-worm, was fome time ago purchafed by the French king, and made public for the benefit of mankind. Not having had an opportunity of trying it, I can fay nothing from experience concerning its efficacy. It feems, however, from its ingredients, to be an active medicine, and ought to be taken with care. The dofe here prefcribed is fufficient for the ftrongeft patient; it muft, therefore, be reduced according to the age and conftitution.

Aftringent Powder.

Take of allum and Japan earth, each two drachms. Pound them together, and divide the whole into ten or twelve dofes.

In an immoderate flow of the *menfes*, and other hæmorrhages, one of thefe powders may be taken every hour, or every half hour, if the difcharge be violent.

PILLS.

Strengthening Pill.

Take foft extract of the bark, and falt of fteel, each a drachm. Make into pills.

In diforders arifing from exceffive debility, or relaxation of the folids, as the *cholorofis*, or green ficknefs, two of the pills may be taken three times a day.

Stomachic

Stomachic Pill.

Take extract of gentian, two drachms; powdered rhubarb and vitriolated tartar, of each one drachm; oil of mint, thirty drops; simple syrup, a sufficient quantity.

Three or four of these pills may be taken twice a day, for invigorating the stomach, and keeping the body gently open.

Composing Pill.

Take of purified opium, ten grains; Castile soap, half a drachm. Beat them together, and form the whole into 20 pills.

When a quieting draught will not sit upon the stomach, one, two, or three of these pills may be taken, as occasion requires.

Pill for the Jaundice.

Take of Castile soap, succotorine aloes, and rhubarb, of each one drachm. Make them into pills with a sufficient quantity of syrup or mucilage.

These pills, as their title expresses, are chiefly intended for the jaundice, which with the assistance of proper diet, they will often cure. Five or six of them may be taken twice a day, more or less, as is necessary to keep the body open. It will be proper, however, during their use, to interpose now and then a vomit of ipecacuanha or tartar emetic.

BURNS AND INFLAMMATIONS, BRUISES, SPRAINS, AND ULCERS, ALL EXTERNAL.

Goulard's Extract of Saturn.

Take of litharge, one pound; vinegar made of French wine two pints. Put them together into a glazed earthen pipkin, and let them boil, or rather simmer, for an hour, or an hour and a quarter, taking care to stir them all the while with a wooden spatula. After the whole has stood to settle, pour off the liquor which is upon the top into bottles for use.

With this extract Goulard makes his *vegeto-mineral water*, which he recommends in a great variety of external disorders, as inflammations, burns, bruises, sprains, ulcers, &c.

Liniment for Burns.

Take equal parts of Florence oil, or of fresh drawn linseed oil, and lime-water; shake them well together in a wide-mouthed bottle, so as to form a liniment.

This is found to be an exceeding proper application for recent scalds or burns. It may either be spread upon a cloth, or the parts affected may be anointed with it twice or thrice a day.

Tar Water.

Pour a gallon of water on two pounds of Norway tar, and stir them strongly together with a wooden rod; after they have stood to settle for two days, pour off the water for use.

DRAUGHTS.

Anodyne Draught.

Take of liquid laudanum, twenty-five drops; simple cinnamon water, an ounce; common syrup, two drachms. Mix them.

In excessive pain, where bleeding is not necessary, and in great restlessness, this composing draught may be taken and repeated occasionally.

Diuretic Draught.

Take of the diuretic salt, two scruples; syrup of poppies, two drachms; simple cinnamon-water and common water, of each an ounce.

This draught is of service in an obstruction or deficiency of urine.

Purging Draughts.

Take of manna an ounce; soluble tartar, or Rochelle salt, from three to four drachms. Dissolve in three ounces of boiling water; to which add Jamacia pepper water, half an ounce,

As manna sometimes will not sit upon the stomach, an ounce, or ten drachms of the bitter purging salts, dissolved in four ounces of water, may be taken instead of the above.

MEDICINAL WINES.

Anthelmintic Wine.

Take of rhubarb, half an ounce; worm-seed, an ounce. Bruise them, and infuse without heat in two pints of red port wine for a few days; then strain off the wine.

As the stomachs of persons afflicted with worms are always delibated, red wine alone will often prove serviceable; it must, however, have still better effects when joined with bitter and purgative ingredients.

A glass of this wine may be taken twice or thrice a day.

Antimonial Wine.

Take glass of antimony, reduced to a fine powder, half an ounce; Lisbon wine, eight ounces. Digest, with heat, for three or four days, now and then shaking the bottle; afterwards filter the wine through paper.

The dose of this wine varies according to the intention. As an alterative and diaphoretic, it may be taken from ten to fifty or sixty drops. In a larger dose it generally proves cathartic, or excites vomiting.

Bitter Wine.

Take of gentian root, yellow rind of lemon-peel, fresh, each one ounce; long pepper, two drachms; mountain wine, two pints. Infuse without heat for a week, and strain out the wine for use.

Iij

In complaint, arising from weakness of the stomach, or indigestion, a glass of this wine may be taken an hour before dinner and supper.

INFUSIONS.

The author of the New Dispensatory observes, that even from those vegetables which are weak in virtue, rich infusions may be obtained, by returning the liquor upon fresh quantities of the subject, the water loading itself more and more with the active parts; and that these loaded infusions are applicable to valuable purposes in medicine, as they contain in a small compass the finer, more subtile, and active principles of vegetables, in a form readily miscible with the fluids of human body.

Bitter Infusion.

Take tops of the lesser centaury and camomile flowers, of each half an ounce; yellow rind of lemon and orange-peel, carefully freed from the inner white part, of each two drachms. Cut them in small pieces, and infuse them in a quart of boiling water.

For indigestion, weakness of the stomach, or want of appetite, a tea-cupful of this infusion may be taken twice or thrice a day.

Infusion of the Bark.

To an ounce of the bark, in powder, add four or five table-spoonfuls of brandy, and a pint of boiling water. Let them infuse for two or three days.

This is one of the best preparations of the bark for weak stomachs. In disorders where the corroborating virtues of that medicine are required, a tea-cupful of it may be taken two or three times a day.

Infusion for the Palsy.

Take of horse-radish root shaved, mustard-seed bruised, each four ounces; outer rind of orange-peel, one ounce. Infuse them in two quarts of boiling water, in a close vessel, for twenty-four hours.

In paralytic complaints, a tea-cupful of this warm stimulating medicine may be taken three or four times a-day. It excites the action of the solids, proves diuretic, and, if the patient be kept warm, promotes perspiration.

If two or three ounces of the dried leaves of marsh trefoil be used instead of the mustard, it will make the *antiscorbutic infusion*.

Conserve of Red Roses.

Take a pound of red rose buds, cleared of their heels; beat them well in a mortar, and, adding by degrees two pound of double-refined sugar, in powder, make a conserve.

After

After the fame manner are prepared the conferves of orange-peel, rofemary flowers, fea-wormood, of the leaves of wood-forrel, &c.

The conferve of rofes is one of the moft agreeable and ufeful preparations belonging to this clafs. A drachm or two of it, diffolved in warm milk, is ordered to be given as a gentle reftringent in weaknefs of the ftomach, and likewife in pthifical coughs, and fpitting of blood. To have any confiderable effects, however, it muft be taken in larger quantities.

Conferve of Sloes.

This may be made by boiling the floes gently in water, being careful to take them out before they burft; afterwards expreffing the juice, and beating it up with three times its weight of fine fugar.

In relaxations of the *uvula* and glands of the throat, this makes an excellent gargle, and may be ufed at difcretion.

Preferves are made by fteeping or boiling frefh vegetables firft in water, and afterwards in fyrup, or a folution of fugar. The fubject is either preferved moift in the fyrup, or taken out and dried, that the fugar may candy upon it. The laft is the moft ufual method.

The following is a moft excellent Remedy for a Cold. I know not one that is fo efficacious.

Take a large tea-cupful of linfeed, two penny worth of ftick-liquorice, and a quarter of a pound of fun raifins. Put thefe into two quarts of foft water, and let it fimmer over a flow fire till it it reduced to one; then add to it a quarter of a pound of brown fugar-candy pounded, a table-fpoonful of old rum, and a table-fpoonful of the beft white wine vinegar, or lemon juice.

Note. The rum and vinegar are beft to be added only to the quantity you are going immediately to take; for, if it is put into the whole, it is apt in a little time to grow flat.

Drink half a pint at going to bed, and take a little when the cough is troublefome.

This receipt generally cures the worft of colds in two or three days, and, if taken in time, may be faid to be almoft an infallible remedy. It is a moft fovereign and balfamic cordial for the lungs, without the opening qualities which endanger frefh colds in going out. It has been known to cure colds that have been almoft fettled into confumptions in lefs than three weeks.

DECOCTIONS.

Decoction of Logwood.

Boil three ounces of the fhaving, or chips, of logwood, in
four

four pints of water, till one half the liquor is wasted. Two or three ounces of simple cinnamon-water may be added to this decoction.

In fluxes of the belly, where the stronger astringents are improper, a tea-cupful of this decoction may be taken with advantage three or four times a-day.

Decoction of Bark.

Boil an ounce of the Peruvian bark, grossly powdered, in a pint and an half of water to one pint; then strain the decoction. If a tea-spoonful of the weak spirit of vitriol be added to this medicine, it will render it both more agreeable and efficacious.

Compound Decoction of the Bark.

Take of Peruvian bark and Virginian snake-root, grossly powdered, each three drachms. Boil them in a pint of water to one half. To the strained liquor add an ounce and an half of aromatic water.

Sir John Pringle recommends this as a proper medicine towards the decline of malignant fevers, when the pulse is low, the voice weak, and the head affected with a stupor but with little delirium.

The dose is four spoonfuls every fourth or sixth hour.

PLASTERS.

Plasters ought to be of a different consistence, according to the purposes for which they are intended. Such as are to be applied to the breasts and stomach, ought to be soft and yielding while those designed for the limbs, should be firm and adhesive.

Stomach Plaster.

Take of gum plaster, half a pound; camphorated oil, an ounce and an half; black pepper, or capsicum, where it can be had, one ounce. Melt the plaster and mix with it the oil; then sprinkle in the pepper, previously reduced to a fine powder.

An ounce or two of this plaster, spread upon soft leather, and applied to the region of the stomach, will be of service in flatulencies arising from hysteric and hypochondraic affections. A little of the expressed oil of mace, or a few drops of the essential oil of mint, may be rubbed upon it before it is applied.

Adhesive Plaster.

Take of common plaster, half a pound; of Burgundy pitch, a quarter of a pound. Melt them together.

This plaster is principally used for keeping on other dressings.

Anodyne

Anodyne Plaster.

Melt an ounce of adhesive plaster, and, when it is cooling, mix with it a drachm of powdered opium, and the same quantity of camphor, previously rubbed up with a little oil.

This plaster generally gives ease in acute pains, especially of the nervous kind.

Blistering Plaster.

Take of Venice turpentine, six ounces; yellow wax, two ounces; Spanish flies, in fine powder, three ounces; powdered mustard, one ounce. Melt the wax, and while it is warm add to it the turpentine, taking care not to evaporate it by too much heat. After the turpentine and wax are sufficiently incorporated, sprinkle in the powders, continually stirring the mass till it be cold.

Though this plaster is made in a variety of ways, one seldom meets with it of a proper consistence. When compounded with oils and other greasy substances, its effects are blunted, and it is apt to run; while pitch and resin render it too hard and very inconvenient.

When the blistering plaster is not at hand, its place may be supplied by mixing with any soft ointment a sufficient quantity of powdered flies; or by forming them into a paste with flour and vinegar.

Gum Plaster.

Take of the common plaster, four pounds; gum ammoniac and galbanum, strained, of each half a pound. Melt them together, and add, of Venice turpentine, six ounces.

This plaster is used as a digestive, and likewise for discussing indolent tumours.

Method of destroying the putrid Smell which Meat acquires during hot Weather.

Put the meat intended for making soup into a sauce-pan full of water, scum it when it boils, and then throw into the saucepan a burning coal, very compact and destitute of smoke; leave it there for two minutes, and it will have contracted all the smell of the meat and soup.

If you wish to roast a piece of meat on the spit, or to bake it, put it into water till it boils, and, after having scummed it, throw in a burning coal as before; at the end of two minutes, take out the meat, and, having wiped it well, put it on the spit, or into the oven.

When fresh butter has not been salted in proper time, or when salt butter has become rancid or musty, after melting and scumming it, dip in a crust of bread well toasted on both sides, and at the end of a minute or two the butter will lose its disagreeable odour, but the bread will be found foetid.

CORNS

CORNS AND TEETH.

A Remedy for Corns on the Feet.

Roaſt a clove of garlic, or an onion, on a live coal, or in hot aſhes; apply it to the corn, and faſten it on with a piece of cloth. This ſoftens the corn to ſuch a degree, as to looſen and wholly remove it in two or three days. Foment the corn every other night in warm water, after which renew the application.

The ſame intention will be yet more effectually anſwered by applying to the corn a bit of the plaſter of Diachylon with the gums, ſpread on a ſmall piece of linen; removing it occaſionally to foment the corn with warm water, and pare off the ſoftened part with a penknife.

To clean the Teeth and Gums, and make the Fleſh grow cloſe to the Root of the Enamel.

Take one ounce of myrrh, in fine powder, two ſpoonfuls of the beſt white honey, and a little green ſage in fine powder; mix them well together, and rub the teeth and gums with a little of this balſam every night and morning.

To ſtrengthen the Gums, and faſten looſe Teeth.

Diſſolve an ounce of myrrh as much as poſſible in half a pint of red wine and the ſame quantity of oil of almonds: waſh the mouth with this fluid every morning.

This is alſo an excellent remedy againſt worms in the teeth.

A ſure Preſervative from the Tooth-Ach.

After having waſhed your mouth with water, as cleanlineſs, and indeed health, requires, you ſhould every morning rince the mouth with a tea-ſpoonful of lavender-water mixed with an equal quantity of warm or cold water, which ever you like beſt, to diminiſh its activity. This ſimple and innocent remedy is a certain preſervative, the ſucceſs of which has been confirmed by long experience.

A Powder to clean the Teeth.

Take dragon's blood and cinnamon, of each one ounce and an half, burnt allum, or cream of tartar, one ounce; beat all together into a very fine powder, and rub a little on the teeth every other day.

The following Powder will be found an excellent Preſerver, as well as Cleaner, of the Teeth; it likewiſe makes them very white.

Take pumice-ſtone prepared, ſealed earth, and red coral prepared, of each an ounce; dragon's-blood, half an ounce; cream of tartar, an ounce and an half; cinnamon, a quarter of an ounce; and cloves, a ſcruple. Beat the whole together into a powder.

C c   WATERS.

WATERS.

A Receipt to make the genuine Hungary Water.

Put into an alembic a pound and an half of fresh picked rose-mary flowers; pennyroyal and marjoram flowers, of each half a pound; three quarts of good Coniac brandy; having close stopped the mouth of the alembic to prevent the spirit from evapo-rating, bury it twenty-eight hours in horse-dung to digest, and then diftil off the spirit in a water-bath.

A drachm of Hungary-water diluted with spring water, may be taken once or twice a week in the morning fasting. It is also used by way of embrocation to bathe the face and limbs, or any part affected with pains or debility. This remedy recruits the strength, difpels gloominefs, and strengthens the fight. It must always be ufed cold, whether taken inwardly as a medi-cine, or applied externally.

To make Rose-Water.

To make an excellent rose-water, let the flowers be gathered two or three hours after fun-rifing in very fine weather; beat them in a marble mortar into a pafte, and leave them in the mortar foaking in their juice, for five or fix hours; then put the mafs into a coarfe canvafs bag, and prefs out the juice; to every quart of which add a pound of frefh damafk rofes, and let them ftand in infufion for twenty-four hours. Then put the whole into a glafs alembic, lute on a head and receiver, and place it on a fand heat. Diftil at firft with a gentle fire, which is to be increafed gradually till the drops follow each other as quick as poffible; draw off the water as long as it continues to run clear, then put out the fire, and let the alembic ftand till cold. The diftilled water at firft will have very little fragrancy, but after being expofed to the heat of the fun about eight days, in a bottle lightly ftopped with a bit of paper, it acquires an admirable fcent.

Rofe-water is an excellent lotion for the eyes, if ufed every morning, and makes a part in collyriums prefcribed for inflam-mations of thefe parts; it is alfo proper in many other com-plaints.

Directions for making Lavender-Water.

Fill a glafs or earthen body two thirds full of lavender flowers, and then fill up the veffel with brandy or molaffes fpirits. Let the flowers ftand in infufion eight days, or lefs if ftraitened for time; then diftil off the fpirit, in a water-bath with a brifk fire, at firft in large drops or even a fmall ftream, that the effential oil of the flowers may rife with the fpirit. But as this cannot be done without the phlegm coming over the helm at the fame time, the fpirit muft be rectified. The firft diftillation being finifhed, unlute the ftill, throw away what remains in the body, and

and fill it with fresh flowers of lavender, in the proportion of two pounds of lavender flowers to one pint of spirit; pour the spirit already distilled according to the foregoing directions, on the lavender flowers, and distil a second time in a vapor bath.

To make Orange-flower Water.

Having gathered (two hours before sun-rise in fine weather) a quantity of orange-flowers, pluck them leaf by leaf, and throw away the stalks and stems: fill a tin cucurbit two thirds full of these picked flowers; lute on a low bolt head, not above two inches higher than the cucurbit; place it in balneo mariæ, or a water-bath, and distil with a strong fire. You run no risk from pressing forward the distillation with violence, the water-bath effectually preventing the flowers from being burnt. In this method you pay no regard to the quantity, but the quality of the water drawn off. If nine pounds of orange flowers were put into the still, be satisfied with three or four quarts of fragrant water; however, you may continue your distillation, and save even the last droppings of the still, which have some small fragrancy. During the operation, be careful to change the water in the refrigeratory vessel as often as it becomes hot. Its being kept cool, prevents the distilled water from having an empyreumatic or burnt smell, and keeps the quintessence of the flowers more intimately united with its phlegm.

Virgin's Milk, a safe and excellent Cosmetic.

Take equal parts of gum benjamin and storax, dissolve them in a sufficient quantity of spirit of wine. The spirit will then become a reddish tincture, and exhale a very fragrant smell. Some people add a little balm of gilead. Drop a few drops into a glass of clear water, and the water, by stirring, will instantly become milky. This may be used with safety and success: it will clear the complexion, for which purpose nothing is better.

To take Iron Mould out of Linen.

Hold the iron mould over the fume of boiling water for some time, then pour on the spot a little juice of sorrel and a little salt, and when the cloth has thoroughly imbibed the juice, wash it in lye.

To take out Stains of Oil.

Take Windsor-soap, shaved thin, put it into a bottle half full of lye, throw in the size of a nut of sal ammoniac, a little cabbage juice, two yolks of new-laid eggs, and ox gall at discretion; and lastly, an ounce of powdered tartar; then cork the bottle, and expose it to the heat of the noon-day sun four days, at the expiration of which time it becomes fit for use. Pour this liquor on the stains, and rub it well on both sides of the cloth; then wash the stains with clear water, or rather with the following foap, and when the cloth is dry they will no longer appear.

To take out the Stains on Cloth of whatever Colour.

Take half a pound of honey, the fize of a nut of fal ammoniac, and the yolk of an egg; mix them together, and put a little of this mixture on the ftain, letting it remain till dry. Then wafh the cloth with fair water, and the ftains will difappear. Water impregnated with mineral alkaline falt, or foda, ox-gall, and black foap, is alfo very good to take out fpots of greafe.

A Soap that takes out all Manner of Spots and Stains.

Take the yolks of fix eggs, half a table-fpoonful of bruifed falt, and a pound of Venetian foap; mix the whole together with the juice of beet-roots, and form it into round balls, that are to be dried in the fhade. The method of ufing this foap is to wet with fair water the ftained part of the cloth, and rub both fides of it well with this foap; then wafh the cloth in water, and the ftain will not long appear.

To cure Warts.

Anoint the warts with the milky juice of the herb mercury feveral times, and they will gradually wafte away.

Another safe and experienced Method.

Rub the warts with a pared pippin, and a few days afterwards they will be found to difappear.

To destroy Fleas.

Sprinkle the room with a decoction of arfmart, bitter apple, briar leaves, or cabbage leaves; or fmoke it with burnt thyme or penny-royal.

Another way.

Put tanfey-leaves about different parts of the bed, viz. under the matrafs, or between the blankets.

Another way.

Rub the bed-pofts well with a ftrong decoction of elder leaves.

A Liniment to destroy Lice.

Take an ounce of vinegar, the fame quantity of ftavefacre, half an ounce of honey, and half an ounce of fulphur. Mix into the confiftence of a foft liniment, with two ounces of falad oil.

A Liniment to destroy Nits.

Take oil of bays, oil of fweet almonds, and old hogs-lard, of each two ounces; powdered ftavefacre, and tanfey-juice, of each half an ounce; aloes and myrrh, of each a quarter of an ounce; the fmaller centaury and falt of fulphur, of each a
drachm;

drachm; mix the whole into a liniment. Before you ufe it, wafh the hair with vinegar.

Receipt to thicken the Hair, and make it grow on a bald part.

Take roots of a maiden vine, roots of hemp, and cores of foft cabbages, of each two handfuls; dry and burn them; afterwards make a lye with the afhes. The head is to be wafhed with this lye three days fucceffively, the part having been previoufly well rubbed with honey.

To make Hair black.

Firft wafh your head with fpring water, then dip your comb in oil of tartar, and comb yourfelf in the fun: repeat this operation three times a day; and at the end of eight days at moft the hair will turn black. If you are defirous of giving the hair a fine fcent, moiften it with oil of Benjamin.

Simple Means of producing the fame Effect.

The leaves of the wild vine change the hairs black, and prevent their falling off. Burnt corks; roots of the holm-oak and caper-tree; barks of willow, walnut-tree, and pomegranate; leaves of artichokes, the mulberry-tree, fig-tree, rafpberry-bufh; fhells of beans; gall and Cyprus nuts; leaves of myrtle; green fhells of walnuts; ivy-berries, cockle and red beet feeds, poppy-flowers, allum, and moft preparations of lead. Thefe ingredients may be boiled in rain-water, wine, or vinegar, with the addition of fome cephalic plant, as fage, marjoram, balm, betony, clove july-flowers, laurel, &c. &c.

Obfervations upon a Leech, by a Gentleman who kept one feveral Years for the purpofe of a Weather-glafs.

A phial of water, containing a leech, I kept on the frame of my lower chamber window fafh, fo that when I looked in the morning, I could know what would be the weather of the following day.

If the weather proves ferene and beautiful, the leech lies motionlefs at the bottom of the glafs, and rolled together in a fpiral form.

If it rains before or after noon, it is found crept up to the top of its lodging, and there it remains till the weather is fettled.

If we are to have wind, the poor prifoner gallops through its limpid habitation with amazing fwiftnefs, and feldom refts till it begins to blow hard.

If a remarkable ftorm of thunder and rain is to fucceed, for fome days before it lodges almoft continually without the water, and difcovers uncommon uneafinefs, in violent throes, and convulfive-like motions.

In

In the froſt, as in clear ſummer weather, it lies conſtantly at the bottom. And in ſnow, as in rainy weather, it pitches its dwelling upon the very mouth of the phial.

What reaſons may be aſſigned for them, I muſt leave philoſophers to determine, though one thing is evident to every body, that it muſt be affected in the ſame way with that of the mercury and ſpirits in the weather-glaſs, and has doubtleſs a very ſurpriſing ſenſation, that the change of weather, even days before, makes a viſible alteration upon its manner of living.

Perhaps it may not be amiſs to note, left any of the curious ſhould try the experiment, that the leech was kept in a common eight ounce phial glaſs, about three-fourths filled with water, and covered on the mouth with a bit of linen-rag. In the ſummer the water is changed once a week, and in the winter once a fortnight. This is a weather-glaſs which may be purchaſed at a very trifling expence, and which will laſt ſome years.

ROYAL HUMANE SOCIETY.

Directions for the recovery of the Apparently Dead.

I. The reſtoration of heat is of the greateſt conſequence to the return of life: when, therefore, the body is taken out of the water, the cloaths ſhould be ſtripped off; or, if naked at the time of the accident, it muſt be covered with two or three coats, or a blanket. The body ſhould then be carefully conveyed to the neareſt houſe, with the head a little raiſed. —In cold and damp weather, the perſon ſhould be laid on a bed, &c. in a room that is moderately heated:—In ſummer, on a bed expoſed to the rays of the ſun, and not more than ſix perſons admitted, as a greater number may retard the return of life. The body is to be well dried with warm cloths, and gently rubbed with flannels ſprinkled with rum, brandy, gin, or muſtard.—Fomentations of ſpirits may be applied to the pit of the ſtomach with advantage.—A warming-pan covered with flannel ſhould be lightly moved up and down the back; bladders, or bottles filled with hot water, heated bricks, or tiles wrapped up in flannel, ſhould be applied to the ſoles of the feet, palms of the hands, and other parts of the body.

II. Reſpiration will be promoted by cloſing the mouth and one noſtril, while, with the pipe of a bellows, you blow into the other with ſufficient force to inflate the lungs; another perſon ſhould then preſs the cheſt gently with his hands, ſo as to expel the air. If the pipe be too large for the noſtrils, the air may be blown in at the mouth. Blowing the breath can only be recommended when bellows cannot be procured.

III. The

III. The bowels fhould be inflated with the fumes of tobacco and repeated three or four times within the firft hour; but if circumftances prevent the ufe of this vapour, then clyfters of this herb, or other acrid infufions with falt, may be thrown up with advantage. The fumigating machine is fo much improved as to be of the higheft importance to the public; and if employed in every inftance of apparent death, it would reftore the lives of many of our fellow creatures, as it now anfwers the important purpofes of fumigation, infpiration, and expiration.

IV. Agitation has proved a powerful auxiliary to the other means of recovery; one or more of the affiftants fhould, therefore, take hold of the legs and arms, particularly of boys, and fhake their bodies for five or fix minutes; this may be repeated feveral times within the firft hour. When the body is wiped perfectly dry, it fhould be placed in bed between two healthy perfons, and the friction chiefly directed, in this cafe, to the left fide, where it will be moft likely to excite the motion of the heart.

V. When thefe methods have been employed for an hour, if any brewhoufe, bakehoufe, or glafshoufe, be near, where warm grains, afhes, lees, &c. can be procured, the body fhould be placed in any of thefe moderated to a degree of heat very little exceeding that of the perfon in health. If the warm bath can be conveniently obtained, it may be advantageoufly ufed in conjunction with the earlieft modes of treatment,

VI. Electricity fhould be early employed, as it will increafe the beneficial effects of the other means of recovery on the fyftem. "The electrical fhock," fays Mr. Kite, in his Effay on the Recovery of the apparently Dead, "is to be admitted "as the teft or difcriminating characteriftic of any remains of "animal life; and fo long as that produces contractions, may "the perfon be faid to be in a recoverable ftate; but when that "effect has ceafed, there can no doubt remain of the party "being abfolutely and pofitively dead." ● ●

●●● convulfions, or other figns of returning life appear, a tea-fpoonful or two of warm water may be put into the ●●●th; and if the power of fwallowing be returned, a little ●●● wine, or brandy and water may be given. When this gradual approach towards recovery is obferved, and breathing returned, let the perfon be put into a warm ●●●, and if difpofed to fleep, as is generally the cafe, give no ●●● urbance, and he will awake ●●●moft perfectly recovered.

The above methods are to be ufed with vigour for three or four hours; for it is a vulgar and dangerous opinion to fuppofe perfons are irrecoverable, becaufe life does not foon make its appearance; an opinion that has configned an immenfe number

ber

ber to the grave, who might have been reſtored to life by reſo-
lution and perſeverance.

Bleeding ſhould never be employed in ſuch caſes, unleſs by
the direction of one of the medical aſſiſtants, or ſome other reſ-
pectable gentleman of the faculty, who has paid attention to the
ſubject of ſuſpended animation.

On the firſt alarm of any perſon being drowned, let hot water, flour of muſtard, warm blankets, hot flannels, flat bottles
filled with hot water, a heated warming-pan, bellows, brandy,
hartſhorn drops, and an electrifying machine, be procured.
Theſe articles being immediately employed, may be productive
of reſtoring many uſeful and valuable lives.

The common people will often reſtore life by purſuing the
plans now recommended ; but if gentlemen of the faculty can
be obtained, their aſſiſtance ſhould be immediately requeſted,
as their ſkill will lead them judiciouſly to vary the methods of
treatment, and, in a variety of accidents, many more lives will
be reſtored to the community and to their families.

The above means of reſtoration have proved efficacious in
apparent ſudden death, by convulſions, ſuffocations, intoxtica-
tion, hanging, intenſe cold, and the tremendous ſtroke of light-
ning.—When perſons are froſt bitten, they ſhould be rubbed
with ſnow, previous to their being brought into a warm room.
In ſuffocation, occaſioned by the fumes of ſulphur, charcoal,
&c. daſhing the face and breaſt with cold water has been known
to reſtore life.

*** Publicans and others, who have been deterred from re-
ceiving the apparently dead into their houſes, or giving immediate aſſiſtance, under an apprehenſion of legal puniſhment or
penalties, are now informed, that the Committee have obtained
the following opinion of an eminent Special Pleader :—" It is a
" miſdemeanour by the common law, and an indictable offence,
" to prevent the Coroner from doing his duty, or to obſtruct
" him in the execution of it. But the medling with a body
" apparently dead for the purpoſe of preſerving life, is not a
" tranſgreſſion of the law in either of theſe reſpects, nor do I
" know any ſtatute by which ſuch an act is prohibited."—All
perſons who immediately admit the drowned, or otherwiſe
ſuffocated and afford aſſiſtance in the various inſtances of apparent death, will be indemnified by the Managers of this
Inſtitution ; and are informed that the charges of burial, in
unſucceſsful caſes, will be paid by the Royal Humane Society.

F I N I S.